THE GREAT DIVIDE

ALSO BY THOMAS FLEMING

NONFICTION

1776: Year of Illusions

Washington's Secret War: The Hidden History of Valley Forge

Duel: Alexander Hamilton, Aaron Burr and the Future of America

The Perils of Peace: America's Struggle for Survival After Yorktown

The Intimate Lives of the Founding Fathers

A Disease in the Public Mind

FICTION

Liberty Tavern

Dreams of Glory

Remember the Morning

The Officers' Wives

Time and Tide

The Secret Trial of Robert E. Lee

THE GREAT DIVIDE

The Conflict Between
Washington and Jefferson
That Defined a Nation

THOMAS FLEMING

DA CAPO PRESS
A Member of the Perseus Books Group

For information, address Da Capo Press, 44 Farnsworth Street, 3rd Floor, Boston, MA 02210.

Designed by BackStory Design
Set in 11 point Adobe Caslon by Marcovaldo Productions, Inc. for the Perseus Books Group

Cataloging-in-Publication data for this book is available from the Library of Congress.
First Da Capo Press edition 2015
ISBN: 978-0-306-82127-1 (Hardcover)
ISBN: 978-0-306-82236-0 (eBook)

Published by Da Capo Press
A Member of the Perseus Books Group
www.dacapopress.com

Da Capo Press books are available at special discounts for bulk purchases in the U.S. by corporations, institutions, and other organizations. For more information, please contact the Special Markets Department at the Perseus Books Group, 2300 Chestnut Street, Suite 200, Philadelphia, PA, 19103, or call (800) 810-4145, ext. 5000, or e-mail special.markets@perseusbooks.com.

10 9 8 7 6 5 4 3 2 1

To Alice

*To see this country happy...is so much the wish of my soul...
nothing on this side of Elysium can be placed in competition
with it.*

GEORGE WASHINGTON[1]

*Rather than it [The French Revolution] should have failed,
I would have seen half the earth desolated. Were there but an
Adam and Eve left in every country, and left free, it would be
better than as it now is.*

THOMAS JEFFERSON[2]

The government we mean to erect is intended to last for ages.

JAMES MADISON[3]

Contents

Introduction

A CONFLICT BETWEEN GEORGE Washington and Thomas Jefferson? Most Americans are unaware that such discord ever existed. Numerous historians have explored Jefferson's clash with Alexander Hamilton. But little has been written about the differences that developed between the two most famous founding fathers.

Two years after her husband's death, Martha Washington told a visiting congressman that she regarded Mr. Jefferson "as one of the most detestable of mankind," and saw his election as president as "the greatest misfortune our country has ever experienced." The congressman agreed with her and recorded these opinions in his diary.[1]

A series of political clashes had gradually destroyed the friendship and mutual respect the two men had enjoyed at the start of Washington's presidency. Ultimately, they became enemies. Small, slight James Madison, whose brilliant political theorizing won the admiration of both men, was forced to choose between these two tall antagonists.

Eleven years older than Jefferson, Washington had almost no formal education. He spent his teenage years as a hardworking surveyor. Jefferson devoured books and ideas at the College of William and Mary. At the age of twenty-two, Washington went to war against the French and Indians in Virginia's western wilderness, and became the colony's best known soldier. Jefferson studied law and became a passionate revolutionist when America's grievances against British rule exploded into rebellion.

During the eight-year struggle for independence, Washington rose to worldwide fame as the commander of the American "Continental" Army. He crowned his victory by rejecting pleas to banish the bankrupt Continental Congress and become the new nation's military dictator. Instead, he resigned his commission and returned to civilian life.

1

Jefferson's chief contribution to the struggle was drafting the Declaration of Independence. The opening paragraph's soaring insistence that every human being was entitled to life, liberty, and the pursuit of happiness would ultimately give the document world-transforming power. But few people emphasized this aspect of the Declaration—or thought of Jefferson as its author—during the War for Independence. Congress had heavily edited and revised his draft before issuing it on July 4, 1776. Jefferson was better known for his two years as governor of Virginia, during which he revealed a dismaying inability to deal with the crises that confronted him.

By 1783, when independence was confirmed by a peace treaty with Great Britain, it had become apparent to many thoughtful men that the Continental Congress and the primitive constitution it had created, the Articles of Confederation, were inadequate to the challenge of governing thirteen contentious states.

In September 1785, Congressman James Madison began visiting General Washington at Mount Vernon to discuss the need for a more effective federal government. Absent from these conversations, which would have a large influence on the as yet unborn constitution, was Washington's and Madison's mutual friend, Thomas Jefferson. He was in France, serving as America's envoy.

If Jefferson had been at Mount Vernon, would Washington have influenced him? Or would Jefferson have influenced Washington? It is one of American history's most intriguing what-ifs.[2]

Washington was first, last, and always a realist. "We must take human nature as we find it. Perfection falls not to the share of mortals," was one of his favorite maxims.[3] But he combined this realism with a surprisingly strong faith that America was destined to become a beacon of freedom for men and women everywhere. One recent biographer has called him a realistic visionary.[4]

Jefferson tended to see men and events through the lens of a pervasive idealism. He believed that if left to their own devices, free men would inevitably find the path to a good government. All they needed were visionary words to inspire them.

Experience had convinced Washington that this happy outcome would only occur with the help of strong leadership. This was the missing ingredient in the Articles of Confederation, which made Congress the ruler of the nation and their presiding officer a powerless factotum. Jefferson was reluctant to exercise political power. "I have no ambition to govern men," he told his friend John Adams. "It is a painful and thankless office." [5]

Against this background, let us begin an exploration of the conflict that arose between these two very different leaders, both of whom cared deeply about the United States of America.

CHAPTER 1

The Man Who Lived Dangerously

A N ADMIRING ENGLISH TRAVELER who saw Mount Vernon be-fore the American Revolution said the house "commands a noble prospect of water, of cliffs, woods, and plantations." Anyone who has vis-ited George Washington's home and gazed out at the broad Potomac River flowing past the green lawn will agree with this description. The similarity of the contemporary landscape makes it easy to imagine Wash-ington and James Madison there on the sunny piazza, discussing what might and should be done to rescue the infant republic they had done so much to launch.

Simultaneously, the house helps us understand its proprietor. As his own architect, Washington had created a mansion from the unassuming one-and-a-half-story building he had inherited from his older brother. He had raised the roof and added four full-sized rooms upstairs. A few years later, he expanded both sides of the house, adding a library on the south end with a bedroom above it, and a double-sized dining room on the north end. He also ordered the exterior "rusticated"—a process that utilized sand-laced paint to make the wooden walls resemble stone. Mount Vernon became a house that revealed its owner's sense of himself as a man of dig-nity and importance. But it retained the simple straightforward lines of a home for a country gentleman.[1]

The erect, soldierly Washington and the slim, short Madison were an unlikely pair of friends. The thirty-four-year-old congressman was nine-teen years younger than the grey-haired retired general. In public, Washington's formal manner could be almost forbidding; his blue eyes often seemed judgmental, even stern. In private, they could sparkle with delight at a witty remark, especially if it came from a clever woman.

Madison, a graduate of the College of New Jersey (now Princeton), impressed most people as a shy, scholarly man with a history of ill-health. But friends found "Jemmy" a lively conversationalist, with an amazingly rich mind, thanks to years of omnivorous reading. He had a wicked eye for the flaws and foibles of human nature. He was fond of wry aphorisms, such as: "If men were angels, no government would be necessary"—a viewpoint that matched nicely with Washington's realism.

Madison's contribution to the Revolution started with his service as a councillor to Governor Patrick Henry in 1778 and to Thomas Jefferson in 1779. The following year, the Virginia legislature elected the talented young man to the Continental Congress. There, Madison soon attracted General Washington's attention because he did his utmost to push two measures that Washington considered vital. One was giving Congress the power to govern the restless states. The second was to raise enough money to pay the back salaries owed to the officers and men of the army he commanded. Almost as important were funds to finance a pension for the army's officers. Washington told Congress, if they did not make good on this long promised reward, they would "embitter every moment of my future life." [2]

Too often, George Washington has been portrayed as a formidable-looking figurehead, whose fame and leadership abilities were exaggerated and even invented by shrewder, more intelligent men, such as Madison or the general's wartime aide, Alexander Hamilton. One of these skeptics, who has published a dozen books on the Revolution, has expressed the opinion that Washington's entire career could be summed up in a single word: luck. Such people may have paid too much attention to Washington's labored speech accepting command of the American army, in which he protested that he was unfit for the large task confronting him.

What singles out Washington as a leader was the way he dealt with challenges to his army and his reputation almost from the day he took command in 1775. Again and again, he revealed an ability to think for himself and find the right solution to the daunting problems that confronted him. Year after year, he maintained an amazing equanimity in spite of the constant awareness that failure meant disgrace and death. He was unquestionably a man ready, willing, and able to live dangerously.

❦

One of General Washington's first tests was his 1775 discovery that he intensely disliked a great many of the New England soldiers he was supposed to command. In a letter to fellow Virginian Richard Henry Lee, he remarked that the Yankee enlisted men were "an exceeding dirty and nasty people" with the "most indifferent" officers he ever saw. His secretary and aide-de-camp, Joseph Reed, warned him that Lee had shown this letter to John Adams, who had undoubtedly shown it to his fiery cousin, Samuel Adams. Sam would almost certainly resent the slur and be quick to seek revenge. That was the last time Washington ever said anything derogatory about a soldier or politician from any part of their embryo nation. In a painful flash, he saw he must become not only a victorious battlefield leader, but the creator of a sense of brotherhood and mission in his "Continental" army.[3]

❦

In 1776, Washington faced a British army three or four times larger than the one that self-appointed military experts such as Thomas Paine had predicted the supposedly bankrupt royal government could send to America. In battles on Long Island and in Manhattan, the redcoated regulars and their hired German allies routed Washington's mix of regulars bolstered by untrained militia. As he watched fleeing Connecticut militiamen race past him, ignoring his orders to stand and fight at present-day Forty-second Street and the East River, the general roared: "Are these the men with which I am to defend America?"[4]

A few nights later, Washington wrote a letter to John Hancock, the president of the Continental Congress, informing him that, henceforth, he would never risk the American army in another all-out confrontation with the British. Instead, he would "protract the war." This meant the Continental Army would frequently retreat in order to fight another day. Washington hoped Congress would see no disgrace in this new strategy.

Not a few military historians have considered this decision to change the basic thinking of the war proof of Washington's ability to make crucial decisions. Many of his staff officers and subordinate generals were too badly rattled by the British victories to do more than wring their hands.

He was well aware that he was abandoning the theory that Congress had formulated in 1775—the war would be won in one titanic battle—a "general action"—in which overwhelming numbers of spirited American amateurs would crush King George III's comparative handful of dispirited mercenaries. [5]

Several days later, General Washington declared that Congress's policy of using untrained militia to save the cost of a large regular army was threatening their cause with ruin. Only a well-trained army, equipped with cannon and cavalry, and strong enough to "look the enemy in the face," would win the war. It took seven often harrowing years but this combination of a protracted war and a dependable regular army proved to be the formula for victory. [6]

A protracted war did not mean that General Washington was unwilling to fight when he thought he had a good chance of winning. In the final weeks of 1776, when the American cause seemed destined for oblivion, he struck two electrifying blows, killing or capturing the German garrison at Trenton, and routing British regiments from Princeton. America, groaned one dismayed loyalist, became "liberty mad again."

A year later, in the army's winter camp at Valley Forge, Washington discovered that the British were not his only enemies. Disillusioned congressmen, under the leadership of Samuel Adams, a foe of a regular army, with neither sympathy nor understanding of the protracted war strategy, tried to oust Washington with a nasty mix of politics and slander. Wealthy Thomas Mifflin, the army's quartermaster general, was also in on the conspiracy.

Their chief complaint was the Continental Army's failure to stop the British army from seizing the American capital, Philadelphia. Adams, Mifflin, and their followers wanted to downgrade Washington and elevate the victor in the 1777 battle of Saratoga, General Horatio Gates. They made Gates chairman of a "Board of War," with the power to issue orders without bothering to consult the commander in chief. They also began smearing Washington as an overcautious, egotistic fake who thought his two small victories at the close of 1776 had won him enduring fame.

A congressional delegation came to Valley Forge, ready, one of its backers smugly told Samuel Adams, "to rap a demigod over the knuckles" and embarrass Washington into resigning. The general invited the chairman to dinner, and in two hours turned him into an ally. Next he presented him and his fellow would-be knuckle-rappers with a twenty thousand-word statement, written by a young West Indian–born aide, Alexander Hamilton, who had recently joined his staff. The essay informed the stunned delegation that Congress was responsible for the mess in the quartermaster and commissary departments that had brought the army to the edge of starvation. The would-be knuckle-rappers returned to Congress with Washington's solution to the problem, plus an insistence on a pension for the officers, to prevent the army's collapse. Despite frantic objections from the Samuel Adams clique in Congress, the pension passed by a single vote.[7]

At the battle of Monmouth, a few months after the ordeal at Valley Forge, Washington placed his second-in-command, former British colonel, Charles Lee, in charge of the advance guard as they pursued the British army retreating from Philadelphia. The French had entered the war as America's ally and the British had abandoned the American capital to concentrate their forces in New York. Like General Gates, the outspoken Lee had many friends in Congress. He scoffed at Washington's strategy and urged them to discharge the regular army and rely completely on militia to fight a "partisan" (guerilla) war—with him in command.

As Washington and the main body of his army approached the British camp near Monmouth Court House, the general was stunned to see Lee's soldiers reeling toward him, panic on their faces. Convinced that Americans could not stand and fight the British in a face-to-face confrontation, Lee had ordered a retreat the moment the enemy attacked. The pursuing redcoats were only fifteen minutes away.

Washington roared curses at Lee and took charge of the situation. In ten frantic minutes, his troops were manning nearby hills and hasty barricades. They fought the King's soldiers to a bloody draw, which Washington called a victory. Soon afterward, he court-martialed Lee, implicitly daring Congress to override him. They glumly confirmed the guilty verdict.[8]

A year later, a French expeditionary force was scheduled to land at Newport, Rhode Island, to bolster the American army. Washington's spies discovered that the British planned a massive assault on the French soldiers as they came ashore, weary from their long Atlantic voyage. The day before the British fleet and army were to depart from New York, a purported American loyalist handed the British commander a packet of letters that an American messenger had apparently dropped on the road. It contained plans for a major assault on New York. The panicked British cancelled their Newport attack and manned fortifications around the city, until it dawned on them that they had been hoodwinked.

After two more years of seesaw warfare, a French fleet helped Washington trap the main British field army at Yorktown, and the fighting war began to dwindle. A weary British parliament pressed King George III into initiating peace talks, which ended in a preliminary treaty negotiated by Ambassador Benjamin Franklin and his fellow diplomats in Europe.

This dawn of peace was suddenly darkened by a threat of a counterrevolution, organized by restless officers in the American army's winter camp at New Windsor, on the Hudson River above New York. Incendiary broadsides urged the army to march on Congress and demand at gunpoint the years of back pay they were owed—and a confirmation of the promised pension for the officers. Behind the conspirators was Washington's old enemy, General Horatio Gates, who was always eager to listen to the voices of the people, especially when they were criticizing Washington.

Without consulting their commander in chief, the conspirators called a meeting to vote on whether to begin their march. Washington coolly asserted his authority by banning the meeting as "disorderly." He summoned another conclave four days later. When the officers convened, Washington strode onto the stage of the large building called "The Temple" and asked the startled chairman, none other than General Gates, if he could say a few words.

With an emotional intensity that few had seen before, Washington asked the officers "in the name of our common country" and "your own sacred honor" to join him in expressing their "detestation" of any man who wanted to "overturn the liberties of our country" and "open the floodgates of civil discord." Instead, he asked them to remain loyal to their dignity and honor as officers and Americans. Someday people would praise their "glorious example." This later generation would say: "Had this day been wanting, the world would never have seen the last stage of perfection to which human nature is capable of attaining."

Washington took from his pocket a message from Virginia congressman Joseph Jones, a close friend. It declared that Congress was still trying to find a way to raise the money it owed the army. After reading a few lines, Washington paused and drew a pair of glasses from an inner pocket of his coat. "Gentleman," he said. "You will permit me to put on my spec-tacles—I have not only grown grey but almost blind in the service of this country."

A rush of emotion swept through the room. Not a few officers wept openly. Washington finished the letter and strode from the stage. Instantly, his most loyal general, artillery commander Henry Knox, took charge. By the time the meeting ended, the officers had voted their complete approval of Washington's words and condemned the incendiary broadsides. The most perilous moment in the brief history of the United States of America ended peacefully, thanks to one extraordinary man.[9]

⚜

Finally came the day in 1783 when the British army rowed the last of its regiments from New York's docks to waiting transports in the harbor. General Washington and his army, reduced to a mere seven hundred men, took possession of the city. Soon Washington rode south to Annapolis, where the Continental Congress was meeting. Although the legislators had failed to heed his plea to pay the officers and men their back pay or their promised pensions, he put aside his personal embitterment and treated Congress with the same respect he had displayed for its dubious authority throughout the war.

Solemnly, earnestly, he congratulated the delegates for their victory in the long struggle, and resigned his commission as lieutenant general and commander in chief. In Europe, amazement was virtually universal. Everyone—especially George III—had expected Washington to take power as a dictator, like Lord Protector Oliver Cromwell, the victor in England's civil war in the previous century.

⚜

By 1785, the defects of the Articles of Confederation had became glar-ingly apparent. The president of Congress—theoretically, the president of the nation—was a powerless figurehead who could not even answer a let-ter addressed to him without the legislators' permission. Congress had no authority to raise money beyond pleading with the states for "requisitions," which they largely ignored. Each state had one vote, and it required nine votes to make a decision. To pass a money bill required unanimous approval. In 1783, twelve states backed James Madison's proposal to levy a 5 percent duty on imports. Tiny Rhode Island voted no, leaving Congress mired in bankruptcy.

General Washington admitted his growing distress about the future of the nation to several of his many correspondents. As the popularity and power of Congress sank to zero-minus, various states became alarmingly autonomous. New York taxed every farmer's rowboat that crossed the Hudson River from New Jersey with produce to sell. Massachusetts was playing a similar game with Connecticut and New Hampshire. Virginia grew truculent when Pennsylvania attempted these extortions. Other states, notably Rhode Island, began printing their own money in reckless amounts, enabling their businessmen to pay debts in depreciated currency. "I see one head turning into thirteen," Washington warned. [10]

Washington's ex-aide, Colonel Alexander Hamilton, quit Congress in disgust, and advised the governor of New York to give land to discharged Continental soldiers. They would be useful if a civil war erupted. He was not alone in seeing bloody internal strife as the next chapter in the American story.

On August 31, 1786, a disgruntled former Continental Army captain named Daniel Shays launched a revolution in western Massachusetts to protest the state government's seizure of farms and houses for failure to pay taxes. Armed Shaysites closed courthouses and sent judges fleeing for their lives. Similar revolts shut down courts in the western counties of nearby states. Former General Henry Knox told Washington the rebels could raise between twelve thousand and fifteen thousand "desperate and unprincipled men."[11]

Massachusetts asked Congress for assistance. The nation's legislators voted to raise $530,000 for an army of forty-four hundred men, and appealed to the supposedly united states to send them the money. Twelve of the thirteen semi-independent legislatures ignored the request. Total disaster was averted when wealthy men in Massachusetts raised enough cash to hire a local army. Led by another former Continental Army general, Benjamin Lincoln, this force routed the Shaysites. But bands of discontented men continued a guerilla war until February 1787, kidnapping merchants and judges, looting and burning stores.

When a worried Virginian asked Washington to go to Massachusetts and lend his "influence" to calm the upheaval, he angrily replied: "Influence is no government!" He saw anarchy in the careening Shaysites—along with the ruin of the central reality that Americans had to preserve if they hoped to escape Europe's history of destructive wars—their national union.[12]

"There are combustibles in every state,"Washington wrote to Madison. "Let us look to our national character and to things beyond the present moment."[13]

After Madison began visiting Mount Vernon in 1785, he advanced steadily in Washington's estimation. The general soon began his letters to the young congressman with "My Dear Sir," an expression he reserved for close friends. (Others received a standard "Dear Sir.") Just as frequently, Washington closed his letters with "Affectionately." It took Madison another year to begin adding that word to his own closing lines, perhaps evidence that Washington's fame—or his age—inhibited easy familiarity.[14]

By this time, the two men realized they were in almost complete agreement on the need for a drastic reform of the federal government. Washington warmly endorsed Madison's call for a conference to be held at Annapolis, Maryland, to discuss the situation. Madison shrewdly described the meeting's purpose as an attempt to find ways to remove barriers that limited trade and commerce between the states.

Complicating the situation was a growing distrust between North and South. Shays' Rebellion was not a factor in this malaise. When the delegates met at Annapolis on September 11, 1786, the size and seriousness of Shays' upheaval was not yet apparent. More divisive was a move by John Jay, the Foreign Secretary of Congress, to negotiate a deal with Madrid, surrendering the right of the United States to use the Mississippi River in return for the lifting of trade restrictions preventing American commerce with Spain and her colonies in the West Indies and South America. Virginia and other southern states with western counties were infuriated when seven northern states, led by Massachusetts, voted in favor of Jay's proposal.[15]

This sectional antagonism discouraged attendance at Annapolis. Only twelve delegates representing five states (New Jersey, New York, Delaware, Pennsylvania, and Virginia) showed up. Madison found an ally in New

Yorker Alexander Hamilton, with whom he had served in Congress in the closing months of the war. Hamilton heartily backed Madison's suggestion that the Annapolis meeting adjourn and issue a call for a truly national convention. Hamilton drafted this exhortation and portrayed the situation as so alarming, Madison had to persuade him to tone it down. In private talks, the two men found they were in almost complete agreement on the need for a drastic overhaul of the federal government.

Back in Richmond, Madison had no trouble persuading the Virginia legislature to send delegates to a convention the following year in Philadelphia. As inhabitants of the nation's largest state, Virginians thought of themselves as America's natural leaders. Madison now went to work behind the scenes to persuade a reluctant ex-General Washington to preside at the convention. Many people have attributed Washington's hesitation to a fear of risking the fame he had achieved in the armed struggle with Britain. This writer is more inclined to see it as another episode in the career of a man who had lived dangerously for a long time.

Washington's well-honed political judgment had convinced him that he would have only one chance to use his reputation to reform the federal government. In every state there were vocal politicians and businessmen who were profiting from the weaknesses of the current government and were ready to defend the status quo with the same savagery that his enemies had displayed at Valley Forge. What Washington needed and wanted to see was evidence that thoughtful men were ready to join him in Philadelphia.

Madison understood this estimate of their situation and soon found an answer to it. He assured numerous Virginians that General Washington planned to attend the convention. This news inspired leaders such as Governor Edmund Randolph and George Mason (author of the 1776 Virginia Declaration of Rights) to volunteer to serve as delegates. When Washington learned that the state's delegation would have so many "respectable" names, he became much more inclined to join them.

Madison combined this canny politicking with long hours spent absorbing dozens of books on government. He found numerous examples in history of weak confederations that were overthrown by a scheming strongman, often with the help of foreign allies. The specter of Britain seducing one of the disunited states was starkly probable in this historical light. Soon Madison was writing an essay, "Of Ancient and Modern Confederacies," in which he noted how often unions of this type had collapsed because the central government was weak or nonexistent. The result of Madison's research was a forty-one-page booklet, which George Washington liked so much, he copied it in his own handwriting. It would prove an invaluable resource for both men in the coming convention.

Early in 1787, Madison undertook an even more important task. In atrocious winter weather, the man whom college friends had considered a chronic invalid rode from Virginia to New York City, where Congress was meeting. Rivers, Madison later told a friend, "were clogged with ice and a half congealed mixture of snow and water." Next came a Northeast blizzard that made the road from Philadelphia to New York an ordeal.[16]

The ex-invalid survived and was soon reporting to General Washington that Congress was financially and politically bankrupt. Few people wanted to waste time serving as delegates. At first, the few congressmen on hand resisted the idea of approving a constitutional convention. But Madison persuaded them to acquiesce in a tepid endorsement, specifying that the convention was "for the sole and express purpose of revising the Articles of Confederation." Madison knew wary states would now be more inclined to send delegates to Philadelphia—and Washington would almost certainly join them.[17]

Madison also spent not a few hours persuading congressmen from the seven northern states who had voted for John Jay's proposed treaty on the Mississippi to abandon the measure. Although the proponents were two states short of the nine votes needed to pass a law or treaty, Madison wanted to eliminate the divisive issue from the agenda of the coming constitutional convention. As a weapon, he used a resolution from former army officers and others settled in what would soon become the state of Kentucky, deploring the idea.

Next, Madison sought out the Spanish ambassador and discovered he and John Jay had abandoned any hope of passing the treaty. The Congressman was able to tell Washington and other influential Virginians the good news that "The Mississippi sleeps." Thus, he removed the last obstacle to the state's participation in the Philadelphia convention.

During these fall and winter weeks, General Washington became more and more radical in his thinking about a new federal government. On

March 31, 1787, he told Madison he would not be satisfied with a few amendments to the Articles of Confederation. He wanted "a thorough reform of the present system"—a new constitution.

In letters to other correspondents, Washington spelled out some of the changes he had in mind. He wanted the federal government to repay the millions of dollars that America had borrowed from France and Holland to finance the War for Independence. Congress had defaulted on paying even the interest, ruining American credit around the world. Washington also wanted a government with the power to control the reckless policies of individual states. Above all, he wanted a government strong enough to suppress any further outbreaks of violence like Shays' Rebellion.

There was another more personal motive for Washington's commitment—one he admitted only to a few close friends. The words are among the most revealing he ever wrote: "To see this country happy is so much the wish of my soul, nothing else can compare to it, this side of Elysium."[18]

Washington's arrival in Philadelphia triggered an explosion of celebration and admiration. A troop of light horse and dozens of prominent men escorted him into the city while artillery thundered a salute and church bells chimed. Thousands of people cheered and waved from packed sidewalks. A local newspaper declared the excitement and ceremony was proof of "the joy of the people on the coming of this great and good man." It was remarkable evidence of the popularity that Washington had won by relinquishing command of the Continental Army.

After accepting an invitation to become the guest of his close friends, merchant Robert Morris and his wife, Mary, in their three-story brick house on High Street, Washington ended his first day with a visit to Benjamin Franklin. Mutual admiration, expressed in many letters, guaranteed a friendly reception. It was also good politics. Franklin had recently been elected President of the Supreme Executive Council of Pennsylvania, in effect, the state's governor. Washington was pleased to learn that the eighty-one-year-old sage was coming to the convention as a delegate. It was reassuring evidence that he too recognized the gathering's importance.

Franklin, in turn, recognized Washington's central role in the creation of the new nation. During his years as America's ambassador in France, he had kept a full length portrait of the general on the wall behind his desk.

He had sent Washington warm letters, telling how the leading soldiers of Europe admired his generalship.

Delegates to the convention trickled into Philadelphia at a pace that Washington found exasperating. But he tried to greet each one cordially and sample his ideas on what they should try to accomplish. He was encouraged by how many of the delegates agreed with his opinion that the federal government needed a major overhaul. It no doubt helped that a hefty percentage of these politicians were former Continental Army officers.

Meanwhile, General Washington joined James Madison, Governor Edmund Randolph, and the other members of the Virginia delegation to discuss their plan of operation. After listening to Washington's opinions, the Virginians agreed to call for the creation of an entirely new government, and to follow that revolutionary idea with a presentation of its structure, which Madison had sketched out in considerable detail. Their proposal became known as "The Virginia Plan." Its most innovative feature was a president to serve as head of the new government, with powers coequal to Congress.

The man who lived dangerously was about to take the riskiest gamble of his drama-filled life.

CHAPTER 2

The Man Who Loved to Legislate— But Hated to Govern

JAMES MADISON'S FRIENDSHIP WITH George Washington never achieved the intimacy of the congressman's relationship with Thomas Jefferson. The twenty-eight-year-old Madison had already served a year as councillor to Governor Patrick Henry when the thirty-six-year-old Jefferson was elected to succeed the famous orator in June 1779. Madison was undoubtedly aware of Jefferson's role in drafting the Declaration of Independence and other noteworthy revolutionary documents, such as his defiant 1774 essay, *A Summary View of the Rights of America*.

In 1777–78, Jefferson had been chairman of a committee in Virginia's legislature that submitted a staggering 126 bills aimed at eliminating "every trace...of ancient or future aristocracy." One wonders how he thought that the delegates, absorbed in the challenge of fighting a war for survival, could be expected to overhaul the structure of their government at the same time. It was a glimpse of a streak of unrealism in Jefferson's personality—an inclination to put words—especially his own words—ahead of practical considerations.

One bill, abolishing the Anglican faith as an established church, engulfed the legislature in angry debate for weeks, without reaching a decision. Another, calling for universal education, was much too expensive for the cash-strapped state to undertake. Only the law abolishing "entail"— making the eldest son the sole inheritor of a father's wealth—won swift passage. The lawmakers failed to act on almost all of Jefferson's other proposals. But the magnitude of the effort made it clear that he saw himself as a man ready to break new ground in the art and science of government.

In 1776, Jefferson had been placed on a five-man committee of the Continental Congress that was charged with producing a Declaration of Independence as soon as possible. A huge British fleet and army was heading for New York and the embryo American nation badly needed a rallying cry. The committee chose Jefferson to write the draft because he was a Virginian—the same reason Congress had chosen George Washington to lead the Continental Army. It was vital to give leadership tasks to the largest state in the rebellious confederation lest the brewing revolution seem like a New England uproar that could be dismissed as all too typical of the argumentative ex-Puritans.

Jefferson worked extremely hard on his appointed task. In 1943, a fragment of one of his early drafts was found in his papers. No less than 43 of the 156 words were additions or substitutions for words and phrases he had deleted. The opening paragraphs throb with a deeper, richer emotion than any other public document Jefferson ever wrote. Best among these sentences was one he never had to change: *"We hold these truths to be self evident; that all men are created equal, that they are endowed by their creator with certain unalienable rights; that among these are life, liberty, and the pursuit of happiness."*

Jefferson's fellow committee members, who included John Adams and Benjamin Franklin, made several word changes in his draft. But their editing was mild compared to the going-over that Congress gave the document. They threw out whole paragraphs and totally revised the ending. Jefferson was outraged—a little known fact that one distinguished historian has wryly mocked. Drafters of documents were not expected to take such a personal interest in their hastily prepared words.

"This was no hack editing job," the same historian acidly added. "The delegates who labored over the draft…had a splendid ear for language." Along with a vastly improved ending, the editors twice added the word "God"—a player in the drama that Jefferson seemed inclined to ignore, if not dismiss. Rather than accept the judgment of his editor-peers, Jefferson laboriously made copies of his original draft and sent them to several friends as proof that his version was far superior. He, of course, got sympathetic replies. Most later readers have concluded that Congress's version was both more powerful—and more eloquent.[1]

All in all, the lanky (6' 2") Virginian from Albermarle County, who lived in a spectacular mansion on the summit of a mountain, probably had an intimidating aura of superiority for slight James Madison. At this point in his life, his public accomplishments had not extended beyond his readiness to serve when summoned. As the oldest son of James Madison, Sr., proprietor of Montpelier, and the most prominent landowner in Orange County, Madison had been elected to the Virginia legislature in 1776. But he was much too self-effacing to make an impression on Jefferson or anyone else at that time.

The long hours the two men spent together as governor and councillor, discussing with the other seven councillors the problems and perils of wartime Virginia, soon created an intimacy that deepened steadily throughout the next six months. Jefferson soon regarded Madison as his most valuable advisor. As Jefferson put it in later years, he learned to rely on "the rich resources of his luminous and discriminating mind and of his extensive information."[2]

The diffident Madison's thinking on government was probably stimulated by the limitations of Virginia's constitution. In their fear of executive tyranny, the Old Dominion's framers had given the governor a minimum of executive power. Madison told one friend the office really consisted of "eight governors and a councillor." Even then, the legislature retained 98 percent of the power. It is interesting and perhaps significant that Thomas Jefferson's 126 proposed new laws made no effort to change this aspect of Virginia's government. He apparently shared the framers' fear of executive tyranny.

At the close of 1779, the Virginia House of Delegates elected Madison to the Continental Congress in Philadelphia, and he began a correspondence with Thomas Jefferson that would eventually number 1,250 letters over the next forty years. Madison was soon signing many of his letters "your friend," an expression that Jefferson quickly reciprocated. In one of his first letters, the new congressman told the governor "our public situation…continues equally perplexed and alarming." It was the first of a series of grim truths about the struggle for independence that intensified Jefferson's already mounting anxiety about Virginia's and the nation's survival.[3]

❦

Six days after Governor Jefferson took office in 1779, he had written to his friend William Fleming (no relation to the author), who was a Virginia delegate in Congress. The new governor asked if there was any truth to the rumor that the British were willing to make peace but Congress was dragging its collective feet on a negotiation. "It would surely be better to carry on a war ten years hence," Jefferson wrote, "than to continue the present [one] an unnecessary moment."[4]

If the British had gotten their hands on that letter, their propagandists would have had a field day chortling about how the drafter of the Declaration of Independence wanted to drop out of the war. The letter again suggests a surprising strain of impracticality in Jefferson's political judgment. No nation can "drop out" of a war and resume it ten years later.

The impulsive words were triggered by Governor Jefferson's discovery of Virginia's daunting problems. Inflation was making the paper money printed by the Continental Congress a bitter joke. The same thing was happening to paper dollars printed by Virginia. Governor Jefferson had no authority to curtail this debilitating flood, which was destroying patriot morale everywhere.

The governor had even less control over defending Virginia from attack. The state's weak militia law enabled men to avoid service for the most trivial excuses, and Jefferson, a stickler about exact obedience to the will of the legislature, was loath to stretch the government's authority, even in a looming crisis. In the spring of 1779, a British fleet had dropped anchor in Chesapeake Bay and sent ashore two thousand men. They captured a supposedly strong seacoast fort, burned the town of Suffolk, and cut a swath of fiery destruction across several dozen square miles of Virginia's Tidewater district, without losing a man.

This foray was the first glimpse of a change in British strategy. After four frustrating years of trying to subdue the Revolution in the North, George III's generals had decided to make the southern states their main target. Governor Jefferson could only watch helplessly while other British troops surged from Florida to conquer Georgia with dismaying ease. Next a redcoated army and fleet descended from New York to besiege Charleston, South Carolina, trapping a five thousand-man American army inside the city.

Congress did nothing but wring its collective hands. Madison reported a vague hope that the defenders could hold out until a French fleet forced the British to retreat. Jefferson wrote urgent letters to General Washington, asking him for help. But Washington, facing a British army in New York that outnumbered his Continentals, 3-1, could do nothing for him.

Other Madison letters from Congress reinforced the harsh limitations that General Washington confronted. The public treasury was empty and the private credit of men trying to buy food for the army was equally exhausted. More and more, the leadership of the war was in Washington's hands. He even began publishing a newspaper to refute the propaganda pouring from British headquarters in New York. As Madison told Governor Jefferson in one of his gloomiest letters, Congress's role had undergone "a total change" since 1776. In those glorious days, the solons printed paper money by the hundreds of thousands of dollars. The cash gave them the power to issue orders to the states. Now, with the money depreciated to wastepaper, Madison wrote that Congress was "as…dependent on the states as the King of England on the Parliament."

Worse, the states exhibited little or no inclination to respond to Congress's pleas to send food and fresh men to the Continental Army. Madison feared they were approaching a moment when "every thing must inevitably go wrong or come to a total stop."[5]

While Madison and a few others tried to rouse the floundering Congress, Charleston's five thousand defenders surrendered on May 12, 1780. The British army promptly invaded the rest of prostrate South Carolina. The Charleston captives included most of Virginia's Continental regiments. A few weeks later, British cavalry destroyed another Virginia regiment that had been fleeing the doomed city. On August 16, 1780, at Camden, South Carolina, bayonet-wielding redcoats routed an army sent south under the command of Congress's favorite general, Horatio Gates. Their ranks included seven hundred Virginia militia that Governor Jefferson had mustered with not a little difficulty. General Gates fled the battlefield and did not stop galloping rearward for 160 miles. His reputation never recovered.

Jefferson's reputation also suffered a dent with some Virginians, who thought he should have accompanied the militia to the battlefield and rallied them with words as stirring as those he wrote in the Declaration of Independence. Joseph Jones, the senior member of Virginia's congressional delegation, went so far as to hope Jefferson would lead these men in the battle. Under Virginia's constitution, the governor was the commander in chief of the militia. The idea had not even occurred to Governor Jefferson. He had no pretensions to expertise—and not much interest—in military matters. [6]

✿

In June of 1780, at the end of his first year as governor, Jefferson tried to resign. Shocked letters from close friends warned him that his reputation would never recover if he abandoned the leadership of the state in the midst of a crisis. It is a first glimpse of Jefferson's reluctance to wield executive power—and his puzzling lack of enthusiasm for playing the role of an effective leader. Wearily, with no uplifting words about patriotism and duty, Jefferson agreed to serve another year.

If Congressman Madison heard about his friend's attempted resignation, he did not mention it in his letters. Madison had more distressing news to report—"the sudden defection of Major General Benedict Arnold and his flight to the enemy." Madison told how Arnold had almost succeeded in surrendering the Hudson River fortress of West Point to the British, trapping General Washington, the French ambassador, and the Marquis de Lafayette in the snare. [7]

Three months later, an agitated messenger galloped into Richmond to warn Governor Jefferson that another enemy fleet and army were in the Chesapeake. The commander was newly minted British Brigadier Benedict Arnold, and he soon headed up the James River with fifteen hundred men. Governor Jefferson had refused to believe the warning and had waited two days to summon the militia in the three counties around Richmond. A paltry two hundred men turned out. Meanwhile, the Governor had to get his terrified wife and three daughters out of the menaced capital to a nearby plantation. Martha Jefferson had given birth to a baby girl only two months earlier and was still far from well.

Riding back to Richmond along the opposite side of the James River, Jefferson arrived to find Arnold burning tobacco warehouses and other property in the capital. A redcoated detachment marched up the river to Westham, where they destroyed the foundry and shops that made Virginia's muskets. With scarcely a hostile shot fired at him, Brigadier Arnold returned to the coast and set up a permanent base at Portsmouth, where he was soon reinforced by another two thousand men.

Although Virginia had at least fifty thousand men on her militia rolls, Governor Jefferson could not raise enough soldiers to dislodge the British, who repeatedly ravaged the countryside, burning shipyards, ships, and huge quantities of tobacco. In the midst of this public ordeal came a wrenching personal loss—five-month-old Lucy Elizabeth Jefferson died in Richmond, leaving her mother prostrate with grief.

Two weeks later, Brigadier Arnold came up the James River again, once more forcing Governor Jefferson to flee into the countryside with his family. The climax to this ordeal was the invasion of Virginia by Charles, General Lord Cornwallis, the British commander in the Carolinas. He had decided that the rest of the South would not be pacified until Virginia was knocked out of the war. Combined with the garrison in Portsmouth, he had eighty-two hundred men.

Governor Jefferson, his councillors, and the legislature fled west to Charlottesville. Cornwallis rumbled through the countryside, burning and looting at will. The state's morale sank to the vanishing point. One of Jefferson's closest friends, John Page, wailed: "I am ashamed and ever shall be to call myself a Virginian."[8]

At this political nadir, Jefferson informed the legislature that June 2, 1781, would mark the end of his second year as governor, and he did not intend to serve another term. The state's desperate situation made his decision even more incredible to people who had witnessed George Washington's refusal to quit after shattering defeats in 1776 and 1777, capped by the ordeal at Valley Forge. It was even more unnerving evidence that Jefferson seemed to place little or no value on his role as the revolutionary leader of Virginia.

Some months earlier, on March 23, 1781, the Governor had told James Madison in a personal letter that he intended to step down. But he seems never to have revealed his intentions to anyone else. Madison had replied, on April 3, that he could not "forbear lamenting that the state in its present crisis is to lose the benefit of your administration." But he was sure that Jefferson had "weighed well the reasons" for the decision, and Madison would lament it henceforth "in silence." This was an extremely polite way of saying Jefferson was making a mistake—and an almost pathetic glimpse of Madison's deference to his friend.[9]

The Governor's political timing could not have been worse. Early on June 4, two days after his resignation, an agitated horseman came pounding up the steep road to Monticello's summit, shouting: "Tarleton is coming!"

Redhaired Colonel Banastre Tarleton was the most feared cavalry leader in the British army. In a bid to demolish the last shreds of Virginia's resistance, General Cornwallis had sent Tarleton and 250 of his green-coated horsemen on a hundred-mile dash west to scatter the legislature and capture Governor Jefferson. They had thudded through the Virginia countryside without a shot fired at them—more evidence of the almost total collapse of Virginia's will to resist the royal invaders.

The ex-governor's only option was another flight with his terrified wife, Martha, and their two daughters, to a nearby plantation. Returning to Monticello to order silver and other valuables hidden, Jefferson had the unpleasant experience of looking down on the main street of Charlottesville through his spyglass and seeing Tarleton's horsemen riding down fleeing members of the legislature. The beat of hooves on Monticello's winding road warned him that a detachment of dragoons was heading his way, making it wise for him to retire from the vicinity as rapidly as possible.

In July, a rump group of legislators assembled at Staunton, Virginia, on the other side of the Blue Ridge Mountains, to affirm that the demoralized state still had a government. They elected a new governor and, at the suggestion of one member, resolved that an inquiry be made "into the conduct of the Executive of this state for the past twelve months." The man behind this nasty proposal was Patrick Henry. He was disgusted with Governor Jefferson's performance and had decided it was time to get rid of him as one of Virginia's leaders.

Nothing in Thomas Jefferson's political career would ever wound him so deeply. He did not write a letter to James Madison for the next five months, nor did Madison write to him. They did not even exchange comments on the extraordinary transformation of the war. In mid-September 1781, General Washington and America's French allies marched to Virginia to cooperate with the French West Indies fleet and trap General Lord Cornwallis and his army in the port of Yorktown. After a bombardment that lasted little more than a week, the British surrendered, rescuing Virginia and the rest of the crumbling American confederacy from imminent collapse.

Although Jefferson wrote a letter congratulating Washington, he was not the same man who, as governor, had exchanged crisp, detailed communications with the general about the war in Virginia. Instead, he humbly explained that he would have come in person to thank him for Yorktown. But he was sure Washington had better things to do than exchange small talk with a mere "private individual." The draft of the letter was crossed out and interlined to an extraordinary degree, suggesting Jefferson's emotional turmoil. It is sad evidence of the deep depression into which Jefferson had plunged after the humiliating close of his governorship.[10]

※

Neither the assembly nor the man who proposed the inquiry into Governor Jefferson's conduct had made any specific charges. But Jefferson magnified the proposal into a grievance that gave him an excuse to withdraw from politics permanently. He told his friend, Edmund Randolph: "I have returned to my farm, my family, and my books, from which I think nothing ever more will separate me." The astounded Randolph replied: "If you can justify this resolution to yourself, I am confident you cannot to the world."[11]

It is more than a little significant that Jefferson said nothing to James Madison about his withdrawal from public life—nor did his younger friend say a word to him, although there is no doubt that Randolph, who was also serving in Congress, had informed Madison of Jefferson's letter. Similarly, neither Jefferson nor Madison mentioned the Virginia Assembly's decision when they considered charges against him, two months after Yorktown. The legislators, their mood transformed by Washington's victory, dismissed the indictment and declared their unwaveringly high opinion of Jefferson's "ability, rectitude, and integrity as chief magistrate of this commonwealth." By this time, not even Patrick Henry saw any point in condemning the drafter of the Declaration of Independence when hopes of ultimate victory were dawning.[12]

※

The legislature's exoneration did not alter Jefferson's determination to quit public life. He reiterated to several friends that he had no plans to leave Monticello for the rest of his days. He declined to serve when his county's voters chose him for the state legislature and ignored a warning from the Speaker of the House of Delegates that he was risking arrest.

James Monroe, nephew of Congressman Joseph Jones, had been elected to the Virginia legislature from another county. Monroe warned the ex-governor that many members were criticizing him. Jefferson replied with an emotional letter. He declared that the threat of censure had inflicted injuries on his feelings that could only be cured by "the all healing grave." He reinforced this pronouncement by refusing an attempt to elect him to Congress.[13]

An obviously troubled Madison admitted to Edmund Randolph that he was partial to Jefferson. But "the mode in which he seems determined to revenge the wrong inflicted by his country does not appear to me to be dictated either by philosophy or patriotism." Madison was much kinder when he wrote to Jefferson. He explained his long silence by saying he was so certain the legislature would exonerate his friend, their decision had made "little impression" on him. But he confessed to personal disappointment because Jefferson had refused the attempt to elect him to Congress. To work with him again would have given Madison "both unexpected and personal satisfaction." The country would also have probably derived "important aid" from his presence. [14]

At the close of his letter to James Monroe, Jefferson revealed an additional reason for his inner turmoil: "Mrs. Jefferson has added another daughter to our family. She has been ever since and still continues very dangerously ill." Six months later, Martha Jefferson died, inflicting a terrific blow to this emotionally fragile man's stability. For a while there was fear Jefferson would commit suicide—he later admitted he had considered it. His sense of responsibility for his three young daughters forced him to cling to a life he no longer valued. But he did little except wander his mansion or ride aimlessly around the countryside in a stupor of grief, sometimes accompanied by his distraught oldest daughter, Martha.

Jefferson did not write a word about this tragic ordeal to Madison. But the younger man soon heard about it from their mutual friend, Edmund Randolph, who described Jefferson as "inconsolable." Madison knew how totally a plantation could become a world in itself, enveloping a man. He decided Jefferson's only hope of recovery was a swift return to public life.

By this time, Madison had become one of the most influential members of Congress. He had no trouble persuading his fellow legislators to appoint Jefferson a commissioner in the peace negotiations that were about to begin in France. A confidential letter whizzed from Madison to Edmund Randolph in Virginia, telling him to let Jefferson know as quickly as possible. "An official notification will follow," Madison added. Showing how well he understood that Jefferson's wounded feelings needed balm, Madison urged Randolph to tell the ex-governor that the resolution "passed unanimously, without a single remark adverse to it."

This long-range psychology worked perfectly. Jefferson accepted the appointment and was soon ready to leave Monticello for France. Accompanied by young Martha, he went first to Philadelphia to get the background he needed for his peace negotiator's role. A smiling Madison greeted him at Virginia's favorite boarding house, run by a genial widow named Mrs. Mary House and her lively daughter, Mrs. Elizabeth Trist. After three years of separation, the two men quickly regained their old intimacy.

Another sign of their renewed friendship was a confession from Madison that he was in love. The young lady was a pretty teenager named Kitty Floyd, daughter of a New York congressman and his wife—also residents of Mrs. House's hostelry. Young women did not go to college or pursue careers in 1782. Kitty, who would soon be sixteen, was considered more than eligible for marriage. Jefferson and his daughter headed for Baltimore, where a French frigate was to take them to France. Winter weather and a British blockade of the Chesapeake delayed his departure.

As he waited in Baltimore, Jefferson exchanged wry letters in cipher with Madison about the foibles of some of their fellow revolutionists. Madison described a stream of imprudent diatribes from John Adams, who was in Europe serving as one of the peace commissioners. These angry screeds exposed his vanity, his prejudice against France, and his "venom" against America's ambassador, Benjamin Franklin. Jefferson tried to defend his colleague from the heroic days of 1776, who had stoutly supported his draft of the Declaration of Independence against congressional editing. He assured Madison that the volatile Yankee had a "sound head" and "integrity."

As Jefferson began to complain of boredom in Baltimore, word arrived from France that the American negotiators had signed a "provisional" treaty of peace. Congress cancelled Jefferson's appointment, but he did not return to Monticello. Instead, he headed for Philadelphia and participated in the celebrations when a copy of the peace treaty arrived from Europe on the ship *Washington*.

Early in the new year (1783), Jefferson proved that he had regained his equilibrium by writing a letter to George Washington in which he expressed his "individual tribute" for all the general "had effected for us." He hesitated to indulge in "warm effusions" because "even the appearance of adulation" was "foreign" to his nature. Washington replied in equally warm terms. He wrote that winning the approval of men like Jefferson was all the reward he sought for his long service in pursuit of the victory that now seemed certain.[15]

✤

Back in Virginia, Jefferson received a letter that exploded his hope that James Madison and Kitty Floyd would happily marry. On her return to New York, Miss Floyd had had second thoughts and written Madison a curt, dismissive letter. Struggling to be philosophical, Madison confided to Jefferson that it was "one of those incidents to which such affairs are liable."

Jefferson tried to console his younger friend, exclaiming that "no event has been more contrary to my expectations." He reminded him that "the world still presents the same and many other resources for happiness," and assured Madison that "firmness of mind and unremitting occupation [hard work]" were the best remedies for his pain.

Madison stayed in Philadelphia until his term in Congress expired in November 1783, trying to take Jefferson's advice about hard work. But circumstances beyond his control made legislative labors difficult. Not long after General Washington persuaded the infuriated officers of the Continental Army at New Windsor to abandon plans to march on the bankrupt Congress to demand their back pay, the nation's legislators found themselves surrounded by a surly regiment of bayonet wielding soldiers who had been stationed in Lancaster, Pennsylvania. They wanted their long unpaid back salaries immediately, if not sooner.

Congress fled to Princeton, New Jersey, a little village with few of the creature comforts of Philadelphia. Madison found himself sharing a bed with six-foot-tall Joseph Jones, which added sleeplessness to his woes. He told one correspondent that he scarcely had room "to move my limbs." Far more distressing was Congress's descent to a new low in the eyes of the nation. One Philadelphia newspaper issued a summary judgment that was soon echoed by editors and readers everywhere. The legislators' decision to cut and run "exhibited neither dignity, fortitude, nor perseverance." In Europe, one American traveler reported, the story had been inflated into "the annihilation of Congress and the utter destruction of the commonwealth."[16]

The American peace commissioners, waiting for a final version of the provisional treaty, warned that the news had "diminished the admiration in which the people of America were held by the nations of Europe." This was James Madison's reward for three years of toil, trying to create a legislature worthy of an independent nation. There can be little doubt that the experience made him begin thinking about a drastic cure for Congress's futility.

In June 1783, the Virginia legislature nominated Thomas Jefferson to replace Madison as the leader of the state's congressional delegation. Congress had moved to Annapolis, the capital of Maryland. There, Jefferson found a pathetic ghost of the legislature he had known in 1776. Only twenty delegates were present from seven states, which meant it was impossible to make any important decisions.

Staring at the delegates was the most significant document that Congress had considered since the Declaration of Independence—the definitive treaty of peace. With it came a letter from Benjamin Franklin, John Adams, and John Jay, the American negotiators, telling them that the "riot in Philadelphia"—the attack by the bayonet-wielding soldiers—had given the British hopes that the United States was about to collapse, making a peace treaty dead on arrival.

The treaty stipulated that the Americans would sign it within six months of its acceptance by the British and the French. On January 1, 1784, an anxious Jefferson was telling Madison that one of the current congressmen had gone home, leaving only six states represented instead of the nine that were required to ratify the treaty. March 3 was the deadline for the signed treaty to be delivered to the British. What to do?

Arthur Lee, a Virginia delegate who specialized in being cantankerous, told Jefferson that seven states would be enough, and soon convinced two other Virginia delegates to join him in "violent" insistence on this solution. They vowed to put the idea to a vote when and if they had seven states represented.

Jefferson demurred. Too much was at stake to risk an accusation of deception from the truculent British. He sought Madison's opinion, and he strongly agreed on the need for nine states. Signing with only seven present might deceive the British, but it would be "immediately detected at home" and the deception would "dishonor...Federal Councils everywhere." This turmoil did not improve the depression that continued to trouble Jefferson. "I have had very ill health since I have been here, and am getting lower rather than otherwise," he told Madison.[17]

Meanwhile, the president of Congress rushed frantic messages to absent members, and they trickled into Annapolis. On January 14, Congress had twenty-three delegates from nine states. To Jefferson's vast relief, the peace treaty was ratified and returned to Europe. Not until May did the British sign it, making peace permanent.

This achievement was to be Jefferson's only legislative satisfaction. Congress continued to behave like a pack of ill-bred adolescents. They came and went at will, repeatedly leaving those still in their seats without a quorum. Even when they managed to muster that minimum requirement, the delegates were so contentious, there was no hope of agreement on anything. An exasperated Jefferson—a lawyer himself—blamed the impasse on the fact that most of the delegates were attorneys, "whose trade it is to question everything, yield nothing, and talk by the hour."

Jefferson's frustrations renewed his wish for the peace and quiet of private life. He urged Madison to buy land near Monticello. He had persuaded James Monroe and another young admirer, William Short, both of whom had studied law under his guidance, to agree with this idea. "In such a society," Jefferson saw himself quitting politics and its contentions once and for all. "Life is of no value but as it brings us gratifications," he avowed, and he saw no hope of pleasure in the "insupportable" arguments that harried him in Congress.

❀

In the light of future years, perhaps the most important topic Jefferson addressed during this sojourn in Congress arrived on his desk in a letter from George Washington. When the Continental Army of the Revolution disbanded in 1783, the officers formed a "Society of the Cincinnati," a name that honored the Roman general, Cincinnatus, who surrendered his military power after he successfully defended Rome, and returned to his farm. It was no accident that the Society elected Washington as their first president. In their eyes, he was a veritable model of this peaceful relinquishment of the honors and privileges of war.

The Society's chief purpose was to offer help to officers who needed aid to reestablish their civilian lives. Another principle was a hereditary right for sons and grandsons of the founders to inherit their membership. This idea stirred violent antipathy among the civilians who had not served in the army. They accused the Cincinnati of conspiring to undermine America's republican principles by creating a new aristocracy. Washington was disturbed by this rancor and asked Jefferson's opinion of the Society, and how he might best deal with its political problems without undermining its commitment to help ex-officers in need of help.

Ex-Governor Jefferson wrote a masterful reply to the retired general. He told Washington the hereditary idea violated the American principle of "the natural equality of man...particularly the idea of preeminence by birth." Most people, including almost all the current members of Congress, disapproved of it. Washington was not immortal, and they feared that future leaders of the Cincinnati would forget that "the moderation of a single character has probably prevented this revolution from being closed as most others have been, by a subversion of that liberty it was intended to establish." The only solution, it seemed to Jefferson, was the abandonment of the hereditary principle. Even better might be the disbandment of the Society.

Jefferson closed his extraordinarily frank reply by assuring Washington that he would mention their discussion to no one. He saw himself as temporarily "thrown back by events on a stage where I had never more thought to appear." He did not think he would stay very long in this role, but "while I remain...I shall be gratified by all occasions of rendering you service & of convincing you there is no one to whom your reputation & happiness are dearer."[18]

Washington was so impressed, he stopped in Annapolis on his way to a meeting of the Cincinnati in Philadelphia. He spent an evening with Jefferson, discussing the best way to preserve the Society. He agreed with Jefferson about the need to eliminate the hereditary idea. But the ex-general felt too committed to the Society's desire to offer mutual aid and brotherhood to urge the harsh final step of disbanding. [19]

After Washington departed, the quarrels of Congress must have seemed even more trivial to the still depressed Jefferson. Suddenly, rescue appeared in the guise of a message from Europe. Peace commissioner John Jay had announced his resignation, and the southern states demanded that someone from their region replace him. Congress had asked the commissioners (Jay, John Adams, and Benjamin Franklin) to remain in Europe and negotiate commercial treaties with several nations. Southerners felt their interests should be represented by one of their own.

To no one's surprise, Congress nominated Jefferson for the post. He accepted without even a moment's hesitation—evidence that he dreaded a return to Monticello and its tragic aura, which would only worsen his depression. At least as influential was his eagerness to visit Europe and explore nations and societies that he had read and thought about since his student days.

"I am now to take leave of the justlings (sic) of the states," Jefferson informed Madison with visible delight. In this new field, "the divisions will be fewer but on a larger scale." He hoped Madison would continue their correspondence. He was especially desirous of hearing from him "at the close of every session" of the Virginia legislature, and of Congress, so Jefferson could remain up-to-date on "general measures and dispositions."[20]

With almost incoherent haste, Jefferson returned to Philadelphia, where he had left his thirteen-year-old daughter, Martha, in the care of poet Francis Hopkinson and his wife. The new diplomat invited William Short to join him as his secretary. In early May 1784, Jefferson and his entourage headed north to Boston, where a ship awaited them. Now and then, he paused to discuss politics with various friends in New England. In a farewell note to Madison, he reported "the conviction growing strongly that nothing can preserve our confederacy unless the band of Union, their common council [Congress], be strengthened."[21]

Those words underscore a significant fact. Thomas Jefferson was out of touch with George Washington's and James Madison's approach to strengthening the federal government. The man from Monticello was thinking about Congress; the man from Mount Vernon and his scholarly young advisor would soon be thinking about a new political entity: the American presidency. This divide in their approach to the nation's government would grow deeper in the years to come.

Simultaneously, the new envoy was sailing toward another divide. France, the nation whose soldiers and warships and money had made a crucial difference in winning the struggle for independence, was almost as bankrupt as the United States. It was a condition that was hard for King Louis XVI in his splendid palace at Versailles and the noblemen in their sumptuous mansions in Paris to understand. But in the winding alleys and backstreets of Paris were people who would soon propose a future for France that would change the way Thomas Jefferson thought about politics forever.

CHAPTER 3

Should This Constitution Be Ratified?

I N PHILADELPHIA DURING THE summer of 1787, George Washington presided over a conclave that fiercely and sometimes frantically debated the new constitution that slowly emerged from James Madison's Virginia plan. As the delegates edged toward agreement, Madison began to think there was only one way to describe the outcome of their hundreds of hours of often abrasive argument: a miracle. At the center of this unlikely outcome was a large fact that Madison also noted in his voluminous notes of the proceedings—that no one signed the Constitution with more enthusiasm than General Washington. [1]

After a farewell dinner with the delegates at the Rising Sun Tavern, Washington returned to Robert Morris's house and wrote a letter to the Marquis de Lafayette about the success of their experiment. His motive was both personal and political. He wanted to get the news of the Constitution and its promise of American stability to their Revolutionary War ally as quickly as possible. At the same time, he was hoping the young man he sometimes called his "adopted son" could use their reconciliation of liberty and power to help him deal with political unrest in France, which showed signs of veering into violence. After describing the Constitution and its hoped-for good effects, he told Lafayette: "I do not believe that providence has done so much for nothing."[2]

Although James Madison publicly praised the Constitution that emerged from the Philadelphia convention, privately, he was a disappointed man. Above all, he had wanted to give Congress the power to veto state legislation. Instead, he had to settle for a vaguely worded assertion that the Constitution was the "supreme law" of the nation. States were barred only from specific tasks, such as coining money.

Madison was even more unhappy with the compromise that gave each state two senators. He had wanted the House of Representatives to elect senators and give them the power to veto both state and federal legislation. Madison succeeded in giving the president enough veto power and authority to make him the guardian of federal unity. But he remained troubled by doubts that the Constitution would be adequate for the hopes of unifying federal power that he and George Washington had shared at Mount Vernon.

Madison's doubts might have become demoralizing, if he had seen Thomas Jefferson's reaction when the Constitution reached him in distant France. In the three years that had passed since Jefferson left America, he and Madison had remained in touch with a steady stream of letters. But it was hardly a normal correspondence. At least two months elapsed between mailing a letter and its delivery, and it often took another two months for the reply to reach the original sender. Events in both countries frequently intervened, prompting sharply different reactions from the two friends. It soon became apparent that they had begun to disagree about the kind of government the nation needed.

A prime example was Shays' Rebellion. Influenced by ex-General Washington and the appalling weakness of Congress in the face of this upheaval, Madison called the Shaysites "a diseased part of the body politic," and suspected that British influence may have been involved. Even after the rebels had been crushed, Madison reported to Jefferson that many of them "remained insolent," and he worried that the new governor of Massachusetts, John Hancock, was "an idolater of popularity" who might be seduced into "dishonorable compliances" to their demands, which included a redistribution of property.[3]

Jefferson's reaction to the Shaysites was almost totally opposite. He saw nothing wrong with "a little rebellion now and then" in a republic. It was a medicine "necessary for the sound health of government." These were ironic opinions from a former governor who twice tried to resign when his state was confronted with armed men determined to kill or capture him and his supporters. Jefferson was even more tolerant in his comments to other correspondents, such as Colonel William Stephens Smith, John Adams's son-in-law. "The tree of liberty must be refreshed from time to time with the blood of patriots and tyrants. It is its natural manure."[4]

When Madison's letter reached France, Jefferson made no attempt to reply to his younger friend's tough-minded view of the Shaysites. The envoy's experience in France undoubtedly had something to do with this silence. He was dismayed by the extreme poverty and powerlessness of the French peasantry compared to the largely untaxed wealth and authority of the king and his fellow aristocrats. Jefferson called it "a government of wolves over sheep."[5]

Madison did not rush a copy of the new constitution to Jefferson. Instead, as the convention drew to a close, he sent him an outline of the document. Meanwhile, the envoy received a copy from John Adams, who was America's minister to Britain. His Massachusetts friend, Elbridge Gerry, had sent it to him, after refusing to sign the document. Jefferson was not happy with what he read. "How do you like our new Constitution?" he asked Adams. "I must confess there are things in it which stagger all my dispositions to subscribe to what such an assembly has proposed."

Jefferson had expected only three or four new enlargements to be added to "the good, old, and venerable fabrick" of the Articles of Confederation." He added an even nastier line about the office Washington and Madison valued most. "Their president seems a bad edition of a Polish king."[6]

In 1783–84, Congressman Jefferson had writhed for six months in the grip of the feckless legislature that the "venerable" Articles of Confederation had created. But his fear of power was so intense, he preferred this ordeal to a government designed to reach decisions and enforce them with the help of this new office, the presidency. Jefferson told Colonel William Stephens Smith he thought the new charter was an overreaction to Shays' rebellion. The Constitutional Convention had "sent up a kite [a predatory bird] to keep the hen yard in order."

The metaphor is revealing. Apparently, Jefferson regarded the people in the yard (the nation) as amiable as clucking hens. Shays' Rebellion was anything but a chorus of innocent fowls. Jefferson also blamed the British for exaggerating American instability in their newspapers. London had repeated this slander for so long, the envoy was convinced that even the Americans had come to believe it—and had constructed a much too powerful response to the problem.

In 1786, Jefferson had visited John Adams in London. His friend had taken him to the royal palace and introduced him to George III. The king had been more than cordial to Adams when he presented himself as the American ambassador. But His Majesty pointedly turned his back on the drafter of the Declaration of Independence, which was filled with insults to his royal person. The thin-skinned Jefferson was deeply offended. A year later he was telling people that the English would have to be "kicked into common good manners." [7]

Not until October 24, 1787, five weeks after the Philadelphia convention adjourned, did Madison send Jefferson a copy of the Constitution. It was accompanied by an extraordinary seventeen-page letter. In this virtual treatise, Madison simultaneously confessed his disappointment with the new charter's shortcomings and defended its value as a practical replacement for the unworkable Articles of Confederation. The delay suggests Madison feared Jefferson would not agree with the outcome of the Philadelphia convention. In particular, the younger man was eager to refute the widely held belief—which Jefferson subscribed to - that only small nations could or would support a republic. Larger countries naturally gravitated to rule by kings or emperors.

In this long letter, Jefferson became the first man to read Madison's breakthrough argument that a large republic would be *less* likely to degenerate into tyranny. Why? A large republic contained so many varied groups, each pursuing their own interests, they would be unlikely to blend into a majority that would engage in "unjust pursuits," such as violating property rights or individual liberties. This was especially true of a republic divided into large states, most of them geographically distant from each other.

Events also played a part in Madison's delay. The campaign to win ratification for the Constitution had begun almost the day the convention adjourned. Madison had hurried to New York to take his seat in the old Congress, where he worked hard to persuade the members to pass the document on to the state legislatures without any negative comments. This was not an easy task. From September 17 to September 28, a heated debate about what to do with the new charter raged virtually nonstop. Virginians such as Richard Henry Lee, one of the earliest supporters of the Revolution, voiced severe criticisms. Soon there was an alarming number of congressmen who wanted to reject the Constitution on the spot. They had authorized the convention only to revise the Articles of Confederation. Instead, the Philadelphia conclave had produced an entirely new government. This was disobedience, and deserved to be punished.

Madison led the fight for a compromise, repeatedly telling people how General Washington had signed the new Constitution with great "cordiality." With both sides weighing each word, the compromise was hammered out. Congress sent the Constitution to the states by a unanimous vote, with neither criticism nor praise. Madison immediately informed General Washington, who replied with evident pleasure—and political sophistication: "This apparent unanimity will have its effect."

The effect was slow to appear. Madison soon discovered considerable opposition outside Congress. Essays written by New Yorkers under pseudonyms such as Cato began appearing in the city's papers, deploring the Constitution as an assault on the nation's peace and prosperity, and a threat to everyone's civil liberties. New York's Governor George Clinton remained hostile to the change in government. He liked the way the Articles of Confederation had allowed him to become a virtual dictator of the so-called "Empire State."

Thomas Jefferson did not even mention the durability of a large republic in his reply to Madison's long letter. Instead, the envoy told the Congressman what he liked and did not like about the new constitution. He liked the way it sidetracked the state legislatures. He also liked Congress's power to levy taxes and the organization of the government into three branches. He especially liked the compromise between the large and small states, which gave every state two senators and based membership in the House of Representatives on a state's population. [8]

Then the envoy told Madison what "I do not like." First and most troubling was the omission of a bill of rights, which would guarantee freedom of religion, habeas corpus, trial by juries, freedom of the press and protection against standing armies. "The people are entitled to a bill of rights against every government on earth," Jefferson insisted.

At the Philadelphia convention, Madison had argued that he thought a bill of rights was superfluous. But he was not opposed to the idea in principle. He had already led an historic struggle in Virginia to pass Jefferson's proposal to discard the Episcopal Church as the state's established religion, and make religious freedom the prevailing policy.

The second feature Jefferson disliked was the abandonment of rotation in office—especially in the case of the president. He was sure that a "first magistrate" would always be reelected if he were permitted to succeed himself. This meant he would become president for life. "The power of removing him every fourth year by a vote of the people is a power that will not be exercised," Jefferson predicted. [9]

Then came words that would echo through the rest of Jefferson's life: "I own I am not a friend to a very energetic government. It is always oppressive...I think our governments will remain virtuous for many centuries, as long as they remain chiefly agricultural, and this will be as long as there are vacant lands in America. When they get piled upon one another in large cities, as in Europe, they will become as corrupt as in Europe."[10]

There was nothing new about most of Jefferson's ideas. They were standard Whig (the eighteenth century word for liberal) doctrine. Central to them was the conviction that power was a threat to liberty. Washington and Madison, on the other hand, had moved beyond this fear to the belief that power could be used positively to control—and even to enlarge—individual liberty. This was one of the central ideas in a series of essays that Madison began writing, in partnership with Alexander Hamilton and John Jay, defending the Constitution against its critics. They kept their identities secret by writing under the pen name Publius, in honor of one of the founders of the Roman Republic, Publius Valerius Publicola.

The trio produced three or four essays a week, which were published in three New York newspapers. Madison wrote twenty-six and Hamilton fifty-one; Jay contributed only six before an attack of rheumatism laid him low. Early in 1788, the essays were collected into a book, *The Federalist*, that became a powerful weapon in the ongoing debate about whether the Constitution should become the law of the land.

George Washington was an enthusiastic admirer of *The Federalist*. He called it one of the most important discussions of government ever written. "When the transient circumstances and fugitive performances which have attended the crisis will have disappeared, this work will have merited the notice of posterity," he told Alexander Hamilton. For a man whose education had ended in the fourth grade, this comment revealed remarkably good judgment. *The Federalist* remains an admired document to this day.[11]

Washington made it clear that this praise was not mere flattery. "I have read every performance which has been printed on one side or another of the great question," he told his ex-aide. None could have more impact on an unbiased mind "as the production of your triumvirate." The ex-general asked Madison to send him a "neatly bound" copy for his library.[12]

Washington's remark about reading every pamphlet or news story written about the Constitution is a glimpse of how intensely he was involved in the fight for ratification. At one point, his secretary at Mount Vernon, his former military aide-de-camp, Colonel David Humphreys, called him "the focus of political intelligence for the New World." The ex-general repeatedly urged the friends of the Constitution to take up their pens to answer the critics.

Speaking as one Virginian to another, Madison remarked that their home state needed these essays as much as New York did. Some of the leaders of the Revolution in the Old Dominion had become strident opponents of the new Constitution—most notably, Patrick Henry. The orator had been joined by another prominent political leader, George Mason, who had published an angry essay condemning the document. Madison suggested that Washington might put the Federalist essays "into the hands of some of your confidential correspondents in Richmond who would have them reprinted there."[13]

Washington sent the essays to Dr. David Stuart, who represented Fairfax County in the state legislature. Stuart had married the widow of Martha Washington's son, John Parke Custis, and was a trusted friend. Washington urged him to find a Richmond printer who would give the essays "a place in his paper." He was not at liberty to disclose the names of the writers, and he was even more emphatic about keeping his role in forwarding the essays a total secret. This powerful political medicine was soon appearing weekly in the *Virginia Independent Chronicle*.

Washington had decided his influence would be strongest if he maintained a detached image. But he remained at the white hot center of the contest. Madison all but deluged him with letters from New York, reporting on the ratification contest in various states, and its prospects of success.

By early 1788, Washington knew that Pennsylvania, Delaware, New Jersey, Georgia, and Connecticut had approved the new government by comfortable margins. But Massachusetts was a large and ominous worry.

Elbridge Gerry, a close friend of John Adams, had been attacking the charter since he returned from the Constitutional Convention. He had aroused serious doubts in Samuel Adams and Governor John Hancock, whose friendship went back to the heady days of 1776. Neither man had any great affection for George Washington, who had outshone the wildly ambitious Hancock during the Revolution, and worsted Adams in contests over control of the Continental Army. Hancock had become governor by placating the Shaysites and their sympathizers with promises of tax relief. He reportedly controlled fifty votes in the Massachusetts ratifying convention.

The federalists, as the proponents of the Constitution began to call themselves, had learned from the earlier contests. In Pennsylvania, they had pushed for immediate ratification. Though they had won a majority, their haste left the anti-federalists infuriated, and the antis took to the newspapers, hurling nasty accusations and dark predictions that soon circulated around the nation. Taking a different tack in Massachusetts, the federalists let the antis talk for weeks and tried to be agreeable. Nor did they object when Samuel Adams and his followers asked if they could recommend amendments, especially a bill of rights.

An anxious Madison, in close touch with the debate, urged Washington to send a Bay State friend "an explicit communication of your good wishes" for the Constitution. The general wrote a strong letter to former Major General Benjamin Lincoln, the man who had crushed Shays' Rebellion. By the time it arrived, Massachusetts had voted to ratify. But Washington's warm words may have helped prevent second thoughts and angry counterattacks a la Pennsylvania from the Adams-Hancock faction.

⚜

The delegates that Virginia's voters sent to the ratifying convention had a worrisome tilt toward the constitution's chief opponents, Patrick Henry and George Mason. Now it was Washington's turn to give some crucial advice to James Madison. The Congressman was reluctant to appear in public as the document's defender. Perhaps his early doubts about its defects resurfaced when he pictured himself in that role. More probably, Madison knew his limitations as a speaker and hesitated to take on Patrick Henry, an acknowledged champion in that department. Washington banished Madison's hesitation with no-nonsense bluntness. "Explanations will be wanting" at the convention, and "none can give them with more precision and accuracy than yourself."[14]

Early in March, Madison left New York and made Mount Vernon his first stop in Virginia. He and Washington spent a full day (March 19, 1788) discussing the political situation in their home state. They apparently agreed that the Massachusetts strategy of tolerating future amendments might work well in Virginia.

At home in Montpelier, Madison learned that in Maryland and South Carolina, anti-federalists had come up with a new strategy. They planned to persuade their ratifying conventions to adjourn without a vote. Madison rushed a letter to one of Maryland's leaders, warning him that such a move could have fatal consequences. He did not know the man's address, and he sent the letter to Washington, leaving it open, inviting him to read it before forwarding it. The general sent it along with a letter of his own, warning that the idea was "tantamount to rejection of the Constitution." At the convention, the Marylander circulated Washington's letter, and ratification won by a comfortable majority.

The Virginia convention was a challenge that could not be solved so easily. George Washington had made a point of sending Patrick Henry a copy of the Constitution as soon as he returned to Mount Vernon. Washington said he wished it "had been made more perfect," but "sincerely believed" it was the best agreement that could be obtained at this time. Perhaps the chief reason to accept it, he added, was his sense that "the political concerns of this country are, in a manner, suspended by a thread."

These sincere and serious words had made no impression on the headstrong orator. He became even more determined to destroy a document that he considered a threat to Virginia's welfare—and his power in the nation's largest state. It was no accident that Henry and George Clinton of New York had similar attitudes. New York was not yet a large state from a population point of view, but its empty northern acres left no doubt that it would eventually join this exclusive club.[15]

By this time, Madison realized he and Washington had another opponent in this looming clash: Thomas Jefferson. The ex-governor's friendly tone in his letter to his former councillor was very different from the note of anger and even contempt that he struck in letters to other men. He told one correspondent that he doubted if Madison could "bear the weight" of contending with Patrick Henry and his eloquent allies in the Virginia ratifying convention. He informed Alexander Donald, a tobacco broker and old friend, that he wished "with all my soul" nine states would endorse the Constitution and the remaining four would reject it until it had a bill of rights.

Such a tactic would have led inevitably to a call for a second convention. Madison—and Washington—knew this was tantamount to a death sentence for the government they had worked so hard and long to create. The anti-federalists would go all out to pack this second convention with their adherents.

Jefferson had written equally critical letters to friends in Maryland as their convention approached, knowing his name had influence there. A federalist delegate saw one of these letters and wrote to Madison, asking: "Can this possibly be Jefferson?" But Washington's name had trumped the man from Monticello there. The Maryland ratification vote had been an anti-federalist rout. [16]

⚬

The Virginia convention was a terrific ordeal for Madison. The conclave lasted twenty-three long, hot June days and Patrick Henry orated almost continuously. Several of his speeches lasted an entire day. His assault was as shrewd as it was savage. His goal was to arouse fear of the Constitution in every listener. He portrayed it as a conspiracy of the rich against the poor. He warned people who owed money to British merchants that federal marshals would drag them before federal judges and bankrupt them. He told slaveholders the new federal government would have the power to free their slaves by taxing them out of existence. Above all, the new government would eventually destroy everyone's liberty. Henry dwelt on this threat so graphically, one listener later recalled feeling his wrists to make sure fetters were not already pressing his flesh. [17]

George Mason seconded Henry's arguments with his own less eloquent brand of righteousness. He could testify that he had sat in the Philadelphia convention and listened to the arguments, and came away unconvinced. He joined Henry in preaching fear and suspicion of the North because of their hostility to slavery. He agreed with Henry that it was folly to entrust Virginia's safety and prosperity to such self-righteous neighbors.

Madison tried to deploy a strategy of his own. He called on the delegates to debate the Constitution clause by clause. No one could match the arguments he planned to muster with this approach. But Henry and Mason paid no attention to this proposal. Day after day, they assaulted the document from all points of the rhetorical compass, forcing Madison to deal with their slanders and exaggeration. The strain brought on an attack of "bilious fever"—an ailment that had troubled Madison since his college days, when he had often studied to the limits of his physical strength. He missed three days of debate, and when he returned, his voice was so weak, oratory was out of the question.

The gap was temporarily filled by Virginia's current governor, Edmund Randolph, probably the only speaker in the chamber who could match Henry's bravura style. Although Randolph had refused to sign the constitution in Philadelphia, he now declared himself in favor of full ratification with no demands for amendments or a second convention. Without Virginia, there would be no union. Raising his right arm, Randolph said he would "assent to lopping off this limb before I assent to the dissolution of the union." Henry, the self-styled people's spokesman, had no ready reply to these vivid words.

Randolph also performed another crucial service. As governor, he had received a letter from George Clinton, proposing that Virginia form an alliance with New York to force a second convention. Instead of reporting it to the ratifying convention, Randolph sent this explosive missive to the Virginia legislature, where it lay untouched and unread, while all its members were absent, listening to the arguments at the ratifying convention.

Madison soon told Washington the good news about Randolph. He kept his silent partner in touch with the drama in terse letters every three or four days, even when his illness left him "extremely feeble." Washington's hopes and fears rose and fell with every message. The thought that his home state might sabotage the Constitution was almost enough to give him an attack of bilious fever. But his nerves had been conditioned to deal with suspense by eight years of wartime uncertainty.[18]

In the last week of the convention, Madison regained his strength and style. Speaking from a bevy of notes he held in his hat, he answered Henry's attacks with steady, irrefutable facts. Another tactic did even more damage to Henry's case. Madison reminded the convention that General

Washington had severely criticized the Articles of Confederation in the circular letter he had sent to the governors of the states shortly before he resigned his commission in 1783.

Henry had an answer that momentarily flustered Madison. The orator wondered why Madison was disagreeing with his good friend, Thomas Jefferson, who had advised numerous men, including Henry, to "reject this government till it be amended" at a second convention. Madison regained his equilibrium and met Henry with a semi-denial that had some—but not much—basis in fact. He declared Mr. Jefferson's generally positive view of the Constitution was being misrepresented by these words.

Finally came Madison's climactic appeal to the relative handful of delegates who were still making up their minds. He urged them to help the United States excite the astonishment and admiration of the world by "peacefully, freely and satisfactorily" establishing a government capable of ruling a large and complex continental nation. Was there a better way to fulfill the promise of the American Revolution?[19]

Henry replied in his florid style, and he was joined by younger anti-federalists, notably Jefferson's new disciple, James Monroe. Future Supreme Court Justice John Marshall and several other speakers answered them. When Henry launched into a disquisition about slavery, George Wythe, the distinguished professor of law at the College of William and Mary, and one of Thomas Jefferson's early mentors, interrupted him and proposed a vote.

First came a tally on Henry's call for amendments. Back and forth the counties seesawed, with the anti-federalists seeming to pull ahead when nine out of twelve votes went their way. But the Tidewater region (which included Washington's Fairfax County) ended the suspense with six straight votes for ratification. The final total was 89-79. A shift of six votes would have condemned the Constitution to oblivion.

Madison's first thought as he contemplated this hard-won victory was George Washington. He joined other federalists in rushing the news to Mount Vernon. Meanwhile, a disappointed James Monroe was telling his mentor, Thomas Jefferson: "Be assured his [Washington's] influence carried this government."[20]

As word of the ratification spread along the Potomac, dozens of Washington's neighbors piled into boats and swarmed to Mount Vernon to congratulate him. They invited him to a celebration the next day at nearby Alexandria. A delighted Washington was soon telling Madison and other veterans of the struggle in Philadelphia how much pleasure it gave him to be a member of the first "public company" to drink a toast to the new federal government.

On June 3, Madison stopped at Mount Vernon on his way to New York to resume his seat in Congress. Washington saw at a glance how exhausted he was. For the first and only time, he showed his paternal feelings for this gifted young man. He urged Madison to "take a little respite from business" and relax at Mount Vernon for a few days. He advised a routine of "moderate exercise" and books only occasionally—books he should read for pleasure, "with the mind unbent." Madison must have been touched by this concern. He spent the next four days at Mount Vernon.

A similar drama was on stage in Poughkeepsie, New York, where that state's delegates had convened with the prospects for ratification looking dire. Anti-federalists outnumbered the federalists 46-19, and the antis gleefully flourished Governor Clinton's letter to Governor Randolph, confident that it would produce an alliance that would demand a second convention and doom the Constitution. Day after day, with Alexander Hamilton as the eloquent floor leader, the federalists argued for the Philadelphia document, clause by clause—and got nowhere. "Our arguments confound but do not convince," a discouraged Hamilton said.

On July 2, the Clintonites were flabbergasted to learn that Virginia had ratified without so much as a mention of a second convention. Frantically scrambling for a new tactic, Clinton turned to the by now tired demand for a bill of rights. Hamilton asked, Why this sudden passion? The New York State Constitution did not have one, and Governor Clinton never stopped praising it. The rattled antis began splitting into moderate and intransigent factions.

Armed with the arguments from *The Federalist*, Hamilton began annihilating anti-speaker after anti-speaker. For a clincher, he issued a threat that pushed the Clintonites to the edge of panic. If the convention failed to ratify, New York City would secede and form a separate state, and ratify the compact without them. The city had sent an overwhelmingly federalist delegation to Poughkeepsie. "Where will the Empire State be without its crown jewel?" Hamilton mockingly asked.

Desperate now, the Clintonites proposed that New York's ratification should be "conditional." They would reserve the right to secede from the union unless all the amendments they proposed were added to the Constitution. The governor and his friends had concocted no less than fifty-five of these changes and additions. Hamilton had anticipated this maneuver, and he had ready a letter from James Madison, who had returned to New York and resumed his seat in the soon-to-expire Congress.

Madison's letter, which Hamilton proceeded to read aloud, could not have been more explicit: the Constitution "requires an adoption in toto and *for ever* ... any condition whatever must vitiate ratification." New York's anti-federalists collapsed. Seven Clintonites abstained and the moderates joined the Hamiltonians to ratify 30-27. Seldom has a legislative body changed its collective mind so completely in less than a month. Madison promptly rushed the good news to Mount Vernon.

It was now only a matter of time before two holdout states, Rhode Island and North Carolina, would have second thoughts and join the union. At Mount Vernon, the prospect of a united nation prompted more thoughts about the narrow margin between victory and defeat. "We may, with a kind of grateful and pious exultation, trace the finger of Providence through these dark and misterious events," Washington wrote to a friend.[21]

In spite of Patrick Henry, George Clinton and other obstructionists, including Thomas Jefferson, the Constitution created by George Washington and James Madison had become the cornerstone of a resurgent American republic.

CHAPTER 4

The President and His Partner
Begin Making History

A FTER THE CONSTITUTION WAS ratified, James Madison wrote to
Thomas Jefferson, telling him how Patrick Henry had used his letter
to portray him as an anti-federalist. He also reported the way Jefferson's
influence had nearly derailed ratification in Maryland. Although Madison's language was diplomatic, the letter remained a reprimand that might
have triggered a negative response in the sensitive envoy. But the gap in
time and distance softened the exchange. Jefferson had learned from other
sources that nine states had ratified, and he wrote cheerfully to Madison:
"I sincerely rejoice [in] the acceptance of our new Constitution. It is a
good canvas, on which only some broad strokes want retouching."[1]

This retouching was anything but pleasant for Madison and Washington. It soon became apparent that a lot of powerful people were unreconciled to the ratified Constitution. A letter from Governor George Clinton
began circulating through the ranks of the anti-federalists. When the new
Congress was elected, Clinton argued, their first order of business should
be a call for a second constitutional convention. Then they should adjourn
and see what transpired in this conclave, which the antis devoutly hoped
would be a death sentence for the Philadelphia charter.

An alarmed Madison informed Washington of this threat. Both men
knew that Patrick Henry was almost certain to endorse it. Madison described it as electing a Congress "that will commit suicide on their own
authority." Washington decided it was of "unspeakable importance" to

47

have Congressman Madison return to the Virginia assembly. But his young partner demurred. He had barely recovered from the bilious attack that his recent confrontation with Patrick Henry had triggered. [2]

Washington fell back to urging Madison to become one of the two senators who would be chosen by the Virginia assembly. Madison, again seeing no hope of victory against Patrick Henry, was inclined to run for the House of Representatives instead. But Washington virtually insisted he become a candidate, to prevent two anti-federalist senators from representing the nation's largest state.

Henry campaigned ferociously against Madison, declaring that he was "unworthy of the confidence of the people." Anyone who wanted to see the Constitution amended should not vote for him. Although everyone knew Madison had Washington's backing, he came in third, with seventy-seven votes in the legislature. He professed surprise that he got that many, but Washington was unreconciled. He growled that "the Edicts of Mr. H" were obeyed with less opposition than "those of the Grand Monarch are in the Parliament of France." He was trying to say he was sorry that he had exposed Madison to this public humiliation.[3]

Delighted with his victory, Henry now tried to prevent Madison from winning a seat in Congress. He persuaded Jefferson's disciple, James Monroe, who was an outspoken anti-federalist, to run against him. Few people were inclined to worry about the probability that Madison would lose again. If he did, they were sure that Washington would become president and give him an important post in his administration. But the general did not want to see his partner suffer another humiliation at Patrick Henry's hands. He strenuously informed his numerous correspondents that he wanted Madison in Congress.

Madison headed south to campaign, and stopped at Mount Vernon from December 19 to Christmas Day. Martha Washington and other members of the family were soon fond of him and vice versa. Politically, this hospitality was news that travelled around Virginia. Madison confided to the ex-general that he had decided to announce that he was in favor of amending the constitution with a bill of rights. Washington had no objections to the idea. He saw that it would be far better for Madison to push this in Congress, rather than entrust it to a potentially disastrous second constitutional convention.

Madison trounced Monroe in the election, and a pleased Washington congratulated him for winning with such a "respectable majority." Monroe, fearful that he might have offended Jefferson by running against his far more intimate friend, rushed to buy an eight hundred-acre farm within sight of Monticello—something Jefferson had urged both him and Madison to do. It was a glimpse of the personal power Jefferson could exercise over a younger man.

⚶

Madison's attention—along with the rest of the country's—now shifted to another large question: Would Washington agree to be the nation's first president? In light of what has already transpired, it may seem hard to believe that anyone, especially the ex-general himself, could entertain any doubts. Close friends and former advisors like Alexander Hamilton had been urging him to accept the nomination almost from the moment the document was ratified.

It is more than a little significant that Madison never sent Washington a word so much as hinting that he might refuse to serve. When Jefferson wrote from France that he assumed "General Washington will be called to the presidency," Madison said nothing to raise even an iota of a doubt.[4]

Several years later, Madison admitted that during his visits to Mount Vernon, Washington had revealed "embarrassments" about accepting the office. He pointed out that he had dramatically announced his retirement from public life when he resigned as commander of the Continental Army. Ever the realist, Washington knew how meanspirited people could be, especially when aroused by political or ideological rancor. It was a fear that would later become a fact.

Madison was too realistic himself to deny the possibility. He offered the worried general a way to deal with it. As soon as the new government was operating smoothly, and the country's prosperity was well established, Washington could return to private life. It would be proof that he had meant what he said at his first withdrawal from public service. If by unhappy chance he should die in office, Madison guaranteed that he and others would take pains to guard his reputation against slurs that he was an insatiably ambitious hypocrite. Privately, Madison may have been pleased that this tactic made it almost certain Washington would refute Thomas Jefferson's prediction that presidents would rule for life.[5]

Although Washington continued to tell some correspondents that he felt unqualified for the complexities of the job, he admitted to others that much as he dreaded the sacrifice of his privacy, "the occasion was still greater." By the spring of 1789, he was wryly telling Henry Knox that his trip to New

York to be inaugurated would resemble "a culprit that is going to his place of execution." Realistically, it made no sense for a man "in the evening of a life nearly consumed in public cares" to undertake this new task.[6]

This was not false modesty at work. Washington was fifty-seven, and he often noted that he did not come from a long-lived family. He was also troubled by his lack of a formal education—a loss he had tried all his life to repair by omnivorous reading. But he often sensed a certain condescension in the company of college graduates such as John Adams and Thomas Jefferson. Nevertheless, he permitted his nomination for president and soon learned that on February 4, 1789, he had been chosen unanimously by the electoral votes of all the states.

It was a unique endorsement—and a stark contrast to the political contest that had erupted for the vice presidency. After some debate, the federalists had agreed to back John Adams, to give New England a feeling of semi-equality in the new government. The anti-federalists pushed Governor George Clinton, whom Madison regarded as a catastrophe in the making.

Hamilton, operating in New York, did not entirely agree. He thought Clinton, as a vice president, would reconcile many moderate anti-federalists and perhaps cement the Union. Washington said he was ready to work with either man. But Madison and others had too many doubts about Clinton, and his candidacy faltered. Many other electors voted for favorite sons from their own states. Adams was chosen with little more than half the total of Washington's unanimous elevation. New England's candidate began brooding about this shortfall almost instantly, with unfortunate consequences in the not-too-distant future.[7]

꧁꧂

At Mount Vernon, Washington had a new worry: his inaugural address. He asked his secretary, Colonel David Humphreys, to write a draft. The former aide-de-camp was one of a group of Connecticut wordsmiths known as "The Hartford Wits." The result was a seventy-two page monstrosity, which would have taken two or three hours to deliver. It not only defended Washington's decision to return to public life, it presented an entire legislative program.

Washington rushed a message to Madison, asking him to work out a way that he could send him a letter with no fear of anyone reading it. The confidential letter, since lost, enclosed Humphreys' draft. Madison stopped at Mount Vernon on his way to his seat in the new Congress and spent a day writing a speech that retained only one idea from Humphreys's draft. It asked Congress to consider amendments to protect the people's liberty.

The new speech, which Washington edited slightly, was four pages long. It urged Congress to think nationally and asked the blessings of God on the new government. Washington may have added a few words about his acceptance of this task as a duty, which overcame his feelings of "incapacity as well as disinclination." That disposed of his uneasiness about returning to public life.

The speech was only one item in a veritable agenda that Washington discussed with Madison. The topics explained why he wanted his young partner in Congress. At the top of the president-elect's concerns was the status of the western territories. He showed Madison letters from frontiersmen warning that the British were intriguing with the Indians to drive the Americans out of these fertile lands between the Appalachian Mountains and the Mississippi River. At least as important was the need to obtain free access to the Mississippi, and restore America's ruined credit by generating federal income with a tariff on imports.[8]

Since Madison would reach New York first, Washington asked his help in finding him a comfortable but modest house, befitting a republican president. They also discussed important matters of protocol. How should the president handle the hundreds of people who would want to see him? Should he accept invitations to dine out? Should he return calls, as the custom of the day required? Madison promised to consult fellow congressmen and see how they felt about these and similar questions.

Also probably discussed was the need for talented men as the president's assistants. The phrase "cabinet officer" had not yet been invented. Washington and Madison spoke of them as "auxiliary offices." For the moment, they saw four posts: a secretary of the Treasury, a secretary of state, an attorney general, and a secretary of war. Washington hoped—but doubted—that his friend, Robert Morris, would take charge of the Treasury. The Philadelphia tycoon was absorbed in running a worldwide business empire. Washington's second choice was Alexander Hamilton; Madison enthusiastically endorsed him.

Washington thought Edmund Randolph would make an excellent attorney general, and Henry Knox a good secretary of war. Again, Madison liked both choices. As for secretary of state—could there be anyone better than Thomas Jefferson? Madison's answer was predictably and enthusiastically affirmative. Washington asked Madison to write to him, and inquire "whether any appointment at home would be agreeable" to him. Madison promised the president-elect that he would do his utmost to persuade Jefferson. Neither man realized that they were writing finis to their partnership—and eventually, to their friendship.[9]

❦

In New York, Congress was slow to assemble. Not until April 1 did a quorum enable the representatives and senators to count the electoral ballots and declare Washington the president and John Adams vice president. Messengers were promptly dispatched to inform them, and Congress got down to the business of launching the nation. Madison introduced the first resolution, calling on his fellow politicians to create a revenue system to keep at bay the bankruptcy that had crippled the old Congress.

Madison proposed import duties on a wide range of luxury items, such as wine, rum, tea, and cocoa, and lower "ad valorem" (according to value) charges on all other imports. He also called for higher tonnage duties on ships from countries with whom the United States had no commercial treaty. He had a very large target in view—the merchant fleet of His Britannic Majesty, George III.

Instantly, there were arguments and dissensions. New Englanders cried that a high duty on rum would wreck their trade with the West Indies. Pennsylvania wanted a higher tariff to protect its infant iron industry. Southerners groused that tonnage discrimination would raise prices on their imports. Madison's goal was to shift some American commerce from Great Britain to France. This proved to be a difficult sell. British credit was far easier to obtain, and southerners were ready and eager to resume doing business with merchants they knew and, in many cases, liked.

Madison argued that they had a chance to continue teaching the British the lesson they should have learned from the Revolution. George III's ministers were treating their former subjects with the same arrogant presumption of superior power that had converted so many loyal colonists into rebels. London barred American ships from her West Indian islands and forbade British ships from seeking repairs in American ports. Only British ships could carry exports from the United States to the mother country. Ultimately, the House of Representatives agreed with Madison, but the bill died in the Senate, which lacked a leader with his persuasive powers.

Fisher Ames, a talented orator who had emerged as New England's spokesman, remarked that Madison was too "Frenchified" for his tastes.

This hostility to America's revolutionary allies pervaded most Yankee congressmen and not a few New Yorkers. Gotham's merchants had a long history of trade with England. Madison blamed a lot of the resistance he encountered on the city's "Anglicanism"—a term that he used in a non-religious way to describe the tilt toward London. These two clashing attitudes were a preview of the politics of the coming decade.

✦

At the end of the new government's first month, politics were discarded on all sides to welcome George Washington to New York. His week-long journey from Mount Vernon had been a pageant of military escorts, cheering crowds, booming cannon, receptions, and salutes in verse and oratory in the towns and cities through which he passed. In Elizabeth, New Jersey, he was greeted by a congressional committee aboard an elaborately decorated fifty-foot barge, which carried him across New York Harbor to the city. Mounting crimson colored steps at Wall Street, he was met with the cheers of almost every man, woman, and child in the budding metropolis. The day ended with a dinner given by Governor Clinton and a stupendous display of fireworks in the night sky.

Inauguration day began at noon when five congressmen, one of whom was Madison, called on the president-elect at his modest Cherry Street residence (long since swallowed by the approaches to the Brooklyn Bridge). Together they strolled down Wall Street to Federal Hall, where Washington was introduced to Congress. Next, on a portico of the building, while an immense crowd watched in respectful silence, Chancellor Robert R. Livingston of New York administered the oath of office. As Washington completed the solemn words, shouts of "God Bless Our President" echoed across the harbor.

Washington wore a dark brown American-made suit with a set of silver buttons featuring eagles with sunburst-like shields on their breasts. Thousands of watching admirers wore the same tribute to liberty and independence. After bowing to the cheers and shouts, Washington returned to the interior of Federal Hall and read his brief inaugural address in the Senate chamber. He spoke in a low, deep voice, without a trace of oratorical gestures, save for a flourish of his right hand when he spoke the words: "all the world." Nevertheless, an orator as gifted as Fisher Ames was "overwhelmed with emotions of the most affecting kind." He found the speech "an allegory in which virtue was personified…addressing those whom he would make her votaries."

Others were less gracious. Senator William Maclay, a blunt anti-feder-alist from western Pennsylvania, thought Washington looked "agitated and embarrassed" and read his speech as if the words were entirely new to him. (Maclay is probably best summed up by his opinion of the Constitu-tion—"the vilest of all traps that was set to ensnare the freedom of an unsuspecting people.") Madison never described his reaction to the inau-gural address, but his feelings must have been at least as deep as Fisher Ames's admiration. For the young Virginian, this was the culmination of almost two years of partnership with a unique man he had grown to like as well as respect.[10]

During this first session of Congress (April–September 1789), Madison remained Washington's confidential advisor. He was also busy on the floor of Congress. His chief task there was persuading his fellow legisla-tors to pass a bill of rights. This proved to be a far from simple matter. The anti-federalists, although a minority in the new legislature, remained vocal and hostile to the Constitution. They tried to insert into the list of rights ingenious clauses that would restore various powers to the states at the expense of the federal government. Not until September was Madi-son able to win agreement for twelve amendments to submit to the states. The ten that a majority approved became the Bill of Rights that today's Americans revere and admire.

Meanwhile, Washington was relying on Madison in a variety of ways. When the House and Senate sent him welcoming addresses in response to his inaugural speech, the President asked Madison to draft answers to both of them. Privately, the two men were probably amused—both had excellent senses of humor—that in effect, Madison was answering himself three times. (He had written the House address.) There is a hint of a smile in Washington's written request: "As you have begun, so I would wish you to finish, the good work in a short reply."

There was a serious side to this formality. The President's replies estab-lished his role in communicating with Congress. Madison also played a part in another issue that would influence the politics of the next ten years. In the Senate, Vice President John Adams, who served as the presiding officer, and Senator Richard Henry Lee of Virginia, jointly decided that the president and vice president, and perhaps the senators, needed sono-rous titles to give them the dignity and authority to function in a republic.

When Adams learned that the House, under Madison's guidance, had addressed Washington simply as the President of the United States, he demanded the formation of a Senate-House conference committee. There he declared that the president should be called "His Highness, the President of the United States and Protector of Their Liberties." The vice president should have an equally resounding title. Madison was appalled—and so was Washington.

The President confided to Madison that he feared people would suspect the gaudy title was "not displeasing to me" and communicate this nasty opinion to "the adversaries of the government." This was exactly what Senator Maclay of Pennsylvania did. He informed his diary that "through the whole of this base business I have endeavored to mark the conduct of General Washington." The senator was hoping to discover the President was behind the idea.[11]

Both Washington and Madison thought the whole affair was trivial—but foresaw that anti-federalists might use it to smear the new government. Madison hoped rejecting titles would prove that neither Congress nor the President favored monarchy or aristocracy. In public, he referred to the Adams title as "tinsel" which "the manly shoulders" of the President did not need. But when he wrote to Thomas Jefferson about it, he was far less restrained. He said Adams' proposal would have "given a deep wound to our infant government."

Jefferson called the titles "the most superlatively ridiculous thing I ever heard of." It proved that Ben Franklin was right when he said Adams "was always an honest man, sometimes a great one but sometimes completely mad." Jefferson wished Adams were with him in Paris. After witnessing what looked more and more like a revolution, if the Vice President had "one fiber of aristocracy left in his frame he would have been a proper subject for bedlam."[12]

Madison also advised Washington about his relationship to the Senate and played a key role in bolstering presidential independence. The Constitution gave the Senate to right to "advise and consent" on executive appointments. Some senators thought that gave them the power to decide whether the president could dismiss a federal official without Congress's approval. Madison firmly disagreed and his influence prevailed.

Similarly, some senators thought that they should have the right to decide, with the president, how much money a diplomat should be paid. Once more Madison backed presidential independence, and Washington soon pressured the Senate into passing a bill specifically endorsing this course. Washington had already written to the major nations of Europe, informing them that, henceforth, all communications with the United States should be addressed to him—not Congress.[13]

⚜

When he was in office only two weeks, Washington asked Madison's advice on how to find a "true medium" between opening his doors to all comers, and shutting them to everyone but selected friends. Washington sent similar requests for advice to John Adams and Alexander Hamilton. Adams predictably favored a style based on the pomp and ceremony he had seen at the court of George III. Hamilton urged him to bar any and all congressmen from access.

The President and Madison worked out a plan that was a reasonable compromise between these extremes. For Tuesday "levees" Washington would wear gloves and a dress sword, and bow formally to each person who presented himself. On Thursday, he would host a dozen congressmen, foreign diplomats, and federal officials at a formal dinner. After Martha Washington arrived at the residence in late May 1789, she held Friday night receptions at which the President greeted visitors of both sexes in a more relaxed and informal style.

Perhaps most important was Madison's role in helping Washington choose the best available men to assist him in running the federal government. There was no shortage of volunteers, "A rage for office" swept the country after the inauguration. Over one thousand jobs, from revenue officials to clerks to postmasters to federal judges, awaited the President's choices. Madison proved extremely helpful in finding pro-federalists in Virginia and Kentucky to build resistance to Patrick Henry.

Both men soon realized, in Washington's words, "it is in the nature of republicans (he was using the word to describe people who favored a government elected by the people) who are nearly in a state of equality, to be extremely jealous as to the disposal of all honorary or lucrative appointments."[14]

To make the right choice, the President investigated job seekers with the help of Madison and others. He especially wanted to know about a candidate's previous support for the Constitution. Opinions of the candidate provided by men of local reputation also came into play. It was hard and often wearisome work. At one point, Washington wrote apologetically to Madison. "I am very troublesome but you must excuse me. Ascribe it to friendship and confidence, and you will do justice to my motives." He asked his young colleague for the names of the men they had chosen for federal attorney and marshal for Kentucky, adding: "Forget not to include their Christian [first] names."[15]

The partnership worked both ways. Washington supplied Madison with a letter, backing the Congressman's attempt to win a tonnage discrimination bill against the British. In the struggle to persuade dubious congressmen to back a bill of rights, Washington declared that Madison's list of amendments "have my wishes for a favorable reception in both houses." The two branches of Congress approved Madison's bill in a joint resolution on September 25, 1789.[16]

Washington's support of the Bill of Rights played a crucial part in bringing North Carolina into the union. The state's governor, Samuel Johnston, had written the President a letter, congratulating him on his election and promising that North Carolina would consider changing its negative stance if a bill of rights was added to the Constitution. Washington wrote a cordial reply, which Madison urged the governor to publish in Tarheel newspapers. Within a few weeks of Congress approving the rights, North Carolina voted to send congressmen and senators to New York. Now Rhode Island was the only state that still declined to join the Union.

❦

When Congress adjourned in September 1789, Washington discussed with Madison an idea he had been thinking about for some time. Did Madison think there was any "impropriety" in his taking a trip through the New England states during the next two months? Madison pronounced it an excellent idea and saw no reason why the President should not undertake it.

As for Congressman Madison, he was heading back to Virginia to mend a few political fences there on behalf of the new government. At least one obstacle to his efforts had been removed. Patrick Henry had recently announced he was leaving politics to practice law and make enough money to feed his numerous children. Madison was also looking forward to a reunion with his old friend, Thomas Jefferson, who was coming home on a five-month leave of absence from his ambassadorship. Madison promised to explore in more detail Jefferson's feelings about becoming Washington's Secretary of State.

CHAPTER 5

The Birth of an Ideologue

I N FRANCE, DURING AMERICA's eighteen-month struggle to create and ratify the Constitution, Thomas Jefferson was having a very different experience. A revolution was rumbling beneath the surface of a country he had grown to love. He considered King Louis XVI "a good man," though he privately deplored the immense unchecked powers he and his ministers wielded, and their apparent indifference to France's numerous poor.

Nevertheless, Jefferson made many friends among upper-class French men and women. Above all, he admired their politeness—to him and to each other. "It is impossible to be among people who wish more to make one happy," he told a correspondent. He was occasionally troubled by the widespread indifference to marital vows among the rich. Domestic happiness, as Jefferson understood it, and had experienced it in America, was dismissed as a myth.

In his many trips around the country, Jefferson talked as well as he could in his halting French (he never learned to speak the language well) to the common people of France. He bought food from them in their kitchens, asked them about the hours they worked, the money they made, their feelings about their country. He acquired a knowledge of their attitudes and problems that filled his heart with pity.

Once, near the chateau of Fontainbleau, Jefferson met a ragged woman trudging along a road. The ambassador asked, Did she work? Yes, she was a day laborer. How much did she make? Eight sous (about eight cents) a day. She had two children to support and the rent for her house was six hundred sous a year. Jefferson realized that that was seventy-five days' wages. Often, the woman continued, there was no work. What then? No bread. They starved.

"We walked together near a mile and a half and she had…served me as my guide," Jefferson said. "I gave her on parting 24 sous. She burst into tears of gratitude."

Jefferson was so moved, he wrote a letter to his friend, the Marquis de Lafayette, urging him to make a similar trip through the countryside. He should travel "absolutely incognito" and "ferret the people out of their hovels as I have done, look into their kettles, eat their bread, loll on their beds…to find out if they are soft. You will feel a sublime pleasure in the course of this investigation, and a sublime one hereafter, when you shall be able to apply your knowledge to the softening of their beds, or the throwing of a morsel of meat into their kettles of vegetables." [1]

The Marquis did not reply to this advice, which he almost certainly thought bizarre. Like most noblemen, Lafayette spent his days in his mansion in Paris and in frequent visits to King Louis XVI's vast palace at nearby Versailles. No ruler in Europe approached the splendor in which Louis XVI lived, surrounded by hundreds of servants and swarms of courtiers. The royal court was an apotheosis of the absolute power that the king's great-great-great grandfather, Louis XIV, had created to make France the ruling power of Europe.

The result was a political vacuum in the rest of the country. "The nation," one of Louis XVI's ministers of finance wrote in a confidential report, "is an aggregate of different and incompatible social groups, whose members have so few links between themselves that everyone thinks solely of his own interests…Your Majesty is obliged to decide everything by yourself or through your agents. Special orders are needed before anyone will contribute in any way to the public good." [2]

Louis XVI's annual revenues were 500 million livres—the equivalent of 100 million dollars or 20 million pounds. (In modern money, 1 billion, 500 million dollars.) This was far more than King George III of England dared to collect from his subjects, and twice as much as the Austrian emperor's income. It was also three or four times the incomes of the kings of Prussia, Russia, or Spain. But the tax system was so antiquated and corrupt, France had long been forced to resort to deficit financing. The government owed hundreds of millions of livres to Dutch and English bankers on which it paid outrageous interest. [3]

Early in 1787, the King and his ministers finally admitted the nation was on the verge of bankruptcy. They summoned an Assembly of Notables to advise them on how to fix the tax system. Essentially, the notables were an expanded version of the king's council, selected by the ruler for their dependability and loyalty. The aristocrats and wealthy bourgeois resisted any and all requests by the King's ministers to join them in raising more revenue. Instead, they accused the ministers—and, by implication, the King and his court—of gross waste and corruption. The Marquis de Lafayette emerged as one of the leaders in this blame game.

The King was forced to call a meeting of a much larger body, the Estates General, in which the aristocrats, the clergy, and the middle class were represented. On May 5, 1789, while Congress was in the opening days of its first session in New York, Ambassador Jefferson was one of the two thousand spectators at this historic conclave. They met in a huge hall constructed in Versailles solely for this purpose.

The chief problem, as Jefferson soon noted in letters to several American correspondents, was the immense size of this ancient parliament—twelve hundred members. He wondered if "tumult and confusion" could be avoided in such a gigantic conclave. There were no rules of procedure or debate. The members were Frenchmen, "among whom there are always more speakers than listeners." Even more unhelpful was the decision to have the three estates meet in separate chambers of the gigantic "hall of states."[4]

There was another problem that Jefferson foresaw in a long letter to George Washington on the eve of the fateful year, 1789. "In my opinion," he wrote, there was "a kind of influence which none of their plans for reform take into account [which] will elude them all; I mean the influence of women in the government. The manners of the nation allow them to visit, alone, all persons in office, to solicit the affairs of husband, family friends, and, [in] their solicitations, bid defiance to laws and regulations."

Growing gloomier with every word, Jefferson declared that no American, without the evidence of his own eyes, would believe "the desperate state to which things are reduced in this country from the omnipotence of [this] influence." Americans did not realize how fortunate they were that in their country, women did not try to extend their influence "beyond the domestic line."[5]

Most of the time, Jefferson tried to be optimistic. He assured James Madison and other friends that the French government would be transformed peacefully. He managed to dismiss the first outbreak of violence in

Paris, shortly before the Estates General met. The army was called in to disperse rioters protesting a paper manufacturer who tried to reduce the wages of his workers. The troops opened fire and killed about one hundred of the protesters. In contrast to the way he had praised the rebellion of Daniel Shays and his followers in Massachusetts, Jefferson described these agitators as "the most abandoned banditti of Paris." Never, he added, was a riot "more unprovoked and unpitied." When similar disturbances erupted in other French cities, he dismissed them as nothing unusual. The cause was probably "want of bread."[6]

It gradually became evident that peaceful progress in the Estates General was virtually impossible. The nobles and the clergy refused to have any serious conversations with the "Third Estate"—the people's representatives. They haughtily rejected the idea that the three estates should merge and vote as individuals, not as separate groups.

Soon rumors swirled through the Third Estate that the King was summoning troops from all parts of France to assert his absolute control. On June 20, 1789, the people's spokesmen found soldiers barring their access to the great hall and retreated to a nearby indoor tennis court, the Jeu de Paume. In a tumultuous meeting, they took an oath to remain in session until they had achieved a constitution, no matter what the King or his ministers said.

The other estates had also been excluded from the hall of states. The King was mourning the death of his son and heir, and had presumed the Estates would join him. The violent reaction of the Third Estate was an ominous sign that they were determined to assert themselves. Soon they began calling for the other estates to join them in a congress or parliament that would speak for the whole nation.

Jefferson had predicted that the nobles, led by Lafayette, would welcome such an invitation. But the majority of the aristocrats, including Lafayette, resisted the idea. To Jefferson's surprise, the clergy were much more receptive. Most of them were parish priests, and they had strong class sympathies.

On June 22, the bourgeoisie, most of the clergy, and numerous moderate nobles like Lafayette marched in a body to The Church of St. Louis, hoping a divine presence would help them resolve their differences. Jefferson and an Italian friend, Philip Mazzei, joined them to hear the discussions. Mazzei later recalled that Jefferson "stopped at the threshold and said: 'This is the first time that churches have ever been made some good use of.'"[7]

By June 29, 1789, Jefferson was telling his American correspondents that "the triumph of the Tiers [the Estates General] is considered complete. Tomorrow they will recommence business, voting by persons on all questions…All danger of civil commotion here is at an end." Little more than a week later, the shocked American envoy was forced to ask the king's foreign minister, the Comte de Montmorin, for a guard of royal troops. His house had been robbed three times by roaming bands of thieves from the Paris slums. Civil commotion would soon become much too tame a term to describe the politics seething through Paris.[8]

On July 10, Lafayette introduced a bill of rights in the National Assembly—the new name for the Estates General. The next day, Jefferson wrote a triumphant letter to Thomas Paine, who was in England, eagerly cheering on events in Paris. The ambassador praised the assembly for having shown "a coolness, wisdom and resolution to set fire to the four quarters of the kingdom and perish with it….rather than relinquish an iota of their plan for a total change of government."

Admittedly, Jefferson was writing in a state of high excitement. Still, the reader of this book may wonder if James Madison or George Washington would have been as thrilled by this vision of total power passing into the hands of the National Assembly. It was precisely the sort of government that Madison had labored to avoid in the Constitutional Convention—an arrangement without a trace of a check or balance to prevent the excesses of majority rule. Jefferson added to the letter a long list of rights and principles that the Assembly would have to incorporate in a constitution. But he soon learned that revolutionary events were outrunning the rational expectations of a man who loved to legislate. Instead, the four corners of the kingdom were about to catch fire.

On July 13, as Jefferson was passing the Tuileries Gardens in his carriage, he witnessed a confrontation between a mob and a detachment of royal cavalry trying to preserve order. The mob attacked the cavalry using stones that had been collected for a new bridge over the Seine, Pont Louis XVI. "The showers of stones forced the horse to retire," Jefferson reported. "The people now armed themselves with such weapons as they could find in armorer's shops and private houses…and were roaming all night through all parts of the city."

The law-abiding citizens realized there was only one way to maintain a semblance of order. They organized a citizen's guard and made the Marquis de Lafayette its commander in chief. Everyone began wearing cockades of white, blue, and pink colored ribbon which bore witness to their support for the revolution.

Still clinging to optimism, Jefferson told Thomas Paine that "the progress of things here will be subject to checks from time to time, of course. Whether they will be great or small depends on the army. But they will be only checks."

That letter was mailed on the thirteenth of July. The next day, the mob, now semi-organized, acquired more weapons when they smashed open the gates of St. Lazare Prison and released the inmates. The rioters seized additional guns and ammunition at nearby armories and headed for the gloomy prison known as the Bastille, where prisoners of state were held. They demanded guns from the prison's governor, who tried to stall them, hoping royal troops would rescue him. The mob exploded and swiftly overwhelmed the small garrison. Seizing the governor and lieutenant governor, they decapitated them on the spot and paraded their bleeding heads through the streets.

Instead of hundreds of prisoners, a grand total of seven were released from the Bastille. Four were convicted forgers, a fifth was an aristocrat incarcerated at the request of his family because his taste in sexual adventures resembled the Marquis de Sade's. The final two were lunatics, one of whom thought he was Julius Caesar; they were swiftly confined in another prison. *Revolutions de Paris,* a newspaper that began publishing on July 17, declared that uncounted innocent victims and venerable old men, imprisoned for generations, had been freed from the Bastille. It was the revolutionists' first, but by no means the last, resort to the fine art of lying to the public.

The truth or falsity of this aspect of the fall of the Bastille became irrelevant as the screaming mob held aloft the decapitated heads and surged through the city. One historian of the event maintains these blood-dripping skulls represented "a kind of revolutionary sacrament." Some people turned away, appalled. They had supported the revolution as long as it was confined to abstractions such as *Liberté.* Others with stronger nerves and tougher stomachs decided, like their future descendants in Moscow, Peking, Havana, Caracas, and other capitals, that violence—blood—was the real key to power.[9]

Few citizens in Paris were more excited by these murders than Thomas Jefferson. He rushed another letter to Thomas Paine, reporting that "the city committee" had organized an impromptu army of forty-eight thousand men with Lafayette as its commander. In Versailles, the king and his government began coming apart. Minister after minister resigned. On July 17, Louis XVI and the National Assembly decided to come to Paris and assure the citizens of their sympathy and support. Jefferson described the incredible sight to John Jay, who was still serving as foreign secretary to the old Congress.

"The King's carriage was in the center, on each side of it the Assembly, in two ranks afoot, at their head, the Marquis de Lafayette on horseback and [the] guards before and behind. About sixty thousand citizens of all forms and conditions, [some] armed with the muskets of the Bastille.... the rest with pistols, swords, pikes, pruning hooks, scythes...saluted them everywhere with cries of 'vive le nation.'"

At the Hotel de Ville (the Paris City Hall), a leader of the city committee pinned a white, blue, and pink cockade on the King's hat, and the people shouted "vive le roi et la nation!" Whereupon Lafayette and his guardsmen escorted the subdued king back to his palace in Versailles, followed by the members of the National Assembly. It was, Jefferson wrote, "such an *amende honorable* [pledge of friendship] as no sovereign ever made and no people ever received."

What did it mean? The power of the National Assembly was "absolutely out of the reach of attack," Jefferson told Paine. They had total "carte blanche." Neither Jefferson nor Paine realized that the "city committee" that had staged this demonstration would soon become the Paris Commune, a power that would make the National Assembly's carte blanche more and more meaningless.

In letters to America, Jefferson repeatedly stressed the impact of the decapitations of the men in charge of the Bastille as a key factor in destroying the King's and his ministers' will to resist. He noted with evident pleasure that the "Aristocrats of the Nobles and Clergy in the Estates General" now "vied with each other in declaring how sincerely they were converted to the justice of voting by persons, and how determined to go with the nation all its lengths." These were the words of frightened men, testifying to the efficacy of terror as a political weapon. But Jefferson seemed unbothered by this harsh fact.[10]

❧

Many nobles and recently resigned government ministers fled Paris. One of them, seventy-four-year-old Joseph Foulon, took refuge with a friend in the country. Hatred for aristocrats was swirling through Paris, and Foulon was among the most detested. He had held many posts in the royal government, most recently the controller general of finances. In a government constantly short of funds, he functioned as a sort of abominable no man in his losing struggle to balance France's books. Vicious stories about him circulated ominously: he supposedly had said, during a famine many years earlier, "If those rascals have no bread, let them eat hay." This was obviously a fiction, in the same category as Queen Marie Antoinette's purported later advice to the poor: "Let them eat cake."

Seized by peasants on his friend's estate, Foulon was transported back to Paris and made to walk barefoot through the streets to the Hotel de Ville. Someone strapped a bundle of hay on his back, and when he begged for water, his captors gave him peppered vinegar. Lafayette and members of his National Guard tried to rescue him, but the mob fought them off and hanged their battered captive. When the rope broke, they decapitated him and paraded his head through the streets with hay jutting from his mouth. His son-in-law, Berthier de Sauvigny, who had served as Intendant [finance minister] of Paris, met a similar fate a few days later.

Jefferson knew neither of these men personally. He reported their deaths to his favorite correspondent, James Madison, without the slightest trace of pity. He saw their fates as further evidence of the decline and fall of the aristocracy, a word that had long stirred his deepest antipathy, when he was in an ideological mood. At other times, he freely admitted many aristocrats were decent men like the Marquis de Lafayette.

⚜

For the next two months, Paris was relatively quiet. In Versailles, the National Assembly began debating what to put in a constitution. In the provinces, there was evidence of growing unrest, and foreign governments were making ominous noises on France's borders. But Jefferson still felt enormously optimistic. For the man who loved to legislate, the situation seemed ideal. There were no legal obstacles left on the path to a satisfying revolutionary outcome: a constitutional monarchy.

The King would become the humble servant of the legislature while French citizens of all descriptions would win a galaxy of human rights, from trial by jury to the vote. Jefferson summed up his feelings and hopes to one of his French correspondents in memorable words: "I have so much confidence in the good sense of man, and his qualifications for self-government, that I am never afraid of the issue where reason is left free to exert her force, and I will agree to be stoned as a false prophet if all does not end well in this country. Nor will it end with this country. Here is but the first chapter in the history of European Liberty."[11]

What was happening to the American envoy? He was having a conversion experience. With no traditional religious faith to balance his intellect and emotions, politics had become Thomas Jefferson's religion. The cause of liberty, sustained by his belief in the essential goodness of human beings, became his chief article of belief. Few people, above all Jefferson himself, have understood his experience this way. Viewed from the distance of two centuries, it was a turning point in American history.

Across the English channel, another student of politics was watching the events in Paris. Edmund Burke had been hailed in America in 1775 when he gave a sensational speech in Parliament, calling on England to grant Americans their rights before it was too late. He had been equally enthusiastic about the French Revolution at first. But now he was growing dubious. Not long after Jefferson expressed his soaring confidence to his French correspondent, Burke wrote a letter to a British friend who had expressed similar optimism.

"That they can settle their constitution, without much struggle, on paper, I can easily believe: because at present the interests of the Crown have no party, certainly no armed party, to support them; but I...very much question...whether they are possessed of any...capacity for the exercise of free judgment...There is a mob of their constituents ready to hang them if they should deviate into moderation..."

Throughout this turbulent summer in Paris, Jefferson's emotions were complicated by a growing desire to go home. In the spring, he had written to John Adams that if he stayed much longer, Europe would begin to feel like a prison to him. He may have been influenced by Adams's decision to go back to America in 1788. A new government was taking charge of the United States, and both men wanted to participate in it.

For Jefferson, the impulse was shadowed by his unhappy experience as governor of Virginia. He concealed his ambivalence by asking for a five-month leave of absence from Paris, to put his American affairs in order. In

September, he was delighted to receive a letter from Foreign Secretary John Jay, approving this plan. This would give him time to observe the American scene and decide whether he approved the new Constitution and the government it had created.

۩

With his departure scheduled for early October, Jefferson began thinking large thoughts about the meaning of the revolutionary upheaval in France. More and more, he focused on an epochal idea that was swirling through Paris. On September 6, 1789, in one of the longest and most important letters of his life, he described it to James Madison. He told his ex-councillor that the central idea was larger than the turbulent scenes he was watching in the streets around his residence. Jefferson had begun to think it justified all revolutions and might be useful to the new government in America.

"The question whether one generation of men has a right to bind another seems never to have been stated on this or our side of the water. Yet it is...of such consequence as ... to merit... place...among the fundamental principles of every government."

What was this huge idea? *The earth belongs to the living.* Jefferson declared the principle was self-evident: no man has power or right over his money or property after his death. It "ceases to be his when himself ceases to be, and reverts to the society." Debts contracted by the dead person should also be cancelled.

Jefferson proceeded to apply this principle to generations. He had studied mortality statistics and concluded that every nineteen years, a new generation took charge of the affairs of a nation. Why should they be obliged to repay the debts of the previous generation? They were also under no obligation to obey the laws that the previous generation may have passed in a legislature or enshrined in a constitution. "Every constitution...and every law, naturally expires at the end of nineteen years. If it be enforced longer, it is an act of force and not of right." The only true test of a government was its support by the will of the majority of the current generation.

Jefferson thought this principle was especially relevant to the situation in France. After hundreds of years, the nation was burdened by huge amounts of land given to the Catholic Church, to hospitals, colleges, and orders of chivalry. Then there were monopolies on commerce, given to or acquired by various groups. One group, "the Farmers General," alone had the right to import tobacco. The legislature should feel free to abolish or alter all these obligations, with the understanding that the next generation might disagree and restore some of them. "The legislature of the day could authorize…appropriations and establishments for their own time, but no longer."[12]

Jefferson urged Madison to "turn this subject in your mind…particularly as to the power of contracting debts, and develope (sic) it with the perspicuity and cogent logic so peculiarly yours." The envoy thought it might be very relevant to "the councils of our country." He knew by this time that Madison was in the new Congress, at work on creating the inner structure of the American government.

Reading over this explosive letter, Jefferson decided not to entrust it to the mails. By the time he finished writing it, he was only two weeks away from boarding a ship and returning to the United States after an absence of five years. He decided to tuck it into his luggage and give it to Madison personally when they met in Virginia.

The letter made one thing very clear. Emotionally and psychologically, Thomas Jefferson was not a friend of this new government that George Washington, James Madison, Alexander Hamilton, and a host of other Americans had labored so hard to create. The idea of a perpetually renewable or readily transformed constitution made a mockery of Madison's letter to Alexander Hamilton, telling him that New York state had to accept the Constitution irrevocably, with no reservations or claims to a right to abandon it if it did not suit them.

Jefferson's tentative and speculative tone, and the request for Madison's help in developing this idea, made it equally clear that the ambassador was not coming home to challenge the new government. He saw himself as a possible participant in its development. But it would slowly become apparent that Thomas Jefferson was determined to make sure this development met the approval of a man who had become a passionate believer in the world-transforming importance of the French Revolution.

CHAPTER 6

The President Takes Charge

THUS FAR, PRESIDENT WASHINGTON had played a largely behind-the-scenes role. Judging him on his first six months in office, one might be tempted to agree with the authors of a recent book that declared: "When he assumed the presidency, Washington intended to preside, not to command or demand." On the contrary, the man who lived dangerously, the general who commanded an army in a seesaw eight-year war, did not "assume" the presidency to be a figurehead. [1]

As a general, he had written bold letters to the frequently feckless Continental Congress, informing them, among other things, to stop relying on patriotism to win "a long and bloody war." As president, he was determined to assert similar leadership to define this new office. When Charles Thomson, the secretary of Congress under the Articles of Confederation, arrived at Mount Vernon to inform Washington that he had been elected president, he replied: "I wish that there may not be reason for regretting the choice, for, indeed, all I can promise is to accomplish that which can be done by honest zeal." [2]

The choice of words is significant. *Zeal* was not the attribute of a presider. The word emanates energy, decision, action. Zeal is what a man brings to a challenge that has to be confronted and resolved. This was Washington's view of the presidency's importance. Congress needed a decisive leader to preserve the unity of a continental-sized nation, already stretching fifteen hundred miles along the Atlantic seaboard, and rapidly expanding westward. The presidency was the essential ingredient in this new federal vision. [3]

At the same time, Washington understood that making a new political system acceptable to four million often skeptical, contentious Americans required a combination of leadership and patience. He did not expect harmony to be achieved overnight, or even in a year.

❦

Washington was convinced that it was important to make the president a visible presence to as many citizens as possible. In New York, he held both formal levees and informal receptions to emphasize that the president was both a figure of authority and a down-to-earth man, ready to exchange jokes and chat about the news of the day. He supplemented this hospitality by occasionally strolling the streets of New York, greeting and being greeted by average citizens. Vice President John Adams, still obsessed with the need to create an aura of importance, was, someone wryly observed, "never seen but in his carriage and six."[4]

During one of these strolls on the street known as "the Broadway," Washington encountered a Scottish maid escorting a young boy. "Please your honor," she said. "Here's a bairn named after you." The President patted six-year-old Washington Irving on the head, instantly creating a legend in the young man's family. Decades later, Irving's three-volume biography would be considered the best account yet written about the complex man who was almost reflexively called the father of his country.[5]

❦

The President's concern about connecting with the public was rooted in one of the primary lessons he had learned as a general. Summer and winter, for eight long and often discouraging years, he had shared camp life with the Continental Army's officers and men. Not once did he retreat to Mount Vernon or move into some similar mansion in New Jersey or Pennsylvania for winter quarters. He refused to leave discipline and morale problems to be solved by lower ranking officers.

Staying in close proximity to his troops had resulted in a steady accumulation of loyalty and respect. This was the experience President Washington hoped to duplicate in the fall of 1789 when he told James Madison of his plans to make a tour of New England. On October 15, he rumbled out of New York in his coach, accompanied by six servants and two aides, Major William Jackson and Tobias Lear.

South Carolinian Jackson had distinguished himself as a fighting soldier during the Revolution and served as Washington's aide-de-camp in the closing years of the war. He later proved himself a capable assistant as secretary of the Constitutional Convention. Tobias Lear was a genial New Hampshireman who became Washington's personal secretary in 1784 and would remain indispensable for the next sixteen years. Both men had the candor and self-confidence that Washington valued in his assistants.

The President had invited Vice President John Adams to join them. Again displaying his almost total lack of political instincts, "Honest John" had curtly declined the invitation. He found it difficult and frequently impossible to restrain his envy of Washington's fame. This flaw would eventually erode his effectiveness as a federal leader.

The purpose of the trip, as Washington explained it in his diary, was to "sample the temper and disposition of the inhabitants toward the new government." He also felt he was entitled to a vacation. He had dealt successfully with Congress and survived a painful illness, a tumor on his thigh that had greatly alarmed his doctors and his wife, Martha. That estimable lady, having devoted a great deal of time to supervising weekly presidential dinners and receptions, had decided to stay in New York and enjoy the company of her two grandchildren, ten-year-old Nelly and eight-year-old George Washington Parke Custis, usually called "Washy."

Martha foresaw that her husband's tour would involve numerous official dinners and parades and speeches that she had little or no desire to endure. The President, on the other hand, seemed to enjoy these ceremonies, which were numerous as they progressed toward Boston. When they approached a town, Washington usually mounted a favorite white charger who spent most of his time trotting behind the baggage wagon that accompanied them. The President was often called the finest horseman of his era. His confident mastery of his steed made a strong impression on the crowds that swarmed to see him.[6]

Any man would have found it hard to dislike the compliments that were showered on the nation's leader. He was regularly called "Columbia's favorite son" and "the man who unites all hearts." Washington regarded these effusions as tributes to the presidency. He also saw the value of a

Virginian winning this affection and admiration from New Englanders. Too often, the Yankees had manifested a sense of moral superiority to the rest of the nation, at times bordering on alienation.

Washington's diary revealed his interest in the physical condition of the country. He noted the quality of the roads (mostly bad) and the inns (mostly mediocre). He jotted down sites where a canal or an improved road would be valuable. He was especially interested in seeing examples of American manufacturing. Already, the energetic New Englanders were in the textile business. In Hartford, he explored a woolen mill and demonstrated his approval of their product by buying a dark blue suit for himself and breeches for his servants.

The President's Virginia eye noted the differences between this society and the Old Dominion. He told his diary there was a remarkable prevalence of small farms, few larger than one hundred acres, a striking contrast to the master of Mount Vernon's three thousand acres, and the equally large domains of his Potomac neighbors. Also absent in the crowds that greeted him were well-dressed gentlemen. But there was also no sign of the ragged poverty that marked poor whites in the South. The "great equality" of the people, especially in western Massachusetts, surprised and pleased the President.

Boston was by far the most important stop on the President's itinerary. Frequently called the capital of both New England and Massachusetts, the city was aware that they had never thanked General Washington for liberating them from a humiliating British occupation in 1775–76. They looked forward with great excitement to his arrival. John Hancock was still the governor of the state. The lieutenant governor was Samuel Adams, who did most, if not all, of Hancock's thinking for him.

While the President was still on the road, he received an invitation to stay at Hancock's mansion. Washington explained that he had made it a rule not to visit any private homes on his trip, lest it arouse an unpleasant competition among would-be hosts. But he politely informed the governor that he would be happy to dine with him, when Mr. Hancock called on him at his inn.

That casual remark was weighted with political significance, Washington was telling the Governor that the presidency was the preeminent office and Hancock must make the first call. The President had not forgotten that

Hancock and Adams had expressed severe doubts about the Constitution in their state's ratifying convention in 1788. Washington undoubtedly also knew that in 1775, several delegates to the Continental Congress had noted the chagrin visible on Mr. Hancock's face when John Adams nominated Colonel Washington to head the Continental Army. Hancock's military experience was close to zero, but he was the wealthiest man in Boston—a fact he apparently thought entitled him to consideration for the post.

As Washington was settling into his quarters on the upper floor of a Boston tavern, a note arrived from Governor Hancock, explaining he was much too crippled by an attack of gout to venture from his house. Back went a note from the President, expressing his sympathy and informing the governor that he would dine at his "lodgings" that evening with Vice President Adams.

After supper, Samuel Adams arrived with two members of the governor's council. There are good grounds for suspecting Sam was behind this scheme to assert the Bay State's political ascendency. In the Continental Congress, his penchant for devious politicking had won him the nickname "Judas Iscariot." The President's diary reports that Mr. Adams said he was there to "express the Governor's concern that he had not been in a condition to call upon me as soon as I came to town."

Washington was not an admirer of Sam Adams. He remembered all too clearly that Sam had been the man behind the scheme to replace him with Horatio Gates. The President's summary of their conversation in his diary bristles with barely concealed dislike. "I informed them in explicit terms that I should not see the Governor unless it was at my own lodgings." The delegation talked and talked about Hancock's crippled state— and got nowhere.

The supposedly ailing governor capitulated the next morning. He rushed a note to the President announcing that "the Governor will do himself the honor of paying his respects in a half hour. This would have been done much sooner had his health in any degree permitted." Hancock was now ready to "hazard everything" to make the required visit. Since it was the Sabbath, Washington was attending a morning service when the note arrived. He did not reply until one o'clock. His answer more than matched Hancock's third person language and left no doubt about the political implications of the contest.

"The President of the United States presents his best respects to the Governor, and has the honor to inform him that he shall be at home 'til 2 o'clock. The President of the United States need not express the pleasure it will give him to see the Governor; but at the same time he most earnestly begs that the Governor will not hazard his health on the occasion."

Soon the street outside the President's lodgings was a scene of a hastily staged drama. Governor Hancock arrived in his splendid coach and was lifted out by a team of brawny servants. His legs were swathed in red flannel bandages. The servants carried him into the inn and he hobbled upstairs to Washington's drawing room. There, the President of the United States wryly informed his diary, he "drank tea with Governor Hancock."[7] Washington and his aides almost certainly celebrated this triumph with not a few private chuckles.

As he toured Boston, the President was in a cheerful mood. When he visited a sailcloth factory, in which the workers were all young women, he told the foreman he had hired "the prettiest girls in Boston." At a sumptuous dinner in his honor, he noted in his diary "there were upwards of 100 ladies. Their appearance was elegant and many of them were very handsome." At this and other banquets, women swirled around the President, all but entranced by his height, his affability, and his fame.

Back in New York, refreshed and satisfied with his trip, the President turned his attention to another large responsibility: America's relations with the Indian tribes on the nation's western frontier. Most troublesome was the large and warlike Creek nation, which had killed numerous Americans migrating into western Georgia. The Creeks were formidable opponents, with no less than five thousand warriors at their command.

President Washington sent a three-man delegation to visit them and negotiate a truce. The diplomats were ordered to urge the tribe to forge a relationship with the United States, rather than Spain. Madrid's power loomed large from the Creeks' point of view. Spain controlled Florida and the Louisiana Territory, which included New Orleans and the vast swath of the continent west of the Mississippi.

Although the United States and Spain had been allies during the Revolution thanks to French persuasions, the Spanish monarchy had few friendly feelings for the new nation. Madrid saw American independence as a threat to Spain's colonies in Mexico and Central and South America. Many people assumed that the Spanish were pleased by the Creeks' random terrorism.

A key figure in this three-cornered game was Alexander McGillivray. He had a French grandfather as well as a Scottish father, but his mother and grandmother were Creek. McGillivray swiftly emerged as a canny leader, adept at playing the white men off against each other. Washington put his secretary of war, Henry Knox, in charge of negotiations.

Knox had persuaded Washington that making the War Department responsible for Indian affairs would strengthen the presidency. The Boston general favored buying the land that the western settlers wanted from the tribes, and persuading the Indians to settle in enclaves where the federal government would guarantee they would not be molested. Whether Knox could persuade someone as slippery as McGillivray to accept this arrangement seemed a dubious bet. But McGillivray and a delegation of his fellow chiefs came to New York and signed a mutually satisfactory treaty of peace.

The Creeks were not the only Indians who worried the President. Further north, the warlike Miamis and Shawnees, armed and encouraged by the British in Canada, had murdered an estimated fifteen hundred would-be settlers by the time Washington became president. Envoys were also dispatched in this direction, hoping that these tribes would accept the Knox approach to peace.

۞

The President had yet to receive a reply from Thomas Jefferson, and had begun fretting over his lack of a secretary of state. Washington wanted to discuss the Creek situation with the Spanish minister to the United States, but the envoy was about to return home and Congress was not in session. Washington wondered if he could consult him without the Senate's "advice and consent." Another worry was the frequent capture of American ships in the Mediterranean by Algerine pirates. The President wrote a letter to the Emperor of Morocco, asking for his help in eliminating these seagoing predators.[8]

Far more important to President Washington was the problem of defending the United States in a war. At the moment, the nation had exactly 840 troops in its regular army. They were stationed at West Point and at Fort Pitt in western Pennsylvania. For a decade, these soldiers had not been asked to do anything more military than guard cannon and ammunition left over from the Revolutionary War. Almost to a man, Congress suffered from a malignant hatred of a regular army. The enmity had erupted in the last years of the war, when the officers insisted Congress should keep its 1778 promise to pay them pensions. Instead of heeding Washington's repeated pleas to establish a small peacetime army, Congress had ordered him to discharge the remaining regiments in service at the end of the Revolution, retaining only the token garrisons at Fort Pitt and West Point.

This was an extremely unwise decision; the British had yet to turn over six western forts they had promised to evacuate under the terms of the peace treaty. With no army to make London think twice about ignoring the treaty, the forts were still in British hands, giving His Majesty's diplomats and soldiers easy access to the already restless northwest tribes. [9]

To relax from his presidential chores, Washington turned to a recreation that many New Englanders and not a few New Yorkers disapproved of— the theater. In 1774, the Continental Congress had banned play-going along with horse racing and other supposedly degenerate pastimes from their virtuous new republic. The New England delegates had been among the leaders in this outbreak of their inherited puritanism. As a result, only the British army staged plays during the early years of the Revolution.

At Valley Forge, this ban had been breached with General Washington's approval. His younger officers began staging plays, at which he was a frequent attendee. The Continental Congress issued a steaming rebuke— which the soldiers and their general ignored.

In 1789, New York's John Street Theater was still frowned upon in many quarters. President Washington soon changed almost everyone's mind. On May 11, he and Martha enjoyed one of their favorite plays, Richard Brinsley Sheridan's *The School for Scandal*. The drama was considered racy even by those who enjoyed a naughty laugh now and then. Soon, Washington was inviting guests to the roomy presidential box.[10]

The President told the new chief justice, John Jay, and his wife, Sarah, that he would understand if they declined. Huguenot Protestants like Jay were known for their puritanism. But Jay's severity had been softened not a little by his attractive New Jersey spouse. They accepted and thanked the President for a very pleasant evening.

Soon the presidential box was regularly packed with government VIPs. Even viper-tongued Senator Maclay, a fierce Presbyterian, accepted an invitation. President watchers began paying close attention to who was invited to enjoy the latest drama. On November 24, 1789, they saw a highly significant set of visitors. The new Secretary of the Treasury, Alexander Hamilton, sat with his wife, Betsy, and her father, Senator Philip Schuyler, one of the nation's wealthiest men. Was it a hint that Washington had seen and approved the plan for a new financial system that Congress had asked Hamilton to submit?

Washington's unique combination of fame and political dexterity was on the way to making the president the central figure in the new federal government. What would Thomas Jefferson think of this phenomenon? He had called the presidency a poor edition of a Polish king. Would Jefferson also be surprised to discover that his former councillor and close friend, James Madison, was working as Washington's partner in the elevation of this new office to such unexpected power?

CHAPTER 7

The Secretary of State from Paris

O N OCTOBER 8, 1789, Thomas Jefferson departed from Le Havre
for America. Like many trans-Atlantic voyagers, he had to sail from
the French port on a packet ship and rendezvous with an America-bound
merchant ship at the English port of Cowes. The envoy went ashore and
bought some British newspapers, hoping to stay in touch with the ongoing
drama of the French Revolution.

The papers described the dramatic events of October 4–5, when the
Paris mob surged into Versailles, slaughtered the bodyguards of the king and
queen and forced them to return to Paris as virtual prisoners. Jefferson was
unperturbed by this violence. He wrote cheerfully to Thomas Paine: "I have
no news but what is given under that name in the English papers. You know
how much of these I believe. So far I collect from them that the king, queen,
and National Assembly are removed to Paris. The mobs and murders under
which they dress this fact are like the rags in which religion robes the true
god." Along with revealing his dislike of traditional Christianity, Jefferson
was again keeping the murderous side of the French Revolution at arm's
length, lest it damage his transcendent faith in its future. [1]

Elsewhere in England, Edmund Burke, the American Revolution's former champion, reacted with horror to the mob's invasion of Versailles. He
focused with special intensity on Queen Marie Antoinette's ordeal. He
portrayed "this gentle soul" forced to flee her rooms "almost naked" while
her guards were being butchered before her eyes. Did a single person, beyond these personal protectors, rise to her defense? Not one. Burke found
it hard to believe that in a nation of men of honor, "ten thousands swords"

had not "leaped from their scabbards to avenge even a look that threatened her with insult."

These words were from an essay that Burke had begun composing, "Reflections on the Revolution in France." It would soon detonate with a large political impact in Britain and America, changing minds and hearts in both countries. [2]

On the day Jefferson sailed, James Madison wrote him an earnest letter, urging him to accept President Washington's offer to become his secretary of state. "It is of infinite importance that you should not disappoint the public wish on this point," Madison declared. "The Southern and Western country have it particularly at heart. To every other part of the Union it will be entirely acceptable." The ex-councillor was still trying to assuage the psychological wound Jefferson had received as Virginia's wartime governor.[3]

Jefferson never received this letter. His ship docked at Norfolk in late November and there he learned from the newspapers that Washington had asked him to be secretary of state. Jefferson promptly wrote to the President, admitting that when he compared his present post with the large and uncharted waters a secretary of state would navigate, he preferred to remain a diplomat.

Jefferson also admitted that he would enter upon the new appointment "with gloomy forebodings from the criticisms and censures of a public just indeed in their intent but sometimes misinformed and misled." But he simultaneously admitted "it is not for an individual to choose his post. You are to marshal us as may be best for the public good."

Washington firmly but cordially declined to play the general and give him an order. "It must be your option," he wrote, making it clear that he would have no objection if Jefferson wished to continue to serve "abroad."[4]

Part of Jefferson's ambivalence reflected his knowledge of the current political situation in Virginia, as his many correspondents had described it to him. Thanks to Patrick Henry, a large portion of the state's electorate remained hostile to the federal government. This was particularly true in the Piedmont section of the state, which included Jefferson's home county of Albermarle.

Not long after Christmas, Congressman Madison and Thomas Jefferson shook hands at Monticello after a five-year separation. There is little doubt that Madison reiterated the advice he had written in his undelivered letter of October. As he saw it, Jefferson's role in the new government was far more important than his own. The symbolic power of his name would do much to win support in Virginia and elsewhere.

Madison had been unable to mount a satisfying counterattack against Patrick Henry in the House of Representatives. But he had pushed through the Bill of Rights, defeated John Adams's call for resounding presidential and vice presidential titles, and emerged as the informal leader of the new Congress. He assured Jefferson that he would remain a strong ally if new disputes with Henry arose. Nevertheless, the envoy remained dubious about the wisdom of accepting the President's offer.

With typical energy and shrewdness, Madison proceeded to orchestrate a letter writing campaign to change Jefferson's mind. One of his first recruits was President Washington, who told the reluctant candidate that "the secretary of state would play a very important role in the successful administration of the general government." This, the President added, was "of almost infinite consequence to the future happiness of the citizens of the United States."

Madison followed up these resounding presidential words with a letter of his own, reporting "a universal anxiety is expressed for your acceptance." By way of further persuasion, Madison recruited James Monroe to head an Albermarle County Committee that sent Jefferson an address of welcome in which they declared "America still has occasion for your services."[5]

These words stirred deep emotions in Jefferson. He replied to his neighbors that he would never forget that they had been the first to summon him to serve "in the holy cause of freedom," and he pledged himself ready to bow "to the will of my country." Two days later, Jefferson accepted Washington's offer and promised to be at the President's service as soon as he could prepare his neglected farms and mansion for another extended absence.

After his meeting with Madison, Jefferson read over the long letter he had written in Paris describing the idea that had seized his mind, *the earth belongs to the living*. He found nothing to change and mailed it to New York, where Madison was back in Congress. When Madison found time to reply, he was torn between friendship and candor. The latter emotion soon prevailed. He diplomatically conceded that the idea was "a great one." But he was skeptical of its value as a political lodestar. He "regretfully" found it "not very compatible with the course of human affairs."

Madison broke the theory into four parts:

1. The living generation can only bind itself.

2. A generation spans nineteen years.

3. A generation's actions are limited to that term, and, to be valid, have to be expressly enacted by its congress or parliament.

4. In every society, the will of the majority binds the minority.

Madison calmly demolished each of these propositions, mostly on the basis of their impracticability. After the ordeal he and George Washington had endured to create the Constitution and the new government, he was especially opposed to the idea of each generation revising all its laws and customs every nineteen years. Such a government would lose "those prejudices in its favor which antiquity inspires." Worse, every revision would arouse pernicious factions.

Even weaker was the contention that the new generation had no obligation to honor the debts of the previous generation. "Debts may be incurred principally for the benefit of posterity," Madison wrote. A good example was the present debt of the United States, which was incurred to win a war bestowing freedom on the next generation and hopefully on all those that would follow it.

Instead of splitting the generations apart, Madison found that the "nature of things" tends to bind them together. In this unity, the principle of "tacit assent"—rather than literal reenactment of all the laws—was indispensible. If explicit assent had to be obtained for every principle and idea in a nation every nineteen years, there was a danger of "subverting the foundation of civil society." As for the majority binding the minority, Madison could find no law of nature that supported the idea.

The Congressman attempted to soothe his friend by assuring him that he was not trying to "impeach either the utility of the principle [that the earth belongs to the living] in some particular cases." But this was a pleasure he had little hope of enjoying. "The spirit of philosophic legislation has never reached some parts of the Union, and is by no means the fashion here [in New York] either within or without Congress." Those last words were very close to being sarcastic. But Madison was confident that Jefferson's friendship was strong enough to tolerate it.[6]

Jefferson never replied to Madison's letter. But he also never abandoned his idea that the earth belongs to the living, and its corollary, the overriding importance of majority rule. From the perspective of two hundred-plus years, it is obvious that the two men had very different political philosophies.

※

While Jefferson was making up his mind to become secretary of state, Congressman Madison was discovering the importance of another member of President Washington's cabinet—Secretary of the Treasury Alexander Hamilton. Born on the small West Indian island of Nevis, Hamilton had survived a troubled childhood. He and his brother were sons of a common-law marriage, which ended when his headstrong mother, Rachel Fawcett Lavien, threw her feckless Scottish-born husband, James Hamilton, out of her bed and house. Thereafter, she had so many affairs with various men, a local court condemned her as a common prostitute. When Alexander was thirteen, she succumbed to one of the many fevers that made life in the West Indies so precarious. A prosperous local merchant, who may have been Hamilton's real father, hired the boy as a clerk.

Young Alexander displayed so much intelligence and self-reliance in the art of buying and selling, his employer persuaded other merchants plus a warm-hearted Presbyterian minister to send him to New York to complete his education. When the Revolution exploded, Hamilton wrote a fierce essay supporting it and organized a company of artillerymen. He soon attracted General Washington's attention and was invited to join his staff as an aide. There, he swiftly became the general's chief ghostwriter and frequent advisor.

In 1780, Hamilton grew ambivalent about the aide's invisible role. His exposure to General Washington had stirred a desire to achieve a reward that only leaders of nations could hope to merit: fame. Hamilton was the first of the founders to articulate this spiritual and psychological goal. In 1778, he wrote an essay under the pen name "Publius" declaring that every American of virtue and ability should rejoice that the Revolution was giving him a chance to help found an "empire" that "would...promote human happiness" and win him the fame that was the topmost rung in the ladder of worldly glory.

Hamilton was echoing the opinions of Sir Francis Bacon, the British Renaissance philosopher, whose *Essays* were extremely popular with the

Founding Fathers. Thomas Jefferson displayed a painting of Bacon wherever he happened to be living, not unlike devout Catholics mounted portraits of favorite saints.

After the war, Washington saw or heard little from Hamilton until the ferment for a new Constitution arose. At the Philadelphia convention, he made a long angry speech, calling for a president who would rule for life. This extreme solution went far beyond Washington's desire for a strong executive. "Not having compared ideas with you, sir," Hamilton wrote from New York after that intemperate speech "I cannot judge how far our sentiments agree." The formal tone made it clear he had had little contact with the civilian Washington, and still thought as a general's aide. But Hamilton's exertions on behalf of the Constitution, above all his masterful performance at New York's ratifying convention, restored their close wartime relationship.[7]

❦

The Treasury Secretary faced a challenge that stirred President Washington's deepest interest—what was the best way to restore America's ruined credit abroad, and place the infant United States on the road to prosperity? Although Washington was not a student of international finance, he was a savvy businessman, who had run Mount Vernon's farms with a keen eye for turning his lands into profitable ventures. He had abandoned tobacco farming for wheat and other grains and sold the harvests to the overcrowded islands of the West Indies. He had launched a distillery which prospered for several years, and has recently been revived for those with a penchant for historic hangovers.

Washington—and others, notably Robert Morris—had acquired an early respect for Hamilton's thinking on finance. In 1782, when he was a mere twenty-four years old, he had published a series of essays entitled "The Continentalist," that laid out a plan to fund the federal government. The essays revealed that Hamilton had read and thought deeply about the problems and perils of financing a nation.

In a letter to Robert Morris around this time, Hamilton condensed his ideas around a central concept: a national bank. This would be a unifying force, both politically and economically. Above all, it would attract wealthy investors, who would buy shares in the bank that would pay them hefty interest. The bank could loan money to the federal government and absorb the huge debts piled up by the eight years of the Revolutionary War.

The new nation's leading merchant was so impressed with the young man's expertise, he told Hamilton that any suggestion from him would "always command the attention of Robert Morris."[8]

During the summer of 1789, Congress organized the executive branch of the new government. There was little dispute about the powers and responsibilities of the secretary of state, secretary of war, and attorney general. But the Treasury made the politicians uneasy for several reasons. As the chief tax collector, the secretary would have the most direct impact on the people. He would supervise the collection of revenue at the nation's ports—the chief—in fact, the only—immediate hope of financing the federal government. Some congressmen feared the office was too powerful to trust to a single man; there was talk of a three-man committee.

Congressman John Page, an old friend of Thomas Jefferson, thought the House of Representatives should come up with a plan for restoring public credit. Ceding it to the Treasury secretary was "a dangerous innovation" that could create a moneyed aristocracy or "a detestable monarchy." Madison came to the rescue, declaring that such dangers were far less than the menace of the House's bungling in a field that most congressmen understood dimly if at all. Fisher Ames of Massachusetts heartily agreed, declaring government finance was "a deep, dark and dreary chaos."[9]

There was not a trace of Jeffersonian-style hesitation in Hamilton's acceptance of his appointment. The President had discussed it with him not long after his inauguration, and Hamilton had immediately accepted. But everyone had to wait until Congress passed the bill that created the department. Washington signed the legislation on September 2, 1789, and appointed Hamilton on September 11. The new cabinet officer immediately gave the President a list of five well-qualified assistants. The Senate confirmed him and the assistants without even the hint of a debate. They were all at work in a matter of hours.

Hamilton's first act was to borrow $50,000 from the Bank of New York, which he had helped to found. The next day was Sunday, but that did not prevent the new secretary from dispatching assistant treasurer William Duer to Philadelphia with orders to borrow an additional $50,000 from Robert Morris's Bank of North America, another institution that owed much to Hamilton's ideas. Little more than a week later, an impressed House of Representatives asked the Secretary for a report on how to fund the federal government.

While Jefferson was sailing home from Paris, Hamilton was at his desk in the Treasury Department offices in Federal Hall, toiling over the first installment of his plan to create a prosperous nation. He sought advice from James Madison and several other people, but he relied chiefly on his own wide reading and thinking about the arcane world of public finance.

In the midst of this daunting task, Hamilton received a visit from Major George Beckwith, a veteran British intelligence officer. In 1780, he had succeeded the unfortunate Major John Andre as leader of the British secret service in America. (Andre had been captured and hanged for his role in the plot with the traitor general, Benedict Arnold.) Technically on the staff of General Sir Guy Carleton (Lord Dorchester), the governor general of Canada, Beckwith had come directly from England, landing in New York in late September 1789. The quondam spy wanted to find out if there was any chance that James Madison's attempt to launch a policy of discrimination against British imports might be revived. If so, Beckwith had orders to warn the Americans that Britain would retaliate ferociously.

Hamilton assured Beckwith that there was little chance of such a policy being adopted by the Senate, no matter how persuasive Madison might be in the House of Representatives. Personally, he would use his utmost influence to defeat it. The Treasury Secretary grandly declared that he favored its polar opposite—a commercial treaty that would attract more British goods and money into the country. President Washington, he added, was of the same opinion. It was the quickest way to start funding the federal government via the tariffs that would flow to the Treasury's coffers.

As for Madison's attempt at discrimination, Hamilton said, there was no doubt that his Virginia friend was a brilliant thinker on government. But he lacked a certain worldly wisdom that occasionally led him astray. A pleased Beckwith hurried a report of this conversation to Lord Dorchester in Canada, where it swiftly crossed the Atlantic to London. To protect Hamilton from potential political enemies, Beckwith gave him a code name, Number 7.

Two hundred years later, some historians would seize on this device to prove that Hamilton was a British agent. Other historians have researched the matter and decided that Hamilton was negotiating with Beckwith and his superiors using a tough mixture of threats and reminders. He boasted that the United States was on its way to great prosperity—and power.

Britain would be wise to avoid antagonizing her. Hamilton demanded the right to trade with the West Indies, and insisted the two nations would never have normal relations as long as the British refused to evacuate the forts they still garrisoned in the Northwest Territory –the area north of the Ohio River and east of the Mississippi River. When the Secretary provided Washington with summaries of his meetings with Beckwith, there was no hint of disapproval from the President's side.[10]

Meanwhile, Hamilton continued to write his report on how to fund the federal government, which aroused stronger interest with each passing day. More and more wealthy Americans, and some not so wealthy, acting for foreign investors, were buying up the paper certificates that Congress and state governments had issued to pay for their purchases during the Revolutionary War. Madison became aware of this financial ferment when he returned to Congress on January 20, 1790. In a letter to Jefferson, he remarked that speculation in the public securities was rampant, and had sent their value soaring. He sourly added: "Emissaries [of the speculators] are still exploring the interior and distant parts of the Union in order to take advantage of the ignorance of holders."[11]

By this time, Hamilton had completed his report, which combined proposals for dealing with the national debt, and pungent arguments defending his solutions. The debt totaled $79 million—over a billion dollars in today's money. About two-thirds was owed by the federal government and a third by the states. Instead of undertaking the Herculean task of paying it all as swiftly as possible, Hamilton proposed "funding" it, setting aside revenues for this purpose, and paying off the debt at regular intervals, convincing creditors that eventually they would be paid in full. Meanwhile, the debt would be "a national blessing." The government would issue new securities to existing creditors, with generous rates of interest. Wealthy investors could trade these bonds for cash, or use them to purchase land or launch businesses.

To achieve this goal, Hamilton urged Congress to make some difficult decisions. Perhaps the toughest was the Secretary's recommendation that the current holders of government certificates should be paid in full, without any consideration of how or when they acquired them. Such a policy was crucial to restoring faith in the nation's credit. At first glance it seemed to penalize the men to whom the certificates had been issued, and who, in the intervening years, had sold them to speculators for far less than their original worth.

Even more unnerving to many congressmen was Hamilton's next recommendation. Instead of repudiating the debts incurred by the states, as
some people were suggesting, Hamilton wanted them to be consolidated
with the federal debt, making the nation as a whole responsible for them.
This, too, was part of the Secretary's conviction that the nation's credit
could only be restored by regarding every debt as a sacred obligation that
must—and would—be paid.

The Secretary also saw consolidating the two debts as a giant step
toward making a unified nation out of the thirteen previously semi-
independent states. At the same time, Hamilton made it clear that he
did not favor a perpetual debt. In his report, he called for the creation of
a "sinking fund"—revenue exclusively devoted to the gradual retirement
of the debt.

🦋

The audacity—and complexity—of Hamilton's system at first stunned his
listeners. But not for long. Rumblings came from southerners and westerners as they watched speculators dispatching agents to their sections of
the country to buy up old certificates. Pennsylvania Senator Maclay, the
quintessential spokesman for anti-federalist suspicions, was soon calling it
"a villainous business" and darkly declaring certain congressmen were
among the eager buyers. Hamilton denied this claim in a note to President
Washington, and incidentally defended the speculators. He thought it
strange that men should be "deemed corrupt and criminal for investing in
the funds of their country."

Congressman James Jackson of Georgia added to the turmoil by denouncing the speculators on the floor of the House: "My soul arises indignant at the avaricious and immoral turpitude which so vile a conduct
displays," he bellowed. Topping him was a blast from Dr. Benjamin Rush
in Philadelphia, who fancied himself a political sage. Rush accused Congress of legislating "for British subjects." He denounced the very idea of a
public debt, as if his opinion would automatically make it disappear. Hamilton was introducing "European vices into our infant republic," the political physician cried. [12]

In spite of his incoherence, Dr. Rush touched on a crucial aspect of
Hamilton's plan that was obvious to many people. It was modeled on the
British system, which funded the nation's debt in the same way and sold
shares to investors on the open market. For British-haters, who were still

numerous among American voters, the mere fact of this similarity was proof that it was evil.

※

Throughout these first acrimonious weeks, James Madison remained silent. On February 11, 1790, he rose in the House—and stunned Hamilton and President Washington by joining the critics. He declared himself in favor of "discrimination"—finding the original holders of the certificates and paying them a just share of their total value. Madison, like good politicians before and since, was paying attention to his Virginia constituents, who shared his dislike of speculators. Madison said he favored paying those who had purchased certificates what they were worth at their current market value plus accrued interest. The difference between the current value and the certificates' full face value should go to the original owners, who had sold them under duress.

A huge argument exploded in both houses of Congress. Hamilton's backers said the task of finding the original owners was virtually insuperable. Madison tartly replied that if Congress put as much effort into the task as the speculators were devoting to buying the certificates, it might be accomplished quite easily. This was an answer that solved nothing and the issue was put to a vote on February 22, 1790.

Early that day, Senator Maclay and his allies thought they saw an opportunity to impose a totally different solution on the nation. Maclay visited Madison and proposed slashing the interest on the entire debt from 6 percent to 3 percent—and making public lands in the west the only payment. Such a move would be a total repudiation of Hamilton's report.

Madison did not even bother to read Maclay's resolutions. He had convinced himself and others that he was only asking for justice for the original owners. He was not trying to reduce the amount the country owed, or indulging in tricks to somehow repudiate part of the debt. The Pennsylvanian went away damning "His Littleness" for refusing to change his ideas.

That afternoon, the House gave Madison a shock; they voted down his proposal, 36–13. Nine of the thirteen negative votes came from Virginia—a good indication of why the Congressman had gone out on this controversial limb. [13]

President Washington's silence throughout the debates in Congress had made it clear to almost everyone that he favored Hamilton's approach. Some outraged critics now accused him of betraying the soldiers of the Continental Army, who held a large share of the original debt certificates. Washington's defenders pointed to advice he had given the men when the certificates were issued to them in 1783. He had cautioned the soldiers against "the foolish practice…of disposing of their notes and securities at a very great discount." Nevertheless, numerous people with anti-federalist leanings were quick to impugn Washington's integrity. The *Pennsylvania Gazette* published a hostile poem with the following sneer as its centerpiece:

> *In war to heroes let's be just*
> *In peace we'll write their toils in the dust.*[14]

President Washington was soon writing to friends in Virginia, expressing his concern about his native state. "Your description of the public mind in Virginia gives me pain," he told one man. "It seems to be more irritable, sour and discontented than it is in any other state in the Union." He—and Madison—were both being forced to confront the baleful negativity of Patrick Henry, who continued to warn all and sundry against the federalist plot to "consolidate" the states out of existence.

Madison was as unhappy about Henry as was the President. Around this time he wrote a letter to one of his older Virginia friends, asking if Henry's contributions to the Revolution were exaggerated. It suggests he was thinking about launching a campaign of political extermination.[15]

On March 21, 1790, Thomas Jefferson finally arrived in New York. He had been delayed for several reasons. Among the less pleasant was a trip to Richmond to arrange payment of the interest on the 7,500 pounds he owed British merchants. (About 600,000 modern dollars.) Much more pleasant was supervising the marriage of his seventeen-year-old daughter, Martha, to her cousin, Thomas Mann Randolph. [16]

Another delay slowed the secretary of state–elect on the trip to New York. Madison explained it to a mutual friend as a recurrence of Jefferson's "periodical head-Ach." These migraine-like attacks were by this time obviously linked to the performance of a task in which Jefferson's feelings were divided. Politics was about to deepen these divisions in ways that would also divide the nation.

CHAPTER 8

Mr. Jefferson Wins a Victory
That He Soon Regrets

JEFFERSON'S FIRST WEEKS IN New York were largely social. President Washington greeted him cordially and invited him to one of his levees. More enjoyable was one of Martha Washington's sumptuous dinners, where the Secretary of State was one of a dozen guests, most of them congressmen and senators and their wives. This may have been where the ever critical Senator Maclay met Jefferson and confided his impression to his diary.

The Pennsylvanian thought the Secretary of State had a "rambling vacant look, and nothing of the firm collected deportment that I thought would dignify a...secretary or minister." The senator also disliked Jefferson's "laxity of manner" and the way he spoke "almost without ceasing" in a "loose and rambling way." He also thought Jefferson's clothes did not fit him very well. Maclay was critical of almost everyone he met in New York, but his description of Jefferson was especially harsh. One suspects the senator thought the Secretary of State acted too much like a Virginia aristocrat for Maclay's hardscrabble taste.[1]

Jefferson did not like or approve of the formality of Washington's levees. Some years later he claimed that Madison had warned him that the people around the President had "wound up the ceremonials of the government to a pitch of stateliness" incompatible with a republican government. It is doubtful that Madison was displaying this kind of animus to Washington in 1790, when he was still the President's frequent advisor

90

and ghostwriter. He had played a part in helping Washington work out his social routine. But the comment is an indication of the way the political current began running, after Jefferson arrived.[2]

✸

The Secretary of State was soon on the prowl for anyone who did not agree with his view of the French Revolution—and/or showed even a hint of what Jefferson deemed favoritism to Great Britain. His first target was John Adams. The Vice President had begun publishing a series of essays, *Discourses on Davila*, which rambled widely about the art and science of government. Enrico Caterno Davila was a long dead historian who had written an eighteen hundred-page chronicle on the French civil wars of the late sixteenth century. The essays were appearing in *The Gazette of the United States*, a semi-official newspaper edited by Boston-born John Fenno. The Gazette had a profitable monopoly on publishing notices and statements by the federal government.

On April 27, 1790, the day that the first of these Davila essays appeared, the Vice President remarked to the Senate that America was being deluged with British pamphlets on the French Revolution—most of them highly favorable. "I despise them all but the production of Mr. Burke," Adams said. Hearing these words caused Senator Maclay to all but levitate from his seat. He knew how little Mr. Burke thought of the French Revolution.

If Maclay had seen the letter Adams had recently written to the liberal English clergyman, Richard Price, a few days earlier, he would have been even more exercised. The Vice President had known and liked Price in the days when Adams had been America's first ambassador to London. The clergyman had sent him a copy of a sermon he had given, praising the French Revolution. Price thanked God he had lived to see "thirty millions of people spurning at slavery and demanding liberty." Adams had replied by telling his "dear friend" that he too rejoiced—but "with trembling."

The American Revolution, Adams reminded him, had been based on the solid principles of English philosopher John Locke. The French were relying on claptrap concocted by erratic savants such as Francois Marie Voltaire and Jean Jacques Rousseau. Worse, Adams added, "I know not what to make of a republic of thirty million atheists." Worst of all, the revolutionists were relying on the National Assembly to lead them. Such legislatures had failed with dismaying regularity since the days of the ancient Greeks. In an ultimate dismissal, Adams told Price the French, like "too many Americans, pant for the equality of persons and property."[3]

Adams was soon saying similar things about the French Revolution in the *Gazette of the United States*. When Jefferson combined these remarks with his old friend's aborted pursuit of elaborate titles for the president and vice president, the Secretary of State concluded that Massachusetts's favorite son should never be trusted with significant political power.

John Adams's skepticism about the French Revolution was mild compared to what Edmund Burke began saying in Parliament. "The French have proved themselves the ablest architects of ruin that ever existed in the world. In one summer....they have completely pulled down to the ground their monarchy; their church; their nobility; their law; their revenue; their army; their navy; their commerce; their arts; and their manufactures...Yet they are so unwise to glory in a revolution which is a shame and a disgrace to them." This rhetoric quickly crossed the Atlantic and also appeared in the *Gazette of the United States*.[4]

Jefferson cited Burke's wild words when he urged President Washington to regard all British commentaries on the French Revolution as tainted. The Secretary of State pointed to promising developments in France. Except for the bloodshed of the Paris mob's invasion of Versailles in October, the year 1790 was relatively calm and seemingly productive politically. France seemed to be evolving into a constitutional monarchy not unlike Britain's.[5]

In fact, the King and Queen were virtual prisoners in their Paris palace. But the National Assembly was still in control of liberal noblemen such as the Marquis de Lafayette and Jefferson's close friend, the Baron de la Rochefoucauld. This apparent calm enabled the Secretary of State to persuade John Fenno to balance his coverage by reprinting stories from pro-French European newspapers. Federal cash played a part in persuading Fenno to be more evenhanded. The Secretary of State was authorized to "print the federal statutes" in three newspapers. Jefferson would soon find out that Secretary Hamilton had even more cash to bestow via Treasury notices about the department's many fingers in the national pie, from tariffs to tax collectors to the operations of the Coast Guard.

Jefferson's first impression of the Secretary of the Treasury was positive. Hamilton invited him to dinner and Jefferson was charmed by his wife, Eliza. But this cordiality was soon disrupted by politics. Hamilton had trounced Madison in Congress, winning a mandate to ignore the Virginian's claim that the original owners of federal securities should be considered in the government's payment for them.

Jefferson went farther than his friend in his comments on this hardnosed policy. "Immense sums" were being "filched from the poor and ignorant" by the "fraudulent purchasers," he claimed. This sentiment collided head-on with Hamilton's contention that there was nothing dishonest or dishonorable in an investor buying this hitherto worthless paper.[6]

By the time Jefferson was settled in a house on Maiden Lane, he had also drawn some dark conclusions about New York City. Although he had five servants, including a slave chef, James Hemings, whom he had taken to Paris for training, as well as a maitre d' hotel (essentially a butler) imported from the French capital, he told one correspondent that he was dismayed by the way hitherto unspoiled Americans were succumbing to extravagance and luxury. It was "a more baneful evil than Toryism was during the war."

We might pause here to note the unreality of these words. Toryism during the Revolution was a matter of life and death. The British and their loyalist American supporters were looking forward to hanging, drawing, and quartering General Washington and dozens of other rebel Whigs, as they had done after quelling revolts in Scotland and Ireland. Extravagance and luxury were hardly comparable, especially since their condemnation was coming from a man who had shipped from France 86 crates of expensive French furniture, dinnerware, silver and paintings, plus 288 bottles of expensive wine.[7]

⚜

The Secretary of State eagerly, if covertly, joined Madison in a new collision with Secretary Hamilton. During the Revolution, the semi-independent states had all contracted large debts—amounting to some 25 million unpaid dollars. Most of this money had been spent fending off British invasions or bombardments, paying militiamen, and recruiting men for the Continental Army with generous bonuses. The Treasury Secretary wanted to buy up these debts, too.

The proposal stirred even more resistance than the quarrel over the federal debt. Virginia, North Carolina, and Georgia had paid off almost half their obligations in the intervening years. Other states, notably Massachusetts and South Carolina, had paid little or next to nothing. On this issue, there is little doubt that Madison felt threatened by a surge of hostility in Virginia, fanned by a sneering Patrick Henry. Hamilton made little attempt to understand or excuse the congressman's decision to oppose the policy. For the Secretary, it was a betrayal of the words Madison had written in *The Federalist* about the importance of minimizing state power to guarantee a strong federal government.[8]

Hamilton maintained that it made political sense for the federal government to assume the states's debts. Arguing over who had repaid and who had not repaid them was beside the point. The money had been spent fighting a common enemy in the name of their country's salvation. But the underlying anti-federalism of thousands of voters dismissed this patriotic appeal as sophistry and a lunge for too much personal power. On April 12, 1790, Madison had the satisfaction of watching the House of Representatives defeat Hamilton's proposal, thirty-two to twenty-nine. When Hamilton partisans attempted to revive the subject two weeks later, Madison was ready with a *coup de grace*—he persuaded the House to vote against further debate on the issue.

Worsening the prospect of a Hamilton comeback was an alarming illness that President Washington contracted on May 7—pneumonia. For a few days, he seemed close to death and New York City was plunged in anxiety and gloom. Confounding the pessimism of his doctors, the President rallied and was soon out of danger. But he was in no condition to give Hamilton any help in the battle over assuming the states' debts, which looked more and more like a total defeat.

✴

There was a contentious issue smoldering in the background of the battle about assumption: where to locate the new nation's capital. New York, having acquired the wandering Continental Congress largely by accident, seemed to think fate had confirmed a well deserved destiny. New Yorkers were sure they were on their way to becoming the nation's largest and wealthiest city.

Philadelphia was quick to point out that Gotham had by no means achieved this supremacy. The City of Brotherly Love was more populous—forty-five thousand industrious citizens—and more civilized than

New York, thanks to founder William Penn's passion for order and cleanliness. New York did not even have an adequate water supply. Moreover, the Quaker city had been the original choice for a capital in 1776.

The nation's most influential politician, George Washington, had been having his own geographical thoughts. He was convinced that a federal city, at the mouth of the Potomac River, would be certain to grow and unite North and South. The Constitutional Convention had voted to create this "federal district" but had not specified its location. The President's fellow Virginians, Jefferson and Madison, agreed with his Potomac River choice, as did numerous voters in the Old Dominion. Washington's vision was linked to a belief that canals could and would remove the many obstacles to making the Potomac a navigable link to the steadily growing settlements in the West.

Thomas Jefferson had a very different motive for favoring the idea: hatred of cities. He was fond of saying that those who "labor in the earth" were nature's true noblemen. He saw a nation of independent farmers as the only hope of preserving America's commitment to liberty. In cities, men were too easily corrupted by money and luxury to worry about fundamental political truths.

Packed with people, cities were also subject to epidemics that spread sudden death. It is hard to see how these convictions jibed with Jefferson's faith in the ultimate triumph of the French Revolution, which was struggling to be born in one of the largest cities in the world, with an addiction to luxury that was second to none.

⚘

Further complicating the location of the national capital was the fact that Secretary Hamilton was strongly in favor of New York. Unfortunately, Hamilton's abrasive tactics in the first stage of assuming the nation's debt, and his overall energy and evident delight in wielding power, had made New York's chances of winning this contest dubious at best. Senator William Maclay was among those who were convinced that Hamilton and his fellow "Yorkers" were ready to try anything, from bribery to threats of secession, rather than "part with Congress." Some senators and congressmen who agreed with the Pennsylanian had begun calling the city "Hamiltonopolis."[9]

According to Jefferson, it was he who wove this web of potentially ruinous disagreements into Congress's first great compromise. He happened to meet Secretary Hamilton at the close of a June day outside President Washington's residence. "His look was somber, haggard and dejected," Jefferson recalled many years later. "Even his dress was uncouth and neglected." Hamilton's conversation was as ragged as his appearance. If assumption failed, he told Jefferson, he would probably resign. God alone knew when and if Congress could work out an agreement on the states' debts. There was so much anger between "creditor" states and those who had paid their debts that secession was a distinct possibility. In desperation, Hamilton wondered if Jefferson could intercede with some of his friends to change their votes.[10]

Jefferson invited the Treasury Secretary to dinner the following night. While the French wine flowed and everyone savored James Hemings's French cooking, Jefferson urged his other guest, Congressman James Madison, to reconsider his opposition to assumption. (Also at the table, though not mentioned by Jefferson, may have been the shrewd, beefy Secretary of War, Henry Knox, as a semi-spokesman for the ailing Washington.) Madison probably sighed heavily, as if he were being asked to sign his own death warrant, and admitted some kind of agreement was a possibility—if he got something in exchange.

Otherwise "the pill would be a bitter one for the Southern states," and Dr. Madison had no intention of administering it. The implication was clear—some highly effective medicine had better be on the table. Hamilton supposedly gnashed his teeth and said he was ready to trade the location of the nation's capital for Madison's support on assumption.

The scene would play well as drama, but the reality was a bit more complicated. We now know that Hamilton had begun negotiating before he went near Thomas Jefferson. The Secretary had persuaded Robert Morris, who was a senator from Pennsylvania, to approve the deal, with a nice proviso to soothe his fellow Philadelphians. The City of Brotherly Love would be the capital for ten years, while the government was building the federal city beside the Potomac. This was long enough to encourage the Keystone Staters to hope they might make their temporary "capitalization" permanent.

However many grains of salt we may want to mix into Thomas Jefferson's version, the deal was soon translated into votes in Congress—although it was a bumpy ride to this destination. Senator Rufus King of New York, hitherto a Hamilton admirer, exploded with rage when the Secretary told him of the swap. Hamilton's wealthy senator father-in-law,

General Philip Schuyler, was equally chagrined. He pointed out that New York City had all but broken ground on a sumptuous official residence for the President.

Meanwhile, Hamilton had to make sure the Pennsylvanians agreed to the bargain. Senator Maclay, still convinced Hamilton was evil incarnate, told his diary that on June 23, Senator Morris was called from the Senate chamber for several minutes. When he returned, he whispered in Maclay's ear: "The business is settled at last." Maclay cared little about Philadelphia; in his western Pennsylvania bailiwick, it was another word for snob. He was far more appalled that Congress would now adopt the "abominations" of Hamilton's funding plan. The Senator blamed President Washington for letting himself become "the dishclout of every dirty speculation."[11]

❦

Here we should pause again to ask a question that few historians have raised about this deal: what America lost by it. Instead of a capital like London, which was also the headquarters of the nation's financial and cultural elite, for the next two hundred years, the American capital would remain a small, isolated town, whose only industry was politics. For the first few decades, it was a swampy, primitive village, in which petty envies and parochial thinking (personified by Senator Maclay) would become the norm. Gone was any hope of writers and artists, as well as businessmen and journalists, unifying the nation around a community that would embody its finest aspirations.

Granted, Washington D.C.'s destiny had complex causes: President Washington's hopes of making the Potomac a waterway to the West never materialized. The preferences of three Virginia presidents (Jefferson and his two disciples, Madison and Monroe) played a significant part in Congress's lack of interest in spending the money to create a federal metropolis. The million young men who died in the Civil War bear mute witness to one of the many prices America paid for this hostility to the kind of unified nation Washington and Hamilton hoped to create in America.

❦

In the second week in July, the House of Representatives approved the Residence Act, which made Philadelphia the capital for ten years, and selected a ten-mile square district on the Potomac as the place for a permanent capital. Two weeks later, the House passed the bill to assume the states' debts. Congressman Madison demonstrated his political stubbornness (and his survival instincts) by voting against it. But he had persuaded four congressmen from Virginia and Maryland to become supporters. Moreover, with the help of some deft accounting, he procured a better deal for Virginia in the final estimate of what the Old Dominion owed.

As Congress ended its session in late August 1790, and the federal government began preparing for the transfer to Philadelphia, Thomas Jefferson and James Madison headed back to Virginia. They were not happy travelers. Treasury Secretary Hamilton had gotten his way on another step in his financial program. The dispute over state debts had demolished the two Virginians' hopes of getting Congress to pass a bill discriminating against the hundreds of British ships arriving in their ports.

Jefferson also may have noticed that on August 21, the *Gazette of the United States* had published a story that cast the French Revolution in the worst possible light. The report dealt with the National Assembly's decision to pass a bill, depriving King Louis XVI of the power to declare war or negotiate peace. "Fifty thousand persons surrounded the place of meeting," the story declared. "Had the decision been different, bloodshed and carnage would probably have been the consequences." Jefferson could not have been pleased with this assertion that the Paris mob was now part of the legislative process. He would have disliked it even more if he knew that, henceforth, editor John Fenno would print almost nothing but bad news about the French Revolution thanks to orders—and cash—from Secretary Hamilton.[12]

Many years later, Jefferson called this agreement with Hamilton the worst mistake of his political life. "I was duped into it by the Secretary of the Treasury and made a tool for forwarding his schemes, not then sufficiently understood by me." The latter part of the statement is especially hard to believe. If the Secretary of State somehow failed to understand what Hamilton was doing, he was in daily conversation with Congressman Madison, who would have been more than willing to explain it to him.

On December 6, 1790, the politicians gathered in Philadelphia to resume governing. President George Washington made financier Robert Morris's mansion his official residence. The house was surrounded by brick walls that guaranteed some much needed privacy. Congress took up its task in the Pennsylvania State House (now Independence Hall) on Chestnut

Street. The congressmen relaxed in sixty-five armchairs upholstered in black leather, while the senators chose red Morocco affixed to the frame with shiny brass tacks.[13]

A visitor would have been inclined to think James Madison still exercised decisive influence with George Washington. Functioning as chief ghostwriter, he composed the President's message to Congress, in which he recommended "encouragements to our Navigation as well to render our commerce less dependent upon foreign bottoms." Once more, Madison replied to the message, in which he had the pleasure of enthusiastically agreeing with his own words. Topping off this seemingly irresistible arrangement, he also wrote the President's reply, in which he looked forward to "the happiest consequences" from their coming deliberations.[14]

Secretary of State Jefferson had meanwhile handed Madison a series of reports that were part of a prearranged plan to ram through tough new legislation against Great Britain. First came a tart narrative describing how the British had left Gouverneur Morris, the special envoy President Washington had sent to England, stewing in London for months, never answering his attempts to negotiate a settlement of the disagreements about the western forts and other matters. The Secretary of State recommended that there should be no attempt to reopen this failed conversation until America was in a position to enforce her demands.

Two weeks later came a report on the sad condition of America's Mediterranean trade, thanks to the depredations of Muslim pirates in Algeria and elsewhere along the coast. Jefferson condemned Great Britain for its policy of paying bribes to these countries to exempt her ships from such attacks. Next came a report on the nation's fishing industry, which had never recovered from its virtual extinction by British warships during the Revolutionary War. The business was still languishing because England either placed high import duties on its catches or excluded them entirely.

The Secretary of State made it clear that the answer to these irritations and insults was a congressional tonnage law, which would favor French ships over British ones by raising import duties on the ships of any country that did not have a reciprocal treaty with the United States to reduce tariffs.

Alas, neither President Washington's warm words in his opening address to Congress nor the wealth of facts that the hardworking Secretary of State poured into these reports produced even a glimmer of a response from Congress. Jefferson and his covert partner, Congressman Madison,

could only watch in dismay while the national legislature was again absorbed and divided by two new proposals from the Secretary of the Treasury, a taxation program on "whiskey and other domestic spirits"—and a
proposal for a national bank.

It was a toss-up which disturbed Senator William Maclay more. He
predicted revolutionary resistance to the liquor tax in the hills and valleys
of western Pennsylvania. As for a national bank, it could only be described
as the ultimate outrage in Hamilton's attempt to turn America into an
outpost of London. No one agreed with the latter accusation more vehemently than Secretary of State Thomas Jefferson. For him, American
politics was rapidly becoming a conspiracy that threatened both the virtuous agricultural republic he saw as the nation's destiny—and his beloved
revolution in France.

CHAPTER 9

From Disagreements to
the First Divide

I T HARDLY NEEDS SAYING that President Washington's attitude toward these two new proposals was a crucial factor in their destiny in
Congress. He had little difficulty favoring the tax on whiskey. Most people, including Thomas Jefferson and James Madison, seemed to think it
was a relatively painless way to increase the flow of revenue into federal
coffers. Hamilton's argument that the money would enable the government to pay its current expenses and make regular payments on the national debt had considerable appeal.

There was a fair amount of debate on the subject. Albert Gallatin, a
newly elected congressman from western Pennsylvania, joined Senator
Maclay in warning that the measure would lead to violent protests. But
the whiskey tax passed the House and Senate with comfortable majorities
early in 1791.

The Bank of the United States was another matter. There was nothing
in the Constitution empowering Congress to launch a bank. Nevertheless,
Washington favored the idea. He had not mastered all the intricacies of
Hamilton's bank, but he was a believer in banks as a crucial way to concentrate a nation's economic strength. During the darkest years of the Revolution, 1780–81, when the nation's currency collapsed and the Continental
Army faced starvation, Philadelphia's Bank of North America had issued
notes that retained their face value and were used to purchase vital supplies
and equipment for the army.[1]

The Bank of the United States was a great deal more complex than the Bank of North America, or the Bank of New York, which Alexander Hamilton had helped to found in his home city. In his proposal to Congress, the Secretary of the Treasury called it "a great engine of state." President Washington's tacit approval was well-known, and this may have had much to do with the way the proposal passed the Senate almost casually, with a voice vote.

In the House of Representatives, a very different scene transpired. James Madison, still the acknowledged leader of this branch of the legislature, took the floor and shocked President Washington and Secretary Hamilton by opposing—and then denouncing—the idea. For a whole day, Madison lectured his fellow congressmen on what was wrong with the proposal. In essence, he argued that the absence of any mention of a bank in the Constitution meant that the framers of the national charter never intended to give the federal government the right to create such an entity.[2]

No one was more astonished by this denunciation than Alexander Hamilton. During the Constitutional Convention, Madison had proposed giving Congress the power to charter banks and other corporations. The delegates had rejected the proposal. Now he cited this rejection but coolly neglected to mention that he had been the author of the proposal. In his *Federalist Papers* essays, Madison had ignored this earlier disapproval and repeatedly insisted there were implied powers in the Constitution that gave Congress the ability to deal with many aspects of federal governance.

Congressman Elias Boudinot of New Jersey was among a number of listeners who did not hesitate to remind Madison of his previous stance. Boudinot read aloud the words from Madison's essay, Federalist No. 44: "There must necessarily be admitted powers by implication unless the Constitution descended to every minutia…No axiom is more clearly established in law or in reason that whenever the end is required, the means are authorized; whenever a general power to do a thing is given, every particular power for doing it is included." Thus the Constitution gave Congress the power to regulate the nation's commerce. Secretary Hamilton saw the Bank of the United States as an essential tool in this crucial task.[3]

The House of Representatives agreed with Boudinot and Madison's other critics, who openly mocked his sudden transformation to a "strict" or literal interpreter of the Constitution he had done so much to create. The bill chartering the Bank of the United States passed the House by almost a two-to-one margin—39 to 20. But this victory, immensely pleasing to Hamilton, soon became only the first act in a drama that would alter America's history.

President Washington, with his acute concern for the nation's unity, was alarmed to note that almost all the congressmen from states north of the Potomac River backed Hamilton's brainchild, while most of the southerners opposed it. Washington asked the lawyers in his cabinet, Secretary of State Jefferson and Attorney General Randolph, to give him their opinion of the bank bill. Soon the President had a strenuous essay by Jefferson on his desk, denouncing the bank with far more vehemence than Madison had exhibited in the House of Representatives. The Secretary of State insisted that permitting the federal government to exercise such an unspecified power could launch the nation toward a centralized federal tyranny.

"To take a single step beyond the boundaries...specifically drawn around the powers of Congress is to take possession of a boundless field of power, no longer susceptible of any definition," the Secretary of State warned. Any extension of Congress's delegated powers had to be truly necessary. Otherwise, the American government would soon become a mirror image of the British model, where the King and Parliament regularly chartered corporations which enriched a privileged few. Jefferson backed up his arguments with a copy of Madison's speech to the House of Representatives.[4]

Attorney General Randolph came to the same conclusion in a far less emotional essay. Washington, obviously upset, sent these opinions to Secretary Hamilton and asked him to reply to them. His covering letter was cold, almost curt, suggesting a loss of faith in Hamilton as an interpreter of the Constitution. Simultaneously, the President asked Madison to prepare a veto message—a glimpse of which way he thought the argument was going.

Literally working day and night, in the next seven days Hamilton produced a fifteen thousand-word treatise that has become one of the most important documents in America's legal and political history. At its climax, he summed it up in a single triumphant sentence: *It is not to be denied that there are implied as well as express powers in the Constitution and the former are as effectually delegated as the latter.* Supporting strict construction, as Jefferson and Madison were doing—arguing that all extensions of government power had to pass a test of being "absolutely necessary"—was madness, Hamilton maintained. It would soon leave the United States with a malfunctioning and ultimately, a nonfunctioning federal government. The states would eagerly rush to fill the power vacuum and would soon reduce federal authority to its pitiful condition under the Articles of Confederation.[5]

In every sense of the word, Hamilton's argument was historic. He simultaneously justified the Bank of the United States and created a rationale for future exercises of federal power that has enabled the United States to function as a nation. President Washington read Hamilton's essay and signed the Bank of the United States into law the following day.

※

This was the moment when Jefferson and Madison began seeing the President as a mere tool in Hamilton's hands. There are strong reasons to challenge this conclusion. Washington was not a man who submitted to anyone's supposed expertise. He had disagreed strongly with Hamilton more than once in earlier years. Once the Secretary convinced him that the Bank of the United States was constitutional, he had no further objections to it. Unlike his fellow Virginians, the President had no difficulty seeing the bank as a dynamic commercial force that would help unite the new nation.

Washington was not in the least bothered by the BUS's similarity to the Bank of England. Unlike Jefferson, the President's view of the mother country was remarkably free of hostility. At a dinner Washington gave for British officers after they surrendered at Yorktown, one of them boldly offered a toast to "The King." Washington raised his glass and added: "Of England. Confine him there and I'll drink him a full bumper."[6]

A few months after the Bank of the United States became law, a delighted President told one of his closest friends: "Our public credit stands on the ground which three years ago it would have been considered a species of madness to have foretold." Thomas Jefferson and James Madison remained violently opposed to the bank. They saw it as an institution designed to enrich the wealthy—and warned it was tempting Americans to risk their money and their peace of mind in what Jefferson called "an appetite for gambling." Madison described the welcome that the bank received as "a mere scramble for public plunder."[7]

※

In the spring of 1791, largely unaware that there was a deepening clash among his cabinet and close advisors, President Washington decided to take a trip through the southern states. He wanted to show the citizens below the Potomac that the President had the same concern for their welfare as he had displayed for the New Englanders the year before. He also wanted to reassure the southerners that signing the bank bill did not mean he was aligned with a so-called "northern phalanx" that, according to some Virginians, was conspiring to seize control of the government.

The trip was no small task. The President's itinerary covered 1,826 miles—a huge distance to traverse by horseback and coach. At every stop there were parades, rallies and dinners, at which he had to appear both affable and presidential to hundreds of strangers. The military side of Washington's character came to the fore. Every day was planned in advance; he let neither rain nor dust-choked roads delay him. His reward was the enormous enthusiasm with which people greeted him everywhere.

At Wilmington, North Carolina, "an astonishing concourse of people" included hundreds of women waving from windows and balconies. At a ball that night, the President was greeted by sixty-two beautifully gowned and coiffed ladies. Simultaneously, he played politics, telling a group of Freemasons led by war hero Mordecai Gist how pleased he was by their statement of support for "our equal government." The adjective was not chosen by accident.

Similar welcomes took place in every city. Washington returned home convinced that the people of the South "appeared to be happy, contented and satisfied" with the federal government. By and large, he found the region prosperous and peaceful with no evidence of hostility to the whiskey tax, the funded debt, or the Bank of the United States.[8]

Only when the President returned to Philadelphia did he discover that not everyone approved of his trip. The most outspoken was a new voice on the newspaper scene, Benjamin Franklin Bache. This grandson of the Founding Father had launched the *General Advertiser*, with an undisguised tilt toward the French Revolution and a hostility to any and all tendencies in American politics that so much as hinted at a British model. Bache thought Washington's tour smacked of the "royal progress" of a king and denounced the "incense" of admiring addresses that greeted the President in every city. He was aware that people were expressing their admiration for "the defender of the liberty of our country," but insisted that it all "favors too much of monarchy to be used by republicans."[9]

Shares in the Bank of the United States went on sale on July 4, 1791, in Philadelphia, New York, and Boston. Rumors had convinced not a few people that the government would pay 12 percent interest. Swarms of investors stormed the Treasury offices in Philadelphia and 26,200 would-be buyers entered bids. The shares sold out within an hour. To widen participation, Hamilton marketed the $400 shares (about $6,000 in today's money) piecemeal; a would-be investor could pay only $25 for a document called "scrip," which entitled him to buy a certain number of shares, for which he would have to pay in full in eighteen months.[10]

For the first month, the price of scrip remained within reasonable bounds. But early in August, it zoomed into the stratosphere. Some people began calling the frenzied market "scrippomania." One friend warned Hamilton that the entire city of New York had become infected with gambling fever. Artisans were deserting their shops, storekeepers were auctioning off their goods to raise cash, and not a few merchants had abandoned their normal business routines to speculate in scrip. Another eyewitness said the city of Philadelphia had become "a great gaming house" with everyone from "merchants to clerks" betting on the soaring scrip. An alarmed Hamilton foresaw the danger of a bubble. He had already warned against "extravagant sallies of speculation" that could injure "the whole system of public credit" that he was struggling to create.[11]

With President Washington's approval, Hamilton decided he had to intervene. He began "talking down" the price of scrip, telling several people he thought it was dangerously overvalued. Next he published a statement in *The Gazette of the United States,* signed by "A Real Friend to Public Credit," warning that the price of scrip was much too high and certain to decline. Next, he ordered the cashier of the Bank of New York to buy $150,000 in government securities. The fever in scrip began to abate.

Nevertheless, Thomas Jefferson predicted serious damage to America's social order. He was convinced that a tailor whose scrip had made him several thousand dollars in a single day would never be willing to work for ordinary wages again. Congressman Madison, who was in New York when the investment fever was raging there, told Jefferson the speculators were all "stockjobbers and tories." Jefferson's comments were equally abusive. In one letter, he told Madison: "Several merchants from Richmond (Scotch,

English, etc.) were here [in Philadelphia] lately. I suspect it was to dabble in federal filth."[12]

In another letter to Jefferson, Madison feared "the stockjobbers will become the praetorian band of the government, at once its tool & its tyrant." (In ancient Rome, the Praetorian Guard was the emperor's private army, which could, and sometimes did, threaten both the unruly populace and the ruler.) Madison was convinced that the stockjobbers could be bribed by Congress's "largesses" or could overawe it "with clamours and combinations." He gloomily concluded that his imagination would not "attempt to set bounds to the daring depravity of the times."[13]

The enthusiasm of these first investors was unquestionably extreme, and merited some concern. But the apocalyptic reaction of Jefferson and Madison was even more extreme. It revealed a profound hostility to the very idea of public finance. Hamilton's successful intervention in the scrippomania bubble enabled President Washington to remain enthusiastic about the new financial system. He told one correspondent that the eagerness to buy shares in the Bank of the United States was "unexampled proof of the resources of our countrymen and their confidence in [the] public measures" of the new federal government.[14]

⸙

What explained the almost instinctive hatred of banks and a stock market that Thomas Jefferson and James Madison displayed? From the perspective of 2014, these two gifted men sound like maniacs. The investors of 1791 were doing something that tens of millions of contemporary Americans do every day—invest in bonds or stocks. Mere dislike of Alexander Hamilton or jealousy of his growing power and influence is not enough to explain such frantic extremism. Why did not President Washington, a man who said seeing America a happy nation was "the first wish" of his soul, watch this birth of a commercial spirit with similar horror and dread? To understand this phenomenon, which continues to have relevance in the twenty-first century, requires a trip back in time to England in the early eighteenth century.

Under Prime Minister Robert Walpole in the 1720s, the British government became a centralized engine that made Britain the strongest nation in Europe. Its taxation system enabled it to sustain a large fleet and a standing army. It chartered and helped finance the East India

Company and other corporations that extended the reach of the empire and earned huge profits for private investors. To manage this international colossus, Walpole used titles, honors, and other favors, including occasional bribery, to persuade leading members of Parliament to support his policies.[15]

Simultaneously, a vocal opposition to this centralization arose. Claiming to speak for the majority of the people, they called themselves the "country" party, who opposed the "corruption" of the "court" party. The very terms were polemical. Soon newspapers and books were full of angry exchanges between true believers on both sides. The argument was followed with fascination by intelligent men in the thirteen colonies. The majority of Americans sympathized with the country party, especially after Parliament began asserting more and more power over all parts of the empire. They adopted the chief argument of the opposition, that the court party was drenched in corruption and was steadily destroying British liberty, both at home and abroad. This rhetoric became an essential part of the vocabulary used to justify the American Revolution.

The country party liked to portray themselves as idealists who wanted to regain a largely mythical past, when stalwart yeomen voted their consciences on behalf of the public good. Over the horizon in an equally mythical future, they saw a land where justice prevailed, under a "patriot king" who adjudicated the differences between the quarreling factions. Both Thomas Jefferson and James Madison had absorbed this ideology in their collegiate youth, and when they saw its supposed lessons being ignored by Alexander Hamilton, they reacted with ideological fury.[16]

Again, we must ask why President Washington did not share these fierce emotions. Here we come close to defining the essential difference between Thomas Jefferson and George Washington. For Jefferson, liberty was a sacred, semi-religious goal. He saw a future in which America's independent farmers were liberty's best guardians. Thanks to them, the nation would demonstrate the perfectability of human nature. This utopian faith was at the root of his passionate support of the French Revolution, as well as his determination to keep the supposed corruptions of commerce out of America's future.

Washington was the polar opposite of a utopian. He drew his own conclusions about politics and business, rooted largely in his experiences. He had no prejudice against the commercial world. Premier merchant Richard Morris was one of his closest friends. Nor was he in the least shocked to hear Hamilton praise merchants and other men of business as vital to America's future.

✸

While President Washington was touring the South, Thomas Jefferson had an encounter with Alexander Hamilton that confirmed his worst suspicions. The President had suggested that the members of the cabinet meet with Vice President John Adams and discuss any decisions that the government needed to make in his absence. One April evening, after discussing official business at a dinner party at Jefferson's residence, the talk turned to theories of government. For a while, Adams pontificated about the virtues of Britain's "balanced" government and its distribution of power between the king, the lords, and the commons. The problem with this arrangement, Adams added, was the "corruption" that gave the king and his ministers too much influence over the House of Commons. This was straight country party doctrine, virtually from the mouth of its most famous spokesman, Lord Bolingbroke.

Hamilton disagreed with the Vice President. He said that if by some miracle the British government were purged of corruption, the result would be "impracticable." In his opinion, the present system, with its supposed corruption, was "the most perfect government that ever existed." Hamilton was expressing his admiration for the way Prime Minister Walpole's successors had created a wealthy and powerful nation. But Jefferson—and probably Adams—heard him with minds steeped in the long struggle between Britain's country and court parties.

To them, Hamilton's words were a veritable confession of his admiration for the ruthless men and evil deeds that would eventually snuff out all traces of liberty in the mother country. For Jefferson, the behavior of the first investors in the Bank of the United States confirmed this judgment with a certainty that would dominate his mind for the rest of his life.

✸

Even before the Bank of the United States began selling its shares to clamorous customers, Jefferson and Madison had decided it was time to do more than express their disapproval of Hamilton's program to a small circle of friends. In the spring of 1791, they took a trip to northern New York, which Jefferson described to President Washington as a remedy for the headaches that kept disturbing his health. In discussing it with others, he called it a "botanical" expedition to discover new flowers and fauna in that part of America.

The journey's real purpose was political. The Virginians spent time with Chancellor Robert R. Livingston, head of a powerful and wealthy Hudson River Valley clan. They also met with Senator Aaron Burr, who had recently defeated Hamilton's father-in-law, Philip Schuyler, in his bid for reelection. They may also have seen Governor George Clinton. These gentlemen, especially Clinton, were united by personal dislike of Secretary of the Treasury Hamilton. Although the word "party" was still taboo, there was little doubt that the Secretary of State and the Congressman were seeking the support of these men in the months to come.

Back in New York City, the peripatetic Virginians spent not a little time with Madison's college roommate, Philip Freneau. Known as "the Poet of the Revolution," for verses he had published about his experience aboard a British prison ship in New York Harbor, the New Jersey–born Freneau was writing a column for a New York newspaper in which he revealed a hatred of all things British. He was more than ready to denounce Hamilton and his rich friends as enemies of the poor and middling classes, of which he was eminently one. Madison and Jefferson urged him to come to Philadelphia and launch a newspaper that would express their mutual fear and detestation of the Treasury Secretary's attempt to shape the federal government along British lines.

The penniless Freneau, with a growing family and no means of support but some unproductive acres of farmland in South Jersey, first said yes, then changed his mind a month later. Jefferson was so disappointed, he journeyed back to New York and spent an entire day trying to repersuade the indecisive poet. It would take another effort by Madison to convince him to enter the political fray. Whereupon a delighted Jefferson offered Freneau a job as a translator in the office of the secretary of state. This was—and remains—a unique performance—giving a newsman a government salary to attack the administration in which his patron was supposedly a loyal partner.[17]

<hr/>

Over the next twelve months, Madison, in close and constant consultation with Jefferson, contributed eighteen unsigned essays to Freneau's paper, the *National Gazette*. All were attacks on Hamilton's program. President Washington remained unaware of this secret assault on his administration by a man whom he still considered his closest advisor. In the same month of October 1791 that Freneau began publishing his paper in Philadelphia, Madison drafted Washington's annual message to Congress and chaired the committee that responded to it. A few days later, in the first edition of the *National Gazette*, Freneau accused Alexander Hamilton of being the head of a "monarchist" group plotting to destroy the republic. He also hailed Thomas Jefferson as a "colossus of liberty." [18]

Perhaps we should pause here to puzzle over Madison's duplicity. In most of the dealings of his long life, he was an honorable and honest man. The best explanation for his becoming two-faced in his relationship to President Washington may well be Thomas Jefferson's role in the Congressman's political and personal life. From the earliest days of their relationship Jefferson had been the leader, Madison his intelligent, but usually subordinate, advisor.

This did not mean subservience. We have seen how Madison tactfully disagreed with some of Jefferson's wilder ideas, such as the earth belongs to the living. But Jefferson's current role in Washington's cabinet fused with his fame as the drafter of the Declaration of Independence and his experience as ambassador to France to become an overpowering combination in 1791. Writing to Jefferson around this time, Madison assured him that he was always ready "to receive your commands with pleasure." [19]

While Freneau published more and more biting attacks on Hamilton, Secretary of State Jefferson remained ostensibly neutral. A Philadelphia printer inadvertently destroyed this disguise. Jefferson had reacted with disgust and rage at Edmund Burke's essay, "Reflections on the Revolution in France." The Irish orator predicted the upheaval's collapse into bloodshed and anarchy, ending in a dictatorship. The Secretary of State was doubly pleased when Thomas Paine responded with a vigorous assault on Burke, *The Rights of Man.*

Jefferson particularly liked Paine's claim that "every age and generation must be free to act for itself *in all cases*…The vanity of governing beyond the grave is the most ridiculous and insolent of all tyrannies." He also approved Paine's condescending view of the British people as passive victims of "the feeble and crazy" George III. He was even more enthusiastic about Paine's denunciation of the British centralized financial system, which resulted in "a monied interest [class]" that controlled the nation. "It is power, not principles, that Mr. Burke venerates," Paine sneered. [20]

Paine was so confident that he was enunciating American principles, he dedicated *The Rights of Man* to George Washington and shipped fifty copies of the polemic to the President. Jefferson sent a copy of the book to a Philadelphia printer with a covering letter expressing his pleasure "that something is at length to be said against the political heresies that have sprung up amongst us." The printer converted the letter into an introduction to the book.

An uproar exploded. The agitated Secretary of State assured President Washington that he had never intended his letter to be made public. Jefferson claimed he was criticizing the essays that Vice President John Adams had been publishing in John Fenno's *Gazette of the United States* about the long-dead historian, Enrico Davila. Recent essays had expressed grave doubts about relying on unstable public opinion and stubbornly called for a society ruled by rank and distinction, in which titles would be conferred on the "natural aristocracy" of America. No one had any trouble agreeing that this was a theory almost laughably wrong for the United States.

Into the uproar barged a talented Adams defender. A series of hard-hitting essays signed by someone using the pseudonym "Publicola" accused Jefferson of being the real heretic for backing Tom Paine's ideas. Jefferson assured Paine that Publicola represented "a sect high in names but small in number." The sarcasm suggests that he assumed Publicola was the Vice President. In fact, the writer was Adams's son, twenty-four-year-old John Quincy Adams, making his first appearance on the public stage. He was writing without asking his father's permission. His eleven Publicola essays were widely read and reprinted as a pamphlet in England, where they were very popular. That was not surprising. John Quincy agreed wholeheartedly with his father's—and Edmund Burke's— pessimistic view of the French Revolution.

Only when the controversy subsided two months later did Jefferson try to rescue his friendship with John Adams. He claimed his letter to the printer grew from his belief that "truth, between candid minds, can never do harm." Adams coolly expressed surprise. He had no recollection of ever discussing theories of government with Jefferson. He also denied he was Publicola but assured Jefferson that their friendship was still "very dear to my heart." [21]

Far more significant are the letters Jefferson exchanged with James Madison about this incident. Jefferson assured Madison that he believed Adams was a heretic, but "certainly never meant to step into a public newspaper with that in my mouth." Then came more revealing words. Colonel Hamilton was "open-mouthed against me," claiming that "it [the introductory letter for *The Rights of Man*] marks my opposition to the government." In a pained tone, Jefferson claimed that Hamilton was attempting to turn on the government "those censures I meant for the enemies of the government, to wit, those who want to change it into a monarchy."

Jefferson added that he "had reason to think he [Hamilton] has been unreserved in uttering these sentiments." This was a glimpse of a distinction that would cause Jefferson trouble for the rest of his life. He drew a line between what he said in a private letter and what he said in public discourse. Hamilton had violated this rule by being "open-mouthed" with his opinion. But Jefferson constantly used private letters to influence public policy—and only retreated to the other meaning of private when his opinions stirred criticism or opposition. As a public man, he also refused to recognize that very little of what he said was a private matter.[22]

Madison replied that he had never entertained for a moment anything but a firm belief that Vice President Adams's ideas were ridiculous. Hamilton's pro-British views—and his growing power—was the heresy they had to fear. Madison said he saw nothing wrong with a public servant—Jefferson—endorsing a book (*The Rights of Man*) that defended "the principles on which 'that Govt is founded'"—and Hamilton was violating.

❦

In view of these convictions, it is not hard to imagine Jefferson's and Madison's reaction to a new report that Secretary of the Treasury Hamilton sent to Congress in mid-December 1791—a proposal to create a Society for the Establishing of Useful Manufactures that the federal government would help to fund, along with private investors. Hamilton wrote a prospectus, with the help of Assistant Secretary of the Treasury Tench Coxe, a strong advocate of an industrial America. The S.U.M. would encourage and promote factories that would launch the United States as an industrial power, aimed at challenging British dominance of this rapidly growing segment of the world's economy. Hamilton summed it up with a bold sentence that was the equivalent of a war cry: "Both theory and experience conspire to prove that a nation...cannot possess *active* wealth but as a result of extensive manufactures."

The Society called for the creation of a city devoted to manufacturing. It would be named Paterson, after the popular governor of New Jersey, who had persuaded his legislature to charter it. Would-be investors rushed to buy shares in the S.U.M, which could be paid for in part with stock in the Bank of the United States. The initial offering of $500,000 sold out almost immediately. Soon the shares were rising dramatically and Americans began discussing the prospect of producing the long list of goods that Hamilton mentioned in his prospectus, from paper to cotton and linen textiles to blankets and beer. [23]

For Jefferson and Madison, this was ultimate proof that Hamilton was determined to transform America along British lines, with an inevitable final touch—the crowning of a king. Soon a pseudonymous James Madison was telling readers of the *National Gazette* that Hamilton's policies were based on "the principles of aristocracy and monarchy, in opposition to the Republican Principles of the Union, and the Republican spirit of the people."[24]

A war had begun—a struggle for the public mind—the political soul—of George Washington's America. At stake was the future of the experiment in independence to which he had devoted his life.

CHAPTER 10

When Best-Laid Plans Go Wrong

NOT MANY PEOPLE SAW George Washington lose his temper. His self-control was legendary. But when he lost it, the explosion was something witnesses never forgot. One of the most historic detonations occurred on December 9, 1791, when a messenger from Secretary of War Henry Knox arrived at the President's Philadelphia mansion while Washington was entertaining guests at dinner. His secretary, Tobias Lear, hurried into the dining room and whispered that there was news from the West.

The President excused himself and rushed to a nearby parlor to glance at a dispatch from the commander of the western army, Major General Arthur St. Clair. The previous day, a newspaper had reported a rumor that the army had been mauled in a clash with hostile Indians. Within minutes Washington returned to the table, where he chatted agreeably with his guests until they departed.

Lear followed Washington into the parlor to see if he were needed for any further duties. The slight, affable secretary found a man he had never seen before. The President's face was red, his eyes wild. His long arms flailed the air. "IT'S ALL OVER!" he roared. "St. Clair's defeated—ROUTED! The officers nearly all KILLED! I told him when I took leave of him—Beware of SURPRISE! He went off with that as MY LAST SOLEMN WARNING! Yet he let his army be cut to pieces—HACKED—BUTCH-ERED—TOMAHAWKED—by SURPRISE—the very thing I warned him against! The blood of the slain is upon him—the curse of widows and orphans—THE CURSE OF HEAVEN!"

For another five minutes, Washington damned General St. Clair using adjectives and adverbs that Lear had never heard before in his genteel life. He had spent the Revolutionary War years at Harvard. The horrified secretary feared the fifty-nine- year-old president would topple to the floor in a fatal fit of apoplexy.

Breathing in rasps, Washington flung himself onto a nearby sofa. When he spoke again, it was in a calm, measured voice. "This must not go beyond this room. General St. Clair shall have justice. I will hear him without prejudice."[1]

Even before Washington became president in 1789, the fledging United States had been fighting an undeclared war in the western territory the Americans had unexpectedly acquired from the British in the treaty of peace that ended the War for Independence. President Washington had sent envoys who attempted to negotiate a peaceful cession of some of the Indians' lands. As we have seen, in the South the Creeks responded, but in the Northwest, the Miamis, Shawnees, and other more warlike tribes evaded or violated agreements.

To the President's frustration, the United States still did not have an army to add some muscle to his diplomacy. If anything, the opposition to paying a regular army had become a permanent prejudice in Congress. Not even President Washington's military prestige could persuade the politicians to recruit more than the single regiment created in 1784. A year before General St. Clair marched to disaster, this regiment, reinforced by over one thousand militia, had launched an attack on a cluster of Miami villages from which many war parties emanated. About one hundred Miami warriors led by a gifted war chief, Little Turtle, had ambushed the advance guard. The panicked militia abandoned the regulars in headlong flight. The army stumbled back to its base at Fort Washington, near present-day Cincinnati, demoralized and humiliated.[2]

A grim President and his Secretary of War, Henry Knox, persuaded Congress to authorize a second regular regiment. They also negotiated permission to raise two thousand "levies" for six months service. These soldiers would be considered regulars even though they were closer to militia. To command this second army, the President chose Arthur St. Clair, who had been a major general during the Revolution, and was currently governor of the Indiana territory.

Simultaneously, anti-army ideologues in Congress undermined St. Clair and the President. Late in 1790 they reduced the regulars' pay, and for an entire year did not bother to send them a penny. Less than 10 percent of the men whose enlistments expired that year signed up again. When St. Clair reached Fort Washington, he found the First Regiment had dwindled to 299 men. Recruiting for the new second regiment faltered disastrously, leaving the regulars 50 percent below their authorized strength. St. Clair's six-month levies were barely trained and he was forced to call out 1,160 militia.[3]

Meanwhile, the Indians gathered a fifteen hundred warrior army under the leadership of Little Turtle. At dawn on November 4, 1791, the war chief attacked. The militia and the six-month levies fled and the American campground became a scene of indescribable slaughter. An appalling 64 officers and 807 enlisted men were killed or wounded, and the casualties among the packhorse drivers and other civilians were even more horrendous. General St. Clair had joined the fugitives on one of the few surviving horses.[4]

The President informed Congress and the newspapers that the country was now embroiled in a full scale war, with the future of the United States at stake. Were we going to let the British and their Indian allies confine America to a strip of states along the Atlantic seaboard? The chastened politicians abandoned their regular army paranoia and gave the President the soldiers he wanted. There would be four regular regiments, with men enlisted for three years service, plus a squadron of cavalry. As a sop to a still vocal minority of regular-haters in Congress, Secretary of War Knox decided the new force would be called "The Legion of the United States" rather than the United States Army.

The President chose Anthony Wayne of Pennsylvania to command this new entity. As a brigadier general in the Revolution, he had acquired a reputation for fierce attacks. Someone who did not relish his headlong battlefield style had called him "Mad Anthony," and the name stuck. Wayne was far from a reckless hothead. In 1782, with only a few hundred regulars, he had wrested control of Georgia from a much larger British army.

Wasting no time, General Wayne headed for Pittsburgh, where he was told his army would await him. He discovered a grand total of forty morose recruits. It took another ten months for the Legion of the United States to reach twelve hundred men. Low pay and the prospect of confronting the tomahawk wielders who had slaughtered St. Clair's army did not attract the best and brightest. A grim Wayne went to work on turning this collection of illiterate farm boys and urban drifters into serious soldiers.

Back in Philadelphia, the man whom President Washington had begun to consider his most important cabinet member was revealing an all too human flaw. On December 15, 1791, ten days after Secretary of the Treasury Alexander Hamilton had submitted his groundbreaking *Report on Manufactures* to Congress, he received a letter from James Reynolds, informing him in outraged terms that he had just discovered the Secretary was conducting a torrid affair with his wife, Maria. By seeming coincidence, Mrs. Reynolds had also written Hamilton an alarmed letter, warning him that her husband had discovered their liaison.

The affair had begun in the summer of 1791, when Hamilton sent his wife and children to spend several weeks with their maternal grandparents in Albany, New York. Philadelphia was notoriously unhealthy when the temperature soared. One humid night not long after their departure, Maria had appeared at Hamilton's door pleading for help from her abusive husband, who had supposedly abandoned her. When Hamilton went to her house with some money that evening, he learned Maria was prepared to express her gratitude in a way that left no doubt about her passion for him.

We now know that Reynolds had been renting his stylish twenty-three-year-old wife to various gentlemen for several years, and quite possibly blackmailing them. It was an early version of what police officers began calling "the badger game." The term came from an eighteenth century English sport that pitted a badger against a dog, which the badger often demolished with his powerful jaws and formidable claws. James Reynolds, the badger in Hamilton's version, was soon regularly demanding money from Hamilton to assuage his wounded "honor."

A sensible public official would have ended the affair the moment he received Reynolds' first letter. But Hamilton was not sensible about the women in his life. Along with the sophisticated man who could analyze and argue economics and politics with an overwhelming cascade of rhetoric and logic, and think brilliantly about the future of his country, there was a primitive Hamilton who remained trapped in his West Indies boyhood watching his beautiful, headstrong mother conduct blazing affairs with wealthy merchants.

Somehow, while enjoying Maria Reynolds and fending off her greedy husband, Hamilton managed to perform his complex duties as Secretary of the Treasury. He exchanged letters with customs officers all over the country, he supervised repaying the nation's international debt and the more intricate task of equalizing payments to states that had paid most of their war debts, and adjusted sums to those that had paid little or nothing. Simultaneously, he produced his *Report on Manufactures* and conducted a growing newspaper war with Thomas Jefferson and James Madison. But Maria Reynolds and her husband may have been one complication too many.

✺

The Secretary of the Treasury should have paid more attention to the activities of his former assistant secretary of the Treasury, William Duer. The son of a rich West Indies planter, Duer came to New York on business in 1768 and joined the American side in the Revolution. He served ably in the Continental Congress, where he won Hamilton's friendship by defending General Washington against his critics.

Duer later became Secretary of the Congressional government's Treasury Board. He also made a good deal of money as a contractor, supplying the Continental Army with food. In 1779, he married Catherine Alexander, daughter of Major General William Alexander of New Jersey, who was also known as Lord Stirling thanks to his somewhat dubious claim to a Scottish title. "Lady Kitty," as she was called, liked a splendid lifestyle as much as Duer. They rode around postwar New York in a coach and four with a coat of arms emblazoned on the doors, and often served fifteen different wines at their dinner parties. They were undoubtedly among the New Yorkers who convinced newly arrived Secretary of State Thomas Jefferson of the city's addiction to luxury.

Duer spent only seven months as an assistant treasury secretary. But he learned enough about Hamilton's financial plans to take advantage of them. When the Bank of the United States sold its first shares and Congress added "scrip" as a way for the less wealthy to acquire a piece of the action, the wildest "scrippomania" boiled up in New York, led by Duer. After Hamilton deflated the bubble, he sent Duer a stiff letter, urging him to exercise more public responsibility. "I have serious fears for you—for your purse and for your reputation," he wrote.

Alas, Hamilton remained fond of Duer personally, and managed to convince himself that his friend had learned a lesson. He also needed

Duer's talent for raising large amounts of money. The Secretary asked him to become governor and chief salesman for the S.U.M. Already regarded as a man with a golden touch, Duer helped raise the $500,000 necessary to capitalize the new government entity.

The mania for paper profits had only been checked, not eliminated. Across the country, state banks were being founded, primarily to loan money for speculation in stock and land. "Bankmania" joined "scrippomania" as part of the national vocabulary. The market in government securities soon resumed its rise. By October 1791, "six-percents" (shares in the Bank of the United States, paying six percent interest) were selling at $500, or $100 over par, and scrip had risen similarly.

William Duer decided to plunge on a grand scale. Forming a partnership with Alexander McComb, a New York businessman and land speculator, he set out to corner the market in six-percents. Duer soon drew in many of the leading investors in the S.U.M., forming what would soon be called "The Six Percent Club." They hoped to achieve a corner by July 1792, when the next installment on stock in the Bank of the United States would be due.

Duer and his allies bought on time as many shares in the bank as they could find. If they pulled off the corner, they planned to sell the six-percents at huge markups to foreign investors eager to buy American securities. With revolutionary France on the brink of exploding, America looked far more stable than any country in Europe. Ultimately, Duer and McComb hoped to buy enough shares to seize control of the Bank of the United States.

As news of Duer's scheme circulated through New York, people rushed to entrust their savings to him. He cheerfully promised to double their money in six months. Even the madam of one of the city's brothels pulled dollars from beneath her much-used mattresses to throw into the promised bonanza. Duer also dipped into the funds of the S.U.M. and persuaded numerous merchant friends to cosign notes to expand his credit.

As with so many other attempted corners, Duer's ploy read better on paper than in reality. Bringing off such a coup required not only nerve, but the ability to keep track of a plethora of details, which was not Duer's strong suit. He had a manic tendency to get involved in more speculations than even the most gifted financier could handle. While impossibly leveraged by buying government stock with McComb, he was also the absentee contractor for the U.S. Army that was preparing to fight the western Indians. Simultaneously, he was heavily involved in the Scioto Company, an immense land speculation that had agents in Europe trying to unload 1,000,0000 acres of the Ohio wilderness.

Duer and his fellow plungers never imagined that another group of investors would try to sabotage their corner. These foes were aligned with Secretary Hamilton's political rival (and Thomas Jefferson's ally), Governor George Clinton of New York. They got into the game on the bear side, selling all the stock they could find to Duer and his partners for payment at a future date. They also withdrew large amounts of money from the city's banks to create a credit shortage. Their goal was to depress stock prices, so they could make a killing on the day of delivery—and force the Duer group to pay ruinous interest rates.

The bears' timing was good. In the spring, much of the cash in New York went into the country to buy produce for export. This put a squeeze on the banks, which began calling in their loans. With the price of their Bank of United States shares remaining flat, Duer and the other members of The Six Percent Club scurried around New York in search of money. They were soon paying interest as high as 1 percent per day—365 percent per year.

Watching from Philadelphia, Alexander Hamilton became increasingly dismayed. Duer and his friends were making a mockery of the system Hamilton had created to give America financial stability. The Secretary knew that Jefferson and his colleague, James Madison, were looking for an opportunity to strike him down. "The enemies to banks and credit are in a fair way to having their utmost malignity gratified," the Secretary of the Treasury lamented.[5]

Meanwhile, Oliver Wolcott, the meticulous comptroller of the Treasury, had been toiling over the books Duer had left behind from his tour of duty on the old Treasury Board of the Confederation Congress. Wolcott found a shortfall of $239,000—money Duer had apparently used for personal investments and expenses. Duer had long acknowledged the deficiency, but ignored Wolcott's demands that he make it good. Rumors of Duer's financial woes reached Wolcott, who called upon the U.S. attorney in New York, Richard Harrison, to sue Duer for the long overdue debt. Wolcott did not want to be responsible for the money, if Duer went bankrupt.

The frantic Duer begged Hamilton to block the suit, which would cripple his ability to borrow. For the Secretary of the Treasury, it was a painful clash between private friendship and public duty. Hamilton told Duer that he was experiencing "all the bitterness of soul on your account which a warm attachment can inspire." But he met this test of his integrity head-on, grimly consigning Duer to his fate: "Tis time there should be a line of separation between honest men and knaves," he told a friend.[6]

On March 9, 1792, Duer failed to meet a number of payments on loans, and his paper pyramid began to crumble. He claimed that the notes had been issued by his agent in his absence, and required "investigation." No one believed a word of this. By March 15, six-percents were in precipitous decline. The bears were throwing all the stock they could find into the market to accelerate the downward plunge. Duer faced a rising volcano of demands for payments of stocks that would soon be delivered, and the falling market combined with the government's lawsuit made it impossible for him to raise another cent.

Duer was soon in danger of physical harm from what one speculator called "the lower class of his creditors." On March 23, he took refuge in the city jail—a place to which most debtors went reluctantly. He saw it as far safer than his mansion on the Broadway. A New York businessman ticked off the names of a veritable gallery of top merchants to whom Duer owed large sums—$80,000 to one man alone. He also owed "shopkeepers, widows, orphans—butchers, carmen, gardeners, market women." Another writer reported: "The town has rec'd a shock which it will not get over for many years. Men look as if some general calamity had taken place."

Soon one of Duer's partners, Walter Livingston, of the powerful Hudson River Valley clan, joined him in debtors' prison. He had cosigned twenty-eight of Duer's notes for a total of $203,875.80. Stock prices continued to fall. Public unrest grew. On April 15, Alexander McComb defaulted on half a million dollars in stock he had purchased from the bears. The following day, he joined Duer and Livingston in the city prison.

On the night of April 17, a mob gathered around the jail, but was dispersed by a sudden rain shower. A few days later, another angry crowd gathered, determined to do someone harm, but they lacked leadership. One jittery Connecticut visitor wrote that all the city needed was a "small riot" to burst into a "general flame" that would "consume the prison & D-r and McComb with it." The city fathers equipped the jailers with small arms and cannon, which helped abort the impulse to violence.

Hamilton's attempts to stabilize the collapsing stock market with infusions from his sinking fund were repeatedly overwhelmed by the growing panic. Even the bears were swallowed in the general collapse. One of their chiefs, Brockholst Livingston, was reported as "nearly ruined," and his fellow speculators were not in much better shape. The commerce of New York all but stopped functioning. An upriver merchant with several tons of wheat on ships refused to unload his cargo because no one could pay him in cash and he did not trust the notes of the people who offered to store it. Philadelphia also felt the shock. Land prices throughout Pennsylvania dropped by two-thirds.

❦

On April 17, 1792, a gloating Thomas Jefferson reported that in New York "bankruptcy is become general, every man concerned in paper being broke." Jefferson estimated that the total loss was $5 million, roughly the value of all the buildings in the city. It was the equivalent, Jefferson said, "of the whole town [being] burnt to the ground." Less well-known is the role Jefferson played in this collapse. He was on a five-man committee that had to approve Hamilton's withdrawals from the sinking fund. Jefferson relentlessly disapproved of all the withdrawals. When one of the committee members was absent, the Secretary of State persuaded Attorney General Randolph to join him to prevent withdrawals for several days.[7]

The Secretary of State's delight in the crash was the signal for a ferocious onslaught upon Hamilton by Jefferson's followers. In the *National Gazette*, Philip Freneau assailed the funding system as evil. He blamed it for "the scenes of speculation calculated to aggrandize the few and the wealthy, while oppressing the great body of the people." There was more irony than fact in this wild-eyed claim; most of the few and wealthy were losing their collective shirts. Never hesitant about replying to critics, Hamilton blasted back under numerous pseudonyms, accusing Jefferson of being behind these assaults.

Another series of letters in Freneau's newspaper assailed the Society for Useful Manufactures. Alas, for the immediate future of American industry, the S.U.M. was an easy target. Its treasury was depleted by Duer's illegal transfers into the speculative whirlwind. Many of its board of governors were either in debtor's prison or in hiding, and the few who showed up for meetings nursed grievous financial wounds inflicted by "The Six Percent Club." The S.U.M. was soon in its death throes.

Thanks largely to new infusions from Hamilton's sinking fund, New York City rode out Jefferson's apocalyptic predictions of doom. Stability and calm slowly returned to the stock market and the city. "Trade of every kind begins to be carried on with spirit and success," reported a New York paper. But the 1792 congressional elections would show that a majority of the voters shared Mr. Jefferson's disgust with the behavior of William Duer and his friends.

❦

While Duer was perpetrating the nation's first stock market crash, President Washington received three anonymous letters, warning him that Thomas Jefferson was scheming to succeed him as president—and detailing James Madison's role as pretended friend and secret foe of the administration. One letter focused on Jefferson's role as a critic of the President's military policy. "Behind your back," the writer declared, "he reviles with the greatest asperity your military measures and ridicules the idea of employing any regular troops…His doctrines are strongly supported by his cunning little friend, Madison."[8]

Another letter told the President about the way Philip Freneau had been hired as a translator by Secretary of State Jefferson to help the poet launch the *National Gazette*. The writer described Jefferson and Madison as secret patrons of Freneau's paper. Their goal was twofold—to "destroy Mr. Hamilton" and make Washington "odious."

The fact that the President saved these letters and included them in his papers after he left the presidency reveals a side of his personality that few people have considered. There has been a tendency to view President George Washington as a new edition—almost a different man from the victorious general. On the contrary, there is an essential continuity between the politician and the soldier who won the Revolutionary War. One of General Washington's crucial talents was his shrewd use of spies and intelligence reports to help him counter the enemy's plans. Saving these letters suggests the President had decided their information might be authentic.

The President did not mention the letters when Secretary of State Jefferson visited him with a request to transfer the postal service to his department. The service was currently under the Treasury's control, because it was supposed to make a profit. The Secretary of State expatiated on how Hamilton's department was already too large, with its dozens of customs officers in various ports and a large staff in Philadelphia. The President listened politely and assured Jefferson he would give the transfer serious consideration.[9]

Toward the close of their conversation, Jefferson asked if Washington planned to retire at the end of his term. If so, Jefferson said he also planned to depart. This seemingly offhand remark disturbed the President. Retirement was a large decision he was privately considering. He invited the Secretary of State to breakfast the following day, and, according to Jefferson, who made notes of their conversation, Washington talked frankly about stepping down.

The President pointed out that he had just celebrated his sixtieth birthday. (The citizens of Philadelphia had given a splendid ball in his honor.) He could discern the debilitating influence of old age. His memory, never very good, was growing worse. He worried that other faculties might be faltering too, without him being aware of the decline. He found the many duties of the presidency were growing "irksome." He yearned for the tranquility of private life at Mount Vernon. But he feared that if the "great officers of the government" departed with him, the result might be "a shock on the public mind of dangerous consequence."[10]

Washington was telling his far younger Secretary of State to stay on the job, no matter what he himself decided. But Jefferson revealed in his note on the talk that he had an even more intense desire to depart for Monticello. He was "heartily tired" of doing combat with Hamilton at cabinet meetings. He would have departed months ago, he added, but he felt a responsibility to stay and oppose Hamilton's influence.

Washington concluded the conversation by saying that he feared retirement might not be an option for him. There were "symptoms of dissatisfaction" with his administration that would make a withdrawal at this point seem like he was yielding to the critics. If the President was hoping to draw out the Secretary of State's personal opinion, he succeeded beautifully.

There was, Jefferson warmly informed him, only one source of discontent in the nation: the Treasury Department. It was responsible for "withdrawing our citizens from…useful industry to occupy themselves in a species of gambling." His temper rising, Jefferson accused Hamilton of encouraging congressmen to "feather their nests" with government paper to guarantee their votes for his system. Now had come an ultimate act of corruption, the *Report on Manufactures*, creating the S.U.M. This put the Secretary of the Treasury in the business of founding corporations. If this venture was tolerated, the Secretary of State declared, it was the end of limited government. The Constitution was on its way to becoming "wastepaper."[11]

If Washington had hoped to discover whether there was anything to the anonymous letters' warning that Mr. Jefferson was a secret enemy of the administration, he had discovered that the answer was yes. We might add that this canny maneuver suggests the President was hardly becoming feebleminded. Nevertheless, Washington still yearned to find a way to broker a truce between the Secretary of State and the Secretary of the Treasury that would enable him to return to Mount Vernon without damaging the public's faith in the office of the presidency.

CHAPTER 11

The President—and the Secretary of State—Make Up Their Minds

During a brief vacation at Mount Vernon in May, President Washington again began to think he might retire at the end of his first term. The impact of the imploded stock market bubble was more or less under control thanks to Secretary of the Treasury Hamilton's intervention. Washington apparently assumed he had persuaded Secretary of State Jefferson to remain in office, and could do the same thing with the other cabinet officers, thus avoiding, or at least minimizing, a shock to the public mind.

On the western frontier, Anthony Wayne was slowly shaping an army out of his raw recruits. How he—and they—would perform without George Washington as their commander in chief was a worry. But the President told himself he could not solve every problem before he left office, whether he served one term or two terms—or stayed for life.

Another worry was the growth of anger in the western counties of Pennsylvania and North Carolina at the tax Congress had imposed on the sale of their whiskey. Washington had spent enough time on the frontier to understand the sense of separation and difference that westerners felt toward the supposedly more civilized easterners. Again, this was a problem that might prove to be an unnecessary worry. Retirement still seemed to him a possibility.

The President invited James Madison to visit him at Mount Vernon to discuss the best way to announce his decision to the nation. Instead, he found himself listening to a strenuous plea to remain in office for another four years. Nothing else would guarantee the survival of their fragile union, Madison claimed. He fretted about the "money men" of the North taking over the government, and infuriating the indebted farmers of the South, who regarded banks as dangerous, even evil enterprises. When Washington admitted that these differences seemed to be coalescing into two political parties, and the problem was creating dissension in his cabinet, Madison said that this fact only made Washington even more indispensible.

Nevertheless, the President asked Madison to compose a farewell address and advise him on the best time to release it to the public. He suggested his advanced age and his belief in rotation in office as the best reasons for his decision. He gave Madison what the congressman called a "comprehensive" outline of the topics he wanted to cover, and soon had a very satisfactory farewell address on his desk.[1]

Returning to Philadelphia in late May 1792, Washington found a letter from Thomas Jefferson, urging him in almost frantic language to serve a second term. The Secretary of State resumed his assault on Secretary of the Treasury Hamilton and his "monarchical federalist" political party. They were plotting to "change from the present republican form of government to that of a monarchy, of which the English constitution is to be the model." The plan would inevitably split the Union; only Washington could prevent this catastrophe. "North and South will hang together if they have you to hang on," Jefferson pleaded.[2]

Back at Mount Vernon, in July, Washington invited Jefferson for a visit to discuss his letter. The President, recalling his early conversations with James Madison, told Jefferson that he originally meant to serve only two years. The unsettled state of the world and the development of political disagreements in America had forced him to change his mind. But he still felt he could and should retire at the close of his first full term—on March 4, 1793.

When Jefferson still resisted the idea, Washington abruptly blamed Philip Freneau for a lot of the dissension that was agitating the nation. He took particular issue with Freneau's claim that he headed a "monarchical party." The President thought this was a ridiculous idea, without an iota of support anywhere. He took even stronger issue with Freneau's description of him as a dimwitted puppet manipulated by Secretary of the Treasury Hamilton. In attacking Hamilton, these critics were also attacking him, Washington said.

With not a little anger in his voice, Washington added that he was neither a careless nor a stupid president. He knew and thoroughly understood Hamilton's financial program and approved it. During the War for Independence, he had seen firsthand what happened when America's credit collapsed. He considered Hamilton's restoration of this vital ingredient in nationhood almost a miracle. The country was prosperous and happy.

If anyone was encouraging a monarchy, Washington continued, his temper still rising, it was Philip Freneau with his irresponsible attacks. Some western farmers were refusing to pay the tax on whiskey and talking of secession because the *National Gazette* was telling them that Alexander Hamilton was using their money to create a bloated aristocracy of stock market swindlers and gamblers. By stirring this sort of opposition to the government, Freneau was emboldening some already disgruntled anti-federalists to talk about defying the administration with guns in their hands. That might make more conservative men wonder if some form of royal rule was a necessity to save the Union.

Was President Washington using the information from those anonymous letters to send the Secretary of State a warning about his clandestine opposition to the administration? One is tempted to consider the possibility, even the probability that this was the case. Once we discard the notion that Washington was a dimwitted figurehead—and remember his shrewd use of secret intelligence during the war—the probability tilts toward certainty. Especially worth noting is the President's angry dismissal of the notion he was being manipulated by Hamilton. Was he covertly saying it was time for the Secretary of State to change his mind?

Thomas Jefferson went back to Monticello a very frustrated man. But he remained convinced that he could change Washington's mind about Hamilton's policies. If there was one certainty that guided Jefferson in almost all the disputes of his life, it was his belief that he was more intelligent than virtually everyone else he had thus far met in his journey. James Madison seems to have been the only person to whom he ceded a certain degree of intellectual superiority.[3]

Washington's New England born secretary, Tobias Lear, took a vacation in his home region and returned to inform the President that everywhere he went, people assumed the President was going to stay for another term. They told Lear that four years was too short a time to decide whether the new government was "beneficial or not." On the heels of this message came a plea from Attorney General Edmund Randolph, begging Washington not to retire.[4]

Meanwhile, Secretary of the Treasury Hamilton was intensifying the Philadelphia newspaper war. Writing under a pseudonym like other contributors to John Fenno's *Gazette of the United States*, he bluntly asked if Jefferson could explain why the U.S. State Department paid Philip Freneau an annual salary to help him publish a newspaper which specialized in vilifying "those to whom the voice of the people has committed the administration of our public affairs."

Four days later, the President wrote a letter to Secretary Hamilton, telling him that on his way to Mount Vernon from Philadelphia, he had asked numerous people what they thought of their government. Almost everyone had admitted they were prosperous and happy, but they were somewhat alarmed at the disputes and criticisms that had erupted about differing interpretations of the Constitution. Washington did not mention Jefferson by name. But there was convincing evidence that he was the President's primary concern.

The President listed the criticisms under twenty-one headings, all taken directly from the Secretary of State's May 23 letter, urging him to serve another term. Could Secretary Hamilton find time to answer these attacks? Washington asked. The closing words of this letter were: "with affectionate regard." We have seen how important such expressions were in his correspondence with James Madison. The words were absent in the letters he was exchanging with Secretary of State Jefferson.[5]

Hamilton's reply was another fourteen thousand-word explosion. It more than matched his defense of the Bank of the United States in the vigor of its reasoning and ingenuity of its arguments. The Treasury Secretary apologized for the "severity" of some of his statements. Many of these criticisms were "calumnies" that accused him of the "basest perfidy." Most of the time Hamilton was factual, sometimes brutally so. At one point, he refuted Jefferson's charge that the public debt was excessive by flatly stating that it was "created by the late war. It is not the fault of the present government that it exists."

Washington was pleased with Hamilton's answers. It was obvious that the President wanted to have some ammunition handy if Jefferson again attempted to change his mind about the financial system. Simultaneously, Washington continued to urge both men to compose their differences, reiterating as his chief reason for urging a reconciliation his desire to end his public career with a single presidential term.

The moment Hamilton read these words, he rushed a letter to the executive mansion urging the President not even to think about retirement. To leave office with so many problems and issues unsolved and undecided would reflect on his character, in the eyes of future generations. For George Washington, no more powerful argument could be made. The only reward he had ever sought for his decades of public service was his reputation as a disinterested patriot—and a country that was prosperous and happy.

❦

Happiness was definitely not on the political horizon. Secretary of State Jefferson summoned two younger supporters to reply to Hamilton's attacks on him. James Monroe, just elected senator from Virginia, joined James Madison in a series of articles in Freneau's newspaper, defending Jefferson and lambasting Hamilton. The Treasury Secretary responded with a biting assault on other aspects of Jefferson's character. He depicted him as a man who pretended to be a defender of the poor and oppressed while living a luxurious lifestyle. Even nastier was another essay, suggesting that Jefferson was a "secret voluptuary"—a hint that the Secretary had a hidden sexual side to his widower's life.

On the same day that Hamilton sent Washington his reply to the "criticisms" of the financial program, drawn from Jefferson's letter, the Secretary of State wrote another long letter to the President. For the first time, Jefferson admitted hiring Freneau, but he told Washington that the journalist had approached him with a proposal to launch his newspaper. This was about as far from the truth that Jefferson could get in describing the week in which he and James Madison labored to persuade Freneau to come to Philadelphia. Topping this whopper, Jefferson claimed he had no influence whatsoever over the newspaper that repeatedly praised him and excoriated Hamilton.

The Secretary of State declared that he would not allow Hamilton to "cloud" his approaching retirement with slanders "from a man whose history, from the moment in which history can stoop to notice him, is a tissue of machinations against the country which has not only received and given him bread, but heaped its honors on his head." Were these words an attempt to appeal to Washington as a fellow Virginia aristocrat? If so, they were sadly wide of the target.

The Secretary of the Treasury had risked his life in too many battles under General Washington's command. There was a bond between these two men that Jefferson could never alter with sneers about Hamilton's low birth in the West Indies. It is far more likely that the words deepened Washington's disillusionment with Jefferson—a process that was already well advanced.

Also worth noting was Jefferson's continued determination to retire. The intention was now stated as a certainty, whether or not Washington served another term. Beneath Jefferson's ostensible deference there seemed to be a growing personal antagonism toward the President. Perhaps the Secretary of State resisted the idea that Washington was certain to be ranked far above everyone else in the competition for fame. Did he find himself wondering if Washington could have managed his military triumph without the inspiring words of the Declaration of Independence to rally the Americans to the cause?

In August 1792, Washington wrote to Hamilton, urging him to moderate his hostility towards Jefferson. He vowed to persuade Jefferson to do likewise. These "wounding suspicions" and "irritating charges" were all too likely to be believed by people on both sides of the quarrel, guaranteeing that the differences would or could grow into disputes that might ultimately rupture the Union. This primary value remained a constant concern for the President, as he struggled to decide whether to spend another four years in office.[6]

In late September, Washington invited Jefferson to have breakfast with him at Mount Vernon for another attempt to resolve their differing opinions of Hamilton's program. Before they sat down to dine, the President told Jefferson about the illness of his nephew, George Augustine Washington, who was managing Mount Vernon's farms. The young man was dying of tuberculosis. It made Washington wish he could devote his full attention to making his three thousand acres more profitable. But he also confessed that he was more and more resigned to serving another term, if his aid was needed to keep the federal government from disintegrating.[7]

Were the words aimed at flattering Jefferson, or at least in persuading him not to think about his own retirement? Jefferson reiterated that he saw Washington as the only man who could rise above the disagreements that were tearing the country apart. With not a little artifice, Washington replied that he had "never suspected" that these conflicts had created "a personal difference" between Jefferson and Hamilton.

Jefferson responded with another outburst against Hamilton's "monarchical" tendencies. It was a turning point. Washington's temper flared. He curtly informed the Secretary of State that he did not believe there were ten men in the country "whose opinions were worth attention" who wanted to be ruled by a king or an imitation of one. Jefferson instantly noted the change in tone. There was contempt as well as anger in the President's voice. In his record of the conversation in the journal Jefferson called his *Anas*, he wrote: "I told him there were many more than he imagined. I told him tho the people were sound, there was a numerous sect that had monarchy in contemplation and the Secretary of the Treasury was one of these."[8]

The conversation staggered on, but the friendship between the two men had received a fatal wound. When Jefferson attempted to regain the offensive by reiterating that Hamilton was corrupting Congress by encouraging the members to buy government securities, the President curtly dismissed the problem as unavoidable. He did not see how they could start barring men from holding public office on the basis of their stock portfolios. With an almost ruthless candor, Washington said the only worthwhile test of Hamilton's system was its effectiveness.

A shocked Jefferson abandoned the argument—and his belief that he could change George Washington's mind. In his recounting of this pivotal meeting, he virtually surrendered, saying: "I avoided going further into the subject." Never again would the Secretary of State see himself as the potential leader of the Washington administration, guiding a passive president down the path of true republicanism.[9]

✣

The impact of this defeat on Jefferson's emotions is starkly visible in a letter he wrote to James Madison later on this momentous day. He began by admitting that he had somehow lost on the road to Bladensburg, Maryland, a packet of papers, including a very confidential letter from Madison. Then Jefferson turned to a topic he and his best friend had been discussing in that letter.

Secretary Hamilton was planning to open a branch of the Bank of the United States in Virginia. Henry Lee, a famous cavalry leader of the Revolution, was governor. The ex-soldier had approached some wealthy Virginians about creating a state bank that would compete with the federal intruder. They had sought Madison's opinion, and he, in turn, had asked Jefferson for his reaction to the idea.

The Congressman got a reply that almost emitted steam in its raging ferocity. Jefferson dismissed a state bank as a "milk and water measure." What he wanted was total opposition to all aspects of the federal bank. His rage building, Jefferson insisted that the federal government had no power to create corporations or banks. That privilege was reserved to the states. "For any Virginian to recognize a foreign legislature"—he was talking about the Congress of the United States—"is an act of *treason* against the state, and whoever shall do any act under the colour of the authority of a foreign legislature—whether by signing notes, issuing or passing them, acting as director, cashier or any other office relating to it shall be adjudged guilty of high treason & suffer death accordingly."

This lunge into blood-drenched violence is the most astonishing letter Thomas Jefferson ever wrote. It makes his epistle on *the earth belongs to the living* almost commonsensical in comparison. Within it are visible his deep-seated hostility to the Constitution that had been created in his absence, and his readiness—at least verbally—to propose the wildest acts and ideas against it. The seeds of a disease in the public mind that would one day flower into the tragedy of the Civil War are lurking in this frantic letter.

Congressman Madison made not the slightest attempt to disagree with his tall friend from Albermarle County. "Your objections to it [the state bank] seem unanswerable," he replied. The once independent thinker had become an echo of Thomas Jefferson's angry ideological voice.[10]

Things were not much happier on the other side of the fractured Washington cabinet. In June of 1792, Secretary of the Treasury Hamilton had finally managed to break off his affair with Maria Reynolds. But getting rid of her husband, James Reynolds, was more difficult. For some time, Hamilton had been paying him small sums they called loans but were obviously blackmail, amounting to about $1,000. (More than $15,000 in 2014 money.) In mid-November, Comptroller General Oliver Wolcott had Reynolds and a fellow swindler, Jacob Clingman, arrested for fraud. They had asserted they were the executors of a deceased former soldier's estate with a $400 claim against the government. Unfortunately, the ex-soldier, one Ephraim Goodenough, was very much alive.

Faced with serious jail time, Reynolds started telling people that he had the power to ruin the Secretary of the Treasury. He claimed that he had helped Hamilton engage in secret speculations based on the Secretary's insider's knowledge that had made him millions of dollars. Soon his partner Clingman was telling the story to Senator James Monroe and two influential congressmen, Abraham Venable of Virginia and Frederick Muhlenberg of Pennsylvania, until recently the Speaker of the House of Representatives. At his suggestion, they questioned Maria Reynolds and she confirmed everything her husband said. Meanwhile, after an early morning interview with Secretary Hamilton, Reynolds vanished from Philadelphia.

The three politicians decided to confront Hamilton with these charges of fraud. Monroe was hardly neutral in this situation. His articles in the *National Gazette* defending Jefferson left no doubt where he stood. He had little difficulty persuading the others that Hamilton was guilty of a serious crime. Why else would he persuade the chief witness to flee the city? On December 15, Monroe, Venable and Muhlenberg strode into the Secretary's office, accompanied by Comptroller Oliver Wolcott. Muhlenberg, ostensibly less hostile than the two Virginians, informed Hamilton of their suspicions.

Hamilton exploded into almost hysterical rage. He seemed ready to deny the charge until Muhlenberg presented him with several handwritten notes to Reynolds, which the swindler had given him. Hamilton calmed down and admitted the letters were authentic. He invited his accusers to visit him at his home that evening. There, he assured them, he would give them an explanation which would refute their suspicions.

That night, Hamilton gave the three politicians evidence they had not anticipated: a cache of letters from Maria Reynolds and her husband. With them came a confession of his year-long affair with Maria, replete with salacious details that left his listeners gasping with dismay. One of the delegation, probably Muhlenberg, assured him they were convinced that he was innocent of any fraud and there was no need to tell them the whole story. But Hamilton insisted on describing the entire sordid affair. Muhlenberg and Venable apologized for intruding on such a private matter and promised to mention it to no one. Monroe's manner was far less friendly. In a cold, matter-of-fact voice, he conceded that Hamilton's confession had convinced him no fraud had been committed by anyone but James Reynolds. He also promised to keep the affair a secret.

Two days later, Hamilton began to worry about the likelihood that the pledge of secrecy would be violated. He asked his three accusers for copies of the letters they had shown him. Senator Monroe gave the documents to John Beckley, the clerk of the House of Representatives, for copying. The Senator must have known what would happen next. Beckley was a Jefferson worshipper, hired thanks to their political party's majority in the House.[11]

Two days later, Thomas Jefferson jotted the following comment in his *Anas*. "Dec. 17. The affair of Reynolds and his wife." The Secretary of State proceeded to list all the characters in the drama, from Jacob Clingman to Muhlenberg to Monroe, Venable, and Wolcott. He also noted others who were in on the secret, such as James Madison and Edmund Randolph.[12]

The paragraph makes it clear that Jefferson knew everything James Monroe had heard at Hamilton's house on December 15. If there were any doubts, a paragraph in another essay in the series that Monroe published on "The Vindication of Mr. Jefferson" made the Senator's readiness to act on the Secretary of State's behalf all too clear. "I shall conclude by observing how much it is to be wished [that] this writer [Hamilton] would exhibit himself to the public view that we might behold in him a living monument of that immaculate purity to which he pretends and which ought to distinguish so bold and arrogant a censor of others."[13]

While this drama held center stage for politicians, President Washington decided to serve another term and permitted his name to be placed on the ballot. He ran without opposition, and on December 5, 1792, when the electoral college delegates met in the capitals of their respective states, they again voted unanimously for him. The Jeffersonians, knowing Washington was unchallengeable, concentrated on marshaling enough votes to unseat Vice President John Adams.

Their choice was Governor George Clinton of New York. He was hardly an ideal candidate. In the spring, Clinton had lost a race for another term in Albany to Chief Justice John Jay, whom Hamilton had persuaded to run. Clinton reclaimed a dubious majority by invalidating the votes of three counties on a technicality. Jefferson was appalled, but he had held his nose and supported the badly soiled candidate for vice president.[14]

The combination of this blatant corruption and strenuous efforts by Hamilton to hold Federalists in line for the unpopular Adams worked, but just barely. Adams got seventy-seven votes to Clinton's fifty. The result by no means ended the Jeffersonians' effort to unseat the Secretary of the Treasury, a man they now hated with almost irrational passion: to handle this task, they turned to a man who was second only to Patrick Henry as an orator, Virginia Congressman William Branch Giles.

A husky, unkempt brawler with a fondness for extreme rhetoric, Giles always looked like he had recently emerged from a wrestling match. The strategy, laid out by Jefferson and Madison, was to make outrageous accusations against Hamilton and force him to go to enormous lengths to refute them. After battering the Secretary ferociously on the floor of the House, Giles demanded a complete accounting of all the foreign loans Hamilton had negotiated, and how he was repaying them, plus records of all transactions between the government and the Bank of the United States. Adding to the enormity of these demands was a deadline of March 3, when Congress would adjourn.

To the dismay of Giles and his allies, Madison and Jefferson, Hamilton produced seven huge reports totaling sixty thousand words, by February 19. The documents were replete with charts, lists, and masses of statistics. The few congressmen who attempted to read them were reduced to awed silence. At the close of one report, Hamilton remarked that he had risked his health to complete it. This achievement only prompted Jefferson to take the field personally. He asked President Washington to order an official inquiry into Hamilton's conduct. Washington curtly refused, making it clear where he stood in this confrontation.

Jefferson drew up a series of resolutions calling on Congress to censure Hamilton and gave them to Congressman Giles. Toward the end of February, Giles submitted no less than nine of these denunciations, condemning Hamilton for various offenses. They reached a climax of sorts with the final shaft: "Resolved, that the Secretary of the Treasury has been guilty of maladministration in the duties of his office and should, in the opinion of Congress, be removed from his office by the President of the United States." Once more the game plan included an impossible deadline for a Hamilton reply. Congress was now scheduled to adjourn within a week.

Congressman James Madison hurled himself into rallying his followers in the House of Representatives to approve Giles's resolutions. To his dismay, the House voted down all nine verbal assaults. Even Virginians deserted Madison's leadership. Only five congressmen, including Madison, voted for every resolution. It was a stunning defeat for Thomas Jefferson—with a bitter personal dimension. He had no doubt that President Washington had exercised a hidden hand to influence numerous votes.[15]

Until this point, the differences between the President and his Secretary of State had revolved almost entirely around American issues. But news from France was about to make the clash into a conflict with global dimensions. On January 21, 1793, King Louis XVI was decapitated in Paris's Place de la Concorde, while a mob of twenty thousand people screamed in delight.

CHAPTER 12

The Problems of the Secretary of State's Polar Star

T HE DRAMA IN FRANCE had not been totally absent from America's temporary capital, Philadelphia, during 1792. By the time this critical year began, Secretary of State Thomas Jefferson had made it clear that he regarded the success of the French Revolution as crucial to the political purity of the United States. In mid-1791, the French *Charge' d'Affaires* in Philadelphia told his foreign minister: "It is M. Jefferson who takes the greatest interest in the success of our great revolution. He has often told me that the work of our National Assembly will serve to regenerate not only France but also the United States, whose principles were beginning to become corrupted."[1]

During these months, the Secretary of State was receiving a flow of reports from his protégé and former secretary, twenty-five-year-old William Short, who was serving as the American Charge' d'Affaires in Paris. During Jefferson's years in Paris, Short had accompanied him to salons and soirees where he met the moderate aristocrats who turned to Jefferson for advice as the revolution became a reality.

Besides Lafayette, one of the most prominent of these noblemen was the Duc de la Rochefoucauld. He had a beautiful wife, Rosalie, who was decades younger than her husband. Gradually, both she and Short realized they were passionately attracted to each other. In America, this might have produced ostracism and violence. But in France, there was nothing unusual about such an affair, except perhaps its blazing intensity.[2]

Throughout 1791 and 1792, Short's eyewitness reports to Jefferson revealed the steady growth of violence in the French capital. At one point, he told Jefferson there was a "degree of fermentation" in the streets of Paris that threatened to create "a new revolution." What would that revolution entail? King Louis XVI had already agreed to become a constitutional monarch like George III of Great Britain. The answer was soon obvious to observers in England and America: a "pure" republic—without a king.

How would this political destination be reached? Here was where Short's dispatches from the scene reported things that Jefferson did not want to hear. The National Assembly, which was writing a constitution under the guidance of the Marquis de Lafayette and his faction, was aiming at a carefully balanced moderation. The King would retain considerable powers, which he would wield in conjunction with the assembly. The finished document, Jefferson had predicted, would be a "superb edifice." Short warned the Secretarty of State that there were a lot of Parisians who were bent on challenging the constitutional moderation of Lafayette and his friends. The American Charge' described these opponents as "a mob of their constituents" who were threatening "to hang them."[3]

By 1792, there was now another player in the Parisian revolutionary game: the Paris Commune, which Jefferson called "the assembly of the people of Paris." They were much more radical than the rest of France. President Washington seems to have been well aware of the Commune's differences with the National Assembly. When Benjamin Franklin died in 1790, the Assembly had declared they would observe three days of mourning for the sage whose diplomatic skills had persuaded France to support the American struggle for independence. The Commune staged its own mourning ceremony featuring a long eulogy by one of their best orators, and sent the speech and other reports of their admiration to "the President and Congress," as if the Commune were France's government.

President Washington did not even open the Commune's package. He sent it to Jefferson, who recommended it should be submitted to Congress for a reply. The President ignored this advice, which signaled his awareness that the House of Representatives under James Madison's leadership was exhibiting tendencies that troubled him. He sent the Commune's package to the Senate. This was in keeping with the Constitution, which gave the Senate a role in foreign policy. The senators ignored it.

Then came an event that revealed to everyone in and out of France what was really happening in Paris: on June 21, 1791, Louis XVI and his Queen and family attempted to escape their semi-imprisonment in the Tuileries Palace and flee to the protection of friendly foreign monarchs. Behind him, the King left a message, declaring he had been a prisoner, acting under duress since he was dragged from Versailles to Paris.

Alas, for the monarch and his moderate supporters in the National Assembly, he was recaptured at Varennes and returned to Paris through streets lined with tens of thousands of silent, glaring spectators. Signs declared that anyone who applauded the King would be beaten. William Short told Jefferson the story in late June, adding: "The Crisis is really tremendous and may have a disastrous issue."

A few days later, another report from Charge' Short made this prophecy more specific: "You will easily conceive that the post of M de la Fayette is the most disagreeable and dangerous that can be imagined....The people of Paris [the Commune] headed by some popular ambitious men declare loudly in favor [of] a republican government."The Jacobins, members of a radical political club who had little or no use for a king, declared that Lafayette was behind the flight and he would pay for it "with his head."[4]

Three months later, Secretary of State Jefferson received these reports and promptly informed the President of the King's failed flight. Later, he wrote that he had never seen George Washington "so dejected by any event in my life." All the President's hopes for the French Revolution—and all his doubts—collapsed into deep gloom—and fear for the safety of Lafayette.[5]

Secretary of State Jefferson refused to accept the meaning of the King's capture, even when Short spelled it out for him. The Secretary continued to talk and write about the Revolution as if the calendar had stopped turning in 1789. Three months later, on August 30, 1791, the day that Jefferson received Short's dispatches about the King's ruinous move, the Secretary of State wrote to a French friend in Paris, congratulating him on the news that the constitution was nearing completion. Two weeks later, when the King's acceptance of the document was announced to the public, Short warned Jefferson that public confidence in the moderate charter—and the King—was close to zero.

Jefferson also ignored this all too accurate prophecy. Soon, James Madison, whose thinking on the French Revolution was now virtually dictated by Jefferson, was hailing the King's acceptance as if he had never heard of the monarch's flight and return to a Paris smoldering with hatred. "The French Revolution seems to have succeeded beyond the most sanguine hopes," he told one correspondent.

It was growing apparent that for both Madison and Jefferson, the French Revolution was only real as an issue in American politics. They saw it could become crucial to the success of their new "Republican" Party. The reader will note that the name is in quotations. Many historians no longer use it. They prefer the name Jeffersonian Republican or Democratic-Republican. Henceforth, we will use the latter term.[6]

❀

Not surprisingly, President Washington had less and less confidence in Jefferson's judgment of the upheaval in Paris. He virtually said as much when he named Gouverneur Morris, a man Jefferson disliked, as America's first minister to the new French government. The wealthy New Yorker had been in Paris when the Revolution began in 1789, and his skepticism about its outcome was soon well-known.

When Jefferson notified Morris of his appointment, the Secretary of State urged him to make frequent attempts to assure everyone of "the spirit of sincere friendship and attachment we bear to the French nation." He should avoid opinions "that might please or offend any party." Jefferson told Morris that the Revolution was immensely popular among "the great mass of our countrymen," not too subtly warning him it would be a mistake to differ with this majority opinion.

Writing from London, Morris accepted the appointment as minister and told the Secretary of State he agreed completely with the wisdom of observing silence about the current government of France. "Changes are now so frequent, and events seem fast ripening to such an awful catastrophe, that no expressions on the subject, however moderate, would be received with indifference." The letter demonstrated that Morris was no slouch at the diplomatic game. He promised obedience to the Secretary of State, and simultaneously told him he did not know what he was talking about.[7]

Meanwhile, the Senate was debating Morris's appointment. Virginia Senator James Monroe, by now competing with James Madison for the role of Jefferson's favorite political combatant, denounced the New Yorker. Monroe relied almost entirely on Jefferson's adverserial vocabulary. Morris was a "monarchy man" whose chief interest in Europe was lining his own pockets. Other senators agreed with Monroe.

Gouverneur Morris had never learned to be a popular politician; he frequently told people they were wrong and proved it in cutting terms. Even the two senators from Massachusetts, both conservatives, disliked him, probably because Morris's penchant for pretty women offended their puritan instincts. But the President's prestige was at stake and enough supporters of Washington rallied to confirm Morris's appointment as minister to France.

⚛

Another reason for Morris's two-sided reply to the Secretary of State was a deeply personal letter that the President had written to him. Washington began by saying he had nominated Morris "with all my heart." He then gave the new minister a pungent summary of the Senate debate on his appointment, and told him that he had better face the fact that he was often charged with "imprudence of conversation and conduct." Especially troubling was a supposed "hauteur disgusting to those who happen to differ with you." Washington hoped these warnings would inspire the circumspection Morris would need to represent America in Paris.

To the President, one fact outweighed all Gouverneur Morris's flaws: Morris would tell him the truth, no matter how much he might be forced to dissemble with others. Washington too saw that the French Revolution was becoming an issue in American politics. The President wanted advice from someone he trusted. He liked the way Morris had dealt with the British in London, making it clear that the "honor and interest of his country" was the only thing that mattered to him. [8]

In early March of 1792, Jefferson informed his *Anas* that Washington had told him he had "begun to doubt very much of affairs in France." The remark was made while they were discussing the letter they had received from King Louis XVI, announcing his approval of his nation's new constitution. At the President's request, the Secretary of State had written a carefully neutral response to it. Jefferson had reluctantly obeyed, blaming Washington's tone on Gouverneur Morris "[who] has kept the president's mind constantly poisoned with his forebodings." [9]

Washington had sent copies of the King's letter to the House of Representatives and the Senate. The President became more than a little annoyed when Congressman James Madison persuaded the House to send an independent reply to the French government, warmly congratulating them on completing a wonderful constitution. It was an almost embarrassing contrast to Washington's cool, neutral response. Washington wondered aloud if he should tell Madison and his House allies that foreign policy was none of their business.

The Secretary of State took not a little pleasure in informing the President that the resolution to send their letter had passed the House with only two dissenting votes. It was evidence of how eagerly most Americans supported France's revolution—something the President could only ignore at his political peril.

The Secretary of State had not a little to do with creating this attitude. Philip Freneau's *National Gazette* printed nothing but gushing praise of France's revolutionaries. Jefferson was so emotionally committed to their success, he did not seem to realize he was creating a dangerous division between a realistic view of the Revolution as a series of potentially tragic events in Paris and the idea of it as a political issue in America.

The Secretary of State was extremely pleased when the President took his advice and decided not to tangle with the House of Representatives for interfering in American foreign policy. Instead, he told Jefferson to revise his noncommittal letter—adding a mention that both the House and Senate had expressed their approval of the new French Constitution.[10]

As Jefferson's failure to change Washington's mind about Hamilton's financial system become apparent to him, the Secretary of State grew more and more pessimistic about American politics and invested even more emotion in the French Revolution. In a letter to Lafayette, he praised his military as well as his political talents, and his use of the latter to exterminate "the monster aristocracy" and pull out "the teeth and fangs of its associate, monarchy."

In America, Jefferson continued, an opposite tendency was becoming visible. "A sect" of wayward greedy political operators saw the Constitution as only a step to the nation's true political destiny—"an English constitution" with a king at the nation's helm. The American legislature had become a hive of "stock jobbers and king jobbers." But the voice of the people was beginning to make itself heard. The next election was likely to rid Congress of most of the jobbers.[11]

Lafayette never received the Secretary of State's letter. Jefferson had written it to ally him with the Democratic-Republican Party, on the assumption that he would wield a great deal of power under France's new

Constitution. By the time the letter reached Paris, the Marquis had heard the voice of the people howling for his blood, and had fled his homeland.

As William Short had predicted, the Marquis's political fortunes had been in decline since Louis XVI's failed flight. When a riotous mob on the Champ de Mars demanded the banishment of the King and the establishment of a republic, the National Assembly asked Lafayette and his guardsman to restore order. The mob opened fire, one bullet whizzing close to the Marquis. He ordered the Guard to fire over the rioters' heads. When the *citoyen*s still refused to disperse, Lafayette ordered the Guard to fire on them. At least twelve people were killed, the mob fled, and Lafayette's popularity plummeted to zero.

In the National Assembly, attention turned to the frontiers, where anti-revolutionary émigrés had established a military presence. These naysayers were backed by King Frederick William of Prussia and Leopold II, the Emperor of Austria, Queen Marie Antoinette's brother. In 1791, the two kings had issued a statement expressing concern for the safety of King Louis and the Queen. On April 20, 1792, the National Assembly declared war on both countries. Hotheads in the Assembly decided that these two "rotting despotisms" would be easy to defeat by appealing to the hunger for *liberté* in the souls of their oppressed subjects.[12]

The shift to overt hostilities added new intensity to the distrust and anger that was sweeping through Paris. Worse, the French army performed poorly in its attempt to seize the frontier cities. The untrained troops fled when the professional soldiers of the Austrian army advanced on them. The Jacobins condemned the French commanders, claiming that they were all attached to the "old order." One failed brigadier general was massacred by an enraged mob in the city of Lille.[13]

In a last desperate attempt to maintain order, Lafayette asked the National Assembly to declare martial law. He was condemned in a raging speech by a leader of the Jacobin Political Club, Maximilian Robespierre, who accused him of plotting a coup d'etat. On August 10, the Jacobins and their supporters in the Paris Commune stormed the Tuileries Palace, massacred the six hundred Swiss Guards, the King's only reliable protectors, and arrested Louis XVI. Lafayette was summoned to Paris for what would obviously be a show trial followed by the guillotine. On Aug 22, 1792, the Marquis and four aides fled France. Lafayette hoped to reach neutral Holland or England and there be joined by his wife and children. Eventually, they planned to seek refuge in America. On the French border, the

Marquis was seized by Austrian soldiers and flung into the first of many vile prisons. The royalist émigrés had convinced the Austrians that Lafayette was as hateful as the Jacobins. [14]

۞

In America, Secretary of State Jefferson was soon hearing the grim news from Paris via William Short. Jefferson had persuaded Washington to appoint Short minister to the Netherlands, but information continued to flow to the young Virginian from the seething French capital. Virtually every intelligent person in Europe waited anxiously to learn what was happening in Paris.

Equally dire reports came from Gouverneur Morris. Describing the attack on the Tuileries Palace, Short had denounced "those mad and corrupted people in France who under the name of liberty have destroyed their own government." Morris was less emotional than Short, and closer to the meaning of the massacre: "Another revolution has been affected (sic) in this city. It was bloody." [15]

Morris went on to describe how the Jacobins were now in control and were outlawing other political clubs and associations, notably the *Feuillants,* who had favored the constitutional monarchy. Morris advised Jefferson to read with caution any French newspapers that came his way. They were being written not only "in the spirit of a party but under the eye of a party." With the coolness of a man who knew he had Washington's backing, Morris closed his letter by asking for "orders from the President respecting my line of conduct."

Jefferson must have twitched with irritation at these words. Morris was all but saying that he did not trust any orders from the Secretary of State. Nonetheless, Jefferson conferred with Washington, and they agreed that Morris should remain at his post. Most of the other diplomats in Paris were leaving—a statement that the emerging republic was illegitimate. But Jefferson told Morris that the United States believed it should recognize any government that had been created by the will of the people. He must have been surprised—and pleased—when he received a letter from Morris, expressing the same opinion. [16]

The Jacobins now issued an Edict of Fraternity, which declared France's support for other revolutionary movements throughout the world. To prove their friendly feelings for America, they conferred honorary citizenship on "Georges Washington, N. Madison, T. Paine, and Jean Hamilton." (sic) Some people have puzzled over the omission of Thomas Jefferson. Perhaps it was a commentary on his association with the moderate Feuillants such as Lafayette during his time in Paris. They—and all their friends—were now scorned, derided, and soon would be on their way to the guillotine.

Washington and Hamilton did not reply to this grant of citizenship, but "N. Madison" wrote an oozingly flattering reply, hailing the "sublime truths and precious sentiments in the revolution of France." T. Paine, who had been banished from England, was in France and accepted the honor by joining the National Assembly in time to participate in the unanimous vote to exterminate royalty in France. "Kings," the deputies proclaimed, "are in the moral order what monsters are in the physical." [17]

The stage was now set for what has become known as the September Massacres. The Secretary of State heard about them first in a letter from William Short. He reported "the arrestation, massacre or flight of all those who should be considered friends of the late constitution…The mob and demagogues of Paris have carried their fury in this line as far as it could go." In a postscript, he told how the rioters were "menacing the assembly to immolate these victims without delay." He predicted there would soon be "proceedings, under the cloak of liberty, égalité, and patriotism, as would disgrace any *chambre ardente* that has ever existed." A chambre ardente was a sixteenth century court in which heretics had been tried and burned at the stake.

A few days later, Jefferson was reading Gouverneur Morris's report on September's tidal wave of blood. The Jacobins and their supporters murdered well over a thousand priests, royalists, judges, editors—anyone decreed an enemy of the state. Morris described the death of the Princess de Lamballe, a member of the Queen's household, in graphic detail. "She was beheaded and disemboweled, the head and entrails paraded on pikes and the body dragged after them through the streets." At the building known as the Temple, where the King and Queen were being held prisoner, Marie Antoinette was forced to look out the window at the gruesome spectacle.[18]

Another victim was Jefferson's friend, the Duke de la Rochefoucauld, and his son. They were in their carriage when a mob attacked them, dragged them into the street, and stabbed and clubbed them to death before the horrified eyes of the Duke's wife, William Short's by now beloved friend, Rosalie. It was not the sort of news that would reconcile Jefferson's protégé to the revolution. In the National Assembly, an ecstatic Maximilian Robespierre called the mass murders proof that they were conducting "the most beautiful revolution that has ever honored humanity." His journalist friend, Jean Paul Marat, agreed wholeheartedly. "Let the blood of traitors flow," he said. "That is the only way to save the country."[19]

The Secretary of State received Morris's letter on January 10, 1793. He already knew about the September Massacres from American newspapers, many of which expressed disgust and outrage. Jefferson's political spokesman, Philip Freneau, displayed a very different point of view. He was irked to see some newspapers censuring the French as "barbarous and inhuman." What had they done? Killed "two or three thousand scoundrels to rescue the liberties of millions of honest men." Freneau compared this to the villainy of the French royal family, "the vain wars of whom covered the earth with the blood of innocent individuals from one end of Europe to another."[20]

Secretary of State Jefferson did not say a word of reproach to Freneau. Nor did James Madison. Meanwhile, Jefferson received another letter from Gouverneur Morris reporting that the National Assembly had put Louis XVI on trial for treason. With not a little irony, Morris wrote that it "would seem strange to a person less intimately acquainted than you are with the history of human affairs," that "the mildest monarch who ever fill'd the French throne...a man whom none can charge with a criminal or crude act, should be prosecuted" as "one of the most nefarious tyrants that ever disgraced the annals of human nature." Morris thought it was very likely that the King would be sentenced to death.

On the French border, a small battle took place in the Argonne Valley near the town of Valmy. The Prussian monarch, King Frederick William, had joined his Austrian counterpart in armed hostility to the Revolution. The French army repulsed the vaunted Prussian regulars, and they retreated back across the border. In Paris, the National Assembly had disbanded and become the National Convention—a term that signified a new revolution was about to be launched. The news of Valmy was hailed as a French Thermopylae. The next day the Convention voted to abandon the monarchy and declared a new era in history had begun. It was "Year One of French Liberty."[21]

More French victories followed. Their revitalized armies drove the Austrians out of what is now Belgium. Other armies occupied many small German principalities to the east. Everywhere, the conquering revolutionaries told the local population that liberty was about to transform their lives. What the locals actually got was massive requisitions of cash and property to finance the penniless government in Paris. As one disillusioned resident of Mainz remarked, they would have felt less cruelly deceived if these apostles of liberty had told them from that start, "We have come to take everything."[22]

In America, the French military victories were hailed by Philip Freneau and other admirers of the Revolution as proof that the upheaval was indeed what Secretary of State Jefferson called it: "The True God." In December of 1792, "Civic Feasts" featuring fine wine, mountains of food, and innumerable toasts to France became frequent events in Philadelphia, Boston, and New York.

For Thomas Jefferson, an even more exciting event was a conversation he had with President Washington on December 27. According to the Secretary's *Anas,* the President told him that he had begun to think America should concentrate on improving its relationship with France. Neither the Spanish nor the British were trustworthy. Both continued to treat America with barely concealed hostility. Jefferson could hardly believe his ears. He noted almost smugly that this idea had been his "polar star" as secretary of state, long before France's armies won any battles.[23]

A few days later, the combination of Washington's change of heart and the French military victories—and the enthusiasm they generated in America—moved Jefferson to write a long, angry letter to William Short, in which he all but demolished the young man for his negative reports on the French Revolution. "The tone of your letters had for some time given me pain on account of the extreme warmth with which you censured the proceedings of the Jacobins of France," the Secretary of State told him. For his part, Jefferson considered the Jacobins "as the same with the Republican patriots of America."

This was an astonishing statement, all by itself. The murderers of over one thousand people were morally equal to James Madison, James Monroe, and other followers of the Secretary of State? Even more amazing was what followed this sanctification. In the struggle to "expunge" the King, "many guilty persons fell without the forms of trial, and with them some innocent. These I deplore as much as any body, and shall deplore some of them to the day of my death. But I deplore them as I would have done if they had fallen in battle....Time and truth will rescue and embalm their memories, while their posterity will be enjoying the very liberty for which they would never have hesitated to offer their lives. The liberty of the whole earth was depending on the issue of the contest, and was there ever such a prize won with so little innocent blood?...Rather than it should have failed, I would have seen half the earth desolated. Were there but an Adam and Eve left in every country, and left free, it would be better than as it now is."[24]

Jefferson went on to claim that his extraordinary sentiments "are really those of 99 in an hundred of our citizens." He cited the feasts and "rejoicings" over France's military successes. Even more important, he told Short that he had recently learned the President felt the same way. His "reserve" had hitherto made it difficult to discover his opinion of the revolution. That was why Jefferson had forwarded all of Short's letters to Washington, even though he was troubled by their abusive tone. The most recent letter had forced the President to "break silence and notice the extreme acrimony of your expressions."

Washington also supposedly said he had been informed that Short's conversations "with our allies" had been as offensive as his letters. The President wanted Jefferson to remind Short that he was "the representative of [his] country and should realize his French listeners might conclude that all or most Americans had similar negative opinions." The President urged Jefferson to remind Short that "France was the sheet anchor of this country." Her friendship should be regarded as "a first object" of an American diplomat.

Diligent research by this and other historians has failed to find President Washington saying these things. In fact, Short is not even mentioned in the notes on Jefferson's conversation with the President that survive in his *Anas*. By this time, it had become apparent to Washington that France was not in any way, shape, or form a sheet anchor to the American ship of state. Most of the government's revenues were coming from duties on imports from Great Britain. France simply lacked the economy that could replicate the volume and variety of Britain's commerce. It seems more than likely that Secretary of State Jefferson was concocting a rather cruel form of intimidation to make sure William Short said nothing else negative about the French Revolution.

William Short never responded to this letter. He also did not change his mind about the French Revolution. Many years later, he remarked on this fundamental disagreement between him and his mentor. "Mr. J's greatest illusions in politics have proceeded from a most amiable error... too favorable an opinion of the animal called man...who, in mass form, [is] in my opinion, only a many headed monster. Mr. J, on the contrary, judging him [man] from himself, conceived that his sense of moral rectitude would suffice to induce him to keep a straight path, & that he had need of little restraint." As a kind of footnote, Short added, "it was most difficult to make him change an opinion."[25]

In Paris, the National Convention had been debating the fate of Louis XVI. By a margin of seventy-five in a legislative body of more than eight hundred, the vote was for death. On January 21, 1793, Louis was awakened in the predawn darkness to receive holy communion from the royal chaplain. He dressed simply and gave his valet his wedding ring to pass on to the Queen. When an escort from the Commune arrived, the King asked if he could have his hair cut now, rather than on the scaffold, like a common criminal. The committee said no.

Next came a two-hour ride in the executioner's cart along Paris streets shrouded in clammy fog. Windows along the route were closed and often shuttered. The immense crowd lining the route was silent, as if they could not quite believe what they were seeing.

The King arrived at the scaffold at ten o'clock. He was helped up the steep steps and submitted to the standard haircut by the executioner. Turning, he spoke to the twenty thousand citizens crammed into the square. "I die innocent of all the crimes with which I have been charged," he cried. "I pardon those who have brought about my death and I pray that the blood you are about to shed will never be required of France."

A roll of drums ended his attempt to say more. Louis was strapped to a plank and pushed forward until his head was in a kind of brace. The executioner pulled a cord and the twelve inch blade hissed down to separate the royal head from its body. The head toppled into a basket; the executioner pulled it out and held it up, dripping blood, for the people to bear witness that France was now a republic.

Schoolboys cheered and rushed to dip their fingers in the royal blood. One tasted it and said it was "well-salted." The executioner sold snippets of hair and fragments of the king's clothes. People strolled away, arm in arm, laughing. No one was even faintly aware that beheading the king would launch a European war of incredible ferocity that would bring tragedy into millions of French lives for the next twenty terrible years.[26]

In America, Thomas Jefferson and his followers received the news with something close to exultation. Philip Freneau set the tone with a mocking announcement in the *National Gazette:* "Louis Capet has lost his caput." He went on to say that from his use of a pun, one might suppose he "thought lightly" of the King's fate. "I certainly do," he agreed. "It affects me no more than the execution of another malefactor." He went on to declare the killing "a great act of justice." Anyone who was shocked by it should be regarded with suspicion "of a strong remaining attachment to royalty."[27]

Jefferson was in complete agreement with his spokesman's sentiments. Although he had once said Louis was a good man, and even an honest man, he now declared that kings should be "amenable to punishment like other criminals." Unsurprisingly, James Madison chimed in, announcing that if the King were a traitor, he should be "punished as well as another man." The Congressman dismissed as "spurious" newspaper stories that argued for the King's innocence. Instead, he continued to praise the Revolution in Paris as "wonderful in its progress and stupendous in its consequences."[28]

Neither the Secretary of State nor his chief follower were aware that the French Revolution was about to arrive on their doorsteps with consequences that were disastrous for them and their new political party.

CHAPTER 13

Can America Remain Neutral in a Warring World?

O N FEBRUARY 1, 1793, the French National Convention declared war on Great Britain and the Netherlands. By the time the news reached America in early April, President Washington had taken his oath of office for a second term. He was relaxing at Mount Vernon when a letter from Treasury Secretary Hamilton reached him, reporting that after several rumors about an outbreak of hostilities between France and England, "there seems to be no room for doubt of the existence of war."

The President instantly saw a crisis in the making and rushed back to Philadelphia. In a letter to Secretary of State Jefferson, Washington said the federal government should use "every means in its power" to prevent citizens of either England or France from forcing America to deviate from "a strict neutrality."[1]

The British had struggled to remain neutral in regard to the French Revolution. Prime Minister William Pitt and his cabinet thought it would be a mistake to try to intervene in the upheaval with force. That would only inspire another round of messianic fervor. But the men in control of the National Convention were already too infected by this emotion to accept a pragmatic arrangement. In January 1793, Armand Kersaint, a former naval officer who had fought in the war for American independence, made an inflammatory speech in the National Convention. He declared the oppressed English "sans-culottes" (without knee breeches—the poor) were ready and eager to join their French brothers and sisters in a war to "establish the liberty of the

153

world." They would greet a French invasion with enormous enthusiasm. The speech was greeted with wild cheers and stamping feet.[2]

The British would be easy to defeat, Kersaint declared. Their national debt was enormous; remove the bankers who funded it and the entire edifice would collapse. With the irony that the gods of history seem to relish, Thomas Paine had said almost exactly the same thing in his 1776 pamphlet, *Common Sense*, assuring the Americans that the British could not afford to send a large army to America. A few months later, the biggest army Britain had ever sent overseas arrived in New York's harbor. Deepening the irony, Kersaint had recently written a pamphlet called *Le Bon Sens* (Common Sense).

In spite of this war talk from Paris, the British clung to a determination to remain neutral—until the National Convention decapitated King Louis XVI. A wave of abhorrence swept Britain. Prime Minister William Pitt called the King's execution "the foulest and most atrocious act the world has ever seen."[3] But George III hesitated to declare war without a better pretext than the regicide. Tom Paine's *The Rights of Man* had sold hundreds of thousands of copies in Britain. There was some truth in Kersaint's portrait of the British lower class.

On February 1, the National Convention made up the King's mind for him. The delegates also declared war on the Dutch Republic for resisting a French invasion. On March 7, deciding Spain was not sufficiently sympathetic to the birth of global *liberté*, another declaration of war placed her on the enemies list. By summer, the Spanish, fearing France intended to stir revolts in their colonies, would negotiate an alliance with their long-standing enemy, Britain.[4]

At a cabinet meeting in Philadelphia, President Washington asked his four advisors to answer thirteen questions. First and most important, should United States proclaim its neutrality? Other questions explored the nation's relationship with the new French republic. Should America receive an ambassador from France? Did the Treaty of Alliance Benjamin Franklin had negotiated in 1778 still apply? Was France waging an offensive or defensive war? In the treaty, both nations had pledged mutual support if attacked by another power.

Secretary of State Jefferson listened with barely controlled outrage. Although the President had written out the questions, the Secretary was convinced that "the language was Hamilton's and the doubts his alone." The letter Washington had written to him from Mount Vernon stating strict neutrality as the centerpiece of America's policy apparently had no impact. The Secretary of State seemed on the verge of paranoia about Secretary of the Treasury Hamilton.[5]

The proceedings of the cabinet meeting did little to lessen Jefferson's agitation. He opposed an immediate declaration of neutrality. He thought it would be better to force both the warring nations to compete for America's support. The idea that the French might make the United States an ally with a plethora of extravagant promises appalled Secretary Hamilton. America did not even have a navy. Its army, defeated twice by western Indians, was close to a joke. Major General Anthony Wayne was still training his raw troops in the western wilderness. The confident Indians, buoyed by British guarantees of support, had sent emissaries to tribes further west and north, urging the creation of an immense native army. On the southern frontier, the Creek Indians and American settlers were virtually at war. The pioneers had ignored the treaty Washington had negotiated with their chiefs in 1790.[6]

Hamilton said a war with England would be "unequal and calamitous" for the nation. America desperately needed more years of peace to create a stable country. The Treasury Secretary argued that France's declaration of war made her the aggressor and the 1778 Treaty of Alliance void. Moreover, the treaty had been signed by Louis XVI's government, which had ceased to exist.

Hamilton also declared that there had been nothing generous or idealistic in France's motives when she supported America in 1778. The move had been part of their policy of weakening the triumphant British empire, which had shattered the French army and navy in the Seven Years War (1756–63). To Jefferson's chagrin, the cabinet voted for an immediate declaration of neutrality.

❦

Not content with this victory, Secretary Hamilton also opposed a friendly reception for the new French ambassador, Edmond-Charles Genet, who had recently landed in Charleston, South Carolina. Secretary of State Jefferson objected with ferocity and skill. Why make an enemy of the ambassador and the new French republic, which had as yet done nothing hostile to America? The President decided Jefferson was right.

The argument now shifted to the wording of the proclamation. The Secretary of State won an important opening point. He objected to the word *neutrality*, insisting that it would offend France. Instead, the final proclamation, drafted by Attorney General Edmund Randolph, simply urged Americans to be "friendly and impartial" toward both warring powers. President Washington insisted that the document should also warn Americans against "committing, aiding or abetting hostilities against any of the said powers," and forbid American ships to carry guns or ammunition to either combatant.

A far more serious dispute erupted over when and how the proclamation should be issued. Secretary of State Jefferson maintained that the president lacked the power to make this crucial choice between peace and war without consulting Congress. President Washington informed the Secretary of State that he considered the proclamation well within the powers of the presidency. Aside from this executive prerogative, Congress would not meet for several months. To summon them for a special session would alarm the nation. Far better to issue the proclamation immediately, without excessive fanfare.[7]

The proclamation became American policy on April 23, 1793—and soon had the word "neutrality" attached to it. Even Secretary of State Jefferson used the term although he remained unreconciled to it. In a letter to James Madison, he sneered at the "cold caution" of the government and the "milk and water views" of the text. Jefferson assured Madison that the British could have been browbeaten into granting "the broadest neutral privileges" if he had been permitted to bargain with them.[8] The Secretary of State told Senator James Monroe that Hamilton—and Washington—were ready to tolerate "every kick" the British may "choose to give" the Americans. Jefferson knew both men would vent these opinions in Congress and in the newspapers.[9]

"I fear a fair neutrality will be a bitter pill to our friends," he told Madison. Madison promptly rushed to assault the proclamation as motivated by "a secret Anglomany." [A term invented by Jefferson to describe partisanship for Great Britain.] Congressman Madison called the proclamation a "most unfortunate error" that "wounds the national honor by seeming to disregard the stipulated duties to France."[10]

The man who had once agreed with Washington that the nation needed a strong presidency also objected to the proclamation's violation of "the forms and spirit" of the national charter. Matters of war and peace had been delegated to "other departments of the government." Descending to nastiness worthy of Philip Freneau, Congressman Madison wondered why the President thought he had anything to fear "from the success of liberty in another country, since he owes his preeminence to the success of it in his own." Madison's devotion to Thomas Jefferson and the Secretary of State's imagined French Revolution was persuading him to dismiss the general who had repeatedly rescued the American Revolution with his military and political skills.

Such details were now irrelevant. Enthusiasm for revolution and liberty was becoming a veritable war cry. Jefferson described the phenomenon in a letter to James Monroe. "The war between France and England seems to be producing an effect not contemplated: all the old spirit of 1776 is rekindling." [11]

In Charleston, South Carolina, the new French minister, Edmond-Charles Genet, was confirming this remark. He was also introducing the first of several lessons about the real French Revolution. Red-haired and ruddy-faced, the stocky, thirty-year-old diplomat was fluent in no less than seven languages. His father had been an expert on American affairs in the French foreign ministry. The son had succeeded him in this role and had been a loyal servant of the *ancien regime* until the Revolution exploded. Thereafter, he had paid close attention to the shifting ideological winds from Paris. [12]

In Charleston, S.C., the new minister asked everyone to call him "Citizen Genet." Titles of all sorts were now passé in Paris. The Palmetto State's residents seemed delighted by the opportunity to adopt this down-to-earth style. Genet told them he was in America to obtain a large advance on the money Congress still owed to France from the loans that had financed the struggle for independence. He planned to use the cash to buy tons of grain to feed France's hungry armies as well as pay for huge shipments of gunpowder and weapons.

Genet also noted that America was bordered by Louisiana, Florida, and Canada, colonies controlled by France's enemies, Spain and England. He was eager to hire secret agents to promote revolutionary activities within these territories. He also had in his luggage dozens of "letters of marque"—certificates that would entitle the holders to launch privateers and attack British and Spanish ships on the ocean.

Gouverneur Morris had written to the President, warning that he would find Genet had "at the first blush, the spirit and manner of an upstart." His conduct in South Carolina deserved a more serious label. Genet was an upstart with imperial ambitions. From the day of his arrival, he invoked the Edict of Fraternity, which claimed spiritual kinship with revolutionaries around the world. Where was there a more logical place to assert this bond than the United States of America, where *liberté* was flourishing, thanks to France's benevolent help in throwing off England's oppressive yoke?[13]

Genet was vastly encouraged by the tumultuous welcome he received in Charleston. Amid the toasts and cheering at banquets and parades, he swiftly commissioned four privateers, *Republican, Anti-George, Sans-Culotte*, and *Citizen Genet*. He also had no trouble mustering on paper sixteen hundred volunteers to invade Spanish Florida.

Thanks to Philip Freneau's *National Gazette*, which was mailed to numerous French leaders in Paris, Genet thought he had an excellent grasp of what was happening inside the American government. He knew that Secretary of State Jefferson was an ardent supporter of the Revolution. So was that good man, President George Washington. But he often listened to advice from a very evil man, Secretary of the Treasury Alexander Hamilton.

Genet's was sure he could force the President to stop listening to Secretary Hamilton. He planned to persuade an overwhelming majority of the American people to demand it. As Genet saw it, he did not need Washington's permission to do or say anything. All he had to do was summon his American sans-culottes to guarantee him impunity.

Some accounts of Genet's mission have portrayed the envoy as an ignorant extremist. But those who have taken the trouble to read his instructions from his government have quickly grasped that he was nothing of the sort. He was a daring servant of France's grandiose ambitions. The new rulers really believed there was an immense army of the deprived and oppressed in the world, waiting to embrace the blessings of *liberté*. These were the *vrais republicanes*—the true republicans. Those who failed to receive the message were false republicans—enemies of the Revolution.

According to his instructions, Genet was "Minister Plenipotentiary of the French Republic to the Congress of the United States." President Washington was not even mentioned. From France's current point of view, any and all executive power was regarded as an alien force, hostile to the

only true power, the will of the people. The French revolutionists had mo-
bilized the people (aka the Paris mob) against the regime of King Louis
XVI and destroyed it. They had done the same thing with the constitutional monarchy and the assembly that had endorsed it. By this light,
Genet had every reason to expect a repetition of this experience with the
peculiar office the Americans called the presidency.[14]

❀

The Minister Plenipotentiary took a month to travel from Charleston to
Philadelphia. In town after town, he was greeted by cheering citizens and
banquets thick with toasts to France. "My journey was a succession of civic
feasts without interruption," he reported to his superiors in Paris. Genet
was in Richmond, Virginia, enjoying still more pro-French plaudits when
the news of the neutrality proclamation reached him. At first he dismissed
it as a "horrendous little pleasantry designed to throw dust in the eyes of
the British." But he decided to depart for Philadelphia immediately to
settle who was in charge of the country.[15]

   The French minister's arrival in the city of brotherly love was, he reported to his government, another "triumph for liberty." The true republicans were "brimming over with joy." Again, Genet was telling nothing less
than the truth, from his point of view. He had barely settled in his lodgings at the City Tavern when a huge crowd jammed the streets outside the
building to present him with an address of welcome signed by leading
citizens of the city. Among the most effusive greeters was Thomas Mifflin,
the governor of Pennsylvania, an enemy of George Washington since Valley Forge days.[16]

   Eagerly participating in the pro-French pageant, Philip Freneau published an open letter to the President in the *National Gazette.* "The cause
of liberty is the cause of man," he warned the President, "and neutrality is
desertion." Two days later, Genet, escorted by Secretary of State Jefferson,
presented his credentials to Washington. Already disturbed by reports of
Genet's arrogant posturing during his monthlong journey from Charleston, the President had told Jefferson he wanted the diplomat to be received without "too much warmth and cordiality." We can be sure the
President's demeanor was dignified but firmly unemotional. By this time,
Genet was so exalted by the rapturous reception he had been receiving
from the true Republicans of Philadelphia, he was incapable of noticing
such a subtle message.[17]

The Minister Plenipotentiary gave a brief speech, in which he assured the President that "We wish to do nothing but what is for your own good, and we will do all in our power to promote it…We see in you the only person on earth who can love us sincerely and merit to be so loved." The realist side of George Washington's mind heard these words as utter nonsense, with an underlying threat. Was this wild-eyed fellow saying he could and would decide what was "good" for America?

The Secretary of State, on the other hand, was charmed. "It is impossible," Jefferson wrote in a letter he rushed to James Madison, "for anything to be more affectionate, more magnanimous than the purport of his [Genet's] mission…he offers everything & asks nothing."[18]

Thanks to Genet's reports to his government, we know that the Secretary of State abandoned all pretensions to neutrality when he met with Genet in private. "Jefferson…gave me useful notions on men in office," the Frenchman wrote. He "did not at all conceal from me that Secretary of the Treasury Hamilton had the greatest influence over the president's mind."

Jefferson also cited Washington's friend, Robert Morris, the wealthy merchant who was serving as U.S. senator from Pennsylvania, as a man who joined Hamilton in pro-British sentiments. It was "only with difficulty that he [Jefferson] counterbalanced their efforts." Nevertheless, the Secretary of State assured Genet that "the people were for us."[19]

That same evening came the strongest proof yet of many *citoyens'* eagerness to support France—a grand banquet at Oeller's Hotel, which had the biggest assembly room in the city. On the immense table stood a "tree of liberty" crowned by a red "liberty cap." This symbol had become enormously popular among French revolutionists. It had its roots in ancient Rome. Freed slaves wore such a cap to signify their right to citizenship.

In the course of the evening, nineteen toasts were drunk "to the glory of America and the French Republic." "An Ode to Liberty," written for the occasion, was read aloud and a Frenchman sang France's new national anthem, the *Marseillaise*. Outside, artillery boomed exuberantly. At the close of the evening, Genet took the liberty cap from the tree of liberty and placed it on his head. He solemnly passed it to the man next to him, and it went around the immense table, each man pledging his loyalty to France and *liberté*.[20]

While these cheers and cannon blasts echoed through the city, a tall figure strode along Philadelphia's darkened streets. President Washington had decided to confer with Attorney General Edmund Randolph, who played a moderating role in his cabinet. Randolph sometimes agreed with Hamilton and sometimes with Jefferson. The President saw him as a voice of reasonable compromise. Unfortunately, the Attorney General was not home. The President returned to his executive mansion to meditate on the meaning of the noisy celebration honoring Citizen Genet at Oeller's Hotel.[21]

Elsewhere, the President knew, people were reading the latest edition of the *National Gazette,* in which Philip Freneau launched a ferocious attack on him. The Secretary of State's hired journalist claimed that Washington was surrounded by aristocrats and friends of England, and was ignoring the people's will by refusing to support France. Freneau sent three copies of every issue of the paper to the executive mansion.

A few days later, the Secretary of State visited the President to find out if he approved a letter that Jefferson had drafted to the French government, accepting the replacement of the current minister by Edmond-Charles Genet. Jefferson used the phrase "our republic" to describe the United States. Washington had marked the phrase with an asterisk, and abruptly asked Jefferson how he could use this terminology while he supported the outrageous things Philip Freneau was saying in his newspaper. Had he read the editor's latest gibe? American "Anglomen" had extorted the proclamation of neutrality by threatening to behead the president!

Washington reiterated the absurdity of claiming he was influenced by pro-British intriguers who wanted to turn the government into a monarchy. That was not what they should be worrying about. It was *anarchy* that Freneau was sowing with his berserk smears and claims. For Washington, the word recalled Shays's Rebellion. That upheaval had fortunately been confined to the Massachusetts countryside. Now Edmond-Charles Genet and Philip Freneau were awakening its possibility in the heart of the nation's capital.

The President might as well have berated—or pleaded with—a statue. An hour or two later, the Secretary of State wrote in his *Anas* that Washington wanted him to "interpose in some way with Freneau, perhaps by withdrawing his appointment of translating clerk in my office. But I will not do it. His paper has saved our constitution, which was galloping fast into monarchy, and has been checked by no one means so powerfully as by that paper." William Short was not the only man who discovered the hard way that Thomas Jefferson seldom if ever changed his mind.[22]

Meanwhile, the President had to cope with Citizen Genet's demand for a new commercial treaty that would unite France and America in an embrace that would virtually guarantee war with England. Simultaneously, protests from the British ambassador cascaded onto Washington's desk, as the privateers that Genet had commissioned with his letters of marque began bringing captured British ships into various American ports and claiming the right to sell them.

Philip Freneau launched a series of open letters signed by one Veritas that denounced Washington's foreign policy all the way back to the start of his first term. Veritas warned the President it was time to realize he was being lulled into complacency by an "opiate of sycophancy." Didn't he realize "principles not men" were the essence of republican government?

By the end of the first week in June, the exasperated President complained of "little lingering fevers." His Secretary of State told James Madison that Washington seemed more sensitive to newspaper abuse "than any person I ever yet met with." He was "sincerely sorry" to see him in such a low state of mind and health. Madison more than matched his leader in schadenfreude. "I regret extremely the position into which the P has been thrown. The unpopular cause of Anglomany is openly laying claim to him."[23]

In France, the real French Revolution was about to make a mockery of the benign view of it the Secretary of State and his two lieutenants, Madison and Monroe, were propagating in America. In the first six months of 1793, everything seemed to go wrong for the cause of *liberté*. French armies in Germany, Belgium, and the Netherlands had retreated back to the theoretical safety of their homeland after their untrained volunteers developed a dismaying habit of running away. Another army, sent to suppress a counterrevolution in the Vendée region of France, was even more totally routed. With no foreign country to plunder, the National Convention could only issue another eight hundred million assignats—paper money that only made the first four hundred million even more worthless.

In hungry Paris, this maneuver produced a group of orators known as the *enrages*, a word that originally meant revolutionary zeal, but soon be-

came viewed (and heard) as maniacal anger. The *enrages* blended wild attacks on the selfish rich with berserk demands to punish traitors.
Simultaneously, they enshrined the supposedly starving sans-culottes in a
haze of saintliness. The streets and squares rang with comparisons between these ragged martyrs and the greed of the *capitaliste* and the *gros-ne-
gociant* [large merchants].

Next, the *enrages* were denouncing the *Girondins*, the men who had
issued the Edict of Fraternity and sent Edmond-Charles Genet to America. (The name was derived from the department of Gironde, in southwest
France from which their leaders came.) The *enrages* claimed they were
secret worshippers of kings, who yielded Louis Capet to the guillotine
only when their appeal for a popular vote on his sentence had failed to win
a majority in the National Convention. In June, an immense crowd, estimated to be eighty thousand people, surrounded the National Convention.
They were responding to a call from the leader of the Jacobins, Maximilian Robespierre, to launch a "moral insurrection" against the corrupt leaders of the Convention.

Soon, most of these delegates could only go to the privy escorted by
armed guards. Expensive scarves and coats were torn from their owners'
throats and backs. The arrest and execution of twenty-two condemned
Girondists became a *sine qua non* to prevent a larger explosion of violence.
The commander of the guards at the entrance to the hall told the president of the Convention, if the twenty-two were not delivered, they would
open fire. Cannon were rolled into position and grimly loaded with balls
and powder. More and more delegates who had remained in "The Plain"—
uncommitted to any party—began moving to the section of the assembly
hall known as "The Mountain" where the Jacobins gathered.

This new revolution had three goals: a confiscatory tax on the rich, the
destruction of the Girondists, and the surrender of almost all power to a
Committee of Public Safety, controlled by the Jacobins. Under the leadership of the ascetic, icy-voiced Robespierre, that twelve-man body subscribed to a new, all consuming motto: "The republic consists in the
extermination of everything that opposes it." In Paris, in the Vendée, in
Lyon and other cities, massacre became the order of the day. [24]

CHAPTER 14

Challenging Old Man Washington

Wild enthusiasm for France continued to rampage through Philadelphia, Vice President Adams reported that Governor Thomas Mifflin offered a toast at one of the ubiquitous banquets: "To the ruling powers of France. May the United States of America, in alliance with them, declare war against England." Mobs regularly paraded past the President's door, shouting praise for France. The Vice President became so alarmed, he persuaded Secretary of War Henry Knox to smuggle him a supply of weapons to defend his house.[1]

When the French frigate *Embuscade*, which had brought Citizen Genet to America, captured the British merchantman *Grange* and escorted it to Philadelphia with the British flag flying upside down, signifying surrender, another stupendous crowd swarmed to the waterfront to cheer and shout. No one was more pleased by the demonstration than Secretary of State Jefferson. "Upon coming into sight, thousands and thousands... crowded and covered the wharves," he told Senator James Monroe. "Never was such a crowd seen there, and when the British colors were seen reversed, and the French flag flying above them, they burst into peals of exultation." The Secretary of State was as thrilled by this expression of the will of the people as the most berserk sans-culotte in Paris. He did not show a trace of concern for the President's *Proclamation of Neutrality*.[2]

Perhaps Jefferson thought the cheers for the Embuscade were a rebuke to President Washington. He had told the Secretary of State that there was no rush to reply to Genet's proposal for a new treaty of commerce, or an advance on the debt to France. "We ought not to go faster than it was obliged, and to walk on cautious ground," Washington said. One can almost hear the growl in these words.

The President was unaware that the Secretary of State was secretly disagreeing with almost everything he communicated to Genet in his official capacity as the nation's chief diplomat. Jefferson's description of Washington in the grip of a pro-monarchist clique inspired Genet to consider extreme statements and acts. The envoy told his superiors in Paris that the President "impedes my course in a thousand ways and forces me to urge secretly the calling of Congress."[3]

For Citizen Genet, Congress was a magic word; it represented the voice of the people. The President represented no one but himself and the Anglomanic Hamilton and his allies. It never seemed to occur to Genet, with his endless apostrophes to the will of the people, that the President had been elected by the people—*unanimously*. Genet's antipathy to "Old Man Washington," as he began calling the President, escalated when the Secretary of State informed him that the British ship *Grange*, would have to be returned to her owners. An investigation by Attorney General Randolph concluded that the vessel had been seized within the territorial waters of the United States.[4]

The Secretary of State also solemnly informed the complaining British minister, George Hammond, that the United States "condemns in the highest degree the conduct of any of our citizens who may personally engage in committing hostilities at sea against any of the nations [that are] parties to the present war." Hammond had good reason to doubt these words. Citizen Genet continued to commission privateers in cities up and down the American seaboard and recruit hundreds of Americans for their crews. French consuls had been dispatched to almost all the nation's ports, with orders to set up courts in which they could condemn and auction off the prizes that these raiders brought in.

Attorney General Edmund Randolph arrested two members of one privateer's crew and ordered them prosecuted for violating the Proclamation of Neutrality. When one of this indicted pair went on trial in Philadelphia, he was promptly acquitted by a feverishly pro-French jury. The Attorney General counterattacked, Washington-style. He sent a stern warning to all state attorneys general that the acquittal did NOT mean American citizens could serve on French privateers. Such service was still considered a *crime*.[5]

This illegal warfare at sea was by no means the only questionable enterprise Genet was sponsoring. He dispatched an envoy to Kentucky, with orders to organize a foray down the Mississippi to capture New Orleans from the Spanish. To lead this expedition, Citizen Genet had discovered in the Blue Grass State a hugely symbolic figure, General George Rogers Clark, the man who had liberated much of the Northwest Territory from Britain in the closing years of the Revolution. The hero had fallen on hard times and was desperate for a way to acquire land and money before old age incapacitated him. He leaped at the offer to become a general in the French army, with suitable pay, rank, and privileges.

To cement the bargain, Genet dispatched to Kentucky a Frenchman named Michaux, who he thought could function as the French consul in that state. He took these plans to the Secretary of State for his approval. Jefferson told him he was pleased and excited by the proposal—Genet described his reaction as a "lively sense of the utility of such a project"— but there were problems.

America was currently negotiating with two Spanish commissioners about the possibility of acquiring a trading post on the Mississippi below New Orleans. In Madrid, Jefferson's protégé, William Short, and another American diplomat, William Carmichael, were trying to persuade the Spanish to lift their ban against western Americans using the Mississippi to export their surplus grain and other farm products. Unless the Spanish broke off the negotiations, "a regard for propriety" would prevent the United States from participating directly in the Clark expedition, Jefferson said.

However, the Secretary of State said he could see how "a little spontaneous irruption of the inhabitants of Kentucky into New Orleans" might get the negotiations "moving." He gave Genet letters of introduction to several congressmen and a senator from Kentucky. Also on the list was Governor Isaac Shelby. They were all more than willing to listen to Genet's proposal that the expedition found an independent state in Louisiana "connected in commerce with France and the United States." It was an unnerving glimpse of how westerners viewed the federal union and its government. Like the Shays' Rebellion protestors, there was an instinctive hostility to obeying laws issued by distant, seemingly alien Atlantic coast legislatures, including Congress.

Genet said he was guaranteeing the raiders the support of two French frigates, who would join them in the climactic attack on New Orleans. All this, Genet continued, he was telling Jefferson not as the Secretary of State, but as "Mr. Jeff," his friend and the friend of France. Mr. Jeff's reply was almost schizophrenic in its division between official and unofficial opinion. First, he told Genet that the Americans in the Clark expedition might wind up on a gallows for waging war against a nation with whom the United States was at peace. But "leaving out that article" he "did not care what insurrection should be excited in Louisiana."

As for Monsieur Michaux, he could not function as a French consul in Kentucky; consuls were permitted only in port cities. Genet cheerfully assented to this distinction—and asked "Mr. Jeff" to give Michaux a letter of introduction to Governor Shelby. Mr. Jeff sent him the letter—which Genet returned. He did not like Mr. Jeff's description of Michaux as a mere botanist on the lookout for new plants. He wanted Governor Shelby to view him as "something more—a French citizen possessing his [Genet's] confidence." Mr. Jeff promptly complied with a revised copy.

It takes a moment, perhaps, for the reader to realize that as Secretary of State, Thomas Jefferson was tolerating and even encouraging an attack on Spain, which he admitted was a crime—and simultaneously, in the guise of "Mr. Jeff," doing everything in his power to help it succeed. He was also encouraging the creation of an independent nation in the West, an idea President Washington considered a deathblow to the primary goal of his presidency—the preservation of the American union. Is it too much of a stretch to suggest that "Mr. Jeff" was being a very disloyal Secretary of State?

Jefferson had apparently convinced himself that some form of western independence was inevitable in the long run—the people (of the west) willed it. The similarity of this kind of thinking to the demagogues who were turning the French Revolution into a bloodbath is striking—and dismaying. The will of the people can be simulated by a mob (Paris) or a swarm of frontiersmen recruited by a bankrupt but popular general and a governor who likes the idea of becoming an independent ruler.

Jefferson told himself the negotiations with Spain were hopelessly stalled, and war seemed probable. So why not accelerate it a little? To add to the unreality, "Mr. Jeff" also warmly approved plans by Citizen Genet to arouse the French in Canada to revolt against their British "oppressors" and join the march to universal *liberté*. It was not difficult to imagine how the British would react to this provocation.[6]

At this point, the two Spanish commissioners wrote an agitated letter to President Washington, claiming that some people in Kentucky were plotting to attack the "Spanish dominions of the Mississippi." Neither Genet nor Mr. Jeff was aware that Madrid had a well-paid spy in Kentucky, General James Wilkinson, a U.S. Army officer who was currently in the force commanded by General Anthony Wayne. The President asked the Secretary of State to find out if there was any substance to the Spanish complaint. If so, he should tell Governor Shelby to end the scheme with the threat of legal action.

Abandoning the sentiments Mr. Jeff had expressed to Citizen Genet, the Secretary of State solemnly warned Governor Shelby that the "interests of Kentucky" were at the center of the negotiations between Spain and the United States, and "nothing could be more inauspicious than an appeal to violence." Governor Shelby, well aware of what Jefferson was covering up with this bland solemnity, assured the Secretary of State that all was peaceful and law-abiding in his state. [7]

In cabinet meetings, the Secretary of State pursued his angry feud with Alexander Hamilton, even when the issue involved matters that were almost entirely within the Treasury Secretary's purview. Hamilton proposed to float a two million florin loan from Holland, although the United States did not have an immediate need for the money. Jefferson vehemently opposed the proposal. He claimed to see no reason to add to America's public debt. In private letters, he told Madison and Monroe that he was convinced Hamilton intended to use the money to bribe the incoming Congress to do his bidding. [8]

The President decided in Hamilton's favor, explaining to Jefferson that if Europe plunged into the titanic war that seemed to be brewing, it might be impossible to borrow money from anyone. Reports he was receiving from Georgia suggested America might soon be at war with the Creek Indians. In the Northwest, diplomacy with the Miami Indians and other warlike tribes was also floundering toward failure, leaving General Anthony Wayne and his army as the only recourse. One wonders what the President would have thought if he had learned of his Secretary of State's encouragement of Genet's schemes to invade Louisiana. [9]

At the end of June, President Washington's overseer at Mount Vernon died unexpectedly and he was forced to make a hurried visit to see what could be done to find a replacement. When he returned to Philadelphia on July 11, he found a packet of papers awaiting him from the Secretary of State, marked "INSTANT ATTENTION." At the top of the pile were two letters from Governor Thomas Mifflin. He had discovered that Citizen Genet was turning a captured British ship, the *Little Sarah*, which the privateer *Citizen Genet* had escorted to Philadelphia, into a privateer. Cannon were being installed. American sailors were being recruited on the waterfront.

Mifflin had told Alexander James Dallas, Pennsylvania's secretary of state, to warn Genet that he was violating the Proclamation of Neutrality. Under no circumstances should the ship, now renamed *La Petite Democrate*, be put to sea before President Washington returned from Mount Vernon. Governor Mifflin was summoning a detachment of militia to make sure the ship stayed at her dock. Citizen Genet exploded into a tirade in which he told Dallas he might publish his correspondence with the American government and combine this gesture with "an appeal from the President to the people."[10]

Governor Mifflin rushed a messenger to Jefferson, who had retreated to a house in Philadelphia's countryside, which he preferred to his quarters in the city. Jefferson hurried back and went to Genet's rooms in the City Tavern to urge him not to let the ship sail until the President returned. The Secretary of State was soon enduring a tirade that far surpassed the verbiage Citizen Genet had flung at Dallas.

Genet accused America of violating her obligations to France under the Treaty of 1778. He veered to denouncing the ridiculous American Constitution which gave a single man, this president, so much power. Old Washington had opposed and thwarted him in everything he had tried to do to help his country. The President obviously had no intention of negotiating a commercial treaty with the French Republic. That left Citizen Genet with only one alternative. He would dare the President to summon Congress to Philadelphia so that he could plead for their help. They were the only voice he would listen to in the American government!

The Secretary of State managed to tell Genet that if he had any complaints about the American government, he should report them to his superiors in Paris. "He was silent and I thought was sensible it [this] was right," Jefferson told Washington in his letter describing the encounter.

But the Secretary of State swiftly learned that Genet was immoveable on the future of the *Little Sarah*. There was no way Jefferson could "justify him detaining her," the red-faced envoy bellowed.[11]

For the moment, Genet said the *Little Sarah* was not ready to sail. However, her crew and a new captain, an ensign from the *Embuscade,* were aboard, and were planning to move the ship to a new anchorage farther down the Delaware, where the final work on turning her into a warship would be completed. Genet warned Jefferson that Governor Mifflin's militiamen should not try to board her. "She is filled with high spirited patriots and will undoubtedly resist," he said.

Although Genet had not explicitly promised that the *Little Sarah* would refrain from heading for the open sea, Jefferson told Governor Mifflin to dismiss the militia. He was horrified by the possibility of blood being spilled in this dispute. The next morning, the Secretary of State met with Secretary of the Treasury Hamilton and Secretary of War Knox. Neither had any confidence in Genet, and wanted to erect a battery of cannon on Mud Island, where a bend in the Delaware River had enabled artillery to block the British fleet in 1777. Jefferson strenuously objected to this idea. He claimed that firing on the *Little Sarah* would infuriate France and possibly lead to war.

Later that day, the cabinet members learned that the ship had passed Mud Island and was now anchored off Chester, obviously about to depart for the open sea. Citizen Genet confirmed this intention with a letter to Jefferson. "When ready I shall dispatch her...When treaties speak, the agents of nations have but to obey," he declared.[12]

The President read all this in Jefferson's account and the accompanying letters. His temper rising, Washington sent a messenger racing to summon the Secretary of State. The messenger returned to inform the President that the Secretary was out of town. He had again retreated to his country house, apparently leaving the entire mess in the President's lap. Washington seized a pen and wrote the angriest letter he had yet written to Thomas Jefferson.

"After I had read the papers put into my hands by you, requiring instant attention, and before a messenger could reach your office, you had left town. What is to be done in the case of the *Little Sarah,* now at Chester? Is the minister of the French Republic to set the acts of this government at defiance with *impunity* and then threaten the executive with an appeal to the people? What must the world think of such conduct, and of the government of the United States for submitting to it?

"These are serious questions. Circumstances press for decision, and as you have had time to consider them (upon me they come unexpected), I wish to know your opinion of them even before tomorrow, for the vessel may then be gone."[13]

That evening, a strange response arrived from the Secretary of State. It was written in the third person. "T.J. has had a fever the last two nights which has held him till the morning. Something of the same is now coming on him. But nothing but absolute inability will prevent his *being in town* early tomorrow morning."[14]

After mocking the harassed President for his bouts of fever, the Secretary of State seemed to be undergoing the same malady. Was the illness real or merely convenient? In his private notes, Jefferson scribbled a revealing sentence. "It appears to me that the President wished the *Little Sarah* had been stopped by military coercion, that is by firing on her. Yet I do not believe he would have ordered it himself if he had been here but he would have been glad if we had ordered it."[15] Psychologists call this thought process projection. Jefferson was attributing to the President a wish that had tormented him.

In the midst of this imbroglio about the *Little Sarah,* Jefferson sent a frantic plea to James Madison to take up his pen and answer Hamilton, who was blasting the Democratic-Republicans under the name Pacificus, accusing them of trying to drag the nation into the war as France's ally. The Secretary begged Madison to "cut him to pieces in the face of the public." Then Jefferson turned his attention to Genet and confessed why their new political party was desperately in need of protection.

"Never in my opinion was so calamitous an appointment made, as that of the present minister of F. here. Hotheaded, all imagination, no judgment, passionate, disrespectful, and even indecent toward the P in his written as well as verbal communications, talking of appeals to Congress and from them to the people, urging the most unreasonable and groundless propositions, and in the most dictatorial style, etc. etc. etc. He renders my position immensely difficult."[16]

Further complicating matters was a note from Genet, informing the Secretary of State that the French West Indies fleet of twenty men of war was coming to the United States to escape the hurricane season in that turbulent part of the world. Admiral François De Grasse had cited the same reason when he sailed north in 1781 to rendezvous with General Washington and trap a British army in the Virginia tobacco port of

Yorktown. Was Genet hoping to remind the Americans of that historic deliverance? Or was he suggesting that an attempt to use force to stop the *Little Sarah* might persuade him to order the French fleet to support an overthrow of Old Man Washington and his clique?

Jefferson kept his promise to return to Philadelphia and the cabinet met on July 12, 1793. Attorney General Randolph was absent—traveling in Virginia, at the President's suggestion, trying to counter the hostility against the administration fueled by Freneau and Genet. The President soon revealed that his anger about the *Little Sarah* had not cooled. He had harsh words about Governor Mifflin, who should have acted against arming the ship early in her transformation into a man of war, when a handful of militia could have stopped the work. Washington listened in seeming agreement when Secretary Hamilton urged Genet's recall and Knox suggested suspending him immediately as France's envoy. Jefferson defended Mifflin by reporting Genet's claim that the *Little Sarah* had been armed by cannon taken from other French ships in the harbor.

Wasn't arming the ship the main point? Secretary Hamilton asked. Not where the cannon had come from? The President decided to ask the Supreme Court to help them decide this and other fine points of a nation's neutrality. He would make no decision on recalling or suspending Genet until he heard from them. Two days later, the *Little Sarah* (now *La Petite Democrate*) went to sea, where it soon began seizing British merchantmen.

In the newspapers, Secretary Hamilton, as Pacificus, continued his strenuous defense of the Proclamation of Neutrality. Congressman Madison struggled to answer him from Virginia, but he had no enthusiasm for the task and his essays were feeble. Hamilton's attacks grew sharper when he learned that on July 4, Genet and his followers had founded a "Democratic Society" in Philadelphia. It was modeled on the Jacobin Clubs of Paris. The plan was to create similar groups throughout the nation to help change the public mind about the Proclamation of Neutrality.

In Virginia, James Madison conferred with Senator James Monroe on plans to overturn the Proclamation in the next session of Congress. They were being advised in strictest secrecy by the Secretary of State. In Philadelphia, newsman Benjamin Franklin Bache turned his editorial guns on the Proclamation, calling it "a perfect nullity." At another point he described it as a pact with the King of England.[17]

⑜

With no warning, President Washington received an evening visit from Citizen Genet. He burst into the executive mansion to find the President chatting with his wife Martha and their good friend, Senator Robert Morris. Genet exchanged pleasantries for a few minutes and abruptly asked Washington if he could speak to him in private. Washington escorted him into a nearby room, and Genet poured out a torrent of words about his desire to win the President's friendship.

The envoy disowned all the harsh things being said against Washington in the newspapers. He believed Washington loved his country and also loved France and was convinced they could come to an understanding. Washington said barely a word. Finally, he escorted Genet to the door, where he calmly told the envoy that he seldom if ever read the newspapers and did not care what they said about him.

Genet went back to his quarters convinced that he had charmed Washington into submission. The next morning, he rushed to Jefferson's house to tell him the good news. As he started describing his triumph, the door swung open and in walked the President. Genet glanced at the Secretary of State, and then at Washington, hoping to hear an invitation to remain. Later, he said he would have given "a part of his life" to hear this friendly summons. But the President said nothing and the Secretary of State, with a slight movement of his hand, told the crestfallen envoy to leave.[18]

An infuriated Genet told his superiors in Paris what he now thought of President Washington. He incidentally revealed his politically induced loathing for the fallen hero of two worlds, the Marquis de Lafayette. "Until now Washington has been depicted as friendly to France, simple, popular, the enemy of show. You have known Lafayette, well you have known *Vasington*...He is easy to approach but in reality he is haughty. His settled expression is always half smiling, he caresses you, but he is thinking of deceiving you..."[19]

⑜

Supreme Court Chief Justice John Jay and two other justices responded to Washington's request to define neutrality by politely explaining that such a task was beyond the court's jurisdiction. It was a landmark decision in its own right, sharply defining the federal judiciary's role. But it left to the president and his cabinet the task of spelling out the rules and regulations of neutrality. It also left to them a final decision on how to deal with Genet.

Every attempt to discuss the envoy left Hamilton and Jefferson at angry odds. Backed by Secretary Knox, Hamilton still insisted the government should not pass up the opportunity to strike a blow, not only at Genet, but at his American supporters. Jefferson stonily maintained that this tactic would be a mistake; it would only further inflame everyone in America—and in France.

On July 23, the President took charge of the meeting. Instead of putting the question on the table for further debate, he announced his decision. They would send the record of Genet's inappropriate letters and actions to Paris, without publishing them in America. Along with this evidence, the Secretary of State would write a "temperate but strong" letter, emphasizing that the government blamed this unfortunate collision entirely on Genet, and suggest his immediate recall. Hamilton still disagreed. He saw much more at stake than Genet's removal. He was convinced that Washington's administration was in serious danger of being overthrown.[20]

The Secretary of State just as strenuously backed the President's proposal. The debate continued through two more cabinet meetings. Hamilton cited the activities of Philadelphia's Democratic Society as further proof that there was an anti-Washington plot in the making. Jefferson maintained that the group was only interested in electing their candidate as governor of Pennsylvania, and after the election they would go out of business.

Taking the offensive, Jefferson argued that publishing the government's correspondence with Genet would reveal that there were disagreements in the cabinet. It was a virtual certainty that the garrulous diplomat would write a reply. Did they want him telling the American public that the President did not represent the people—that Washington was the head of a pro-English political party? As for Genet's superiors in Paris, they would almost certainly feel that the publication was unkind. "Friendly nations usually negotiate little differences in private," Jefferson said.

The Secretary's choice of the phrase "little differences" is rather startling, if Hamilton were correct about Genet encouraging Americans to overthrow their government. Jefferson tried to counter this claim by asserting that the Edict of Fraternity was being used to subvert only royal governments. It was an act of self- defense. There was simply no evidence that Genet was trying to do the same thing in America, which already had a republican government.

At this point, Secretary of War Knox produced a copy of Freneau's *National Gazette.* The front page featured a satiric article and cartoon, *The Funeral Dirge of George Washington,* in which the paper described the President being condemned for his aristocratic pretensions and thrust beneath the blade of a guillotine.

Although Jefferson's account of the incident in his *Anas* sneered at Knox's "foolish incoherent sort of a speech," the move was devastatingly effective. The President exploded into one of his awesome rages. He roared that he wished he had retired at the end of his first term and swore that he would rather be a simple farmer at Mount Vernon than be "emperor of the world." That rascal Freneau still sent him three copies of his paper every day, as if he expected him to be his distributor. It was further proof that the chief purpose of this worthless sheet was "to insult him."

The cabinet sat in mortified silence for several minutes. Then, as he usually did after one of these detonations, the President resumed speaking in a calm, quiet voice. They would go ahead with a compilation of their correspondence with Genet and decide later whether to publish it in America or send it to Paris. Washington asked the Secretary of State to begin drafting the letter that would explain their unhappiness with the envoy to his superiors.

۞

The Secretary of State never admitted to himself or anyone else the whole truth about Genet: he was the personification of the French Revolution's arrogant face in America. The current rulers in Paris presumed that the sovereignty of the United States was a mere blip in a worldwide tornado of enthusiasm for their empire of *liberté*. But Jefferson decided to give up on defending Citizen Genet. In private letters, he carefully spelled out to Madison and Monroe why they had to jettison the reckless envoy. On August 18, the Secretary of State sent Madison a copy of his message requesting Genet's recall, and urged him to show it to Monroe.[21]

A lot had been happening in American ports—all of it bad, from Jefferson's point of view. In Boston, a judge had ordered the arrest of the French consul for using force to prevent a captured British ship from being returned to its owners. The consul denounced the judge, and the French frigate *Concorde*, which had captured the ship, flew from her masthead the names of eleven Bostonians who were proscribed as "aristocrats" and enemies of France. Genet wrote an open letter, calling on the republicans of Boston to acquit the consul, which they did, three times.[22]

In New York, the French consul declared that any captured ship was as out of the reach of American jurisdiction as if she were in a French harbor. At another point the New York consul described Jefferson as "this minister of a day and of a republic which owes us the light of day." The consul wondered how the Secretary "dares to speak to men representing the most powerful nation on earth in the language of the old tyrants."[23]

These glimpses of the incredible arrogance of this phase of the French Revolution convinced Alexander Hamilton it was time to demolish Genet. The Secretary of the Treasury persuaded Chief Justice John Jay and Senator Rufus King to publish in a New York newspaper a report that Genet was threatening to appeal to the American people over the head of President George Washington.

The story sent indignation simmering up and down the continent. Pledges of devotion to the President poured into Philadelphia from mass meetings in cities, towns, and villages everywhere. A frantic Genet demanded the right to sue the Chief Justice and the Senator for libel. Secretary of State Jefferson informed him that a foreigner had no right to sue anyone in an American court. Genet responded by publishing his letter and Jefferson's answer.

On August 25, the Secretary of State, acting as the anxious leader of the Democratic-Republican Party, wrote to James Monroe, who was more violently pro-French than Madison. "You will perceive by the enclosed [news] papers that Genet has thrown down the gauntlet to the President by the publication of his letter & my answer, and is…risking that disgust which I had so much wished could have been avoided. The indications from different parts of the continent are already sufficient to shew that the mass of the Republican interest has no hesitation to disapprove of this intermeddling by a foreigner…"[24]

These are significant words. Genet was no longer a spokesman for the glorious French Revolution, the Secretary of State's "polar star." He was a menace to the success of the Democratic-Republican Party, and therefore must be discarded. This was the point that Jefferson wanted his chief lieutenants to make clear to everyone who shared their hope of future political power. To Monroe he lamented that he feared "the more furious Republicans" may "schismatize" with Genet. This was, among other things, evidence of the way Jefferson spoke of their new political party as if it were a religion.

One of these furious schismatizing Republicans turned out to be Alexander James Dallas. Jay and King had cited him as the source of their story. Dallas denied he had ever heard Genet say anything about an appeal to the people against President Washington. But Jefferson, relying on what he had heard Dallas say in their month-ago meeting about the *Little Sarah,* told James Madison on September 1: "You will see much said and again said about G's [Genet's] threat to appeal to the people. I can assure you it is a fact."[25]

CHAPTER 15

The Secretary of State
Calls It Quits

O N GEORGE WASHINGTON'S DESK, while the President and the cabinet were wrestling with the Genet crisis, was a letter from the Secretary of State, announcing that he wished to resign at the end of September. He reminded the President that he had intended to retire at the end of Washington's first term, but "circumstances" had prompted "some of my friends" to persuade him to stay longer. Now he saw no obstacle to leaving by the proposed date.

This letter was almost as curious as the third person message the Secretary of State had sent the President in early July. Jefferson made no mention of Washington's earlier attempts to persuade him not to resign; nor is there even a hint of apology to the man who was bearing by far the greater burden in the government. The coolness that was permeating their relationship was all too evident.

The Secretary added that the circumstances that had persuaded him to stay had now "abated" and he wanted—or needed—to seek "scenes of greater tranquility." Jefferson was referring to the attacks on him by Hamilton and his allies; they had now shifted their verbal artillery to Genet as a better target. The Secretary was speaking as the leader of the Democratic-Republican Party, and the tranquility he sought might be better described as cover. For the time being, the Federalists were in the ascendant and Jefferson saw no point in staying around as a probable target.

On August 6, the President rode out to Jefferson's country house hoping to change his mind. Washington began by revealing that Alexander Hamilton had also told him he wanted to resign. His growing family made life on a federal salary more and more difficult. The President reminded Jefferson that he had accepted another term with reluctance. He was not happy to find that he was about to lose two of his chief advisors.

The Secretary of the Treasury had promised to stay until the end of the next Congressional session, which would begin in December 1793 and end in March or April 1794. Would Jefferson do likewise? His advice might be helpful in dealing with this new Congress. The President did not mention what they both knew—that the Democratic-Republicans would probably have a majority in the House of Representatives, as well as almost equal strength in the Senate.

Jefferson responded with a veritable jeremiad on his "repugnance for public life." He found service in Philadelphia caused him "particular uneasiness" because much of his time he was forced to associate with the wealthy leaders of the city's society and their wives—a circle that "I know to bear me peculiar hatred." He despised these "aristocrats and merchants closely associated with England with their "paper fortunes" and their penchant for spreading stories about him "to my injury."

Jefferson said nothing about his repeated disagreements with Alexander Hamilton. That may surprise some who subscribe to the widely held belief that Washington had constantly favored Hamilton in these disputes. An examination of the record shows the President sided with Jefferson at least as often as he favored Hamilton. This was especially true in the Genet affair.

The Secretary of State assured the President that the new Congress would be basically loyal to him. Jefferson said he had had no communication with "what is called the Republican Party" since the last Congress met, but he was sure there was no desire to oppose the President's leadership. All they might want to do was make Congress "independent." He added that many Republicans were embarrassed by Genet, but most of them would abandon the envoy when they gave further thought to "the nature of his conduct." Quite simply, there was "no crisis" in that quarter—no one in America wanted to overthrow the government.

The President told Jefferson he was ready to believe the views of his followers were "perfectly pure." But he worried that it was not easy, once men "put a machine in motion" to stop it where they wanted it. Washington reiterated his satisfaction with their present Constitution and again dismissed the idea that there was a plot to change the government into a monarchy. If such a movement ever appeared, there is no man who would "set his face against it more decidedly" than him.

The Secretary of State intervened to say no "rational man" suspected Washington of "any other disposition." But a week did not pass in which "we cannot prove" there was a "monarchical party" calling the government a "milk and water thing" which must be knocked down to create one with more energy. The President could barely control his exasperation at finding that the Secretary of State still nursed this conviction. If such people existed, Washington said, it was "proof of their insanity."[1]

They turned to discussing a possible successor. Washington said his first choice was James Madison, but he was sure there was no hope of persuading him. He had already approached Chief Justice John Jay, hoping to profit from his experience as Secretary for Foreign Affairs under the old Congress. But he preferred to stay in his judicial robes. They discussed a number of other men without finding anyone who satisfied the President's requirements.

With a sigh, Washington suggested a compromise. Would Jefferson agree to stay until the end of December? That would get them through the first weeks of the new Congress, and by that time France would almost certainly have recalled Genet. In Europe, the French might well win a decisive victory against their royalist attackers—or vice versa. Either way, it would make for a more peaceful world.

The Secretary of State advanced another clause in the emerging contract. Could he go home to Monticello in September for three or four weeks? The President quickly agreed—and gave Jefferson a few days to say yes to the final arrangement.

Five days later, Jefferson attached a detailed report of this interview to a long letter to James Madison. It was the second letter Jefferson wrote to him that day (August 11, 1793). He called the letters and the interview "timely information" which might help in formulating plans for "the state of things which is actually to take place" when Congress met in December. He insisted the report must be "sacredly kept to yourself unless you have an opportunity of communicating...to Monroe." This abrupt about-face after assuring Washington he had had "no communication" with the

Democratic-Republican Party makes it all too obvious that Thomas Jefferson had become a passionate player of power politics.

Crisply, almost bluntly, he gave Madison his recommendations for the coming session of Congress. He hoped the lawmakers would agree to divide the Treasury Department into two "equal chiefs," one to supervise the customs, the other to oversee internal taxes. That would eliminate Alexander Hamilton's accumulating power. A declaration of the true sense of the Constitution in regard to the Bank of the United States, even if it were made only by the House of Representatives, would suffice to divorce that entity from the government. Jefferson also urged a vote to censure Hamilton on some of the Treasury's practices that had emerged in the failed investigation by Congressman William Branch Giles.

As for the Proclamation of Neutrality—Jefferson told Madison to junk his plans for attacking it. Genet's antics had all but guaranteed that the "great body of the people" desired neutrality in the war between Britain and France. It would also be political suicide to "find fault with the President"—especially in regard to the Proclamation. In New York, when Genet went there to greet the French fleet, the vote at a "full [public] meeting of all classes" was nine out of ten against the diplomat. In Congress, therefore, it will be "true wisdom" for the Democratic-Republican Party "to approve unequivocally of a state of neutrality....In this way we shall keep the people on our side by keeping ourselves in the right."

To this battle plan the Secretary added a P.S. "The Pres is anxious to know your sentiments on the Proclamation. He has asked me several times. I tell him you are so absorbed in farming you write to me always about ploughs, rotations, etc." This addendum was probably designed to distance Madison from Washington, and reduce the chances of an invitation to join the cabinet.[2]

Some readers may puzzle over the President's desire to keep Jefferson or his alter ego, Madison, in the cabinet. What did Washington gain from such an arrangement? Madison's reply to Jefferson reported a conference with Monroe. They decided Washington had been using Jefferson as a "shield." There was a core of truth in this observation. The President, confronted by the emergence of a new political party, saw the value of keeping its founder or one of its leaders in the cabinet. The arrangement gave the administration an aura of neutrality—and a largely invisible way of communicating either disagreement or agreement with the opposition. Here was more evidence of George Washington's political skills.

Jefferson soon accepted Washington's proposal to stay until December and got to work on the letter to the French government requesting Genet's recall. The eight thousand-word message was a masterful balancing act. Instead of denouncing Genet's reckless statements, Jefferson wrote: "We draw a veil over the sensations which these expressions excite…We see in them neither a portrait of ourselves nor the pencil of our friends, but an attempt to embroil both." Two decades later, another secretary of state, John Quincy Adams, read a copy in the State Department's files, and called it a "perfect model of diplomatic discussion."[3]

It would take another six months for the French government to order Genet home. By that time, all the men who had sent him to America had been guillotined by the Jacobin Committee of Safety under that implacable moralist, Maximilian Robespierre. Among the dead was Armand Kersaint, the delegate who had assured the National Convention that Britain would be easy to conquer.

When the Committee of Safety read Jefferson's letter, they apologized profusely for Genet's wild schemes and repudiated all of them—including the attack on New Orleans and the insurrection in Canada. Having rediscovered the importance of executive power in government, Robespierre was reportedly fascinated by the American presidency and doubly appalled by Genet's personal attacks on Washington.

In Philadelphia, the frenzy over Genet was all but snuffed out by a ghastly visitation of the eighteenth century's most fearsome disease, yellow fever. People began taking to their beds, terrified as the fatal color spread up their arms and down their bodies. Within twenty-four hours, many were dead. By August 25, President Washington was telling correspondents that he and Martha were well but "the city is very sickly and numbers are dying daily." Thousands began fleeing to the healthier countryside along the winding Schuykill River. Philadelphia soon resembled a ghost town, with empty streets and shuttered houses everywhere.[4]

One by one, newspapers ceased to publish. Business came to a virtual standstill. For Washington, the disease acquired a personal dimension when Secretary of the Treasury Hamilton and his wife contracted it. Fortunately for them, they had a friend in the medical profession, Edward

Stevens, the son of the merchant for whom Hamilton had clerked in his youth in the West Indies. A brilliant doctor, he scorned the primitive tactics of Dr. Benjamin Rush and other physicians—bleeding and purging, until the patient was often too weak to resist the disease. Stevens's treatment saved both Hamiltons. But for a few weeks, the Secretary of the Treasury was a shattered ghost of the vigorous warrior of the political wars.

Philip Freneau was one of the few editors who persisted in publishing the *National Gazette* throughout the worst of the epidemic. But he pursued an editorial policy that did nothing to soften the impact of the catastrophe on his circulation. He continued to rhapsodize about the wisdom of Citizen Genet and the French Revolution. By mid-October, yellow fever had all but vanished and the city's normal life began to resume. But the plague, combined with the editor's stubbornness, became a literary death sentence. On October 27, 1793, the *National Gazette* published its last issue.

Neither Thomas Jefferson nor James Madison said a word on the paper's behalf. The editor's violently pro-French politics no longer fit into their plans for the future of the Democratic-Republican Party. They let Freneau write frantic letters, vainly begging subscribers to renew. The editor retreated to his sandy acres in New Jersey and tried to start another paper there. He got nowhere, suggesting that without Jefferson's backing he would never have achieved his brief flirtation with fame.

Not until November 1 did President Washington summon the cabinet to meet with him in Germantown—eight miles outside Philadelphia. Washington rented a mansion owned by Colonel David Franks, former aide to Major General Benedict Arnold. Jefferson spent a very unpleasant first night on a bed in the corner of the public room of a tavern, before obtaining decent quarters. This inconvenience did nothing to improve his mood. After almost two months at Monticello, he had no appetite for more political combat.

At the head of the list of issues the cabinet discussed was whether to lay before Congress Jefferson's letter requesting Genet's recall, and the envoy's intemperate correspondence with the American government. Jefferson had strongly opposed this move a few months earlier. Now, with his chief lieutenants in agreement on the Democratic-Republican Party's new policy of dumping Genet, he acquiesced.

There were other more alarming problems to discuss. Late in August, a few days before the yellow fever outbreak, the President had learned that the British government had issued new Orders in Council. They authorized His Majesty's navy to seize the cargoes of any and all neutral ships carrying corn, flour, or grain to France or its West Indies islands. Britain's web of intelligence agents had informed London of their enemy's desperate need for food to feed their armies. This was Britain's answer—even grain became contraband of war.

The President and his cabinet agreed unanimously to protest this ukase. But their angry words did not prevent the seizure of the cargoes of over two hundred American ships. Orders were sent to Thomas Pinckney, the American minister in London, to lodge strenuous protests over this violation of America's neutral rights.

From the Northwest frontier came more grim news. A final attempt to negotiate with the Indians had gone nowhere. The recent conference had been little more than the delivery of an ultimatum from the tribesmen: they wanted every American settler to retreat south of the Ohio River. Behind this arrogance were assurances of support from the British in Canada.

Meanwhile, Citizen Genet, unaware of the request for his recall, was still trying to spread France's influence up and down the continent. The Spanish commissioners continued to complain about French agents in Kentucky, plotting an attack on New Orleans. Rumors from South Carolina renewed fears that Genet was recruiting volunteers for an assault on Spanish Florida. The President told his cabinet that it was time to revoke Genet's powers. Hamilton and Knox heartily agreed, but Jefferson argued it would be wiser to let the French remove him. Attorney General Randolph agreed with the Secretary of State and the President dropped the subject.

Next they began discussing the President's fifth annual message to Congress. A fierce debate exploded about how to describe the Proclamation of Neutrality. Hamilton argued for claiming it was an unequivocal example of the president's power to define the nation's foreign policy. Jefferson insisted it should be described as a mere statement of the status quo—America was at peace and was determined to remain that way. To Hamilton's dismay, the President agreed with the Secretary of State. Washington said he had no intention of interfering with Congress's power to choose between peace and war.

Next came an even more heated discussion of what to say about British depredations against American commerce. Hamilton vehemently protested a draft in which the Orders in Council were described in harsh terms. As usual, Jefferson disagreed. Attorney General Randolph argued for a compromise. He said it was important to keep the door open to negotiations with London. The President amazed everyone by insisting that the entire story of the British abuse of American rights and seamen be told without the slightest reserve. He spoke, Jefferson told his *Anas*, "with more vehemence than I have seen him show."[5]

The result was an address to Congress that won praise from both Federalists and Republicans. Even Benjamin Franklin Bache, who had replaced Philip Freneau as the most outspoken newspaper critic of the President, was delighted. Bache said the address had "universally pleased" and its "energetic simplicity of expression" proved Washington was truly "the Man of the People." [6] He might have added it also proved that the President was a very good politician.

A few days before Christmas, President Washington had another conversation with the Secretary of State. He wanted to know if Jefferson would consider staying in office for a few more months—or possibly a year. But Jefferson's mind was made up. He turned the President down "so decidedly," Washington said he could not even "hint this to him" again. He soon asked Edmund Randolph to become Secretary of State, and he accepted without hesitation.[7]

On the last day of 1793, Jefferson submitted his letter of resignation. "I carry into retirement a lively sense of your goodness, and shall continue gratefully to remember it," he wrote. Washington's reply also rose to the occasion. He assured Jefferson that "the opinion which I had formed of your integrity and talents…has been confirmed by the fullest experience, and that both have been eminently displayed in the discharge of your duties."

There were deep reservations on both sides. Washington could not help thinking that Jefferson was retreating for self-serving reasons—his dislike of Philadelphia's aristocrats, a weariness with public office. Jefferson had to admit that Washington had agreed with him in at least half of the nineteen disputed issues that roiled the cabinet during his years as Secretary of State. But there were constant "moral" issues involved. Every time Washington decided in Hamilton's favor, he was violating a "sacred" principle of good government by siding with "the monocrats of our country."

As the departing Secretary saw their disagreements, it was "immoral to pursue a middle line" and admit the possibility of compromise between "honest men and rogues." In a word, Thomas Jefferson remained that most troublesome of politicians—an ideologue.[8]

৭৬

Ex-General Horatio Gates wrote the Secretary of State a warm letter of congratulation on his retirement. Jefferson replied that he hated politics, "both in theory and practice." He told Senator John Langdon of New Hampshire that he would "never touch a newspaper again nor meddle in politics more." From Monticello, Jefferson informed Madison that "the little spice of ambition which I had in my younger days has long since evaporated…the question is forever closed to me." [9]

Secretary Hamilton did not believe a word of Jefferson's intention to abandon politics. He was convinced that it was "evident beyond question that Mr. Jefferson aims with ardent desire at the presidential chair." Vice President John Adams was even more cynical. He greeted Jefferson's pro-claimed retirement with "a good riddance of bad ware…He is as ambitious as Oliver Cromwell…his soul is poisoned with ambition."[10]

One is tempted to agree with these skeptics. In October 1793, when Jefferson was at Monticello, he had spent hours with Madison and Monroe discussing political strategy for the coming year. In late December, as a parting gift, he presented to Congress, "A Report on the Privileges and Restrictions of Commerce of the United States in Foreign Countries." It was an all out attack on British dominance of America's trade and an attempt to prove Revolutionary France could replace Britain as America's most important trading partner. This would require heavy tariffs on British goods to destroy their "unnatural" monopoly of American imports and exports. [11]

An enraged Secretary Hamilton snarled that Jefferson "threw this firebrand of discord" into the heavily Democratic-Republican Congress "and instantly decamped to Monticello."[12] There would seem to be little doubt that Mr. Jefferson's "retirement" was more myth than fact. But the coming year would produce events that made Democratic-Republican hopes of majority power turn to chimeras. Politics, as Jefferson had already discovered thanks to Citizen Genet, was quintessentially unpredictable.

CHAPTER 16

Shooting Wars Loom on Several Doorsteps

THE YEAR 1794 BEGAN with James Madison launching an attack on the nation's policy toward trade with the British, using the former Secretary of State's report as ammunition. Madison introduced resolutions calling for higher duties and charges on tonnage for imports from countries lacking a commercial treaty with the United States. His target, of course, was Great Britain. The Congressman argued that even if the irate British stopped trading with America, the nation could remain prosperous by finding other outlets for its food and raw materials. British imports were mostly "luxuries" he maintained, and many of them could be replaced by domestic manufacturers.

The Federalists responded with vigor. Congressman William Loughton Smith of South Carolina staggered Madison with statistics (supplied by Secretary of the Treasury Hamilton) that showed two-thirds of America's exports went to Britain while only one-seventh of Britain's came to America. Who was more likely to get hurt by declaring a trade war? In monetary terms, the British took $8.5 million worth of American exports, France only $4.9 million. The import picture was even more starkly in Britain's favor. America had welcomed $15.28 million worth of goods from the erstwhile mother country, and only $2.06 million from France. Moreover, British merchants had millions of pounds in their banks and gave Americans "extensive credit." Was Madison urging the United States to commit economic suicide?[1]

Samuel Smith of Maryland noted that Britain supplied Americans with textiles, leather goods, and tools while French imports were almost entirely fans, combs, perfumes, silk stockings, lute-strings, walking canes, and umbrellas—in a word, luxuries. Madison had predicted an embargo on British trade would throw 250,000 British men and women out of work. What would it do to the same number of American farmers? With no place to sell their surplus crops, they would be forced to borrow to pay for their "necessary supplies" such as fertilizer and tools.[2]

Fisher Ames of Massachusetts wondered if Madison knew what he was talking about. "Trade flourishes at our wharves," he sneered, "And droops in speeches." Americans were building new ships at an astonishing rate, and Ames had the numbers to prove it (again thanks to Hamilton). By the end of 1792, American vessels carrying imports and exports exceeded British and other foreign vessels by 108,067 tons, and Ames predicted the figure would rise even higher in 1793 when statistics were computed for that year. He was right and then some. The proportion in America's favor would soar to four times British tonnage. This meant huge profits and prosperity for the United States.[3]

Madison fought back by descanting on the evils of British influence. He cast doubt on any figures from merchants who traded with Britain. They were not "American" opinions. He noted that the British had broadened the definition of contraband and were responsible for emboldening the Northwest Indians. He tried to include the costs of these acts of hostility in his anti-British statistics. Soon Ames and other orators were pointing out that "Madison & Co." now avowed that these political wrongs were *the* wrongs to be cured by commercial restrictions. How this miracle would take place, Madison did not bother to discuss.[4]

Democratic-Republican congressmen began deserting their leader's sinking ship. A desperate Madison delayed a vote on his proposals. In a discouraged letter to his supposedly retired leader, Farmer Jefferson, Madison admitted he was reduced to the hope that England would commit yet more outrages on American ships and seamen. "The intelligence would strengthen the arguments for retaliation," he wrote. In cities such as New York and Boston, where Democratic Societies and other groups tried to organize support for Madison's contentions, his backers were voted down by huge majorities—as high as two-thirds in commercial-minded Boston.

Soon a lot of people were saying that Madison's resolves were a not too subtle plot to benefit France. A Boston newspaper went into overkill mode, declaring Madison had been "a corrupt tool of France since he entered the Continental Congress in 1780."[5] None of the angry critics mentioned the man behind Madison—Thomas Jefferson. His pseudo-retirement was working well as political cover. But President Washington undoubtedly watched with not a little satisfaction the way a tough response soon extinguished the former Secretary of State's "firebrand" on trade with Britain.[6]

※

More satisfaction enriched the President's political plate from another quarter of the continent. Citizen Genet's plans to invade Florida and Louisiana remained very much alive, and Secretary of the Treasury Hamilton resumed his attempt to persuade Washington to condemn and sequester the pretentious envoy. It would, among other things, be a statement of the President's executive power. But a letter from Gouverneur Morris arrived from Paris, assuring Washington that Genet was political toast, and the President put off a decision.

In the Senate, the Federalists passed a bill forbidding Americans to attack a nation with whom they were at peace. In the House, Congressman Madison and his friends strangled this infant in its cradle. Kentucky Governor Shelby backed this vote with a defiant letter, claiming he had no authority to stop anyone from seizing New Orleans. Washington decided to exercise some of that executive power he believed was crucial to a successful presidency. He issued a proclamation, forbidding the Kentucky expedition. To show he meant business, he ordered General Anthony Wayne to intercept any and all armed men moving down the Ohio River to the Mississippi.

Secretary of State Edmund Randolph wrung his hands over this step. He feared the threat of force would offend westerners and southerners. In December, the Democratic Society of Kentucky had issued a call to "all the inhabitants west of the Allegheny and Appalachian Mountains" to join an attack on Spain's colonies. Adding paranoia to their message, they claimed the federal government was conspiring to keep the Mississippi River off-limits to Americans. President Washington left no doubt of what he thought of this defiance. He told Governor Henry Lee of Virginia that some people were "aiming at nothing less than the subversion" of the government.[7]

In the midst of this tension, the new French minister, Joseph Fauchet, arrived on President Washington's birthday with a very welcome present—a

message of peace and apology. He assured the President that his government disapproved of all Genet's schemes. He would soon prove these
words with a proclamation of his own, revoking all French support and
commissions. It marked *finis* to George Rogers Clark's dream of becoming
a French general.[8]

⚜

The French frigate that brought Minister Fauchet had orders to take Citizen Genet back to Paris. It was said to be carrying a guillotine on its main
deck. Many thought the ship had orders to bring back not the envoy but
his decapitated corpse. A frantic Genet begged President Washington for
asylum. He granted it without the slightest hesitation, and Genet retreated
to New York, where he soon married Cornelia Clinton, the daughter of
Democratic-Republican Governor George Clinton.

Most histories of Genet's explosive career consign him to a rural non-
political existence henceforth. But two years later—two years of brooding
on the way Thomas Jefferson had deceived him—Citizen Genet would
reveal he still had the power to destroy "Mr Jeff's" hopes of becoming
president.

⚜

The promise of peace in the Southwest was nullified by the latest news
from London. A new Order in Council had been issued in November
1793, empowering His Majesty's men of war to seize every American ship
carrying products to the ports of the French West Indies. This was one of
America's prime markets, and in a few months a staggering 250 ships were
captured, their cargoes sold and their crews stripped of their money and
freedom.[9]

On top of this came a report forwarded by New York Governor George
Clinton to the President, revealing that Lord Dorchester, the governor
general of Canada, had virtually invited the Indians of the Northwest to
make war on the Americans. Dorchester told a gathering of chiefs that he
expected hostilities between Britain and America to begin within a year. If
the tribes remained loyal to their benevolent "father," George III, they
would regain all the land they had lost since 1783. The Americans would
be scoured from every foot of ground west of the Appalachian Mountains.

To prove his sincerity, Dorchester ordered another Revolutionary War
veteran, Lieutenant Governor John Graves Simcoe, to build a fort on the

Maumee River, well within American territory, and call it Fort Miami, in honor of the most warlike tribe in the Indian confederacy. The six forts the British had built in the last years of the Revolution also remained in their hands.

Worsening matters was bad news from the Mediterranean. The British had signed a treaty with their traditional ally, Portugal, and the Algerines. It permitted Muslim warships to pass through the Straits of Gibraltar and assault neutral ships in the Atlantic. American vessels were the chief victims—a fate that meant either sudden death or a lifetime of slavery for their captured crews. The British saw the treaty as a way to protect their merchantmen. Americans saw it as another plot to cripple their prosperity.

Indignation about the Orders in Council and the Algerines simmered in every port. The stunned Federalists did not know what to think or say. Congressman Fisher Ames of Massachusetts could only gasp: "The English are absolutely madmen." Even moderate Democratic-Republicans, remembering that the President had won fame as a general, were sure he would soon call for a declaration of war.

Ironically, the most dismayed politician in Philadelphia was Congressman James Madison. The uproar cast his Jefferson-inspired attack on British trade supremacy into virtual oblivion. Even his most loyal supporters began telling him that "more vigorous measures" were called for. Congress began discussing the need to create a strong army and navy to deal with the crisis. They voted to build six frigates to confront the Algerines and began fortifying America's ports. Madison, still the leader of the House, vehemently opposed arming America. He killed a proposal to recruit ten thousand soldiers. He told Jefferson that the Federalists were up to the "old trick of turning every contingency into a resource for accumulating force in the government."[10]

Madison's fellow Jeffersonian lieutenant, Senator James Monroe, told the retired Secretary of State that an army was a plot to "destroy the happiness of America." Hamilton would be put in command of it. Next would come an attempt to achieve "the great object of a change in government." The Senator did not have to add the nasty word, monarchism.[11] Jefferson's obsession with this idea had total control of both men's minds. Obviously, he had never told either man about the President's vehement denials that he would ever even consider such a move.

Although enthusiasm among his Democratic-Republican followers was now close to zero, Madison made another push at Jefferson's retaliatory regulations. Fisher Ames demolished him. "When our commerce is nearly annihilated, it is trifling to talk of regulating it," he told the House. The congressmen voted to postpone Madison's proposals indefinitely. Madison retreated to a demand for an embargo on all trade with Britain. Congress agreed to a one-month suspension, and President Washington signed the bill into law.[12]

A group of senators came up with another alternative. They asked Washington to consider sending a special envoy to London to find a way to avoid gunfire. Washington was not enthusiastic at first. The combination of the Dorchester speech to the Indians and the French West Indies Orders in Council had convinced him that declaring war might well be the best solution.

Another message from London changed his mind. The Order in Council banning American ships from the French West Indies had been revoked. Prime Minister William Pitt had met with a delegation of British merchants in the American trade and admitted the order had been a mistake. He promised those who had been injured by the measure would receive "MOST ample compensation."[13]

The idea of sending a special envoy to London acquired new appeal. It was infinitely preferable to Madison's idea of a lengthy embargo on all trade with Britain. Attention now shifted to the President's choice of the envoy. Senator Monroe offered to explain to Washington why he should NOT name Alexander Hamilton. He got a curt reply from the President, who told him that "I *alone* am responsible for a proper nomination"—and Hamilton was one of the men he was considering. If the Senator wanted to express an opinion, he could put it in writing.[14]

In the House of Representatives, anti-British extremism became the order of the day. Abraham Clark of New Jersey proposed that Congress should end trade with Great Britain until the seized West Indies ships were returned with the value of their cargoes paid in full, and the forts in the Northwest evacuated. Clark also wanted to sequester all debts to British merchants until London capitulated. Madison suggested tempering this plunge to war by not inflicting the punishment immediately. The boycott would begin on November 1 if the British failed to meet these demands. The President was appalled. This was hardly the way to persuade anyone to negotiate, above all a nation as proud and powerful as Britain.

Secretary Hamilton wrote Washington an urgent letter, begging him to speak out against the boycott. The President refused; he had made it his policy not to intervene in Congress's deliberations. But the extremism of the measure made up his mind to send an envoy. The President asked Chief Justice John Jay to undertake the mission. After a day of hesitation, he accepted. Democratic-Republicans immediately heaped insults on Jay and the President. They claimed the Chief Justice could not be trusted to represent the best interests of the whole country. They dredged up his 1786 proposal to swap the right to use the Mississippi River for New England's right to trade with Britain.

Congressman Madison continued to push Abraham Clark's embargo bill. It passed the House, 58–38, and went to the Senate on April 25. After an angry debate, the vote ended in a tie. Vice President John Adams cast an emphatic "NO" and the measure was dead. But the bill was a grim omen of the Democratic-Republicans's hostility to the idea of negotiating with the British.

✣

The President temporarily solved this problem with a masterful pivot that left Madison and his fellow Democratic-Republicans floundering. Washington asked Senator James Monroe to become minister to France, replacing Gouverneur Morris. Madison's trade restrictions against British commerce became as irrelevant as yesterday's news. In a mournful letter to his pseudo-retired chief at Monticello, Madison lamented that the "influence of the Ex [the Executive] on events and the public confidence in the P [President] are an overmatch for all the efforts that Republicanism can make. The party of that sentiment in the Senate is completely wrecked; and in the H. of Reps, in a much worse condition than at an earlier period in this session."[15]

In New York, a crowd estimated at one thousand well-wishers saw John Jay off on his voyage to London. They were really cheering the President. Once more, Washington had added new power to his office. In a very good mood, he permitted himself a little wry humor in a letter to a friend: "The affairs of this country cannot go amiss. There are *so many watchful guardians* of them and such *infallible* guides, that one is at no loss for a director at every turn."[16]

In Virginia, Jefferson began showing symptoms of the French fever he had brought back from Paris in 1790. Some "very quiet" people, he told Senator Monroe, were in favor of continuing to tolerate the "kicks and cuffs Great Britain has been giving us." But they were obviously a tiny minority. "The great mass of thinking men seem to be of the opinion that we have borne as much as to invite eternal insults in the future should not a very spirited conduct be assumed." In other words, he—and supposedly, the great mass of thinking men—were in favor of war.

Jefferson hastily added that he still "wished for peace" if it could be preserved with some shreds of honor. Citizen Genet would have recognized this outburst instantly as his friend "Mr. Jeff" speaking—with even less inhibition—and the former Secretary of State supplying a pro-forma denial.[17]

In a letter to Madison, Jefferson veered into a total fantasy. He thought the Americans should publicly declare their intention of defending the French West Indies against the British fleet. The ex-secretary of state argued that the United States was obligated to make this pledge under the terms of the Treaty of Alliance America had signed with France in 1778. How this feat would be accomplished without a navy, Mr. Jeff did not bother to discuss.

In other letters, Jefferson revealed fierce enthusiasm for the news of French army triumphs in Europe. He told one correspondent he longed for a complete French victory that would bring all Europe's "kings, nobles, and priests to the scaffolds which they have so long been deluging with human blood." He said nothing about the fervor with which the Jacobin Reign of Terror was tackling that task in France. In Paris, Robespierre and his friends were guillotining nine hundred people a month; in Lyons, the scene was even gorier. Mr. Jeff undoubtedly dismissed reports of these massacres as British propaganda.

Throughout the first months of 1794, President Washington wrote only one letter to his former secretary of state. It was mostly about how to obtain and use the best available fertilizer. At its close, there was a cryptic political comment. "We are going on in the old way, 'and slow' I hope events will justify me in saying 'sure.'"[18]

A thick envelope from the Democratic Society of Lexington, Kentucky, momentarily made the President think he might need Jefferson's services. The packet contained a letter from a Frenchman in Louisiana, wondering what had happened to the army of "brave Kentuckians" that was going to free him and his friends from Spain's yoke. The Democratic Society responded with a mass meeting that forwarded a "remonstrance to the President of the United States." They wanted Washington to send an ultimatum to the Spanish king, demanding free navigation of the Mississippi, or the United States would declare war.

Washington had an anxious conference with his new Secretary of State, Edmund Randolph, who suggested persuading Jefferson to be a special envoy to Spain. Kentuckians, Democratic-Republicans almost to a man, trusted him. The President had to admit there was much to be said for this idea. For one thing, it would silence the Kentucky radicals—and demonstrate to Spain that America wanted peace. But he worried that he and Jefferson might disagree over what terms they should propose to Madrid.

The President allowed Secretary Randolph to explore the appointment with Jefferson. The former secretary of state returned an instant refusal, claiming that the "torments" of rheumatism had convinced him that his public life was at an end. A relieved Washington decided to send the current minister to London, Thomas Pinckney, to Madrid. He would be more or less superfluous in the British capital while John Jay was trying to negotiate a treaty.

❧

As the President pondered the pros and cons of a Jefferson mission, he received a letter from Governor Henry Lee of Virginia who told him "a very respectable gentleman" had asked Jefferson if Washington was "really governed by the British interest." Jefferson had sarcastically replied that as long as the President had the "wise advice" of his present cabinet, there was no danger of this becoming a fact.

Washington was infuriated. He told Lee he could not believe there was any doubt in Jefferson's mind that he had not an iota of predilection toward Britain, "unless he set me down as one of the most deceitful and uncandid men living." The ex-secretary of state had had innumerable opportunities to hear Washington "express very different sentiments with an energy that could not be mistaken by *anyone* present."[19]

This exchange would be the first—but not the last—evidence that Thomas Jefferson was ready and willing to demolish George Washington's reputation. The President considered it an unforgivably low blow. The friendship was teetering toward collapse. A gathering crisis in western Pennsylvania would damage it beyond repair.

CHAPTER 17

Will Whiskey Rebels Unravel
the Union?

WITH CONGRESS ADJOURNED, THE President looked forward to a visit to Mount Vernon to talk with his new overseer. He had scarcely arrived in his beloved home when trouble flared in another part of America—the western counties of Pennsylvania. There were about seventy thousand pioneers in this part of the Keystone State. They—and compatriots in the western counties of Virginia and North Carolina and Maryland—still nursed a grievance against the federal government's 1791 decision to lay a tax on the most lucrative product of their labors—whiskey. Almost every good-sized farm had a still where grain was turned into alcohol.[1]

The tax was crucial to Secretary of the Treasury Hamilton's plan to reduce the national debt. That made the President and the Secretary doubly sensitive to protests from the region, which were frequent. In 1792 and 1793, there were mass meetings, and angry demands for repeal of the tax were forwarded to Philadelphia. The government tried to meet some of these objections. Congress agreed to reduce the tax, and exempted farmers from paying it in cash, which was scarce on their side of the mountains. In June 1794, Congress dropped the requirement that accused violators had to travel all the way to Philadelphia to be tried in a federal court. Local state courts were permitted to handle the cases.

But resentment remained strong. Not a little of it was fanned by the growth of Citizen Genet's brainchild, the Democratic Societies. The original, personally founded by the envoy in Philadelphia, had been busy exporting the idea that the federal government was in the hands of would be aristocrats and British sympathizers. Democratic-Republican newspapers frequently said the same thing. The slander found an enthusiastic reception in the West. Local Democratic Societies became proponents of extreme measures to oppose the tax.

Federal collectors were beaten up as they travelled the roads; some were tarred and feathered. A character named "Tom the Tinker" sent threatening letters to owners of large stills that were complying with the law. Those who did not respond had their tanks shot full of holes—a gesture the rebels called Tom's way of "mending" a still. Several of Tom's friends torched the house of John Neville, the regional supervisor in charge of collecting the tax. A bullet whistled close to the federal marshal who was protecting him.

On August 1, 1794, some seven thousand protestors gathered at Braddock's Field, near Pittsburgh. The site was named for the British general, Edward Braddock, whose army had been routed there by the French and their Indian allies in 1755. A young George Washington had been the luckless general's aide. The principal orator at the gathering was a popular attorney named David Bradford, who appeared in the uniform of a major general, and urged the mob to join him in forming a new state—or better, an independent country. Other speakers called Pittsburgh, "Sodom," and recommended looting and burning it. Women among the rioters talked eagerly of the fine clothes they hoped to procure from the houses of the Sodomites before they went up in smoke.

Above the mob floated a flag with six stripes, representing four Pennsylvania counties and two in Virginia. Everyone knew that Kentucky, the next state down the mountain line, was already talking about secession, and the word was soon adopted by the orators. One speaker revealed his admiration for France's Jacobins by urging the construction of a guillotine and the formation of a Committee of Safety. No one knew that by this time Robespierre and many of his fellow fanatics had been guillotined in yet another transfer of power in Paris.[2]

Similar unrest erupted in western Maryland when emissaries from the Pennsylvania protestors arrived, looking for additional guns and ammunition. They told wild stories of the federal government's plan to tax wheat, rye, and oats, and even male and female children. Soon there was talk of attacking the federal arsenal at Frederick. Liberty poles went up in Hagerstown and violence erupted when less convinced residents tried to tear them down. Maryland Governor Thomas Simms Lee ordered eight hundred militia, backed by artillery and cavalry, to crush the insurrection. One government supporter declared "ANTIFEDERALISM" was the rebels' order of march."[3]

⚜

Studying reports of what was being said at Braddock's Field, President Washington concluded that most of the listeners were "dupes." But it was clear that "artful and designing men" were in charge of things. For the President, it was a replay of Shays' Rebellion, whose tentacles had also reached into nearby states. In both cases, the underlying threat was the destruction of the Union. It was time to act.

Washington summoned his cabinet to discuss the situation. Hamilton, Knox, and the new attorney general, William Bradford, favored force. Secretary of State Randolph feared an army would enrage Democratic-Republicans in other states. The President asked Pennsylvania Governor Thomas Mifflin to summon his state militia to intimidate the rioters. Displaying his concealed hatred of Washington, the governor declined to act. He claimed local law enforcement officials could handle the situation. Washington did not even bother to reply to this absurdity.

On August 7, the President issued a proclamation, calling on the protestors to disperse, and announcing his intention to summon thirteen thousand militia from Pennsylvania, Maryland, Virginia, and New Jersey. As a last-ditch effort to achieve a peaceful solution, he asked Attorney General Bradford and two distinguished Pennsylvanians, U.S. Senator James Ross and state Supreme Court Justice Jasper Yeates, to go to Pittsburgh and negotiate with the rebels.

These federal commissioners soon reported that there was no sign of a willingness to accept even a truce. The rebels were full of bravado; they talked of fighting to the death. The President asked Secretary of War Knox to call out the militia, and announced he would put Governor Henry Lee of Virginia in command of it. This was good politics—bringing the largest state in the Union into the game. The President told Lee the upheaval was "the first formidable fruit" of the Democratic Societies.

Soon, thirteen thousand men were marching west through Pennsylvania. The President added to the rebels' apprehension by announcing that he would join the army as they advanced from Carlisle in late September. Simultaneously, he issued another proclamation, calling on the rest of the nation for support. "The people of the United States," he declared, had been permitted, thanks to "divine favor," the freedom to elect their own government. He hoped that gratitude for this "inestimable blessing" would inspire "firm exertions to maintain the Constitution and the laws."[4]

Welcome news came from the President's brother-in-law, Burgess Ball, who told him that Virginia's militia were with him heart and soul and ready to reinforce the army if he needed them. Similar news arrived from other states. Washington's prestige and the impact of his proclamations had aroused a widespread detestation of the whiskey rebels. Democratic-Republicans by the hundreds declared themselves ready to join Governor Lee's army. They saw it was their only hope of retaining some popularity.[5]

One of the most ironic examples of this turnaround was Governor Mifflin. Having sniffed the political winds, he became all warrior. Trying to certify his aging manhood, he drank so hard he gave confused commands that resulted in Pennsylvania cavalry firing on a detachment of New Jersey militia. Fortunately, the bullets flew high. Washington with, we can be sure, not a little pleasure, urged the governor to concentrate on making sure the army was well supplied. The words were a wry reference to the fact that Mifflin had been quartermaster general of the Continental Army in 1778 until he resigned to play anti-Washington intriguer.

※

On September 30, en route to join the army, the President heard news that enormously strengthened his hand. Major General Anthony Wayne reported that his army, still called the Legion of the United States, had won a huge victory over the largest Indian army ever assembled on the continent. The warriors had chosen to fight in a part of a forest that had been struck by a tornado, leaving hundreds of felled trees in a gigantic tangle. The site (not far from present-day Toledo, Ohio) already had a name, Fallen Timbers. To the Indians, it seemed heaven sent as a place that Wayne's cavalry could not penetrate and his infantry would find difficult to attack in a compact mass, wielding the weapon the Indians feared, the bayonet.

The Indians' opening volley killed the two leaders of Wayne's advanced guard, and the rest of the Americans began falling back, firing as they retreated, not a few turning to run. It had all the appearances of the rout that had led to the massacre of the army led by General St. Clair. The howling warriors charged from their tangled timber defense line expecting a harvest of scalps. They collided with the main body of Wayne's well-trained army and found themselves fighting in tall grass and open forest, where American marksmanship took a stunning toll.

"Charge the damned rascals with the bayonet!" General Wayne roared, and his men obeyed with alacrity. The Indians took one look at the on-coming "long knives" and ran. A company of white Canadians recruited by Governor General Lord Dorchester tried to make a stand but Kentucky militia hit them from the flank. The entire enemy line broke in disorder. Some fled across open ground and Wayne's cavalry ruthlessly rode them down.

The fugitives headed for nearby Fort Miami, which the British had built to encourage the tribes to resist the Americans. The fort's command-ing officer refused to open the gates. The humiliated warriors could only continue their panicky flight. It was the end of their illusion that the Brit-ish were on their side, ready to help drive the Americans east of the moun-tains. The battle of Fallen Timbers also annihilated British hopes of siding with the whiskey rebels, and recruiting them into an army strong enough to create a separate frontier nation beholden to Britain.

The victory sent an unnerving chill through the bravado that was animat-ing the whiskey rebels. They turned their anger against people of wealth and property. A rider cantered through the streets of Pittsburgh, waving a tomahawk, and chanting: "It is not the excise law that must go down; your district and associate judges must go down; your high offices and salaries. A great deal more is to be done. I am but beginning yet." The majority of these protestors had little or nothing to do with making or selling whiskey. They had almost no land and no knowledge of how to build a still.[6]

In Europe, the British and French governments were watching the cri-sis. The British minister in Philadelphia, George Hammond, was con-vinced that the United States was too large and geographically divided to survive as a nation. Hammond thought most Americans had a "rooted aversion" to a central government. This belief had been bolstered by clan-destine visits from westerners "of very decent manners and appearance,"

CHAPTER 18

A Master Politician Takes Charge

HE PASSIONATE LOVE AFFAIR with the French Revolution that Thomas Jefferson had contracted in Paris was still alive in his own and heart—and in the minds and hearts of James Madison and Monroe and tens of thousands of other members of the Democrat-ublican Party. They seethed with rage about the way President gton had turned the Whiskey Rebellion into a political triumph—identally added that dreadful (to them) word *force* to the power of sidency. Even more infuriating was the President's demolition of hocratic Societies.

hington strengthened the latter maneuver by having Secretary of mund Randolph write a series of newspaper essays under the sig-Germanicus," which explained the Societies' treasonous role in the Rebellion. The pen name was a clever use of Roman history. cus was a general who crushed a rebellion by German tribes on r of the Roman Empire.[1]

꽃

ocratic-Republicans' frustration did not find any plausible tar- closing months of 1794. But James Madison was soothed by a temporarily transcended politics: love. On September 15, 1794, gress was in adjournment, he married an attractive Philadelphia lley Payne Todd. Among those who played important roles in their meeting and engagement was Martha Washington. She old Dolley that in spite of their political differences, the Presi-

who told him they were "dissatisfied with the U.S. government and were determined to separate from it."

The Spanish minister, Joseph de Jaudene, received similar visits. Secretary of the Treasury Hamilton learned of the reports both ministers were sending to their governments, and informed President Washington. The information had further convinced him of the need for a massive display of federal force.[7]

After reviewing the militia army, Washington received a visit from two envoys from the rebels, Congressman William Findley, and David Redick, a former member of the Pennsylvania Executive Council. They did their utmost to dissuade the federal army from marching to Pittsburgh. They told the President that the protestors were now ready to pay the tax. They claimed there was evidence of "a vengeful spirit" in the army—another reason why they should not be allowed to pillage and plunder in their search for culprits.

The President assured the envoys he would handle this supposed problem. He made it clear he was no longer interested in an easily broken promise to resume paying the tax. He wanted "unequivocal proofs of absolute submission" to federal authority and a confession from the rebels that they had committed treason by attacking Tax Supervisor John Neville and his federal marshal escort.[8]

Another reason for Washington's sternness was the season of the year. By now his militiamen were feeling the chilly winds of October. He wanted to complete this demonstration of federal authority before the freezing temperatures of November arrived. Meanwhile, he made sure that the story of his reviewing the army was published in newspapers throughout America.

Beside Washington strode Governor Lee and his fellow officers, many of them also veterans of the struggle for independence. The President told the soldiers it was not their task to punish the whiskey rebels unless they resisted their orders. Courts of law would decide who was guilty of treason, and determine their fate.[9]

On October 21, the army marched west in two columns. The President headed back to Philadelphia, where Congress was gathering for its next session. Secretary of the Treasury Hamilton was left behind to supervise—but not to command—the army. Nonetheless, Democratic-Republican newspapers went berserk, claiming Hamilton's "appointment" was a first step to a dictatorship. Unperturbed and confident, the President reached the City of Brotherly Love in ample time to work on his address to Congress.

In western Pennsylvania, there were sporadic bursts of resistance, such as the appearance of liberty poles along the army's line of march. But the size of the army dissolved any organized resistance. The would-be leader of the proto-revolution, David Bradford, fled west into Indian territory, followed by several hundred of his followers. The would-be Robespierre who recommended importing a guillotine presumably went with him. The army eventually rounded up about 150 suspects, who were not treated gently while in captivity. But only two people were killed—an amazingly low figure, considering the ferocity of the defiance voiced in Braddock's Field and elsewhere.

In Philadelphia, the President went before Congress in mid-November. Most of his speech was devoted to the Whiskey Rebellion. He described how "symptoms of riot and violence" began to appear when "certain self-created societies" began condemning the federal government. Next came attempts to intimidate "federal officers" by "the vengeance of armed men," which destroyed their ability to sustain the laws. He discussed his attempt to achieve a peaceful solution and his decision to order the army to march when he saw that "malevolence was not pointed merely to a single law...A spirit inimical to all order actuated many of the offenders." He closed with the hope that all Americans would continue to support "that precious depository of American happiness, the Constitution of the United States." [10]

In the Senate, there was widespread approval for the President. The solons made a point of endorsing his condemnation of the "self-created" Democratic Societies. But in the House, there was antipathy. James Madison later told James Monroe that Washington's attack on the Societies was "the greatest error of his political life." [11]

At Monticello, Thomas Jefferson took an even darker view. He called Washington's denunciation of the Democratic Societies "one of the most extraordinary acts of boldness of which we have seen so many from the faction of the monocrats." He could only wonder why and how "the President should have permitted himself to be the organ of such an attack on the freedom of discussion, the freedom of writing, printing and publishing." [12]

Washington had done no such thing. For six years, he had tolerated the freest imaginable press in Philadelphia and other cities. His condemnation of the Democratic Societies was specific—their role in fomenting rebellion and disunion. Jefferson's generalizations were easy to proclaim from Monticello's hilltop, several hundred miles from the m Field, calling for guillotines and looting defenseless Pitts

Several months later, the ex-secretary of state wand into disdainful unrealism, telling James Monroe, in dist insurrection was announced and proclaimed and arme never be found." [13]

In their reply to the President's speech, Madison ar ocratic-Republicans omitted the term "self-created so sage. But they made it clear that they too denounced were devoted to the Constitution. "When viewed i House (in Madison's words) told Washington, the "s rection and its collapse demonstrated "the virtues of ter and the value of republican government."

Washington did not change his mind about the In a letter to John Jay around this time, he wrote societies have been the fomenters of the Western no doubt in the mind of anyone who will examine what Jefferson and Madison refused to do. They h violence that had swirled beyond the Allegheny the gruesome realities of the French Revolution.

Within a year, the victor in this contest woul The replacement of Citizen Genet and France's schemes—and the overthrow of the Jacobins i cratic Societies and their wild-eyed, pro-Fre President Washington's condemnation of thei derscored their extremism. They dwindled f these survivors disappeared before the end of

The presidency and the American people of their commitment to the Union until the difficult challenge awaited Washington in h with Great Britain. [15]

dent retained his affection for the "great little Madison," as some people still called him for his leadership at the Constitutional Convention.

When the Madisons returned to Philadelphia as a married couple later in the fall of 1794, they received an invitation to dine with the Washingtons "in a family way." This was a private meal with several other couples, far more intimate than the President's weekly official dinners. Martha also demonstrated her fondness for Dolley by giving her a wedding present—an exquisite cream pitcher given to the President by a French nobleman.[2]

On November 19, 1794, the day that President Washington reported the end of the Whiskey Rebellion to Congress, John Jay signed a treaty of "Amity, Commerce and Navigation" with Great Britain in London. For the rest of 1794, Philadelphians exchanged rumors about the treaty and paid desultory attention to the aftermath of the Whiskey Rebellion—the treason trials of the twenty men Governor Henry Lee's army had shipped to the nation's capital. Only two of the accused rebels were convicted by federal juries, and President Washington pardoned both of them. They were obviously men of limited brainpower, duped into acts of rebellion by leaders like David Bradford, who remained beyond the reach of the law somewhere in the West. [3]

Washington was not optimistic about Jay's treaty. In several letters to the envoy, he expressed his disgust with the anti-American hostility that prevailed in all parts of the British empire. He had no hope of achieving "any cordiality between the two countries." He would be satisfied if the treaty avoided a war. But if London refused to surrender those forts in the West, "war will be inevitable."[4]

From France, meanwhile, came reports that did not please the President any more than Britain's arrogance. James Monroe had made a speech to the French National Convention, congratulating them on their revolution, and presenting them with an American flag. This was a bizarre move against the background of the hundreds of innocent men and women being guillotined daily. Monroe went on to say that America admired "the wisdom and firmness" of France's current rulers, the Jacobins, as well as the valor of her armies, who continued to win victories on the battle-field. Jefferson's disciple also declared French and American interests were "identical."[5]

President Washington recommended and quickly approved a strong letter from Secretary of State Randolph, reminding Monroe that America was neutral and planned to stay that way. Randolph told the new diplomat that nothing in his instructions authorized "the extreme glow" of his speech. But the rebuke was neutered by another letter from the indecisive Randolph, admitting that the friendship of the French Republic was a matter of great importance, and should be promoted "with zeal."[6]

On another front, the President had to endure further political extrem-ism in the House of Representatives. When someone proposed that the House vote its thanks to General Anthony Wayne for his victory at Fallen Timbers, some Democratic-Republicans argued against the idea. Giving thanks to generals was the President's job, not Congress's, which repre-sented the voice of the people, a large majority of whom hated standing armies. After more debate, the Congress decided to thank Wayne's troops but conspicuously omitted their commander's name. Secretary of War Knox, with Washington's emphatic approval, ignored this idiocy and in-formed the general that he and his army had been voted "the unanimous thanks of the House of Representatives."[7]

In Georgia, the legislature opened fifty million acres of Creek Indian land to white settlers. President Washington warned that the state's deci-sion might "deeply affect the peace and welfare of the United States." But Congress was eager to adjourn. They did nothing about Georgia. The President dispatched three commissioners to talk with the Creeks and try to prevent another frontier war.

As the legislators departed, Washington informed each member of the Senate that he wanted them to return to Philadelphia for a special session on June 8, 1795. Their advice and consent was needed to deal with "certain matters affecting the public good." Everyone knew he was talking about the Jay Treaty, which would almost certainly arrive by that time, and re-quire their approval.

On March 7, 1795, three days after Congress adjourned, a weary Vir-ginian named David Blaney stumbled into Washington's residence. In his luggage was a copy of Jay's treaty, which he embellished with a description of his harrowing three-month voyage in mountainous seas, capped by a temporary capture and search for contraband by a French cruiser.

Accompanying the treaty were numerous letters from Jay to Washington and other men in the government. The envoy told the President the document was the best agreement he could get, and he challenged anyone to do better. "It must speak for itself," he wrote. "To do more was not possible." He added that nothing would have been achieved without "the confidence reposed in your personal character" by the English negotiators. To his friend Tench Coxe, whom the President had briefly considered as Thomas Jefferson's successor, Jay added even more surprising words: "It may seem strange…but next to the King, our President is more popular in this country (England) than any man in it."[8]

If that were true, it was grim testimony to how bad the treaty might have been without Washington's popularity as an inducement. The President's heart sank as he read the twenty-eight clauses of the document on his desk. Only one paragraph cheered him—an agreement to evacuate the forts in the Northwest Territory. Another positive clause promised to reimburse Americans for the hundreds of ships and cargoes that had been seized in the West Indies when those "mistaken" Orders in Council were issued. But it would take months, possibly years, to agree on the amount of money owed for each ship. Otherwise, the paragraphs were a litany of British arrogance—or negotiating skills—or both.

Americans would be permitted to trade with the West Indies. Good news, until the President read the stipulation that no ships larger than seventy tons would be allowed. Not a word was said about the Royal Navy's habit of kidnapping American sailors on the high seas. Nor was there even a murmur about paying Americans for the thousands of slaves the British took with them when they retreated from New York at the close of the War for Independence. One clause granted Britain most favored nation status—without conferring a similar privilege for American exports to Britain! (The term means that two countries agree to lower tariffs and/ or high import quotas in their commerce with each other.) Another clause permitted the British to seize as contraband almost any cargo bound for France that Royal Navy captains thought would enable the enemy "to carry on the war."[9]

It is not hard to imagine the President wondering if the document were a bad dream. But that massive calm George Washington was able to summon when confronting a crisis proved an invaluable resource. He focused for a long moment on the opening words: *A Treaty of Amity*. That was the essential phrase, the key to evaluating this lopsided diplomacy.

Those words stated in the clearest possible terms that the British did not want a war with the United States. Keeping America neutral was the central reason Washington had sent Jay to London. But how could he persuade Congress or the voters to see this treaty as a bargain worth accepting?

The President summoned Secretary of State Randolph. After a single reading, he agreed that there was only one policy for the moment—absolute, total secrecy. No one else should see this creature until the Senate returned on June 8. If it got into the newspapers now, the uproar would make it impossible for the solons to consider it objectively.

On June 8, 1795, the Senate reconvened on schedule and found copies of the treaty resting on each of the thirty desks in their chamber. With them was a terse message from the President, asking them to decide "in their wisdom" whether to advise and consent to it. He urged all the members to discuss it behind closed doors, under a binding promise of secrecy until they reached a decision.

From the Federalists, the first reaction was horror; from the Democratic-Republicans, predictable rage. The New England Federalists were especially upset by the limitation on the size of American ships trading with the West Indies. They were mollified when one of their senators suggested they demand a revision of that clause. This proposal enabled the Senate leaders to call for a vote. The treaty was approved, 20–10. A single defection would have failed to achieve the two-thirds majority.

The treaty was rushed back to President Washington, who now had to decide whether to sign it. He decided it was time to listen to the voice of the people. With the treaty ratified, there was no longer any need for secrecy. Before he could release it to the press with an appropriate message, Benjamin Franklin Bache published a summary in his newspaper, now called the *Aurora,* and followed it with a twenty-seven-page pamphlet, containing the full text. It had been leaked to him by a Democratic-Republican senator from Virginia. Bache was thus able to crow that he was letting "the people" read what the President had withheld from them for months.[10]

A delighted James Madison told James Monroe that the treaty "flew with an electric velocity to every part of the union." There was an explosion of fury from North to South and East to West. One of the wildest attacks came from New York, where Eleazer Oswald, a Washington enemy from Continental Army days, was publishing the *Independent Gazetteer.* Oswald had recently returned from France, where he had served as a lieutenant colonel of artillery in several battles. In his Fourth of July edition, Oswald proclaimed that "Mrs. Liberty" had died from a dose of "subtile (sic) poison" from King George III. The Jay Treaty made "our independence…not even nominal….Our sun, which rose with awful splendor, has sunk in pristine darkness."[11]

This rant was reprinted in dozens of other Democratic-Republican papers. Late in the evening of July 4, an intoxicated crowd carried an effigy of Jay through the streets of Philadelphia and burned it, after fighting a battle with a troop of the city's light horsemen who tried to disperse them. Soon other effigies of the envoy were burning in cities and towns across America.

The treaty was condemned in mass meetings in Boston, Charleston, and New York. Accelerating the process was editor Bache, who had departed from Philadelphia in a coach loaded with hundreds of copies of his pamphlet. In New York, on the wall of a building near Governor Jay's home, a gigantic early venture in graffiti shouted: DAMN JOHN JAY. DAMN EVERYONE THAT WON'T DAMN JOHN JAY. DAMN EVERYONE THAT WON'T PUT LIGHTS IN THE WINDOWS AND SIT UP ALL NIGHT DAMNING JOHN JAY.

Jay wryly remarked that on the night of the Fourth of July, so many effigies of him were burning, he could have walked from Georgia to Massachusetts by the light of their flames. In Charleston, South Carolina, the rioters revealed their political orientation: they celebrated Bastille Day by burning the Union Jack in front of the British consul's house.[12]

In Virginia, the "retired" ex-secretary of state was one of the most inflamed critics. The treaty's only value, Jefferson wrote, was that it prevented war. But this supposed virtue ignored "an eternal truth, that acquiescence under insult is not the way to escape war." This supposed axiom would come back to haunt him a decade later.[13]

The more Jefferson thought about the treaty in the quiet of his hilltop mansion, he saw it in purely political terms. Two months later, he told Madison that "a bolder party stroke was never struck." It was an attempt to stifle the Democratic-Republican majority in one branch of the legislature (The House of Representatives) by using the presidency and the Senate to prevent the House from "restraining the commerce of their patron-nation."

In another letter, Jefferson called the treaty "a monument of folly or venality." To a third friend, he described it as "an infamous act, which is nothing more than a treaty of alliance between England and the Anglo-men of this country against the legislature and people of the United States." Straining to put a positive gloss on these remarks, Jefferson's defenders have claimed he wrote only a comparative handful of letters containing such imprecations. But his correspondents included John Rutledge, the governor of South Carolina, and other men of distinction. There is little doubt that most of the nation's politicians were aware that the former secretary of state, who had supposedly retired from politics, was among the most violent critics of John Jay's Treaty of Amity.[14]

In Philadelphia, the President discussed the treaty with his new cabinet, and was not reassured by what they had to say. He sensed Secretary of State Edmund Randolph had serious doubts about the venture. The new Secretary of the Treasury, Oliver Wolcott of Connecticut, was a convinced Federalist. So was Timothy Pickering, the secretary of war. Their support of the treaty was political. The attorney general, William Bradford, had no experience in foreign policy, and had been chosen largely for his Virginia birth. Reluctantly, the President turned to a man who had given him a great deal of advice in the past: Alexander Hamilton. They had had almost no contact since he left office in January. On July 3, 1795, the President sent him a letter marked "private and entirely confidential."

Washington apologized for disrupting Hamilton's private life. But he would appreciate an analysis of the pros and cons of the treaty as soon as possible. Six days later, a masterfully organized avalanche of arguments and analyses began appearing on the President's desk. It confirmed almost all of Washington's thinking on the treaty. Two more installments arrived on the following two days.

Like Washington, Hamilton condemned the article banning all but toy sailboat-sized ships from the West Indies trade, and denounced the absurd attempt to make almost anything aboard a ship contraband of war if the British were so inclined. Once these were corrected, Hamilton maintained, the President should sign the treaty and America would be at peace with England. Then, "the force of circumstances will enable us to make our way sufficiently fast in trade." Like Washington, Hamilton was convinced that it would not take long for a prosperous America to be strong enough to deal with the British as equals. War at this time would only delay and possibly ruin this happy prospect.[15]

There it was, the difficult but crucial truth, stated with almost uncanny matter-of- factness. Surrounded by screaming mobs and mass meetings in Philadelphia, the President must have regarded the words as unreal. But they gathered power from the promise that they held out. Here, in spite of the chaos that the treaty seemed to be causing, was the thorny path to the happiness he must somehow persuade America to pursue.

§2

In Europe, the British and the French were still locked in all-out war, and American grain became a crucial commodity. The French were again facing famine and the British winter wheat crop had failed, exposing them to the same threat. Inevitably, the British resorted to the Royal Navy. They issued orders to begin seizing grain on American ships en route to France as contraband. This bad news reached Philadelphia as Washington pondered whether to sign the Jay Treaty. His reaction was instantaneous and decisive. He sent Secretary of State Randolph to the British envoy to tell him the treaty would never be signed until this latest contraband gambit was repealed. [16]

Washington made no attempt to answer the protestors in the streets of Philadelphia. During the worst of the uproar, he retreated to Mount Vernon and pretended to be absorbed in improving the operation of his farms. On his six-day trip south, the President talked with numerous men about the treaty, and found all of them hostile. In a letter to Hamilton, he revealed what he had learned. "The string which is most played on," he reported, "is the violation, as they term it, of our engagements with France." People saw the treaty as a "predilection to Great Britain at the expense of the French nation." This opinion was, of course, an endlessly reiterated point in the massive Democratic-Republican assault on the treaty.

Proof of the accuracy of this presidential discovery is a letter that the gleeful but still retired ex-secretary of state wrote to James Monroe around this time. He told the envoy that the treaty had "completely demolished the monarchical party here." The reason was delightfully simple. There was no need for anyone to try to "understand the particular articles" of the proposed agreement. "The whole body of the people" was condemning it because it wore "a hostile face to France."[17]

In New York, Alexander Hamilton launched a vigorous counterattack against the Democratic-Republicans under another classical pen name that commented sharply on the contemporary clash—Camillus. In Plutarch's

Lives, he was a wise and virtuous Roman general who tried to tell hard truths to the people, and was exiled by the hotheads in their midst. But Camillus was recalled and played a hero's role when an invading army of Gauls threatened to overrun the city. Along with vigorous arguments defending the treaty, Hamilton was suggesting that an army of Gauls (French) might descend on America if the Democratic-Republicans got their way, and the citizens might need George Washington's military skills to deal with them.

Over the next six months, Hamilton published twenty-eight of these hard-hitting essays, which were reprinted in newspapers everywhere. His first effort was aimed at a target who was doing his best to stay hidden. Hamilton accused the Democratic-Republicans of using the protests to destroy John Jay as a future presidential candidate and elect their leader, Thomas Jefferson. From Mount Vernon came a letter that made it clear one of Hamilton's readers was in agreement. "To judge of this work from the first number," the President wrote, "I augur well of the performance." He praised Hamilton's "clear, distinct and satisfactory" style. This was a covert way of saying he agreed with every word of it.[18]

The President's augury proved prophetic. As essay after trenchant essay appeared, many intimidated Federalist politicians began to take heart and join in defending the treaty. Hamilton was aided not a little by the news that in mid-August, Washington had signed the treaty, with the proviso that the disputed articles would be corrected in final negotiations.

In Virginia, another Hamilton reader grew more and more anxious. On September 21, 1795, Jefferson rushed a letter to James Madison, confessing that the former Secretary of the Treasury was a "colossus to the anti-republican party." It began to look like he was going to "extricate" the monarchists and Anglomen from the trap they had sprung on themselves. Democratic-Republican attempts to answer him had been "only middling performances." No one but Madison had the ability to challenge Hamilton's arguments.[19]

To Jefferson's dismay, Congressman Madison declined. He had his own plan to torpedo the treaty. It was based on Jefferson's claim that the Federalists were working for their "patron-nation," Britain. The Congressman began expounding a new theory: the House of Representatives could veto the agreement because the Constitution gave them the power to regulate commerce.

Madison must have known he was standing on its head the arguments he and Hamilton had made in *The Federalist* that the Senate alone should have this responsibility. His retired mentor at Monticello, who had warned him that the Constitution would not last very long in its original form, was enthusiastic about this total reversal. "I trust the popular branch of our legislature will….thus rid us of this infamous act," Jefferson wrote.[20]

Hamilton, hearing of their scheme, pointed out what it would mean if Madison won. America's foreign relations would no longer be primarily the president's responsibility. Almost every "species of treaty," Hamilton wrote, would be thrust into the hands of a Congress all too likely to talk it to death. An alarmed John Adams told his wife that if the Democratic-Republicans remained "desperate and unreasonable….this Constitution cannot stand. I see nothing but a dissolution of the government and immediate war."

Other thinking men agreed with Adams. Treasury Secretary Oliver Wolcott predicted, "One month will decide the fate of our country." Alexander Hamilton warned that if the treaty were not accepted, there would be a "foreign war" (with England), and if it were ratified in the present atmosphere, there might well be a "civil war."[21]

In Philadelphia, hundreds of violent resolutions damning the treaty piled up on Washington's desk. Most were too insulting to answer. Newspapers accused the President of plotting to dissolve all connections with France because he preferred a "monarchic ally"—England. Philip Freneau materialized from the pine trees of South Jersey to accuse Washington of planning to become King George I of America. Others told the President that Jefferson was describing him as senile and helpless in the hands of Hamilton and his friends.

In the midst of this barrage of insult and innuendo, Washington had to deal with an upheaval in his cabinet. The British had intercepted a ship carrying mail from Citizen Genet's replacement, Minister Joseph Fauchet, to his government. In one letter, he informed his superiors of confidential conversations he had conducted with Secretary of State Randolph, in which the latter confirmed his deep sympathy for revolutionary France and offered to put pressure on the President if Fauchet would advance him enough money to buy the loyalty of certain Virginians. The British rushed the letter to George Hammond, their envoy in Philadelphia, who gave it to Secretary of War Timothy Pickering. This acerbic gentleman accused Randolph of treason.

In a painful scene, the President challenged Randolph to explain himself. Stunned and floundering, the Secretary of State called the demand an insult and resigned. He was soon at work on a long essay, defending his reputation and accusing Washington of betraying him to the Federalists in his cabinet. The President struggled for weeks to find a replacement for Randolph. A half-dozen prospects, from New Jersey's William Paterson to Virginia's Patrick Henry, turned him down. No one wanted to share the cascade of abuse that was descending on the President.

Washington finally offered the job to the admittedly undiplomatic Timothy Pickering, who accepted it with reluctance. That meant he had to be replaced as secretary of war. At this point, Attorney General William Bradford died, which led to a double round of offers, refusals, and final acceptances from two fairly distinguished men. Marylander James McHenry, a popular aide to General Washington during the struggle for independence, became secretary of war, and Charles Lee, brother of Governor Henry Lee, attorney general.

Somehow, in the midst of these distractions, Washington kept his temper under control and focused on the most important task on his presidential agenda—his annual message to Congress. He sent Alexander Hamilton a detailed outline of his remarks, and worked closely with him on the text. At one point, he told Hamilton to call a halt and wait until Washington sent him a new "ground plan" for the speech. It was a sign not only of how important the President sensed this public appearance was, but of how much he wanted it to reflect his own thinking.

Tension ran high in Congress and in the spectators' gallery when Washington mounted the rostrum on December 8, 1795. They remembered the man who had condemned the Democratic Societies the year before. They expected even more thunderous denunciations of the mobs in the streets and the torrent of personal denunciations that were in every Democratic-Republican paper. Everyone knew how thin-skinned this man was—and how hot his temper could be. Senators and congressmen braced themselves for a memorable explosion.

Instead, the man who stood on the rostrum *smiled* solemnly at them and began speaking in a soft, unmistakably agreeable voice. "Fellow citizens," he began. Never before had he come before them so convinced that they had "just cause for mutual congratulations." He invited them to join him "in profound gratitude to the Author of all Good for the numerous and extraordinary blessings we enjoy."

Gasps of astonishment, gapes of amazement, blinks of disbelief circulated through Congress. The President began to describe these blessings. General Anthony Wayne, the man James Madison and his colleagues had refused to thank for the victory at Fallen Timbers, had just negotiated a treaty with five of the most warlike tribes in the Northwest Territory, promising peace and the opening of millions of acres of land to settlement. At the other end of the thousand-mile western frontier, the commissioners he had dispatched to the Creeks had persuaded the Indians to confirm treaties negotiated in past years. Not even "wanton murders" perpetrated by frontier Georgians had deterred them.

Next the President reported peace with the Emperor of Morocco and the Algerine pirates, thanks to another treaty. The Algerines had even promised to restore "our unfortunate fellow citizens from a grievous captivity." Then came truly sensational news. The special envoy to Madrid, Thomas Pinckney, had informed him that Spain had agreed to open the Mississippi River to American ships and products for export through New Orleans. This meant the discontent that was souring the public mind of Kentucky was banished, forever. The news would be greeted with equal pleasure by westerners in Virginia and Pennsylvania.

In the same mild voice, the President turned to Jay's Treaty. Now would come the explosion, everyone thought. But all he said was what the legislators already knew. He had signed it with "a condition that excepts part of one article." He had summoned the "best judgment" he "was able to form of the public interest" and with "full and mature deliberation added my sanction." It was now up to "His Britannic Majesty" to accept the change.

Whereupon the President urged Congress to join him in "consoling and gratifying reflections" on the promising future these agreements offered to the nation. He could only hope that "prudence and moderation on every side" would produce an end to the "external discord" that had recently "menaced our tranquility."

The dazed legislators were by now almost numb with surprise—or in some cases—disappointment. The President began discussing domestic matters. Now, surely, he would let the protestors and calumniators have it. Instead, he found "equal cause for contentment and satisfaction." While

Europe was being desolated by war and famine, our "favored country" was enjoying peace and prosperity. The President wondered if "it was too much to say" that America was becoming "a spectacle of national happiness" hitherto unseen in human history. He could only hope that Congress would continue to "unite" their efforts "to…improve our immense advantages." It was the "fervent and favorite" wish of his heart to "cooperate with you in this desirable work." Washington added a brief summary of what he called "internal disturbances." He swiftly made it clear he was talking about the Whiskey Rebellion. "The blessings of quiet and order" now prevailed in western Pennsylvania. Next he urged Congress to do more for the nation's defense. It was time to create a standing army and a decent-sized navy. Even more important was legislation to promote peace and understanding with their Indian neighbors. He spent several earnest minutes discussing how much this would please him and cast "luster on our national character."

Finally came closing words in the same mild, cordial voice. There would no doubt be "important subjects" for them to consider in the coming session of Congress. "Mutual forbearance" when there was a difference of opinion was "too obvious and necessary" to need any recommendation from him.

It was perhaps the most extraordinary performance of George Washington's life. The only comparable event was his resignation as commander in chief of the Continental Army in 1783. Then, he had rejected a crown and chosen to become a mere citizen again, subject to laws passed by a Congress that was almost hopelessly inept. Here, he was rescuing another Congress—and the entire federal government—as well as the nation he loved—from imminent dissolution. He was incidentally proving he was the master politician of his era. [22]

Painted after the 1777 battle of Princeton, this portrait reveals the inner confidence of a man who lived dangerously. General George Washington won America's independence by repeatedly out-thinking the British army as well as out-fighting it in a grueling eight-year war.

This is the youthful Thomas Jefferson who drafted the Declaration of Independence, failed disastrously as wartime Governor of Virginia, and became America's ambassador to France. There, another revolution became his "polar star"— immensely complicating his life as President Washington's secretary of state.

James Madison committed his brilliant intellect to creating a Constitution in response to his friend George Washington's call for a strong federal government. But Madison's much closer friendship with Thomas Jefferson eventually made him Washington's enemy.

West Indian born Alexander Hamilton went from General Washington's valued aide to President Washington's controversial Secretary of the Treasury. Washington shared Hamilton's vision of an industrialized America—a future Thomas Jefferson loathed.

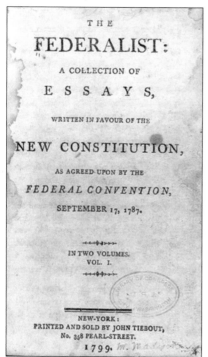

THE

FEDERALIST:

A COLLECTION OF

ESSAYS,

WRITTEN IN FAVOUR OF THE

NEW CONSTITUTION,

AS AGREED UPON BY THE

FEDERAL CONVENTION,

SEPTEMBER 17, 1787.

IN TWO VOLUMES.
VOL. I.

NEW-YORK:
PRINTED AND SOLD BY JOHN TIEBOUT,
No. 358 PEARL-STREET.
1799.

James Madison and Alexander Hamilton wrote almost all *The Federalist* essays—a brilliant defense of the new Constitution. George Washington predicted the essays would "merit the notice of posterity."

Thomas Paine's 1776 pamphlet, *Common Sense*, inspired Americans to fight for independence. The French Revolution was a different story. Paine narrowly escaped the guillotine. Convinced that Washington should have rescued him, the pamphleteer compared the President to the French mass executioner Maximilian Robespierre.

Unanimously elected in 1789, George Washington took the oath of office as first president on the balcony of Federal Hall in New York. He promised to bring "honest zeal" to the new office. The phrase underscores Washington's view of the presidency's crucial importance.

Ambassador Edmond-Charles Genet came to America certain he could convert the United States into a French satellite. Secretary of State Thomas Jefferson eagerly cooperated with him. But when Genet threatened to appeal to the American people to get rid of "Old Man Washington," Jefferson was forced to abandon the arrogant envoy.

In 1794 angry mobs in western Pennsylvania tarred and feathered federal agents trying to collect the tax on whiskey—and talked of seceding from the union. President Washington summoned 13,000 militia and smashed the proto-rebellion. Thomas Jefferson sneered that "an insurrection was proclaimed but could never be found."

President Washington asked Chief Justice of the Supreme Court John Jay to negotiate a treaty with Britain to avert a war. Jefferson and Madison denounced the document. Jay was burned in effigy everywhere. Washington persuaded Alexander Hamilton to defend the treaty in a series of newspaper articles that convinced most people peace was preferable to war.

An aging President Washington remained a masterful politician. In his Farewell Address, he underscored the vital importance of the federal union and deplored Americans who favored foreign countries above their own. Everyone realized he was stating fundamental principles—and also criticizing Thomas Jefferson.

With Washington's covert backing, John Adams defeated Thomas Jefferson to become the second president of the United States. Confronted by a hostile France and an even more hostile pro-French American press, Adams fell into a depression and stayed home in Massachusetts for seven months, governing the country by mail.

When President Adams appointed erratic Elbridge Gerry to negotiate peace with France, ex-President Washington—and many other people—feared the worst.

Vermont Congressman Matthew Lyon, a volatile Jeffersonian, spit in Connecticut Congressman Roger Griswold's face for calling him a coward. The next day the Jefferson-hating Griswold assaulted Lyon with his cane. The Vermont firebrand defended himself with a poker.

Thomas Jefferson called his presidency "The Revolution of 1800." He tried to do almost everything differently from President George Washington. When he mentioned Washington in speeches or letters, he referred to him as "our greatest revolutionary character" or "the General." His presidency was largely ignored.

New York Senator Aaron Burr ran as Jefferson's vice president in 1800. When both men received the same number of electoral votes, the election was thrown into the House of Representatives. Jefferson became convinced Burr was conniving to elbow him aside and become president.

President Jefferson refused to endorse Aaron Burr's run for governor of New York and encouraged local newspapers to destroy him. Alexander Hamilton claimed to be neutral but said damaging things about Burr's character. Burr challenged Hamilton to a duel and killed him with his first shot on July 11, 1804.

As First Consul for Life, Napoleon Bonaparte made it clear that France's 1789 revolution had become a cynical dictatorship. Nevertheless, President Jefferson approved Napoleon's desire to send an army to Santo Domingo— a move George Washington would almost certainly have opposed as menacing America's security.

When yellow fever destroyed the French army in Santo Domingo, Napoleon abandoned his plan to restore France's empire in America and sold the Louisiana Territory to an astonished Thomas Jefferson. Here troops raise the American flag in New Orleans' Place D'Armes making Jefferson's popularity immense.

President Washington dismissed James Monroe as a biased ambassador to France. With Jefferson's help, Monroe wrote a 400-page book attacking the President. When Monroe helped negotiate the Louisiana Purchase, he gave President Jefferson all the credit for it.

Convinced that the Louisiana Purchase meant Virginia would rule the nation, former Secretary of State Timothy Pickering launched a campaign to persuade New England to secede from the Union.

General James Wilkinson was commander in chief of the American army during President Jefferson's administration. The General secretly hated Jefferson and was a well-paid spy, known as Agent 13 in the Spanish secret service.

Defeated President John Adams appointed John Marshall Chief Justice of the United States. He began issuing decisions that enlarged the powers of the Federal government—and enraged President Jefferson. Marshall also wrote a biography of George Washington, refuting Jefferson's dismissive version of his presidency.

CHAPTER 19

The End of Three Friendships

T HE DEMOCRATIC-REPUBLICANS WERE BEWILDERED by the President's speech. A Virginia senator predicted it was a prelude to Washington's resignation. Congressman William Branch Giles, still thirsting for someone's blood, and having failed to spill Hamilton's, told Jefferson the speech was a Washington retreat that virtually conceded the Democratic-Republicans were now in control of the country's destiny.

James Madison was too intelligent to indulge in such fantasies. But he was still hoping to torpedo the Jay Treaty. He opened his campaign by persuading the House to delete a sentence in their response to the President's speech, in which they affirmed their "undiminished confidence" in his leadership. Madison thought it "squinted too favorably toward the [Jay] Treaty."[1]

Some still inflamed Democratic-Republicans, especially from New York, where they had lost the governorship to John Jay, wanted a more explicitly hostile stance. But Madison quailed at the thought of another confrontation with the President, which he was now sure his party would lose. What did these hotheads want him to do—declare himself opposed to the "state of national happiness" that Washington had affirmed? Everyone in a position to judge the matter knew the nation was more prosperous than anyone had imagined it could become in the days of the Continental Congress.

Demonstrating again the flexibility of the presidency, Washington further paralyzed the Democratic-Republicans by outmaneuvering a French attempt to embarrass him. Taking their cue from Minister James Monroe's gift of an American flag to hang in the chamber of the French National Convention, on January 1, 1796, the new French minister, Pierre-Auguste Adet, presented a handsome, gold-fringed tricolor to the President. He added an address that virtually proclaimed the identity of the two republics. Citizen Genet in his wildest moments could not have topped it.

Washington was unfazed. He calmly informed Minister Adet that he would deposit the beautiful flag in the "National Archives" and inform Congress of its reception. (In other words, it would NOT hang in Congress.) Then he launched into a paean of praise for France and the two nations' friendship. He himself, he noted, had been born in "a land of liberty" and had fought a "perilous conflict" to sustain it. His deepest and most sympathetic feelings had been aroused by France's struggle for her liberty. It would be a grievous understatement "to call your nation brave." He hoped "the friendship of the two republics" would endure forever.[2]

Once more, the Democratic-Republicans were reduced to baffled silence. All James Madison could do was tell Monroe that the "pro-British party" must be mortified to hear this presidential praise of France. Unfortunately, the Federalists were "cunning enough" to remain silent. He wished he could persuade inflamed Democratic-Republicans such as Congressman Edward Livingston of New York and Philadelphia newsman Benjamin Franklin Bache to also hold their tongues—and discard their pens.

Madison—and the retired Secretary of State in Virginia—would have been even more astonished—and perhaps mortified—if they had seen a letter that the President wrote to Gouverneur Morris around this time. The wealthy Morris had moved to London, where he was operating as a private businessman. But his connections inside the British government were strong. He sent a letter to Washington reporting that Prime Minister William Pitt's government was angry about the hostile tone of American newspapers. Washington sensed the behind-the-scenes touch of someone high in the London establishment.

Depending on Morris's discretion and friendship, the President wrote a reply that he hoped Morris would forward to some appropriate high-level official—perhaps Prime Minister Pitt or the foreign minister, Lord Grenville. The letter was nothing less than a compact history of British-American antagonism. Washington did not hesitate to mention his own anger and hostility in 1776—feelings that were shared by the vast majority of Americans at that time. Ever since, the British had done nothing to ameliorate these emotions. On the contrary, they had worsened them by sending as ministers, consuls, and other spokesmen nothing but the most "ungracious and obnoxious characters." They had incited the Indians to murder hundreds of Americans on the frontier and were now trying to block the treaty that General Wayne had negotiated.

Britain's conduct on the ocean was even worse. They blockaded American ports, kidnapped American seamen, and allowed "pirates" on the island of Bermuda to prey on American ships. The idea behind the ill-defined contraband policy remained in place, even though the latest version of it had been withdrawn. Why couldn't the British see that a liberal approach might win America's friendship? Why did she persist in virtually pushing her into the arms of France?

Would this have changed Madison and Jefferson's conviction that Washington was a passive tool of Federalist "Anglomen"? Probably not. Men in the grip of an ideology have little or no interest in contrary facts.

In Philadelphia, the seething Democratic-Republicans in the House of Representatives were spoiling for a brawl that would make the President their humbled servant. On Washington's sixty-fourth birthday, a Federalist congressman made a motion to adjourn for a half hour and call on the President to give him their best wishes. The proposal was put to a vote, and lost 50-38. Few people in the City of Brotherly Love paid the slightest attention to this snub. Madison nervously informed Jefferson that the birthday was celebrated in the city with "unexampled splendor." Church bells clanged and cannon boomed a salute, while a veritable horde of well-wishers crowded into and around the executive mansion.[3]

A jittery Congressman Madison continued to perfect his plan to ambush the Jay Treaty. His weapon was the Constitution's provision that money bills had to originate in the House. The treaty had several provisions that would require an expenditure of about $80,000. He intended to argue that this meant the House could veto the Jay Treaty. His supposedly retired mentor at Monticello thought this was a brilliant idea.

The war of words began on March 1 when the President sent the treaty to the House with a confirmation that it was the law of the land. British ratification had yet to arrive, so he was not yet asking for the money to fund it. Nevertheless, Congressman Livingston of New York leaped to his feet and demanded that the President transmit to the House all the correspondence about the treaty, including Jay's instructions. Madison shuddered. He told Jefferson that "the state of the business" was much too precarious for such a move.[4]

The House plunged into a wild debate, with the Federalists firing back at the Democratic-Republicans for trying to rewrite the Constitution. For a while, it looked like the Jeffersonians were winning. "At present," Madison told the ex-secretary of state, a majority of the House favored a Constitutional right to refuse to pass laws for executing a treaty. It came down to the question of whether "the people's chamber," as the Democratic-Republicans called the House, should vote money for a treaty that offended their pro-French sensibilities.[5]

The master of Monticello was delighted with the crisis. He told Monroe in Paris that a "precedent" was about to be set that would change everyone's "construction" [interpretation] of the Constitution. It would transfer "the powers of legislation" from the President and the Senate to the entire Congress.

As things stood, Jefferson continued, laws were being legislated by the first two entities, and anyone and everyone with whom the President signed a treaty. Indian chiefs and Algerine pirates were writing laws Americans had to obey. The former Secretary of State became so enthralled with his own arguments in favor of giving the House of Representatives a role in foreign policy, he told Monroe maybe "annihilating the whole treaty making power" of the president and Senate, "except as to making peace," might be the best way to go. Seldom did Jefferson more nakedly expose his hostility to the Constitution's separation of powers and its wariness of majority rule—the essence of the national charter.[6]

Beyond all doubt, Jefferson told Madison, the Jay Treaty was the issue on which such a large reversal of the current Constitution could deservedly be based. "The rights, the interest, the honor and faith of our nation" were in danger of being "grossly sacrificed." Jefferson reiterated his conviction that a "faction has entered into a conspiracy with the enemies of their country to chain down the legislature at the feet of both." It was time to undo this awful crime and rescue the nation from "the incomprehensible acquiescence of the only honest man [Washington] who has assented to it." Otherwise, they would have to exclaim "Curse on his virtues, they have undone his country."[7]

If ever a great man allowed his own arguments to make him a victim of paranoia, this letter was a prime example. Jefferson's aberration was reinforced when he learned that Madison had put Livingston's demand for the treaty's papers to a vote and it had carried by an encouraging 62–37. But this was only the first round in an epic brawl. Back to the House came President Washington's response—an absolute refusal. He said the House of Representatives had no right to see the documents. He cited the theoretically secret journal of the Constitutional Convention to prove that there were strong reasons why the treaty making power was confined to the president and the Senate.

Madison was shocked by the totality of the President's stand. Drifting into his own brand of paranoia, he was convinced that a message from Hamilton in distant New York was behind this reply. The fiendish Federalists were ready to "hazard" Washington's reputation "to save the faction agst the Reps of the people." The Congressman raved to Jefferson that the journal of the [Constitutional] Convention was "to be kept sacred until called for by some competent authority." Madison asked his mentor how this principle could be "reconciled with the use he [Washington] has made of it?" So far gone was the Congressman's once objective judgment, he did not seem to think the President was a competent authority.[8]

The House Democratic-Republicans now resorted to a caucus—the first use of this political weapon in American history. They obviously were hoping to keep everyone in line. Madison was soon telling Jefferson there was "sufficient firmness" displayed to make him think they would win the contest. But a great deal depended on whether they could avoid "an overt recontre with the Executive." It is fascinating, the way President Washington's former partner could not pronounce his name when Madison went head-to-head with him. Then Washington became an abstraction, "The Executive." Was guilt at work here? Deep in Madison's mind, did he know he was betraying Washington—and the Constitution—by his all-out embrace of Jefferson?[9]

Going for the jugular, Madison proposed two wily resolutions, declaring that the House was not claiming a right to make treaties, only to judge of "the expedience of treaties…on legislative subjects." The other asserted the congressmen had no obligation to tell the president what use they planned to make of the papers they were demanding. Both carried by 57–35, Madison triumphantly reported to Jefferson. Emboldened, he became as inflamed as Edward Livingston. He declared that the House should refuse to vote the money that the treaty was requesting. Instead, a new treaty should be negotiated, presumably by someone other than an "Angloman" like John Jay.[10]

Suddenly, the Democratic-Republicans began to hear things that lessened their confidence. Huge rallies in favor of the treaty were taking place in every major city. Bankers, merchants, and other community leaders were vociferously denouncing Madison and his supporters as warmongers and madmen. A dismayed Madison was soon reporting to Monticello that their majority had somehow "melted" to eight or nine votes. Previously inflamed Democratic-Republican congressmen were finding excuses to rush home to see sick wives or children in distant states.[11]

Next came a battle between the best orators on both sides. Pennsylvanian Albert Gallatin made one of the more noteworthy assaults, speaking in a thick French-Swiss accent, which did nothing to disguise his all-out approval of France and detestation of England. On the other side, the Federalist champion, Fisher Ames, was seriously ill; he wavered beside his chair more than once, seemingly on the brink of collapse. But his ninety minutes of denunciation of the attempt to dismiss the Jay Treaty were mesmerizing. Many consider it one of the half-dozen historic speeches in Congress's oratorical history. Madison could only watch as shaken Democratic-Republicans continued to melt away from his majority.

Then came a blow from an even more unexpected quarter. Thomas Pinckney's treaty with Spain had arrived on the President's desk on his birthday. It was as generous and comprehensive as the early reports had predicted. Fearful of a British-American alliance, Spain had broken its ties with Britain and was eager to do everything to mollify the United States into becoming a semi-ally. The Spaniards assured the President that the Mississippi would soon be an American waterway and New Orleans would welcome ships eager to buy grain from Kentucky and the western counties of Pennsylvania and the Carolinas. Madison nervously reported to Monticello that these hitherto passionately Democratic-Republican counties were sending numerous petitions in favor of Jay's Treaty. Worse, the Senate was talking of not ratifying the Spanish treaty until Madison and his followers accepted John Jay's document.[12]

A distraught Madison began telling his equally aghast mentor at Monticello that "the Banks, the British Merchts, the insurance comps" were "influencing individuals [in Congress] and frightening others" by "sounding the tocksin (sic) of foreign war and domestic convulsions." Soon Vice President Adams was wryly noting that "Mr. Madison looks worried to death. Pale, withered, haggard." The next vote on Madison's no-treaty resolution was 49–49. The chairman of the Committee of the Whole, a Democratic-Republican of course, took a deep breath and voted to accept the treaty. It was *finis* to Madison's—and Jefferson's—dreams of unconstitutional pro-French glory.[13]

A despairing Madison tried for a consolation prize, a preamble calling the treaty objectionable but acceptable, if the British promised to stop seizing American cargoes and seamen. A mournful final report went to Monticello: "A few wrongheads" had abandoned the party and the preamble lost by one vote. The game was truly over now. Madison could only add a self-pitying bulletin. The business "had been the most worrying and vexatious that [he] ever encountered."

At the end of May, as Congress headed for adjournment, a badly wounded Madison summed up the debacle for his commander in chief. "The people have been everywhere made to believe that the object of the H of Reps in resisting the treaty was war; and have thence listened to the summons 'to follow where Washington leads.'" Was it mere coincidence that this avoidance of war was the central reason why the President had accepted the treaty?[14]

Gradually, the weary Madison would discover another outcome of his attempt to cross swords with George Washington. Henceforth, the President regarded him as a traitorous former partner and ex-friend. He seldom wrote to or spoke to James Madison again. Never again was he invited to Mount Vernon. While Washington's disillusionment was silent and accumulative, others in the political arena were less inclined to say nothing. They rejoiced in Madison's new status as the ex-champion of Democratic-Republicanism. One of the more malevolent Federalist writers, a recent British arrival who used the nom de plume "Peter Porcupine," declared that Madison had dwindled to "a mere aide de camp without even the hope of retrieving his reputation."[15]

As Congress adjourned, Madison seemed to agree with him. "A crisis which ought to have been so managed as to fortify the Republican cause has left it in a very crippled condition," he glumly informed Jefferson. From Monticello came a mournful valedictory: "Republicanism must lie on its oars, resign the vessel to its pilot [Washington] and resign themselves to the course he thinks best for them."[16]

Gone were the claims of Hamilton's secret advice and innuendos about the President's incipient senility. Were Jefferson and Madison tacitly admitting they had been defeated by a shrewder politician? Of course not. But the high priest of the American incarnation of the French Revolution and his chief acolyte came very close to admitting this unswallowable truth.

The attacks on the President by newspapermen did not cease with this victory in the House of Representatives. Typical was an open letter from William Duane, one of Philadelphia's nastiest editors. He accused Washington of a "tyrannical act" in refusing the House's demand for the papers, of creating "fatal forms of state secrecy" and conspiring to attach "monarchical privilege to the presidency." Meanest—or silliest—of all was the claim that hypocrisy—the knowledge that all these acts were virtually crimes—had caused the President's "bright countenance" to fade like a wilting flower.

Benjamin Franklin Bache filled his paper with similar attacks. On June 30, he commented that only George Washington had anything to celebrate on the fast approaching Fourth of July. How long, he all but shrieked, would the American people allow themselves "to be *awed* by one man"?

The President grimly told his ex-aide, David Humphreys, that such attacks "will occasion no change in my conduct." He insisted that not once in his seven years as president had he been guilty of a "willful [deliberate] error." When Congress adjourned on June 1, Fisher Ames wryly remarked that he was amazed to find the world was still "right up." Washington may have had similar feelings, as he and Martha headed south to Mount Vernon for the first time in eight months.[17]

Early in July, when the President had barely begun to enjoy the tranquility that he so badly needed, a letter from Thomas Jefferson disturbed his vacation. The ex-secretary of state informed the President that he had just read in Benjamin Bache's *Aurora* a leaked copy of a document Washington had circulated among his cabinet members in 1793. It was a list of the issues raised by the outbreak of war between France and England, including the question of America's obligations under the 1778 Treaty of Alliance with France. During the House debate on the Jay Treaty, this document had been introduced by the Democratic-Republicans, in an attempt to prove that Washington had always intended to sever America's ties with France.

The mere mention of this issue proved no such thing. Moreover, the President had adjourned the cabinet meeting before it was discussed. But Jefferson was in a frenzy about it. He was afraid Washington thought he was the leaker. The man who had retired from politics invoked "everything sacred and honorable" to deny it. Not content with this guarantee, Jefferson launched into a passionate assurance that he had never written for any newspaper. Except for a single essay, he had never even corrected a political article composed by a friend. He had heard that a "miserable tergiversator [liar]" had told Washington he was "engaged in the bustle of politics and in turbulence and intrigue against the government."

It is painful to indict Jefferson for a bold-faced lie. These words suggest, 1: A defeated Jefferson feared Washington's wrath; 2: In spite of all the evidence that he had experienced firsthand, Jefferson still regarded Washington as some sort of uneducated simpleton, whom he, the brilliant graduate of the College of William and Mary, could manipulate at will.

Continuing, the man from Monticello claimed to be sure Washington did not believe this "tergiversator," but he felt compelled to reiterate how much he loathed "political discussion" and only rarely even expressed an opinion when asked explicitly by a friend. Jefferson now asked the President to search his files and return to him a document written by Alexander Hamilton that Jefferson had given him when they were embroiled with Citizen Genet and the ship *Little Sarah*. Mr. Jefferson's explanation for this request? "One loves to possess arms though they hope never to have occasion for them. They possess my paper in my own handwriting. It is just I should possess theirs."

One is left wondering why this brilliant man did not see any incongruity in these words from someone who repeatedly insisted he had no interest in politics, and even loathed the word. Is it further evidence that Jefferson considered the President too far gone in senility or original simplicity or both to ask this question?

Washington's reply soon made it clear that he had asked himself this question. He undoubtedly noted that his former friend and cabinet member did not mention writing political letters. As we have seen, Jefferson produced these in abundance, and Washington, who had once proved himself adept at finding out what his enemies were thinking while fighting a war, almost certainly had learned about more than a few of these exercises. The President began by admitting that people had told him that Jefferson had circulated "derogatory" opinions about him. In fact, they said Jefferson "denounced" him as a man in the grip of a "dangerous influence."

Washington, of course, knew this "influence" was named Alexander Hamilton. He proceeded to remind Jefferson that there were "as many instances when he decided against as in favor of the person alluded to." He also reminded him that in all the issues they had debated during Jefferson's cabinet years, as president, his sole interest had been to find the truth and make the right decisions. He *never* for a moment suspected Mr. Jefferson would be so insincere as to think otherwise. At the same time, he never saw himself—or anyone else—as infallible. That was something only a "party man" thought. He had never been one of these people. "The first wish of my heart, if parties did exist, was to reconcile them."

Then came a blast that became nothing less than a lecture on the danger of political extremism. Until the last year or two, Washington wrote, "I had no conception that parties would, or even could go the length I have been witness to." While he was using "his utmost exertions to establish a national character of our own, independent...of every nation of the earth, and wished, by steering a steady course, to preserve this country from the horrors of a desolating war...I was accused of being the enemy of one nation and subject to the influence of another." Every act of his administration was "tortured and the grossest and most insinuating misrepresentations made...The attackers resorted to "such exaggerated and indecent terms as could commonly be applied to a Nero, a notorious defaulter, or a common pickpocket.

"But enough of this..."

The President regained control of his temper. He had said enough in more ways than one. Mr. Jefferson had been forced to read in considerable detail what he had perpetrated with his passion for "the French Revolution. "This letter made it clear that it had cost him the friendship of the greatest man of their era.

Washington never wrote Jefferson another personal letter. Communication between them was, henceforth, in the words of one of Washington's best biographers, James Thomas Flexner, "pure routine." Unlike personal letters of earlier years, which were signed, "Affectionately yours," the farewell for this final one was a perfunctory "With great esteem."[18]

Later in the summer, another Jefferson lieutenant experienced the results of adhering too enthusiastically to the political creed of his retired chief at Monticello. In Paris, Minister James Monroe had continued to embrace France and the French Revolution with unbecoming fervor. He had ignored the warning letter he had received about his ecstatic speech to the National Convention and continued to talk in extravagant terms about the destiny of the two republics. When the Jay Treaty became an issue in American politics, Monroe did nothing to present it to the French as part of the President's policy of neutrality. Instead, he echoed Jefferson and Madison, and described it as the triumph of the British faction in American politics.

By this time, France was under the control of a five-man council known as the Directory. The radicalism of the Jacobins had been banished, along with Robespierre and his friends. Military victories, some of them won by a promising young general named Napoleon Bonaparte, fed the arrogance of the survivors, who still thought they could claim the magical word, *liberté* as their key to world power.

In early 1796, the French Minister of Foreign Affairs told Monroe that France now considered the 1778 Treaty of Alliance a dead letter. They were planning to send an envoy extraordinary to America to present President Washington with an ultimatum: France wanted a new treaty, giving them the same privileges and respect that the British had achieved in the Jay negotiation. Next the President received a letter from Gouverneur Morris in London, warning him of a rumor that this envoy extraordinary would be accompanied by a French fleet which had orders to start attacking American ships if Washington did not capitulate.[19]

An irked President blamed France's attitude on Madison's attempt to rewrite the Constitution to wreck the Jay Treaty, and "perhaps by communications of influential men in this country through a medium which ought to be the last to engage in it." The influential men were Jefferson and Madison and the medium was Monroe. It is another glimpse of the extent to which the ex-spymaster of Revolutionary days was aware of what the Democratic-Republicans were doing. Along with receiving a stream of letters from Jefferson and Madison, Monroe was sending them copies of what he was reporting to the President about French-American relations.

The coup de grace in this underhanded game was an essay that Monroe wrote for publication in Benjamin Franklin Bache's *Aurora*. It was supposedly a report from an anonymous American gentleman about "the state of things" in France. This diplomatic double-cross had been "inter-cepted"—no one has ever said how—and given to Secretary of State Pick-ering, who rushed it to the President. It was an all- out attack on the Jay Treaty and Washington's supposedly pro-British foreign policy. The essay was to be the first of a series that would be delivered to the salivating Bache for instant publication. Washington showed it to his new attorney general, Charles Lee, who told him Monroe's immediate recall was "indis-pensably necessary."[20]

On the heels of this discovery, gossip swirled through Philadelphia about a Paris dinner party Monroe attended on July 4. When someone proposed a toast to President Washington, several outspoken members of the party objected. Monroe suggested they might raise their glasses to "the Executive"—eliminating the supposedly detested name. Then came news from Secretary of the Treasury Oliver Wolcott that leaders in Kentucky and nearby states were receiving letters reviving Genet's scheme of a pro-French nation in the West. The final nail in Monroe's diplomatic coffin was a letter from John Quincy Adams, now envoy to the Netherlands, to his father that described how Monroe and others in Paris, notably Tom Paine, were telling the French that the United States had become a British ally.[21]

The President decided to recall Monroe, even though he knew the move would "set all the envenomed pens" to work. While Secretary of State Pickering's letter informing Monroe of the President's decision be-gan its voyage to France, Washington sent letters to several men who might be worthwhile replacements. He soon learned that Charles Cotesworth Pinckney, older brother of the man who had negotiated the Spanish treaty, was willing and able.

From Paris, Monroe wrote to James Madison, describing Secretary of State Pickering's letter of recall as something that might have been "ad-dressed as from an overseer on the farm to one of his gang ascribing...that it is altogether owing to my misconduct."[22]

Monroe wrote an infuriated reply to Pickering, claiming he had fol-lowed Washington's instructions to the letter and done everything in his power to prevent a rupture between France and America. The swelling discontent with the United States was not his fault. He had warned the President of the "probable ill consequences" of the Jay Treaty, and Wash-ington had ignored him.

Rather than return home and become the focus of a dispute between the two political parties, Monroe decided to travel in Europe for several months. He may have been aware that his defense would be difficult, once the Federalists produced his intercepted essay to Benjamin Franklin Bache. Another reason was almost certainly news from Madison that President Washington had decided not to run for another term, and the Democratic-Republicans were backing Thomas Jefferson against Vice President John Adams in the fall election. In an earlier letter to Madison, the envoy had remarked: "I most sincerely hope that Mr. Jefferson will be elected and that he will serve. If he is elected, everything will most probably be right here [in Paris] from that moment."

For Monroe, the master of Monticello still had almost magical powers. The ex-envoy began work on a book that that would eventually total 473 pages. Its title was as forbidding as its length: "*A View of the Conduct of the Executive, in the Foreign Affairs of the United States, connected to the mission to the French Republic during the years 1794, 5 and 6.*" Monroe's goal was the annihilation of George Washington's reputation. His editorial advisor—in deep background, of course—was Thomas Jefferson. He was soon telling Madison the book was "masterly…and unanswerable."[23]

CHAPTER 20

A Very Political Farewell

E VEN BEFORE HIS VICTORY over James Madison in the Jay Treaty
clash, George Washington had begun thinking about retirement.
Shrewd politician that he was, he realized the decision was not a simple
one. He worried about what the public would say when he made the announcement. He was still under almost daily attack from Benjamin Franklin Bache and other Democratic-Republican editors. Even his old nemesis,
Philip Freneau, got back in the game again with a short-lived paper he
floated from New Jersey, thick with the usual insults.

Would people be influenced by these partisans and sneer that he was
quitting because he knew there was no hope of being elected again—certainly not unanimously? The more he thought about it, the more convinced Washington became that it would be a good idea to issue a
statement, defending his reputation against the slanderers. He exhumed
from his files the brief speech he had prepared with James Madison's help
in 1792. Rereading it, he decided to make it the opening section of this
new message. It would prove that he had not desired a second term; even
better would be the evidence that it was "known to one or two of these
characters" [Madison and Jefferson] who were now bent on demolishing
him as a power hungry monocrat. [1]

When he sat down to write the statement, the President realized it
would be a mistake to say Madison had been involved in the draft of the
earlier announcement. The bipartisanship of the first term had become a
distant memory. Things had deteriorated so totally between the President

230

and the erudite little Congressman, the mere mention of Madison's name would make Washington look foolish.

Instead, he devoted the opening lines of his statement to discussing how rotation in the office of the presidency would be a bulwark of liberty for future generations. Turning to contemporary politics, he wrote a fierce attack on his critics. He accused them of filling newspapers "with all the invective that disappointment, ignorance of facts and malicious falsehoods could invent to misrepresent my politics." [2]

After reading over these first pages, the President decided to consult the man who had written so many of the documents that had played major roles in his presidency. The ex-secretary of the treasury, now working fifteen or sixteen hours a day as one of New York's busiest lawyers, responded with deep emotion. Alexander Hamilton immediately grasped the momentous nature of the statement the President was asking his help to create.

Over the next months, the two men worked their way through several drafts. Each felt free to add and discard, as their thinking about the statement evolved. Hamilton, for instance, jettisoned Washington's attack on his critics, arguing it made the address too blatantly political. The President tried to insert a paragraph on the importance of a national university in Washington, D.C.—an idea he fervently espoused. Hamilton persuaded him to shift this to his final message to Congress. The President warned Hamilton against being too wordy. Washington feared one of his early drafts would take up an entire edition of a newspaper.

In the final draft, the address of 1792 was only mentioned in passing, with the explanation that the "perplexed and critical posture of our affairs with foreign nations" had impelled him to abandon it. Now, Washington was glad to say that "the present circumstances of our country"—America's prosperity and peace—made him think no one would disapprove of his determination to retire. Then came deeply moving sentences about how grateful he was for "the constancy" of the American people's support when, at times, "the spirit of criticism" might have discouraged him. He would carry this gratitude with him to his grave, with the prayer that the Union, and the "brotherly affection" that sustained it, would be perpetual. He hoped with equal intensity that their "free constitution" would also be "sacredly maintained."

At this point, President Washington admitted he could and perhaps should stop. But "a solicitude for your welfare" prompted him to discuss dangers that he hoped Americans would avoid—now and in the future. He also hoped men and women would hear the advice he was about to offer as "disinterested warnings of a parting friend" who had "no personal motive" to distort his words.

At the top of the President's list was the crucial importance of "the unity of government which constitutes you one people." It was "the main pillar" in the edifice of "your real independence." It was also "the support of your tranquility at home, your peace abroad, of your safety, your prosperity, of that very Liberty which you so highly prize."

For a dozen paragraphs, Washington stressed the crucial importance of the federal union. He discussed the strengths of the different sections, North and South, East and West, and how they blended to create a thriving nation. A strong Union would enable them to avoid becoming like the Europeans, fighting endless wars between various sections of their continent. It would also help America avoid an "overgrown military establishment." If there were fears that a "common government" could not deal with so large a nation, let experience resolve their doubts.

Washington also warned against "geographical" prejudices which "designing men" may try to exploit. That was where the "fraternal affection" they had created in their struggle for independence should come into play. He admitted that political parties may be inevitable in a free society. But the "spirit of party" must never lose sight of the central value of the Union.

Then he turned to a subject that brought him into direct conflict with Thomas Jefferson and his followers. Nothing was more essential to a nation's happiness, the President declared, "than that permanent inveterate antipathies against particular nations and passionate attachments for others should be excluded" from the public mind. "Just and amicable feelings" toward all nations should be the rule. "The nation that indulges toward another a habitual hatred, or an habitual fondness, is in some degree a slave." Such a habit of mind will only lead to magnifying "accidental or trifling…disputes" into bloody contests.

Obviously remembering the storms of emotion he had endured as president, Washington dwelt on how a "passionate attachment" to one foreign nation "produces a variety of evils. It leads not only to wars but conceding to the favorite nation 'privileges denied to others.'" It also inclines "ambitious, corrupted or deluded citizens" an excuse to "betray or sacrifice the interests of their own country." The President was undoubtedly thinking of James Monroe in Paris when he wrote these words.

With a surge of emotion, Washington reiterated the importance of this point. "Against the insidious wiles of foreign influence (I conjure you to believe me, fellow citizens) the jealousy of a free people ought to be *constantly* awake." Foreign influence was particularly fatal to republican government. It led those who have succumbed to partiality to condemn those who disagree with them. "Real patriots...are liable to become suspected and odious." While the "tools and dupes" usurp the applause and confidence of the people. Can there be any doubt that he was talking about Thomas Jefferson and his followers, here?

Next, Washington turned to another aspect of the danger of favoring a foreign nation. "'Tis folly in one nation to look for disinterested favors from another." It is too likely to pay "with a portion of its independence" for accepting privileges offered under this guise. Here the words stirred memories of Citizen Genet and his hopes of turning America into a French satellite. "There can be no greater error than to expect or calculate upon real favors from Nation to Nation." It was "an illusion which experience must cure, which a just pride ought to discard."

The President closed with a statement of the policy that had guided his administration in foreign affairs. It was summed up in his *Proclamation of Neutrality*. "The spirit of this measure has continually governed me; uninfluenced by attempts to deter or avert me from it." Once more, there is little doubt that Washington was thinking of Thomas Jefferson and James Madison.

Solemnly, the President asked his fellow Americans to accept these words in the spirit in which he had composed them. He freely admitted that in his years of service, he had committed more than a few errors. He never claimed to be infallible. But he prayed to the Almighty to "mitigate" any evils that these mistakes may have caused.

Meanwhile, he hoped that the American people "under the benign influence of good laws under a free government" would achieve the happiness he wished for them. He saw this contentment as "the happy reward... of our mutual cares, labours, and dangers."[3]

In a decade or two, as the issues that animated these words faded away, the Farewell Address would acquire an oracular quality. By the time America entered the twentieth century, it had achieved fame on a par with the Declaration of Independence and the Gettysburg Address. But it can and should also be read as it was by men and women in 1796—as a demolition of Thomas Jefferson and his political party.

President Washington had no such anticipation of the address's enduring fame when he released it to the public. If a president wrote anything similar to it today, the words would vibrate from every newspaper, radio station, and television screen around the world. In 1796 Philadelphia, Washington summoned David Claypoole, publisher of the *American Daily Advertiser,* to his executive mansion. He gave the newsman his only copy of the manuscript, and asked him to print it as soon as possible.

The paper had a tradition of publishing important government documents, including the Declaration of Independence and the Constitution. Claypoole soon had the manuscript in type, and the President made several corrections on the proofs. When Washington gave his final approval, Claypoole returned the handwritten version. He confessed he had been so moved by it, he regretted letting it leave his hands.

The pleased President said, if he felt that way, he could keep it. This offhand act is an insight into Washington's innate modesty. It would also give generations of archivists and historians the bends whenever they thought of it. The handwritten copy has never been found.[4]

On September 19, 1796, the *Daily Advertiser* ran the address on page two of its four-page edition. As was customary, the front page was devoted to ads. There was no comment by the editor. He obviously thought the document needed none. The headline on the second page was only one column wide, in somewhat enlarged type.

TO THE PEOPLE OF THE UNITED STATES.
FRIENDS AND FELLOW CITIZENS.

The text filled the entire page and most of the next page. For the rest of the day, copies of the *Daily Advertiser* sold at an unprecedented rate. The edition also stirred wild excitement among other Philadelphia newspapers, who frantically ordered their typesetters to get to work. Three papers had copies on the street by that afternoon. Post riders galloped to New York, Boston, and other major cities with copies in their saddlebags.

In Philadelphia, Benjamin Franklin Bache published the address in the *Aurora* in two installments, without any comment—his way of saying that he considered it unworthy of his notice. His friend William Duane, who would later assume Bache's editorship of the *Aurora* and role as chief Democratic-Republican defender, published a long pamphlet, in which he abused Washington on every page. Another opposition paper summed up the address as the "loathings of a sick mind."

The Boston *Gazette* damned Washington's pretensions to saintliness and sneered at those who "worship at the shrine of Mt. Vernon." An angry James Madison vented his hostility to James Monroe in Paris, denouncing the President's "suspicion" of anyone who sympathized with France and her revolution. Like his mentor, Jefferson, he remained impervious to the Jacobin bloodbath.[5]

Unrelated to the Farewell Address but beautifully timed from Benjamin Franklin Bache's point of view, was a long open letter from Thomas Paine to President Washington. This passionate backer of the French Revolution had not approved its plunge into mass murder. In the National Convention, he had even opposed the execution of Louis XVI, predicting it would make him a martyr. This benevolence earned him the murderous enmity of Robespierre and his fellow Jacobins.

Arrested, Paine was flung into a fetid prison where he was soon a very sick man, physically and mentally. Envoy James Monroe procured his release, and discovered Paine was nursing a violent hatred of George Washington for failing to rescue him from his ordeal. One suspects, in spite of later denials, that Monroe's negative view of the President's politics had something to do with this antipathy.

The letter began by accusing the President of conniving at Paine's imprisonment. Washington had supposedly declined to inform the French government that Paine was an American citizen. This was, to say the least, a stretch, since Paine had accepted French citizenship and had served as a delegate in the National Convention. Brushing these facts aside, Paine claimed that Washington had secretly encouraged Robespierre to guillotine him to make sure he did not reveal the ugly truths about America's hero that he was now about to tell the world.

For pages, Paine blasted Washington as a liar and a secret enemy of liberty. "Almost the whole of your administration," he ranted, was "deceitful if not perfidious." Everything Washington did and said was part of a desire to destroy France and appease England. Turning to the President's military career, he sneered at his abilities as a general. "You slept away your time in the field till the finances of the country were completely exhausted," he raged. He gave Washington no credit for the victorious war.

Other generals, such as Horatio Gates and Nathanael Greene, won the crucial battles. Without aid from France, Washington's "cold and unmilitary conduct" would have "lost America."

Equally unimpressive was Washington's political career. Paine went on. The Constitution he had helped produce was "a copy, not quite so base as the original model—the British government." The essence of Washington's politics was meanness. He had no friendships. He was "incapable of forming any." He was "constitutionally" ready "to desert a man or a cause" whenever he saw it was to his advantage. Finally, the era's best known pamphleteer lunged to a peroration that was a cross between a roar and a howl: "Treacherous in private friendship...and a hypocrite in public life, the world will be puzzled to decide whether you are an impostate or an imposter, whether you have abandoned good principles or ever had any."[6]

The President did not stay in Philadelphia long enough to read Paine's diatribe or sample the reactions to The Farewell Address. He was in his carriage, on his way to Mount Vernon, the day the address was published. There, he was soon reading letters from friends and admirers, praising it extravagantly. Most Americans were deeply moved by the calm tone and wise sentiments. Few beside active politicians commented on the implied attack on Thomas Jefferson and his Democratic-Republican Party's policies. The majority of the readers were awed as well as exalted to realize that Washington was again relinquishing political power without bloodshed. In England, George III said this made it a certainty that the President would become "the greatest character of his age."[7]

CHAPTER 21

Martha Washington Sends
a Message

ORATOR FISHER AMES TOLD Secretary of the Treasury Oliver Wolcott that the Farewell Address was "a signal, like the dropping of a hat, for party racers to start." Everyone knew what Ames meant. With Washington out of the running, the presidential election of 1796 had begun. Even before the Farewell Address made this clear, many people had been predicting that the contestants would be John Adams and Thomas Jefferson. Alexander Hamilton confirmed this probability when he published a savage attack on Jefferson in the *Gazette of the United States* on October 16, 1796. The blast was the first of twenty-five equally fierce assaults in the next five weeks. [1]

It seems more than likely that Hamilton—and Washington—saw these articles as making explicit what was implied in the Farewell Address: Thomas Jefferson was unfit to be the next president. Using the pen name Phocion, Hamilton repeatedly dwelt on Jefferson's blind worship of the French Revolution. Other rhetorical flights mocked his lack of physical courage—dramatized by his flight from British dragoons when he was governor of Virginia. Hamilton saw similar cowardice in Jefferson's retreat from Washington's cabinet when the nation was confronting international threats that should have been the special concern of a secretary of state.

Especially mocked was Jefferson's repeated claim that he had no political ambitions—and detested all aspects of seeking and wielding power. Far from it, Phocion/Hamilton declared. He was a proto-Caesar who "coyly refused the proffered diadem" while secretly doing everything in his power to obtain it. In a word, he was a hypocrite.[2]

Phocion/Hamilton's view of John Adams was drastically different. He was a man "pure and unspotted in private life" and a citizen "preeminent for his early, intrepid, faithful, persevering and comprehensively useful services" to his country. He was also no monarchist. Jefferson's followers in the press had spread this smear about the Vice President. True, he believed in checks and balances in the federal government, on the British model. But that was a long way from seeking kingship for himself or anyone else.[3]

❦

Neither candidate campaigned in any modern sense of that word. Jefferson did not move off his mountaintop, and John Adams spent much of the time on his farm in Braintree, Massachusetts. But spokesmen supplied verbiage by the ton in their newspapers and pamphlets. The Federalists followed Phocion/Hamilton's lead, portraying Jefferson as a deeply flawed, dangerous man. The Democratic-Republicans insisted Adams was a closet monarchist.

When voters got beyond the rhetoric and compared the careers of the two men, Adams was clearly superior in terms of public achievements. In the Continental Congress, he had been the "Atlas of Independence," whose speeches had persuaded Congress to approve America's break with England. In Europe, he had played an equally major role in the peace negotiations. Jefferson's backers replied by hailing their candidate as the author—not the mere drafter—of the Declaration of Independence.

Adding to the drama was the discovery that Hamilton was secretly backing a third candidate, South Carolina's Thomas Pinckney, the negotiator of the treaty with Spain that opened the Mississippi. He was popular in both the West and South. Hamilton hoped that enough members of the electoral college would vote for him as their second choice, and the total would exceed both Adams and Jefferson. Hamilton thought Pinckney would be far more amenable to party politics than the stubborn, opinionated Adams.[4]

❦

Early in the contest, the Democratic-Republicans discovered they had an unexpected ally—the French envoy, Pierre-Auguste Adet. When he forwarded the Farewell Address to Paris, Adet had denounced "the lies it contains, the insolent tone that governs it, the immorality which characterizes it." President Washington had scarcely returned from his visit to Mount Vernon at the close of October 1796, when Adet published a violent letter in the *Aurora,* addressed to Secretary of State Pickering. He excoriated Washington's administration for its hostility to France and announced that the French would start seizing American ships and searching them for contraband, in the English style.

This was grim news. Even worse was Adet's studied insult to the President—to go public with such a drastic change in policy before submitting it to the Secretary of State for possible negotiation.

Behind this unpleasant shift to outright hostility was a letter that Thomas Jefferson had written to Adet in October of the preceding year. The retired Secretary of State had launched into a passionate declaration of the virtual identity of Revolutionary France and America. "Two people(s) whose interests, whose principles, whose habits of attachment, founded on fellowship in war and mutual kindnesses, have so many points of union, cannot but be easily kept together," Jefferson declared. A veritable explosion of adoration followed, ending with: "our struggles for liberty keep alive the only sensation which public affairs now excite in me."[5]

Jefferson knew people were talking about him as a possible successor to Washington. He also knew Adet would communicate this embrace of France to his superiors in Paris. The diplomat was soon telling his foreign minister how pleased he was by "the trust which the leaders of the Republican Party reposed in me." The Farewell Address had almost made him request a recall to Paris. But "the approach of the nominations for President, the necessity to get out the vote for a man devoted to France, the services I could render to the Republic after his election" changed the envoy's mind about going home. Adet was soon telling his foreign minister about "the friendship and confidence which the leaders of the Republican Party have shown to me...the share I have had in...their projects and plans, my perfect knowledge of the means they intend to employ."

In New York, another Frenchman, Edmond Genet, was reading the newspapers and brooding not a little about his old friend, "Mr. Jeff," running for president. Genet wrote a thirty-eight-page letter to the candidate, which was anything but complimentary. His motive was a speech that William Branch Giles had made in Congress, describing the ex-envoy as a wild man who had threatened to oust President Washington and other-wise made Secretary of State Jefferson's life miserable.

Genet began with a savage comment on Jefferson's career. "I only knew you, sir, before my nomination to the United States mission, through the useful, however timid, role you played in the American Revolution." As Secretary of State, Jefferson had initiated him into "the foibles and secrets of your cabinet, of the political divisions of your country." So he decided to "give myself up to you who seemed so well disposed."

Then, as the political tumult intensified, "Fear took possession of your soul" and Jefferson cruelly sought "to deprive me of the weapons which you had given me, to unpopularize me and to smother the republican fires which were being kindled on all sides." Now it was time for Thomas Jefferson to admit this betrayal, which he had helped to perpetrate, while pretending a weariness with politics. Genet wanted "a reparation as brilliant as the outrages which I endured…"

The letter was nothing less than a keg of gunpowder, with the fuse sizzling. Fortunately for candidate Jefferson, Citizen Genet showed it to his father-in-law, Governor George Clinton. This horrified gentleman persuaded the enraged ex-envoy not to send it to the newspapers—thereby acquiring a debt of gratitude that candidate Jefferson would one day have to repay.[6]

There was as yet no national election day, only clusters of state election days. Theoretically, Vice President John Adams was running with Pinckney on the Federalist ticket and Jefferson was running with Senator Aaron Burr of New York on the Republican ticket. Any one of the four could win the presidency if he garnered enough electoral votes. The Twelfth Amendment, making a two-man presidential ticket a single entity, was still in the future. But electioneering tactics were in full flower. The New England states, aware of Hamilton's secret backing of Pinckney, made a point of not making the South Carolinian their second choice.

By December, the electoral votes had been counted and it was soon—if not officially—known that John Adams had won with seventy-one yeas, and Thomas Jefferson had finished second with sixty-eight. Thomas Pinckney was third with fifty-nine, and Aaron Burr a poor fourth with thirty. That meant Jefferson would be vice president—a job that Adams had frequently described as a political nullity. Fisher Ames was not so sure this would be the case with Jefferson. Party politics was in the saddle and Ames foresaw that "two presidents, like two suns in the meridian, would meet and jostle for four years." Then, he feared, "vice would be first."[7]

When the new Vice President heard the news, he rushed a letter to James Madison assuring him he was not in the least disturbed by his second-place finish. With the French in a rage at America, Jefferson thought foreign affairs "never [had] so gloomy an aspect since the year 1783. Let those come to the helm who think they can steer clear of the difficulties. I have no confidence in myself for the undertaking."[8]

If Jefferson was apparently not disappointed, the same could not be said for envoy Pierre-Auguste Adet. He had discovered his influence was neither wanted nor approved by most Americans. He glumly informed his foreign minister that he had begun to doubt that Jefferson "was entirely devoted to our interest." He liked France largely because "he detests England." When and if Great Britain "ceased to frighten him, he would change his feelings toward us." Jefferson, the minister Adet sourly concluded, "is an American."

❦

In mid-December, at a reception, Martha Washington found a moment for a confidential exchange with John Adams. She congratulated him on his victory and told him that her husband was equally delighted. It was a revealing moment in several ways. Martha would not have been entrusted with such an important message if she abided by the prevailing idea that politics was not a woman's sphere. Thomas Jefferson was firmly of this opinion. The contrary would seem to be true in the Washington marriage. As Martha and her husband testified in their letters, they regarded each other as friends—a word with large meaning in their era. A friend was someone to whom a man or a woman could and would share his most significant thoughts and feelings.

Another implication of Martha's message was all too clear. The President had not wanted Thomas Jefferson to become his successor. Can we doubt that he had communicated this opinion to numerous people, starting with Martha and Alexander Hamilton? That night, John Adams rushed a letter to Abigail, who was still at home in Massachusetts. "John Adams never felt more serene in his life," he told her.

Adding to the President-elect's pleasure was the soon-confirmed rumor that James Madison was abandoning politics for the peace and quiet of his Orange County mansion, Montpelier. With a wry glance at Jefferson's supposed retirement, Adams scoffed at the idea that the Congressman's retreat would be permanent: "It is amazing how some political trees grow in the shade." [9]

☘

Around the time that Martha Washington was conveying her husband's congratulations to Adams, Thomas Jefferson wrote the President-elect a note saying far more extravagant things. He hoped his old friend's term would be "filled with glory and happiness to yourself and advantage to us." He felt not the slightest envy—he had "no ambition to govern men."

With that marvelous ability to pursue his own political agenda in spite of repeated denials, Jefferson launched a savage attack on Alexander Hamilton for trying to intrigue Adams out of his triumph with his secret backing of Thomas Pinckney. Jefferson called it "a trick worthy of the subtlety of your arch-friend of New York." He compared this attempt to convert men into "tools" with his own warm memories of the time when "we were working for our independence."

Confirming the fact that his letter was a political weapon, Jefferson sent it to Madison, asking his opinion on the wisdom of sending it. He had written it, he explained, hoping to induce Adams "to administer the government on it's (sic) true principles and to relinquish his bias to an English constitution." Jefferson also thought it was important to "come to a good understanding with him as to his future elections. He is perhaps the only sure barrier against Hamilton getting in."

If Jefferson meant that last sentence, he had inexplicably forgotten that James Monroe had long ago told him the story of Hamilton's affair with Maria Reynolds. It was a virtual guarantee of Hamilton not becoming president. Jefferson's real purpose here was an attempt to damage Adams's relationship with the chief spokesman of the Federalist Party—and make his election to a second term improbable.

Madison told Jefferson not to send the letter. He feared Adams might view the attack on Hamilton as an attempt to rupture the Federalist Party. (Yet another instance of Madison's superior political judgment.) He also warned his once and future candidate that the new president's policies might "force an opposition" to them. That could create "real embarrassments" if President Adams possessed a letter full of "the degree of compliment" that Jefferson had given him.

Jefferson decided on a better approach. He had received a congratulatory letter from Senator John Langdon of New Hampshire, a warm friend of Adams. He would respond with "exactly the [same] things he had written to Adams," knowing that the Senator would repeat them to the new president.[10]

Here was additional evidence that Fisher Ames might be right about the "Vice" becoming first in four years. As for George Washington, he had no idea that a climactic clash with his ex-secretary of state was awaiting him during John Adams's presidency.

CHAPTER 22

The Vice President
as Party Boss

O N MARCH 2, 1797, when Thomas Jefferson arrived in Philadelphia to take the oath of office as vice president, he was greeted by a
large crowd plus a company of artillery hauling two twelve-pound cannon.
The guns boomed sixteen rounds, one for each state in the Union, and the
cheering crowd waved a flag that read: JEFFERSON, THE FRIEND OF
THE PEOPLE. Thomas Mifflin, still the governor of Pennsylvania, was
once more trying to discomfit George Washington. Mifflin's right-hand
man, Alexander James Dallas, who was often the acting governor, since
Mifflin was drunk a great deal of the time, was no doubt on hand, direct-
ing the celebration. The message was unmistakable. Jefferson's followers
considered the vice presidency a mere pause on his way to the nation's
highest office.[1]

Although Jefferson had made a pro forma statement to James Madison
that he wanted to avoid all such displays, he was not entirely averse to accepting this greeting from one of the President's oldest enemies. George
Washington's impending departure had stirred not a little bitterness in his
soul. As General and President, Washington had survived so many challenges and difficulties, while Jefferson's career was stained by his failures
and flights as wartime governor of Virginia and his inglorious retreat from
the President's cabinet.

In a letter to Madison, the Vice President-elect virtually snarled that
Washington was "fortunate to get off just as the bubble is bursting, leaving

others to hold the bag." The coming difficulties "would be ascribed to the new administration and…he will have his usual good fortune of reaping credit for the good acts of others and leaving to them that of his errors." [2]

Jefferson still found it impossible to credit Washington for the political skills that had piloted the ship of state between the reefs of a war with England and the shoals of a takeover by France. Worse, the men in charge of his beloved French Revolution—the Directory—were very close to declaring war on the United States.

Further irritating Jefferson was the contentment that pervaded most of the nation. Thanks to Hamilton's financial system and a huge increase in commerce with the West Indies and Europe, America was incredibly prosperous. Salaries of skilled workers and laborers in Philadelphia and other cities had doubled in the previous four years. Farmers were getting ever higher prices for their corn and wheat and cotton. On February 22, twelve hundred well-dressed admirers celebrated Washington's birthday at Philadelphia's sprawling Ricketts Amphitheater, normally the site of visiting circuses. "For splendor, taste and elegance," wrote David Claypoole, the publisher of the Farewell Address, the affair "was perhaps never excelled by any entertainment in the United States." Martha Washington reportedly shed tears of happiness to see and hear so much affection heaped on her smiling husband. [3]

On inauguration day (March 4, 1797), the departing President walked alone to Congress Hall. He wore a simple black suit and a military hat with a black cockade. Jefferson, too, walked, wearing a long, blue frock coat. President-elect John Adams arrived in a gleaming new two-horse carriage with a coachman and footman. The incoming chief executive wore a pearl colored broadcloth suit with wrist ruffles and a powdered wig. Some Democratic-Republicans sneered that he was trying to look like a man of the people by using only two horses, whereas "monarchical" President Washington had preferred four steeds and sometimes six.

When the crowd around Congress Hall saw Washington approach, there was a tremendous explosion of cheers. In the House of Representatives, the applause was thunderous. President-elect Adams and Vice President-elect Jefferson also got hearty bursts of clapping. It was a day of more than justified rejoicing. The United States was witnessing a peaceful transfer of political power, something so rare it won exclamations of amazement around the nation and the world. Congressman William Loughton Smith of South Carolina described it as happening with "a facility and calm which has astonished even those of us who always augured well of the government and the good sense of our citizens. The machine has worked without a creak."[4]

Almost everyone gave Washington most of the credit for this semi-miracle. Some people disagreed, of course. Benjamin Franklin Bache's editorial in the *Aurora* declared the departing president had done everything in his power to "canker the principles of republicanism in an enlightened people." Not content with this canard, Bache went back to the first military action of Washington's career. In 1754, he had been leading a reconnaissance party on the Virginia frontier and collided with a French patrol. In Bache's version, Washington ordered his men to open fire, even though the French were displaying a flag of truce. The French commander was killed in the first volley. Bache called it "an act of assassination." For Democratic-Republican readers in 1797, this fictionalized history proved that Washington had always hated the French and it was no surprise to see him so violently opposed to an alliance with Paris.[5]

⚜

In the chamber of the House of Representatives, President Adams gave an inaugural address that was brief but very much to the point. He paid tribute to ex-President Washington and declared his deep admiration for the Constitution. He alluded almost offhandedly to his narrow victory and affirmed his desire for peace with France. But he also warned in sharp language against the danger of "foreign intrigue" in America's politics. This was an undoubted reference—and rebuke—to Minister Plenipotentiary Adet's barefaced campaigning for the Democratic-Republican ticket. In a more subtle rebuke to the opposition's obsession with monarchical tendencies, Adams denied he had ever entertained the slightest fondness for royal government and affirmed his faith in the republican brand.

While he spoke, Adams noticed tears streaming down the faces of numerous listeners, both in the galleries and on the floor of the House. It dawned on him that they were weeping over Washington's departure. In a letter to Abigail, he wryly pretended he was unsure whether they were grieving for "the loss of their beloved President [or the arrival] of an unbeloved one." Or maybe it was "the joy of exchanging presidents without tumult." Or maybe it was the sheer "sublimity" of his speech.[6]

On March 3, the day before the inauguration, Adams had called on Jefferson at the Madisons' home, where the incoming Vice President was staying. The President-elect was upset about the looming crisis with France. The French had recalled Minister Plenipotentiary Adet and refused to accept Charles Cotesworth Pinckney as James Monroe's replacement. Such gestures often preceded a declaration of war. Adams told Jefferson he wished he could send him to Paris as a special ambassador.

That was impossible, of course. But perhaps Jefferson could persuade James Madison to go. Adams had a bipartisan commission in mind, men from both parties. Jefferson said he would consult Madison, but he warned it was a hopeless task. The Congressman was unalterably opposed to risking his fragile health in a six- or eight-week voyage across the Atlantic Ocean.

Three days later, after a pleasant farewell dinner with George Washington, at which politics was somehow avoided, Jefferson and Adams again discussed Madison as an envoy. As Jefferson had predicted, the Congressman had turned down the proposal. Adams confessed that after conferring for the first time with his cabinet, he now had second thoughts about the idea.

To reassure the public that he was following in Washington's footsteps, Adams had retained all of the first president's cabinet officers. They had told him that Madison would just be Monroe with a different name. When Adams lamented this adherence to "party passions," Secretary of the Treasury Oliver Wolcott threatened to resign. It was grim evidence of the gulf between the two parties—and an ominous hint of a possible gulf between the new president and the Federalist Party that had elected him.[7]

✤

Relations with France continued to deteriorate. Before 1797 ended, French warships would seize over three hundred American merchantmen. A troubled President Adams called Congress into special session in May. He reiterated his desire to achieve a peaceful understanding with Paris. But he thought it equally important to prepare for war. He called on Congress to put cannon on American cargo ships, fortify American ports, and create an adequate U.S. Navy.

In 1794, during the crisis over the Jay Treaty, President Washington had made a similar request, and Congress had commissioned six warships. But the trickle of money they voted for their construction had turned the process into a slow-motion charade. Only three frigates were anywhere near the point of being launched. Congress insisted these would be enough to masquerade as a navy.

Vice President Jefferson was dismayed by the President's belligerent stance. He told acquaintances and newspapermen such as Benjamin Franklin Bache that Adams was a warmonger. This rhetoric had not a little to do with Congress's resistance to the President's proposals. It is easy to see why wiser men soon realized that it was necessary to amend the Constitution and ensure that the vice president and the president belonged to the same party. The memory of Vice President Jefferson sabotaging President Adams's policies was a convincing argument, in itself.[8]

⚜

To prove his peaceful intentions, the President launched a three-man commission to negotiate an agreement with Paris. Repudiated minister Charles Cotesworth Pinckney would be joined by Federalist Congressman John Marshall of Virginia and Democratic-Republican Elbridge Gerry of Massachusetts. The cabinet begged Adams not to send the erratic, argumentative Gerry, but he was an old friend and the President insisted on having his way.

The new President's stubbornness was a fact of life to which the cabinet was becoming unhappily accustomed. Oliver Wolcott compared it to the way the god Jupiter supposedly governed from Olympus: "Without regarding the opinions of friends or enemies, all are summoned to hear, reverence and obey."[9]

In the Senate, Vice President Jefferson swiftly took command of the Democratic-Republican Party. It was another ironic comment on his supposed distaste for politics. He was soon reporting to retired James Madison how the party voted in the House as well as in the upper chamber where he presided. When the Federalists fired his friend and backstage operator John Beckley as clerk of the House, Jefferson saw it as a blow to "the Republican interest." When three Virginians started voting with the Federalists in the House, the Vice President called them "renegadoes."[10]

Jefferson lived at the St. Francis Hotel, where, one Federalist sourly remarked, he was surrounded by a "knot of Jacobins"—also known as

Democratic-Republican senators and congressmen. He eagerly thrust his oar into the nomination of Elbridge Gerry as a peace commissioner. In a letter to Gerry, Jefferson said he was "a spring of hope" in the darkness of Federalist hostility to France.[11]

When dismissed envoy James Monroe returned to Philadelphia during the special session of Congress, Jefferson and fifty Democratic-Republican congressmen gave him a sumptuous dinner at Oeller's Hotel. Federalists were outraged. They regarded Monroe as a virtual traitor to his country for his sycophantic worship of the French Revolution during his days in Paris.

There was more than an undercurrent of defiance in Jefferson's public embrace of Monroe. As the special session of Congress began, Federalist newspapers had gotten their hands on a copy of a letter he had written to his Italian friend Philip Mazzei at the height of the controversy over the Jay Treaty. Reporting on the state of American politics, Jefferson described the Federalists as "an Anglican, monarchical and aristocratic party." Shifting to individuals, he told Mazzei it "would give you a fever were I to pass on to you the apostates who have gone over to these heresies, men who were Samsons in the field & Solomons in the council, who have had their heads shorn by the harlot, England."

Mazzei had sent this explosive message to friends in Paris, who were delighted to publish it. Soon it was translated back into English for London readers and inevitably made its way to America. Federalists declared the letter was an insult to George Washington. Who else had been a "Samson" on the field of battle as well as a "Solomon" in the nation's councils?

Monroe urged Jefferson to publish a defense. Madison advised him to remain silent. Such a statement might lead to "disagreeable explanations or…tacit confessions." Jefferson took this advice but it was not a pleasant solution. More than one Philadelphia gentleman and/or his wife crossed the street when they saw the Vice President approaching. Federalist newspapermen began calling him "Monsieur Jefferson." One editor called his opinion treasonous. [12]

During this same summer of 1797, Jefferson's ousted follower, John Beckley, counterattacked with a revelation he had been hoarding for six years.

He gave Scottish-born James Thomson Callender, a Democratic-Republican journalist who had once offered a toast to "the speedy death" of President Washington, the papers he had acquired from James Monroe about Hamilton's affair with Maria Reynolds. Callender published these documents in a murky "History of the United States for 1796." Jefferson liked it so much, he visited Callender's rooming house to congratulate him and bought several copies of his book.

The Vice President was soon calling the author a "man of genius" and "a man of science, fled from persecution." Callender had been run out of Britain for calling the English constitution a "conspiracy of the rich against the poor." Exactly why Jefferson considered him a scientist remains a mystery—unless it was his talent for twisting the truth into venomous accusations. Callender defended his exposure of the long-dead affair as justified by the "unfounded reproaches heaped on Mr. Monroe" for which he claimed Hamilton was responsible.[13]

Instead of adopting the policy of dignified silence that Madison had urged on Jefferson, Hamilton reached for his pen. The result was an erotically detailed thirty-seven-page confession bolstered by fifty-seven pages of documents. Hamilton claimed he was forced to undergo this public humiliation because Callender had asserted the affair with Maria Reynolds was a device to conceal his corrupt dealings with her husband. Hamilton fiercely refuted this accusation, and added denunciations of the politicians behind this plot to destroy him—notably Thomas Jefferson.

Vice President Jefferson and retired Congressman Madison read this unwise exercise with undisguised pleasure—at least in their private correspondence. Jefferson told a Virginia friend that Hamilton's "willingness to plead guilty seems rather to have strengthened than to have weakened; that he was, in truth, guilty of the speculations." Madison was somewhat kinder. He called the pamphlet "a curious example of the ingenious folly of its author." Was he remembering those days of friendship, when he and Hamilton wrote the *Federalist*? If so, Madison swiftly returned to politics and dismissed the ex-treasury secretary's "malignant insinuation" against Jefferson as "a masterpiece of folly, because its impotence is in exact proportion to its venom."[14]

But Hamilton was not quite as impotent—or as foolish—as this tormented confession made him look in Jefferson/Madison/Monroe's eyes. While the nation's political class reeled with the double shocks of the Mazzei letter and Hamilton's admissions, a package from Virginia arrived on the doorstep of the troubled ex-secretary's household on Cedar Street in New York. In the package was a four-bottle silver wine cooler—and a message from George Washington.

The ostensible reason was the recent birth of another Hamilton son. But the message went far beyond this pretext. The ex-president said he was sending it, "not for any intrinsic value the thing possesses, but as a token of my sincere regard and friendship for you." Washington was saying he still had confidence in Hamilton's integrity—and his patriotism. [15]

In Virginia, Jefferson was troubled by something he regarded as far more serious than the destruction of political reputations. Congressman James J. Cabell, from the district that included Monticello, was accused of writing a letter to his constituents that endangered the peace and prosperity of the nation. The message was severely critical of the Adams administration's foreign policy toward France. Supreme Court Justice James Iredell, sitting as a federal judge on circuit, told a Richmond grand jury that "some foreign nation" might use such statements "to take advantage of our internal discords, first making us the dupe and then the prey" of their ambition to control our government. The grand jury indicted Cabell for threatening "the happy government of the United States."

Jefferson called the indictment an invitation to federal judges to become "inquisitors on the freedom of...their fellow citizens." The Vice President drafted a "Protest against the interference of the [Federal] judiciary between Representative and Constituent" for forwarding to the Virginia Assembly. The document claimed that the federal grand jury had committed a crime "of the highest and most alarming nature." The members should be promptly impeached and punished.

The Vice President first sent copies of the protest to Madison and Monroe. Both dutifully praised it, but Madison wondered about the wisdom of "embarking the legislature in the business." This was his polite way of saying he did not think it was a good idea to promote a clash between states' rights and federal rights—one of the chief problems he and George Washington had tried to solve in the Constitution. Monroe confessed a similar worry.

Jefferson ignored his two lieutenants. He sent the protest to the Virginia House of Delegates, where the members angrily denounced Congressman Cabell's indictment. But they ignored Jefferson's call to punish the grand jurors. In fact, they did not even send their wrathful resolutions to the state senate. Nor did they forward them to Congress. The inaction suggests others were uneasy about promoting a clash with the federal government.[16]

Back in the Senate, early in 1798, Jefferson told one friend that "party animosities" had "raised a wall of separation between those who differ in political sentiments." After examining the various names being called, he told one correspondent that Whig (liberal) and Tory (conservative) were the only meaningful terms for the "two sects." He never admitted to himself or to anyone else that he was among the most reckless users of slanderous terms, such as the ones he had produced for the Mazzei letter.[17]

Determined to defend Jefferson as their once and future candidate, the Democratic-Republicans in the House, led by Albert Gallatin, objected to Federalist criticism of the Mazzei letter—especially when a Connecticut representative read it into the congressional record. The Federalists were trying to link Jefferson to Democratic-Republican policies in the current Congress, where the party resisted President Adams's call to raise money for an army and a navy to deal with the threat of French aggression. Federalists declared the Mazzei episode proved Jefferson was "the life and soul of the opposition" to protecting America's independence.[18]

This invective would have been dismissed as far too mild if the Federalists knew what Jefferson told the latest French envoy, Philippe Henri Letombe. He was only a *Charge' d'Affaires* instead of a Minister Plenipotentiary—a diminishment that underscored French hostility. On June 7, 1797, Letombe reported to Paris that he had enjoyed a "long and tranquil" conversation with "the wise Jefferson." The Vice President had assured him that America had "broken...forever the chains which attached it to England" and the nation "was penetrated with gratitude to France."[19]

Jefferson swiftly segued to the underlying reason for these declarations. President John Adams was a disaster—"vain, irritable, stubborn, endowed with excessive amour-propre and still suffering pique at the preference accorded Franklin over him in Paris." But his presidency would last "only five (sic) years." He had only became president by three electoral votes, and "the system of the United States will change" with his departure.[20]

The Vice President launched into a rhapsody of praise for the recent French military triumphs in Europe. France was "at the summit of her glory." She could afford to wait, "to precipitate nothing," and soon "everything would return to order." President Adams's envoys should be received peacefully. But there was no need to accede to their demands. Instead, the Directory should "allow the negotiations to drag on," softening matters whenever possible with the requisite "urbanity." Letombe added that Jefferson "repeats to me incessantly…Machievelli's maxim. *Nil repente* [never repent] is the soul of great affairs." [21]

It was a truly astonishing performance. The Vice President, not content with undercutting the President in Congress, was now telling the French how to talk his foreign policy to a humiliating political death. If this was not treason to the nation, it was certainly a betrayal of his supposedly revered friendship with John Adams. Jefferson rationalized this policy by convincing himself he was preventing a war. He closed by telling Letombe it was time to arrange reciprocal citizenship between the two republics. He hoped France would soon invade England and dictate a peace that would guarantee "a purer government" for export to "other portions of mankind." [22]

There is a touching nobility—and a dismaying naivete—about these ideas. In a country already boiling with antipathy to France, as their men of war seized American merchantmen by the dozen, why would Americans embrace reciprocal citizenship, which would entitle future Citizen Genets to operate with virtual impunity in the United States? Did the Vice President really think that a French army in the ruins of London would inspire the dictatorial Directory to create a purer government?

❧

In Congress, the political atmosphere became so rancid, Vermont Congressman Matthew Lyon, a volatile Democratic-Republican, spit in Connecticut Federalist Roger Griswold's face when the latter suggested he had been a less than heroic soldier in the American Revolution. Griswold responded the next day by assaulting Lyon with his cane. The Vermont firebrand defended himself with a poker.

Jefferson found this violence distasteful. But he told Madison it might have one beneficial outcome. "These proceedings must degrade the federal government, and lead the people to lean more on their state governments, which have been sunk under the early popularity of the former." This was a shift in loyalty that Jefferson approved and even welcomed. It was one more piece of evidence of his underlying hostility to the Constitution. The so-called "father" of that document made no attempt to disagree.

※

A few weeks later, the Vice President was gleefully telling Madison a more entertaining story. "The late birthnight," he wrote, "has sown tares among the exclusive Federals." He was talking about a ball that Washington devotees had proposed to celebrate the ex-president's birthday, even though the man being honored had retired to Mount Vernon. The organizers had invited President Adams and his wife, assuming they would endorse the festivities.

Revealing in stark detail his political limitations, Adams exploded and declared himself insulted. Abigail, badly damaging her reputation as the person who prevented her dearest friend from going to extremes, agreed with him. The contretemps split the Federalist Party and the Adams administration. The President's four cabinet members attended the ball. Those who stayed home drew glares of disapproval from the Washington devotees.

Jefferson described all this in delighted terms. He added a touch for which he may have been responsible. The Democratic-Republicans went "in number," he told Madison. This encouraged the idea that all the previous celebrations had been "for the General and not the President." It was a neat way of dismissing Washington's presidency as worthy of no more than a glimmer of respect. [23]

※

Across the wintry Atlantic came only silence from the three envoys to France. Jefferson convinced himself that this non-communication was an omen of peace. He did not respond to a Madison letter, which compared Adams to Washington. After complimenting the first president in a half-dozen ways and criticizing Adams, the retired Congressman feared serious trouble lay over the horizon.

The confirmation of this pessimism came in March. In phrases charged with tension, Adams reported the peace mission was a failure and there was immediate need to take seriously his call to prepare the nation to defend itself. Vice President Jefferson called the announcement "an insane message." His first instinct was to rally his party to dismiss the President's summons to war. He could think of no reason for such a move that would be plausible even to "the weakest mind."

The Federalists lacked a majority in the House of Representatives, which would vote the money for this preparedness. Jefferson thought the Democratic-Republicans should call for an adjournment, so everyone could go home and consult their constituents. He was sure a vast majority of the people were opposed to both war and the new taxes it would require.

The Vice President swiftly learned no one in the party had the nerve to propose such a move. The best he could get was a lame statement that it was "inexpedient" to go to war with "the French Republic." This weak reed was soon in grave danger of crumpling under pressure from the President, two-thirds of the Senate, and the Federalist share of the House. Madison suggested another tactic. Demand from the President "the intelligence" which led him to his brusque demands.

✠

In the executive mansion, President Adams and Secretary of State Pickering were reading dispatches from envoy John Marshall that revealed the latest truth about the rulers of France. The Directory were revolutionists in name only. Their power depended almost totally on the tolerance of the generals who had won the victories that Vice President Jefferson applauded. With their reign precarious, these pseudo-rulers were eager to line their own pockets should a hasty departure be just around the corner.

When the three envoys arrived at the offices of Foreign Minister Charles Maurice de Talleyrand-Perigord, they were greeted with cool politeness. A former priest, Talleyrand had the most flexible conscience in Europe. Through three spokesmen, he delivered a message to the shocked Americans: it would take money, a lot of money, to reach an understanding.

The spokesmen had no compunction about suggesting a down payment of $50,000. That might enable the envoys to begin conversing with Foreign Minister Talleyrand. Up the road, if some understanding was reached, the French Republic expected a very large loan from her sister republic across the Atlantic. Also needed were profuse apologies for President Adams's speech to the special session of Congress, which had left the Directory "extremely exasperated." This ominous word was succeeded by boastful descriptions of the "power and violence" of the French Republic, demonstrated within a week of the envoys' arrival by Austria's surrender of Italy to General Napoleon Bonaparte.[24]

Here, surely, was the reductio ad absurdum of the French Revolution as Thomas Jefferson's "polar star." Adding to the intended humiliation of the envoys was a warning from one of Talleyand's messengers that if they went home and accused the French of unreasonable demands, the "French party" in America would unite with skillful French diplomats and "throw the blame for the rupture of negotiations on the Federalists"—the British Party, "as France terms you."[25]

When the House Democratic-Republicans took Madison's advice (via Jefferson) and demanded to see the "intelligence" which made the supposedly vain, irritable, stubborn, pique-ish President Adams so anxious to prepare the United States for war, Secretary of State Pickering described the confrontation with Talleyrand's spokesmen in acid detail. As a gesture of decorum, the foreign minister's agents were not named. They were called X, Y and Z. But the size and arrogance of their demands was not withheld. Nor was Charles Cotesworth Pinckney's response: "No! Not a sixpence!" This was soon improved by a Federalist congressman to "Millions for defense but not one cent for tribute!"[26]

A bewildered Vice President Jefferson described the impact to James Madison: "Such a shock on the Republican Mind...has never been seen since our independence." A gleeful Abigail Adams revealed what she thought of Jefferson and his followers: "The Jacobins in the Senate and the House were struck dumb and opend (sic) not their mouths." On March 23, 1798, the President proved he was not quite as politically inept as Jefferson portrayed him; he called for a national day of fasting and prayer to seek God's protection from an amoral, voracious enemy.[27]

Vice President Jefferson knew defeat when it stared him in the face. He told Madison the Democratic-Republicans in the House had abandoned their resolution calling war inexpedient. It made it look like they were in agreement with the XYZ swindlers. The best they could do now was resist "war measures externally" while voting approval of "every rational measure of internal defence."

Behind the scenes, however, the Jefferson/Madison love affair with the French Revolution continued. The Vice President called the XYZ demands "very unworthy of a great nation," and doubted they were the official policy of France's rulers. Madison agreed. Unless proof was "perfectly conclusive," the decision should be "agst the evidence rather than on the side of infatuation."[28]

Like a good president should, Adams sought advice on his next moves from all quarters. Swallowing his hostility, he even invited Alexander Hamilton to dine with him and Abigail to discuss the administration's response. Benjamin Franklin Bache was soon telling readers of the *Aurora* about this dinner party with the "adulterous" Hamilton. He claimed to be aghast at the President's selection of such company for the entertainment of his wife. "Oh Johnny! Johnny!" he mocked. [29]

No one paid the slightest attention to this desperation tactic. Letters and addresses of support poured across President Adams's desk. "The Students of Harvard University" joined "the inhabitants of Providence, R.I. and the 'Soldier Citizens' of New Jersey" in affirming their admiration. When Adams attended the theater, the audience went berserk. The orchestra played "The President's March" a dozen times and people danced to it. Robert Treat Paine wrote a song, "To Adams and Liberty" to the melody of an old tune, "Anacreon in Heaven." Its final line had words that soon became ominous to Democratic-Republicans: "Her pride is her Adams—his laws are her own."[30]

Meanwhile, the "heavy" frigates *United States, Constitution,* and *Constellation* slid down the ways and headed for the open seas to take on French raiders. These ships wielded forty-four guns and were more stoutly built than any ship of their class on the high seas. Other American men of war were also on the prowl. On July 7, 1798, the USS *Delaware's* twenty guns subdued a French schooner, *Le Croyable,* that had seized and looted an American merchantman, the *Alexander Hamilton.* The citizens of Charleston, S.C. launched a warship they had paid for out of their own pockets, the USS *John Adams.* The President decided it was time to take his warrior sailors seriously and created a Department of the Navy to supervise and supply them.[31]

In May, Congress voted to raise a regular army of ten thousand men for active duty and a "provisional" or backup force of twelve thousand. President Adams, facing the fact that he had not an iota of military experience, rushed a letter to Mount Vernon, asking George Washington to emerge from retirement. "If the Constitution and your convenience would permit of my changing places," he wrote, "or of taking my old station as your Lieutenant Civil, I should have no doubts about the ultimate prosperity and glory of the country." To the President's dismay, Washington accepted the task on one condition—that Adams would appoint Alexander Hamilton as a major general and his second-in-command.[32]

By now, Congress had no doubt whatsoever it was preparing for war with France. This stirred a worry about enemies on American soil. There were at least thirty thousand French men and women in the United States. Most were fugitives from their murderous revolution. But there was more than a possibility that many were secret agents, ready, willing, and able to sabotage the American war effort from within. Didn't they have vivid evidence in the XYZ revelations, with their boast of the readiness of their so-called diplomats to work with the "French Party" to overthrow the U.S. government? Federalist congressmen easily convinced themselves that it was time to pass a law giving the president the power to order any and all of these aliens out of the country.

As for the "French Party," what better way to keep the Democratic-Republicans and their devious vice presidential leader under control than a law to silence—or at least, subdue—their obnoxious newspapers? Soon Congress was crafting an "Act for the Punishment of Certain Crimes." This "Sedition Act" made it a criminal offense to speak or print "any false, scandalous and malicious writing or writings against the Government of the United States, or either House of the Congress of the United States, with intent to defame...or to bring them...into contempt or disrepute." The law gave the accused newspaper editor the right to defend himself in court. If he could prove the truth of his statements, he would walk out a free man. If he was found guilty? A federal judge would decide his fate.

President Adams had not requested these proposals. But he was in wholehearted agreement with them. So was his dearest friend and advisor, Abigail. He signed both bills into law. Neither he nor the congressmen and senators who wrote them were aware that they were committing political suicide. They were also triggering a final clash between George Washington and Thomas Jefferson that would profoundly affect the future of the nation. [33]

CHAPTER 23

The Ultimate Divide

W HEN EX-PRESIDENT WASHINGTON FIRST reached Mount
Vernon, he told himself he had left politics behind him, once and
for all. He cancelled all his newspaper subscriptions. But he soon found it
was not easy to make this gesture a reality. Some editors, like his original
gadfly, Philip Freneau, mailed him copies of their latest productions. He
wrote Freneau a stiff letter requesting him to cease and desist. Other papers, with stories that friends thought the ex-President should or might
want to read, arrived in a steady stream. Soon he found the ongoing quarrel
with France an irresistible topic and resubscribed to no less than ten papers.

Obviously, Washington was still in the grip of the primary emotion
that had persuaded him to become president: *To see this country happy is so
much the wish of my soul, nothing this side of Elysium can be placed in competition with it.* Almost from the beginning of his presidential career, Washington's relationship to Thomas Jefferson was central to this epochal
drama. That may have been why he devoted so many hours to reading
James Monroe's attack on the ex-president and his administration when it
was published in 1797.

Monroe claimed he had been an innocent victim in a presidential plot
to convince the American people that the Jay Treaty was a better alternative than an alliance with France. The ex-diplomat heaped abuse on the
treaty and the man who signed it. The notes the ex-president scribbled
in the margins of the book come to sixty-six typed pages; they ranged
from sarcastic to infuriated. Washington found particular fault with Monroe revealing his private instructions and his correspondence with the

administration. It did not much matter that Washington probably never learned that Jefferson had been a combination ghost writer/editor in this venture. Washington already regarded Monroe as little more than a Jeffersonian mouthpiece. [1]

On May 2 ,1797, came the revelation of Jefferson's letter to the Italian radical, Mazzei. Washington did not care whether Jefferson considered him one of the Samsons "shorn by the harlot, England" that supposedly peopled the federal government during his two terms. The description of his administration was more than enough to infuriate him. He dismissed Jefferson's defense—that the phrase referred to the Society of the Cincinnati. These ex-officers of the Continental Army had made Washington their organization's first president. Was being included in a generic smear supposed to make him feel better about his ex-secretary of state?[2]

✾

In the fall of 1797, Washington had another experience that convinced him his friendship with Thomas Jefferson had ended forever. In the mail came a letter from a man who signed himself John Langhorne, a resident of Albermarle County, Virginia, where Monticello loomed on its small mountain. The author described himself as deeply disturbed by the "unmerited calumny" and "villainous machinations" that Washington had endured as president. He was writing in the hope of providing some "comfort to a mind eminently just and virtuous." Langhorne was almost too good to be true, and Washington's reply to him was brief, polite, and cautious. He thanked the writer for his "favorable sentiments" and assured him his retirement was "perfectly tranquil," thanks to his inner conviction that he had never merited such "envenomed darts" from his critics.

A month later, another letter added a swirl of malice to Langhorne's sympathy. John Nicholas, the clerk of Albermarle County, informed Washington that his reply had spent more than a month in the Charlottesville post office, exciting not a little comment. Like all the ex-president's letters, it was sent with a frank bearing his signature. The letter was finally picked up by "a certain character in this county closely connected to some of your greatest and bitterest enemies." Although the man's name was not Langhorne, he claimed the letter was a reply to one he had written.

John Nicholas described himself as "living within cannon shot of the headquarters of Jacobinism in America"—an unmistakable reference to Monticello. He knew that Washington had once been deceived by the

"Chief Jacobin's" pretensions to friendship, and wanted to warn him of a possible plot to embarrass and humiliate him. The ex-president told Nicholas that if such a plot existed, the conspirator had fallen "far short of his mark." But he enclosed copies of his correspondence with Langhorne for possible use in revealing "any nefarious plan" against him or the federal government.[3]

Langhorne soon replied with explosive news. "John Langhorne" was really Peter Carr, a "favorite nephew of *your very sincere friend* Thomas Jefferson." Carr had been raised at Monticello since childhood as "a constant dependent and resident" in the Chief Jacobin's mansion. This description of Peter Carr was accurate; he was a son of Jefferson's sister and his close friend, Dabney Carr, who had died young, leaving his wife virtually penniless. Jefferson had raised Peter Carr and his brother at Monticello.

When Washington did not respond to this startling news, Nicholas wrote to him once more, on the retired President's sixty-sixth birthday. In raging prose, Nicholas described how eager he was to punish Jefferson for this "very extraordinary" and "even infamous affair." Proving himself in touch with all the latest examples of Jefferson's hypocrisy, Nicholas denounced the Mazzei letter and Monroe's obnoxious defense of his mission to France. The Langhorne letter was further proof, Nicholas declared, that Jefferson was "one of the most artful, intriguing…double-faced politicians" on the planet.[4]

These epithets fit perfectly into what Washington saw as the Democratic-Republican party's policy of attempting to ruin "men who stand well in the estimation of the people and are stumbling blocks" to their long-range program—to assail the federal government "without hesitation or remorse" until "the Constitution [is] destroyed." He did not realize he was about to encounter an all too specific example of this dark prophecy, emanating from Monticello.

The Alien and Sedition Acts inflamed Vice President Jefferson and his retired friend James Madison like no issue since Hamilton's Report on the Bank of the United States. Madison labeled the Alien Act "a monster that must forever disgrace its parents." Jefferson called it legislation "worthy of the 8th or 9th Century"—Europe's dark ages. The sedition bill made the Vice President's pulse pound. "Among other enormities," he told Madison, it "undertakes to make printing certain matters criminal, tho one of the amendments to the Constitution, has so expressly taken religion, printing presses, etc. out of their [Congress's] coercion." Both bills were "palpably in the teeth of the Constitution."[5]

In the midst of this political firestorm, the Vice President was caught sponsoring an unauthorized peace mission to France. The envoy was a Quaker friend, Dr. George Logan. Jefferson had given him a "letter of credence" describing him as a visitor to Europe on private business. Logan disappeared so suddenly, friends and acquaintances began talking about it. Soon Federalist newspapers were calling the self-appointed diplomat a "seditious envoy" from the Democratic-Republicans whose mission was to invite a French Army to teach the Americans "the genuine value of true and essential liberty," French style, through the "blessed operation of the bayonet and the guillotine." Jefferson ruefully admitted to Madison that "this extravagance produced a real panic among the citizens" of Philadelphia.[6]

The Vice President rushed to visit Logan's wife, who lived on the outskirts of the city, to make sure she was not abused by irate Federalists. She told him that she was only suffering from "political excommunication." She later recalled that Jefferson "spoke of the late acts of the legislature with a sort of despair."

Heightening the tension was a letter from French Foreign Minister Talleyrand to President Adams, offering to negotiate with Elbridge Gerry, the Democratic-Republican member of President Adams's three-man mission, but not with the other two men, John Marshall and Thomas Pinckney. The *Aurora* published this epistle two days before President Adams announced its receipt. It was an all too obvious attempt to embarrass or intimidate the President with a direct appeal to the people a la Citizen Genet.

Federalist newspapers screamed that Bache was a French agent and Paris was trying to disrupt American preparations for war, leaving them exposed to an invading army. Federalist congressmen connected it to the Logan mission and its sponsor, Jefferson. The Vice President was soon being accused of conducting a "treasonous correspondence" with the French Directory.

So alarmed was the Adams administration, Secretary of the Treasury Oliver Wolcott rushed to New York to interview a man who had just arrived carrying letters from France addressed to Bache, Monroe, and other

Democratic-Republican politicians. Wolcott asked the messenger if he had any envelopes "for the leader of the traitors, Vice President Jefferson." Examining the letters, Wolcott seized one addressed to Jefferson from Fulwar Skipwith, the American consul in Paris. Though there was no proof of sedition in the letter, the Secretary never bothered to deliver it. [7]

Jefferson told Madison he was almost praying for Congress to adjourn. Nothing else would "withdraw the fire under [the] boiling pot." On June 21, President Adams sent a message to the legislature, declaring negotiations with France were "at an end." That same day, the Federalists introduced a bill in the Senate declaring the 1778 Treaty of Alliance with France was "null and void." It passed by an almost 3–1 margin. [8]

As Vice President, Jefferson could only sit in the Senate as a writhing silent witness to the torrent of rage ignited by the XYZ revelations. In a letter to his son-in-law, Thomas Mann Randolph, he groaned that he "had neither ears to hear, eyes to see or tongue to speak, but as the Senate direct me." In a letter to his daughter Martha, he deplored "the rancorous passions that tear every breast here, even of the sex which should be a stranger to them. Politics and party hatreds destroy the happiness of every being" in Philadelphia. [9]

As usual, the Vice President seemed oblivious to his role in creating this conflagration, starting with Philip Freneau. Nor did he ever admit to himself or anyone else that the degeneration of his "polar star," the French Revolution, was playing an equally large role in stoking the blaze. "I never was more home sick or heart sick," he told Martha. "The life of this place [Philadelphia] is particularly hateful to me." Self-pity was unquestionably one of Thomas Jefferson's less admirable traits. [10]

The Vice President was especially troubled by the rain of personal attacks on him, which he described as feeling that he was "a fair mark for every man's dirt." He decided to go home without waiting for Congress to adjourn. The day before he left the nation's capital, he had to sit silent as usual when the Federalists introduced their sedition bill in the Senate. Without waiting for it to pass, the government arrested Benjamin Franklin Bache as their first and most detested violator of the law.

The *Gazette of the United States* published an essay written under the name of the Roman historian, Pliny, urging Jefferson not to depart. "Pray stay a little longer and aid the public councils with your wisdom; leave not your country at this critical period when it is seeking the most effectual means to self preservation," Pliny mocked. If that appeal failed, Pliny hoped his friendship for Benjamin Franklin Bache would persuade the Vice President to "tarry a day or two."

Pliny unctuously urged Jefferson to remember how much help Bache had given him and "his fellow laborers in the iniquitous work of alienating the affections and confidence of the people…in their government." Who else but Franklin's despicable grandson had "a direct intercourse with the Office of Foreign Affairs at Paris?" Another Federalist newspaper claimed to have proof that when the French invaded, they would carry plans to establish an American Directory—an exact imitation of the current rulers of France. The directors would include Jefferson, Madison, and Monroe.[11]

The sedition bill passed the Senate on July 4, 1798, while Jefferson was en route to Monticello. One of Virginia's senators told him "there seemed to be a particular solicitude to pass it on that day." The Federalists especially enjoyed the "drums and trumpets and other martial music" from a military parade that passed the Congress Hall in the midst of their debate, drowning out Democratic-Republican protests. Later, a Federalist rally offered a toast to President Adams: "May he, like Samson, slay thousands of French, with the jawbone of Jefferson." For modern readers without an eighteenth century knowledge of the Bible, it might be worth adding that the jawbone Samson wielded originally belonged to an ass.[12]

In the House of Representatives, Federalist congressmen repeatedly linked Jefferson with Bache, calling him the editor's confidential advisor, who was often seen walking the city's streets arm-in-arm with him. They were undoubtedly "part of a treasonable conspiracy that constituted an internal threat to the nation," one Federalist newspaper concluded. A Democratic-Republican congressman from Maryland took these charges of treason seriously, and asked Jefferson to reply to them.

The Vice President defended his friendship with Bache, calling him a man with "principles the most friendly to liberty and our present form of government." As for the abuse he (Jefferson) was receiving, he did not feel the need of a sedition law to repel it. He was not and never would be ashamed of his political principles, which were the same ones that had motivated him in 1775. He was sure that they were the same as "the great body of the American people."[13]

This was Jefferson's mood when, back in Virginia, the Vice President conferred with James Madison about how to respond to the Alien and Sedition Acts. As usual, Jefferson was the leader. He wanted to prepare two sets of protests, one for the legislature of Virginia, the other for North Carolina's lawmakers. Madison would work on the Virginia version. It was Jefferson's idea to use state legislatures to defy the federal government. It was the method he had adopted to defend Congressman Cabell from the wrath of the circuit-riding Supreme Court justice in the previous year. Madison did not say a negative word about this new move in the same dangerous direction.

The two men spent much of the summer of 1798 working on their protest essays. Jefferson's version reflected the abuse he had endured in Philadelphia. Its language was ferocious from the first paragraph. He condemned the sedition law as "a nullity as absolute and palpable as if Congress had ordered us to fall down and worship a golden image." The Constitution's delegation of power to the national government was severely limited. The Sedition Act violated the First Amendment to the Constitution, which guaranteed freedom of religion, speech, and the press.

To justify a state legislature's right to criticize the federal government, Jefferson declared that the union created in 1787–88 had been a "compact between the states." He seems to have forgotten or decided to ignore the preamble to the Constitution, which expressly declared that "We the people of the United States" were the creators of the national charter. Working from the state compact thesis, Jefferson concluded that acts exceeding the delegated powers were not only unconstitutional, but a state had the power to "nullify" them. He based this on his claim that "every state had a 'natural right'" to resist "all assumptions of power by others" within their borders.

This was not a new idea for Thomas Jefferson. From it had flowed his call to punish—and even to execute—Virginians who worked for the supposedly unconstitutional Bank of the United States, created by a Congress he saw as a "foreign power." In these new resolutions, he did not call for such drastic action. Instead, he urged that a nullifying state communicate its views to other states, asking them to declare "whether these acts are or are not authorized by the federal compact." He was confident that most states would make sure that neither the Alien nor the Sedition Act would be "exercised within their borders." The goal remained nullification, even if that explosive word was not applied to it.[14]

Jefferson did not seem to know—or care—that he was introducing an idea that in the coming decades would play a deadly role in undermining the authority of the federal government and the value of the Union that

George Washington had labored so hard to convince people to cherish above all other political values. It was dismayingly typical of the way Jefferson could ignore the darker side of human nature and the danger of preaching ideological hatred. The French Revolution had demonstrated this grim truth to a hefty portion of the world by 1798. But for Thomas Jefferson, this evidence simply did not exist.

Madison took a very different approach in his protest essay for the Virginia legislature. He made no reference to nullification or a state's natural right to defy the federal Congress. Instead, he began by affirming his deep affection for the union of the states. He saw the Alien and Sedition Acts as "alarming infractions" of the Constitution. He then lurched into standard Jeffersonian jargon, claiming that the acts, along with several measures in Washington's administration, added up to a plan to turn the American government into "an absolute, or at best, a mixed monarchy." He urged the Virginia legislature to "interpose" against this threat by persuading other states to repeal the detested laws.

Madison sent his set of resolutions to Jefferson via a Monticello neighbor, Senator Wilson Cary Nicholas. While the essay was en route, Jefferson learned that Congressman Matthew Lyon of Vermont had been convicted under the Sedition Act for attacking President Adams in a letter to his constituents. Jefferson already felt threatened by the accusations hurled at him in Philadelphia, and he identified deeply with Lyon. He confessed his fear that he too might be prosecuted, if someone leaked one of his political letters to the Federalists. He decided to make Madison's version much harsher. He persuaded Senator Nicholas, who was going to deliver the resolution to the Virginia legislature, to add a sentence declaring the acts were "null, void and of no effect." This was nothing less than nullification with a rhetorical flourish.[15]

Madison happened to be visiting friends in Richmond when the resolutions were introduced in the legislature. He calmly removed Jefferson's insertion, and gave Nicholas a cogent explanation. State legislatures never had anything to do with ratifying the Constitution. That was done by conventions chosen by the people. If a state legislature undertook to call an act of Congress null and void, it could be accused of usurping powers it did not possess. [16]

Jefferson did not share this concern for the union of the states. He was emotionally committed to enlarging the distinctions between state and federal powers. If the Alien and Sedition Acts were accepted, he predicted,

"We shall immediately see attempted another act of Congress declaring that the President shall continue in office during life, reserving to another occasion the transfer of succession to his heirs, and the establishment of the Senate for life. ...That these things are in contemplation, I have no doubt; nor can I be confident of their failure, after the dupery of which our countrymen have shown themselves to be susceptible."[17]

There is no evidence that any Federalist was contemplating such a step. The claim that John Adams would be made president for life is so divorced from political reality, it deserves satire rather than refutation. But these words, written to Virginia's senator, Stevens T. Mason, are dolorous proof of the frenzy that was gripping Thomas Jefferson's mind in October 1798.

※

Thousands of miles away, on the coast of Egypt, another drama was unfolding that would underscore the mysterious way good luck—or destiny—influenced Thomas Jefferson's life and career. Revolutionary France, under the nominal rule of the Directory, was now a nation virtually under the control of one man: General Napoleon Bonaparte. Having smashed the royalist coalition in Europe, he forced Austria to accept a humiliating peace, and reduced Italy to a French protectorate. The Corsican-born adventurer decided on an unexpected strategy to defeat Britain, the one enemy that remained formidable.

Napoleon planned to invade Egypt and swiftly conquer the Middle East. Next, his seemingly unbeatable army would march on India, where numerous British-hating native leaders were ready and eager to join forces with him. With the British empire virtually dismantled, George III and his shaken ministers would be ready to surrender—or at the very least, be easily crushed in battle, leaving Bonaparte dictating peace to the humbled Britons in London.

Virtually the entire French battle fleet escorted the ships that brought Bonaparte's army to Egypt. By dint of absolute secrecy, and not a little good fortune, they had managed to escape a pursuing British fleet led by Rear Admiral Sir Horatio Nelson. Bonaparte had even managed to capture Malta in his zigzag course to Alexandria. Ashore, the French army soon had Egypt prostrate at their feet. Their fleet anchored in Aboukir Bay, twenty miles northeast of Alexandria, ready to fend off any British attempt to regain the initiative with a new army.

The French admiral totally underestimated Nelson's daring. When the British commander saw the enemy men of war arraigned across the bay, he instantly went to general quarters. His ships split into two groups. One got between the French and the shore, the other assailed them from the seaward side. Caught between two fires, the French men of war were battered by a veritable hurricane of cannonballs. Some surrendered, others exploded and sank in demoralizing flames. The French commanding admiral was killed. The survivors attempted to escape. Only two reached the open sea.

The battle had a stunning impact in Europe. Nation after nation revolted against French *liberté*. Another coalition of royal armies was soon in the field. A desperate Bonaparte tried to march overland into Palestine and the rest of the Middle East, but he ran out of supplies and men. He finally abandoned the despairing remnant of his army and made his way back to France in a small ship that eluded British patrols. There, he found the Paris mob was ready to reenact the rule by guillotine of the Jacobins. He swiftly discouraged such an enterprise with point blank artillery fire. But it was more than clear that France's ability to send an army overseas to attack America was no longer a possibility.

When this news reached President John Adams, he began to ask himself why America was spending millions of dollars on an army that no longer had an enemy to fight. He embarked on a policy that would split the Federalist Party and make Thomas Jefferson the next president of the United States.

⚜

Since the news of the XYZ demand for bribes, George Washington's already grave doubts about revolutionary France had turned to grim convictions. "What a scene of corruption and profligacy has these communications disclosed in the Directors of a people whom the United States have endeavored to treat upon fair, just and honorable ground!" the ex-president wrote in a letter to a U.S. senator. His wife Martha shared his dark view of the French. In a letter to the wife of Charles Cotesworth Pinckney, who had been appointed a general in the new army that her husband now led, Martha called France "a faithless nation whose injustice and ambition know no bounds."[18]

When Congress passed the Alien and Sedition Acts in 1798 Washington considered the United States a threatened republic, already at war with France on the ocean, and liable to be attacked by an invading army in the near future. He pointed to the fate of the Republic of Venice, which had thought of itself as a French ally, and was now a mere province of their empire. For the ex-president, the possibility of such a fate justified both the Alien and the Sedition Acts. They were war measures, needed for the security of the nation in a time of crisis. Congress stipulated that they would expire in two years, when the lawmakers assumed the conflict would be over.

Future presidents, such as Abraham Lincoln, Woodrow Wilson, and Franklin D. Roosevelt, would sponsor far harsher measures during the wars of their time. Lincoln suspended habeas corpus, imprisoned thousands of government critics in federal jails for indeterminate sentences, and looked the other way while hostile newspapers were wrecked and burned by rioters often led by Union soldiers. Wilson's administration created the American Protective League—some two hundred fifty thousand volunteer enforcers who tapped telephones, opened letters, and otherwise spied on those suspected of disloyalty and treason. Roosevelt arrested tens of thousands of innocent Japanese Americans, and confined them in detention camps for the duration of the war.[19]

Washington saw the nation as similarly threatened in 1798. The French government's fondness for publishing official letters in anti-Federalist newspapers was, for him, a vivid example of divide and conquer tactics. He saw the French refusal to negotiate with Federalist envoys John Marshall and Charles Cotesworth Pinckney, and their readiness to parley with Democratic-Republican Elbridge Gerry, as part of the same strategy.

❦

When Washington read Thomas Jefferson's Kentucky resolutions and James Madison's Virginia version, he was appalled. He saw both as horrendous threats to the future of the American union. He wrote to Patrick Henry, urging him to emerge from retirement and become a candidate for the Virginia Assembly, so he could launch a movement to repeal Madison's resolutions. "The tranquility of the Union and of this state in particular is hastening to an awful crisis," he wrote. The ex-president cited the Madison claim that the offending acts had violated the compact between the states, giving Virginia the right "to *interpose* for arresting the progress of the evil." For Washington, the word "interpose" meant the same thing as Thomas Jefferson's "nullify"—the dissolution of the American union. In both words, he saw the hand of the leader of the Democratic-Republican Party and the chief appeaser of France. [20]

Although the sixty-three-year-old Henry had recently told a friend he was "too old and infirm" to venture into politics again, he recognized a solemn summons to duty in Washington's letter. He immediately responded, declaring himself a candidate. "My children would blush to know that you and their father were contemporaries, and that when you asked him to throw in his mite for the public happiness, he refused to do it."[21]

In the same spirit, Washington wrote to John Marshall and Henry Lee, urging them to run for Congress as Federalists in the upcoming elections to defend the country against Jefferson's subversion. The ex-president was providing the kind of political leadership the Federalists desperately needed—and President Adams was not giving them. Depressed by the constant barrage of criticism from the *Aurora* and other papers, the President began retreating to his farm in Massachusetts for months at a time, running the government by mail. His absence demoralized his cabinet and his supporters in Congress.

In December 1798, when Generals Washington and Hamilton met in Philadelphia to discuss the organization of the new army, they listened closely to President Adams's second annual address to Congress. He called for continuing defensive preparations for war, but repeatedly said the United States was ready and willing to achieve a peaceful understanding with France. These words proved to be a prelude to an even more unexpected message. On February 18, 1799, Adams went before the Senate and informed them that he had appointed a new envoy to France—William Vans Murray, the American minister to the Netherlands.

Everyone, including Washington, Hamilton, and President Adams's cabinet, was astounded. The President had consulted no one before making this move. It was based on an extremely unorthodox French diplomatic maneuver. Foreign Minister Talleyrand had sent a letter to Louis Andre Pichon, the French *Chargé d'Affaires* in the Netherlands, declaring France was sincerely interested in peace negotiations with America. Pichon had passed the letter to Murray, who forwarded it to Adams. The President instantly decided to respond to it.

Washington had grave doubts about this decision. He suspected Talleyrand was playing "the same loose and round-about game he had attempted the year before with our envoys" in the XYZ affair. The ex-president thought Adams should have made it clear that he would only negotiate when he was sure that the rulers of France, the Directory, were involved in the process. But Washington told Secretary of State Pickering he would make no public comment on the President's decision. He was only a spectator in this drama, without access to all the information that he assumed President Adams possessed.

The ex-president feared that Adams's impulsive response would deflate the defiant mood in Congress and the nation that had induced them to spend millions for an army and navy. As Washington knew from experience, Americans did not like the discipline and hardships of military service. Only a fervent belief that the country was in danger persuaded them to accept it. "Unless a material change takes place, our military theater affords but a gloomy prospect to those who are to perform the principal parts in the drama," he warned Major General Alexander Hamilton.[22]

This grim prophecy was fulfilled in the next few months. General Washington was soon asking Secretary of War James McHenry why recruiting for the army was moving so slowly. A letter from General Hamilton reported that he was getting no help in New England from friends and allies of President Adams. Even worse was the disarray on the political front. Secretary of State Pickering called the Murray mission "a degrading and mischievous measure...dishonorable to the United States." Massachusetts Senator George Cabot described his own reaction as: "Surprise, indignation, grief and disgust." Senator Theodore Sedgwick of Massachusetts told General Hamilton: "Had the foulest heart and the ablest head in the world have been permitted to select the most embarrassing and ruinous measure, perhaps it would have been precisely the one which has been adopted."[23]

Among the Democratic-Republicans, no one was more pleased with President Adams than his vice president. Thomas Jefferson called the decision to send Murray to France "the event of events." Delight was in every phrase of his letter to James Madison, describing Murray's appointment. "This had obviously been kept secret from the Feds of both houses, as appeared to their dismay." Jefferson concluded that the Federalists' "mortification" proved that "war had been their object."

In the grip of his partisanship, Jefferson could not see that the Federalists were dismayed not by the possibility of peace with France, but by President Adams's timing. The nation was approaching the presidential election year of 1800. It was vital to keep their followers in an anti-French mood until John Adams was reelected for another four years. Then would come the right time to negotiate from strength with the arrogant French.[24]

The politically inept Adams could not or would not see that if the French responded to Murray's mission, the Democratic-Republicans would cry "We told you so." They would claim the French about-face proved that the Federalist Party were warmongers, rushing to create an army and navy to fight an enemy that did not exist. Vice President Jefferson had intimated this all too clearly in his letter to Madison. The *Aurora*, eager to widen the breach in the enemy party, hailed the President's decision, declaring that it was about time Adams realized he had, like Washington, been "deluded and deceived" by their corrupt pro-British advisors. This swiftly became a party line repeated by other Democratic-Republican editors.

The desperate Federalists conferred with President Adams, who remained adamant. When they threatened to veto Murray's appointment, Adams agreed to name two other men, both dependable Federalists, to bolster the youthful Murray—Patrick Henry and Chief Justice of the Supreme Court Oliver Ellsworth. When Henry declined because of his faltering health, Adams chose another southern Federalist, Governor William Davie of North Carolina. Watching from the sidelines, a gloomy George Washington sensed this concession would prove to be only a bandage on a fatal political wound.[25]

CHAPTER 24

The Death That Changed Everything

To George Washington's intense satisfaction, John Marshall, Henry Lee, and Patrick Henry, the three candidates whom he had urged to run for office to combat Thomas Jefferson and James Madison's attacks on the Alien and Sedition Acts—and the federal union—all won their elections in the spring of 1799. But bad news came on the heels of these victories. In June, before Patrick Henry could take his seat in the Virginia legislature, he succumbed to chronic ill-health.

From Philadelphia came word that President Adams's peace mission to France had brought recruiting for the army to a virtual halt. Washington told Hamilton he now doubted if they would achieve more than the "embryo" of an army. One of Hamilton's New York friends told him it was progressing "like a wounded snake." With the threat of war removed, the Democratic-Republicans were protesting the trials of several other editors under the Sedition Act with devastating effect.[1]

More and more Federalist leaders began to give up on President Adams as a candidate for reelection. In mid-July 1799, Washington received a letter from his old friend, Governor Jonathan Trumbull of Connecticut, which had taken more than a month to reach him. Washington instantly concluded that it had been circulated to a number of prominent Federalists before it went into the mail. Trumbull urged Washington to consider running for a third term. He was the nation's only hope of avoiding a "French president"—Thomas Jefferson.

Washington's reply could not have been more forthright. He told Trumbull that even if he agreed to run, he did not think he could win. The opposition could "set up a broomstick, call it a true son of liberty, a democrat, or give it any other epithet that will suit their purpose, and it will command their votes in toto." He would be charged "with concealed ambition which waits only an occasion to blaze out—in short, with dotage and imbecility."

The ex-president was telling Trumbull that a man who had written a Farewell Address and rejected another term in 1796 could not reverse himself without permanent damage to his reputation. Washington responded to a second letter from Trumbull with unequivocal words: "I must again express a strong and ardent wish and desire that no eye, no tongue, no thought" may be turned toward him as a potential candidate.[2]

In October 1799, President Adams, ignoring desperate objections from his cabinet and Federalists in Congress, dispatched his two-man delegation to join William Vans Murray in negotiating a peace with France. Also ignored was a huge upheaval in the government of France. Shattered by defeat and headlong retreat from their conquests in Europe, the virtually bankrupt former revolutionists reeled toward collapse.

General Napoleon Bonaparte decided that leadership by a corrupt and divided Directory no longer made sense. In November 1799, his soldiers ousted these feckless executives and created government by a Consulate, which had a vague echo of the ancient Roman Republic, with its reputation for integrity. But this government was a consulate that Emperor Augustus Caesar would have understood at a glance. Bonaparte was the First Consul, and he had far more power than the two other members of the pseudo-triumvirate.

George Washington was baffled and not a little appalled by Adams's decision to send envoys to a seemingly disintegrating France. He thought fate had handed the President a perfect opportunity to abandon the idea. But Adams had become determined to have his way, no matter what anyone told him. Frantic Federalist politicians again wrote to Washington, begging him to make a public statement, disagreeing with the President. Washington admitted that an "awful crisis" seemed to be brewing on the political front, but he did not feel it was his duty to speak out. He was "a passenger only" and he would "trust to the mariners" whose duty it was to steer the national vessel to "a safe port."[3]

On December 12, General Washington wrote a cordial letter to General Alexander Hamilton, praising his proposal to establish a military academy to produce trained and educated officers for the American army. He had repeatedly called for creating this institution while he was president, but Congress, still locked in their opposition to a standing army, had ignored him. Once more, he reiterated his enthusiasm for the idea.

Within an hour of signing his name to this letter, Washington was on his horse, riding through wintry gusts of rain and snow to confer with the overseers of his five farms. He came back to Mount Vernon not a little damp and chilled, and awoke the next morning with a cold and sore throat. He stayed indoors until about four o'clock, when he went out to mark some trees that he wanted removed to broaden Mount Vernon's view of the Potomac.

That evening, Washington's voice was noticeably hoarse as he read to Martha and his secretary, Tobias Lear, the latest political news and editorials from various papers. When Martha withdrew to visit her granddaughter, Nelly, who had recently had a baby, Lear shared some news he had picked up from a neighbor: the state legislature had elected James Monroe governor of Virginia.

The ex-president said he could not imagine a worse choice. He suspected the Jeffersonian majority in the legislature intended their vote to be an insult to him. Lear listened politely and said nothing. He had long since made it clear that he favored the Democratic-Republicans. Washington accepted his stance without acrimony.

Perhaps trying to change the subject, or show he was in other respects a loyal secretary and friend, Lear expressed concern for Washington's sore throat. He urged him to take some medicine. "You know I never take anything for a cold," he replied. "Let it go as it came."[4]

At Monticello, Vice President Thomas Jefferson, alarmed at Patrick Henry's return to politics as a Federalist, had persuaded James Madison to run for the Virginia Assembly to oppose him. Their alarm had deepened when they learned that ex-President Washington was Henry's backer, and was recruiting men like John Marshall and Henry Lee to run for Congress.

The prospect of Washington as an active opponent was bad news for Jefferson's hopes of becoming the next president.

Both men were also dismayed by the icy reception their protests against the Alien and Sedition Acts had received. Not one other state legislature had joined Virginia and Kentucky. Every northern state had rejected the protests and the southern states, where Democratic-Republicans had a majority, remained mute. Massachusetts and a half-dozen other states had passed resolutions endorsing the laws. No less than sixty-three members of the Virginia legislature had voted against Madison's resolutions. At the urging of this group, John Marshall wrote a hard-hitting pamphlet, defending the acts as constitutional.[5]

More and more, both sides began talking about a resort to force. The *Gazette of the United States* called the Address of the Virginia Assembly, enlarging on Madison's resolutions, "little short of treasonable." Senator Theodore Sedgwick thought it was virtually "a declaration of war." General Alexander Hamilton agreed with him. He wondered if his regular army might be needed "to subdue a refractory and powerful state."[6]

John Nicholas, the Albemarle County Federalist who had warned George Washington about Jefferson's possible role in the Langhorne letter, charged that the Virginia government was collecting weapons and ammunition in Richmond. A Federalist leader in North Carolina claimed that "Jacobins" in Virginia were talking loudly about secession and were doing everything in their power to prepare the state's militia for battle. Vice President Jefferson opposed this talk of violence. "Firmness on our part, but a passive firmness, is the true course," he told Madison.[7]

The Vice President saw signs that the Middle States were leaning in their direction. But he could not have been happy with the outcome of the congressional elections in Virginia. Eight Federalists had won seats—an increase of four in their delegation. But in the elections for the state legislature, the Democratic-Republicans had won in a landslide. Among the victors was James Madison.

During the summer of 1799, Jefferson had invited Madison to Monticello to discuss their next move. In a note, he explained that he felt a need to do something about the states that were "disregarding the limitations of the Federal compact" by supporting the Alien and Sedition Acts. He wanted to express in "affectionate and conciliatory language our warm attachment to union with our sister states." They should declare that they were willing to sacrifice "every thing except [the]… rights of self government."They did not want to make every error or wrong "a cause of scission [secession]." They were willing to wait patiently until "the passions and delusions" that the federal government had "artfully and successfully excited …to conceal its designs" subsided.[8]

However, Jefferson continued, they should make it clear Virginia was determined, if disappointed, in this expectation, "to sever ourselves from that union we so much value, rather than give up the rights of self government…in which alone we see liberty, safety and happiness." As some historians have wryly pointed out, the author of the Declaration of Independence here wrote a Declaration of Divorce. The fact that the writer was Thomas Jefferson gave it a resonance that would echo down the decades.[9]

Instead of writing a polite refutation, as he had done when Jefferson sent him his earlier political aberration, "The Earth Belongs to the Living," James Madison leaped on his horse and rode the thirty-five miles from Montpelier to Monticello at a reckless gallop. Jefferson saw the anxiety on his face when his friend came in the door and reassured him that he had changed his mind. He did not think a threat of secession was the right solution for their current crisis. But he did not repudiate the idea.[10]

The Vice President was now convinced that he could not safely write a letter to Madison or anyone else without the danger of some Federalist spy opening it. When James Monroe warned him not to see Madison again for a further political discussion, lest they be accused of conspiring against the government, Jefferson cancelled their planned meeting at Monticello. Simultaneously, Jefferson exhibited a new ability to change his opinion of the French Revolution as France slid from the bribe-greased hands of the Directory into the bayonet-backed grip of Napoleon Bonaparte. The Vice President told Elbridge Gerry that the "atrocious depredations" the French had been committing on American ships in the West Indies had shocked him. "The first object" of his heart had become "my own country." He solemnly assured Gerry that he had "not one farthing of interest, nor one fiber of attachment out of it, nor a single motive of preference for any one nation to another but in proportion as they are more or less friendly to us."

Did Jefferson realize that he was all but reciting one of the central messages of George Washington's Farewell Address, which he had previously called an insult to France? Perhaps he thought it was time to change his mind about that political stance, too. More and more, he was acting like a presidential candidate.[11]

Prevented from meeting with James Madison by Monroe's conspiratorial dictum, Jefferson sent a new Democratic-Republican strategy to Montpelier by private messenger. He thought they should now call for peace "even with Great Britain." They should repeatedly declare their veneration of the federal union. Simultaneously, they should agitate for the disbandment of the federal army, citing its cost and the fear of a military dictatorship. They could and should protest prosecutions under the Sedition Act as "violations of the true principles of our constitution." But nothing should be said or done that "shall look or lead to force and give any pretext for keeping up the army."

The goal was to avoid giving the splintered Federalists a reason to unite. Jefferson saw them as divided into "Adamsites," who backed the peace mission to France, and "Hamiltonians," who were mesmerized by the army led by the ex-secretary of the treasury under General Washington's supervision. Jefferson urged Madison to send his own ideas about these matters as soon as possible.

Meanwhile, Madison headed for Richmond for the winter session of the Virginia legislature. There, he used the prestige he had acquired as a leader in Congress to nominate James Monroe as the next governor. The candidate won by an overwhelming majority. It was a move that clearly established Jefferson's power in the Old Dominion. It was also Madison's way of telling Virginians that George Washington was no longer a political force. To nominate as governor a man who had recently published a book loaded with insults to the first president was a virtual declaration of Washington's political irrelevance.

It was also a very risky move. The ex-president was sure to be infuriated. He would undoubtedly vow to retaliate in every possible way, summoning Alexander Hamilton and other eloquent Federalists to his aid. The presidential campaign of 1800 began to look like it would be a no-holds-barred struggle.

On December 14, 1799, totally unexpected news from Mount Vernon shook politicians and policies everywhere. George Washington was dead.

His cold and sore throat had led to an infection of the epiglottis, a small flap of tissue in the throat, that controls the entrance to the windpipe. Little understood in 1799, the condition had slowly destroyed his ability to breathe. In Richmond, James Madison rose in the House of Delegates to report that "Death has robbed our country of its most distinguished ornament and the world of one of its greatest benefactors."

In imitation of a tradition he had launched in the Federal Congress when Benjamin Franklin died, Madison proposed that all the members of the state legislature should wear black armbands for the rest of their current session. In spite of his devotion to Thomas Jefferson, did Madison still cherish the memory of his lost friendship with George Washington? Perhaps. But it was also shrewd politics to claim a reverential admiration for the departed father of the country.[12]

Madison's cousin, Bishop James Madison, president of the College of William and Mary, prescribed similar armbands for his students—and was startled when not a few refused to wear them. It was a grim indication of how virulent party politics had become. Additional evidence was the reaction of the House of Delegates when someone proposed a statement honoring the late Patrick Henry's "eloquence and superior talents." It was voted down—punishment for Henry's attacks on the Virginia Resolutions in his final campaign for election.[13]

Thomas Jefferson heard the news of Washington's death while he was at Monticello, preparing to return to Philadelphia for the second session of the Fifth Congress. He did not issue a statement, and made no effort to reach Philadelphia in time to participate in the day set aside for formal mourning—December 26, 1799. More than a few people have suspected this act of avoidance testified to the bitter dislike of Washington that Jefferson had exhibited more than once since their friendship collapsed.

There is no doubt that the U.S. Senate's memorial statement would have been difficult for the Vice President to read aloud, as he might have been asked to do as the body's president. "Ancient and modern names are diminished before him. Greatness and guilt have too often been allied, but his fame is whiter than it is brilliant..." The Senate and the House of Representatives joined a huge procession to Philadelphia's Lutheran Church, where Congressman Henry Lee spoke from the pulpit. His opening words achieved immortality—and summed up the national mood. George Washington was "First in war, first in peace, and first in the hearts of his countrymen."[14]

The next two months must have been an ordeal for the Vice President. One historian has counted three hundred ceremonies mourning George Washington throughout the nation. In Boston, Fisher Ames praised his political skills. "His presidency will form an epoch and be distinguished as the Age of Washington....He changed mankind's idea of political greatness." Many orators compared him to Moses. Others chose Alexander the Great. Dozens extolled the Farewell Address. In Boston, women wore black for weeks. Even the chair in which Vice President Jefferson sat in the Senate was draped in black.[15]

It seems almost inevitable that one of the first dissenting voices was Philip Freneau. He emerged from the sand dunes of South Jersey with a poem that simultaneously mocked Washington's eulogists and pseudo-praised the newsman's favorite target.

> *No tongue can tell, no pen describe*
> *The phrenzy of a numerous tribe*
> *Who by distemper'd fancy led*
> *Insult the memory of the dead*
> *He was no god, ye flattering knaves*
> *He owned no world, he ruled no waves*
> *But—exalt it if you can*
> *He was the upright, Honest man.* [16]

This was a good summary of what became the Democratic-Republican party line. President Washington had been a noble but aging soul, deceived by Hamilton and other corrupt Federalists into letting the country slide into the hands of Anglomen and monocrats. Jefferson led the way down this nasty path, more than once describing the departed hero as close to senile in his presidential days. Anyone who takes the trouble to read the vigorous letters Washington wrote up to the day of his last illness knows this is nonsense.[17]

CHAPTER 25

The Race to Make the Vice First

HAVING SATISFIED HIS CONSCIENCE—AND protected his political back—by acknowledging Washington's greatness, James Madison now turned all his energy to making Thomas Jefferson the next president.

On January 7, 1800, less than a month after Washington's death, the Virginia assembly published Madison's "Report on the Resolutions"—a brilliant defense of his objections to the Alien and Sedition Act. He began by affirming his devotion to the Union and muted to the point of extinction Jefferson's threats of nullification and secession. He called the Virginia Resolutions "expressions of opinion" that only aimed at "exciting reflection" in their readers. But he insisted the Sedition Act was a menace, because it threatened free speech, which he asserted was the core of a republican government. This point was especially important because they would soon be involved in a presidential election. How could voters find out the truth about the candidates if newspapers were silenced?[1]

Madison called a caucus of Democratic-Republican members of the House of Delegates to discuss how Virginia could play a leading role in electing Jefferson. They approved a plan to consolidate the state's electoral vote. Previously, individual electors had been chosen by districts. Now there would be one electoral ticket for the whole state. This guaranteed their candidate a handsome bloc of votes from the nation's most populous state. Next, Madison's old Congressional friend, William Branch Giles, proposed a set of resolutions calling on Virginia's congressmen and senators to push for repeal of the Alien and Sedition laws and the disbandment of the army.

In Philadelphia, Vice President Jefferson worked on changing the Democratic-Republican stance toward France. The "dictatorial Consulate" established by Napoleon had convinced him it was time to divorce the party from the expired French Revolution. He told his Kentucky friend, John Breckinridge, that Americans should realize that "their...character and situation was materially different from the French...Whatever the fate of republicanism there," America still had the ability "to preserve it inviolate here." [2] Madison added a thought that would provide ammunition in the coming campaign. The French transfer of the destiny of the Revolution from "the Civil to the military authority" was a good argument for disbanding the American army as soon as possible. "A stronger lesson has seldom been given to the world, nor has there ever been a country "more in a situation to profit from it." Jefferson promptly agreed. He claimed to be worried that Alexander Hamilton, "our Buonaparte" might try to "give us political salvation in his own way." [3]

With France eliminated as a bone of contention, the focus of the Democratic-Republican campaign shifted to saying positive things about Thomas Jefferson. Madison and his fellow campaign managers decided to present him as the man who wrote the Declaration of Independence. Throughout the 1790s, more and more Democratic-Republicans had chosen this achievement as the reason for their admiration of their leader.

With the Declaration came a widely circulated pamphlet portraying the candidate as "mild, amiable, and philanthropic, refined in manners and enlightened in mind, the philosopher of the world, whose name adds luster to our national character, and as a legislator and statesman, stands second to no man's...On him concentrate your present views and future hopes." The pamphlet was written under a pseudonym by one of Jefferson's most fanatic supporters, John Beckley, the former clerk of the House of Representatives, who had ruined Alexander Hamilton's reputation in 1797 by leaking the story of his adultery. [4]

Federalist newspapers and orators struck back with savage accusations. Jefferson was an atheist; like his Jacobin friends in Paris, he would attempt to shut, and if necessary, burn America's churches. Timothy Dwight, the President of Yale, saw Jefferson as one of the French "Illuminati"—the haters of religion. He foresaw the prospect of Americans burning bibles in public, the chalices used in Holy Communion displayed on the back of an ass (as they were in France), "our children, either wheedled or terrified, chanting mockeries of God…our wives and daughters lured into legal prostitution." All these Jacobin horrors would flow from a Jeffersonian presidency.[5]

In many states, the Mazzei letter was reprinted with charges of Jefferson's disrespect to the revered Washington. In Virginia, the anti-Jefferson party referred to themselves as "Washingtonians"—an indication that they were well aware of the late President's dislike of the Democratic-Republican candidate. It is telling evidence of what might have happened on a far larger scale if Washington had been alive to tell people what he thought of the race.[6]

The possible presence and the tragic absence of Washington is the great "What If?" of the 1800 election. The Federalists desperately needed him to hold their party together. President Adams was totally inadequate to this challenge. He added insults to his hatred and jealousy of the party's leader, Alexander Hamilton, calling him "the bastard brat of a Scotch peddler"—a cruel description of his West Indian mother's relationship to his Scottish-born father, whose common-law marriage had never been legalized.

An infuriated Hamilton wrote a scathing fifty-page attack on Adams, which he tried to circulate secretly to Federalist leaders in key states. Hamilton hoped to persuade them to switch their electoral votes to Adams's running mate, Charles Cotesworth Pinckney of South Carolina, making him president and Adams a three-term vice president. Thomas Jefferson's running mate, former Senator Aaron Burr of New York, got his hands on a copy and soon Democratic-Republican newspapers were printing excerpts from it to a chorus of hoots and jeers.

If Washington had been alive, he would never have allowed Hamilton to inflict such suicidal political wounds on the Federalist party. A distraught Noah Webster said the ex-treasury secretary's "ambition, pride, and overbearing temper" were in danger of making him "the evil genius of his country." One of Hamilton's closest friends, fellow attorney Robert Troup, said his character was "radically lacking in discretion."[7]

A politically active Washington would also have disapproved of the Federalist use of the Sedition Act to harass and punish Democratic-Republican editors throughout the year 1800. During his presidency, Washington had never tried to silence any of his newspaper critics, no matter how much they exasperated him. He would have urged the same policy in 1800, when all threat of a French invasion had vanished, and Congress, with the cooperation of many moderate Federalists, disbanded most of General Hamilton's army. No longer could a government attempt to control the press be justified as a war measure.

☙

Also in the drama in a murky way was President Adams's peace initiative. Like everything else this unpolitical politician did, his envoys ignored the very real possibility that a successful negotiation with France might have given Adams's run for reelection a badly needed boost. Instead, the negotiators did not reach an agreement with the French until September 30, 1800—much too late for the news to get to America and influence the election. The treaty was far from a triumph. Sensing Adams wanted peace at almost any price, the negotiators abandoned the $12 million in claims for the seizures of hundreds of American ships during the year of hostilities that historians now call the Quasi War. In return, France grandly released the United States from the 1778 Treaty of Alliance, which the Federalist Fifth Congress had already declared defunct. Still, the agreement was a proclamation of peace that might have changed many voters' minds. But a copy of the treaty did not arrive in Washington, D.C. until December 11, 1800. By that time, John Adams had lost the election.

☙

The contest between the two formerly close friends came down to a struggle for two key states, New York and South Carolina. In both, the Federalists seemed to have an advantage—John Jay was governor of New York and South Carolina was naturally inclined to favor the Federalist candidate for vice president, native son Charles Cotesworth Pinckney. But cool, canny Aaron Burr proved himself a far better politician than the Adams-hating Hamilton. Burr put together a ticket of famous names for New York's state legislature, led by Washington's old and still active enemy, ex-General Horatio Gates. In April, the Democratic-Republicans carried every electoral district in New York City, guaranteeing them control of the legislature and the Empire State's electoral votes.

In South Carolina, another member of the talented Pinckney clan, also named Charles, concentrated on winning Democratic-Republican votes among the small farmers in the backcountry. They were traditionally jealous of the dominance of the state's politics by the Federalist "grandees" of Charleston.

At Monticello, Thomas Jefferson kept in close touch with the political contests in the various states. His hopes had risen with Burr's victory in New York, but a seesaw motion soon prevailed, as New England voted in a bloc for Adams. In a letter to Madison, Jefferson reported a hairbreadth victory in North Carolina and a landslide win in Georgia, counterbalanced by news that New Jersey and South Carolina were too close to call. Madison replied with his own assessments. South Carolina looked "ominous" but they had not yet heard from the backcountry. Maryland was "neither flattering nor altogether hopeless" and Pennsylvania was "uncertain."[8]

By November, the candidate and his campaign manager waited with growing tension for news from South Carolina. The Palmetto State's vote would decide the election. Pennsylvania had divided its electoral votes, New Jersey had gone Federalist, and Maryland had swung to Jefferson. To make sure no Federalist snoopers interfered, all the letters from and to Charles Pinckney came and went to Madison, who was not on any ballot.

On November 24, another letter reached Montpelier. Almost simultaneously, Vice President Jefferson cantered up the drive to Madison's home, planning to stay overnight. He was on his way to Washington, D.C., which had become the nation's capital in accordance with the compromise he had negotiated with Alexander Hamilton ten years ago.

Madison opened the letter and read an exultant message from Charles Pinckney. The Democratic-Republicans had carried South Carolina. Charles Cotesworthy Pinckney had repudiated Alexander Hamilton and announced he would not accept any electoral vote that was not also pledged to President Adams. The Federalists had won a majority of the state's voters, but many of their electors had been convinced by Hamilton's attack on the President and declared they would vote for Pinckney, but not Adams. After ten days of wrangling, a majority of the electors gave their votes to Jefferson and Burr.

A beaming Madison handed the letter to President-elect Thomas Jefferson, who instantly asked Madison to be his secretary of state. He just as instantly accepted. There can be little doubt there was a veritable flood of good cheer at the Montpelier dinner table that night. An ebullient Dolley Madison probably joined them, adding to the festive mood.[9]

In Washington, D.C., Thomas Jefferson learned that a bizarre problem might keep him from occupying the presidential "palace," as many people were calling the huge, unfinished, not yet designated White House. Jefferson and Aaron Burr had both received the same number of electoral votes. Burr had been angered by the failure of Southern electors to vote for him when he ran with Jefferson in 1796. He had exacted a solemn promise from Madison that this would not happen again. But at least one elector in some southern state was supposed to vote for someone—anyone—else to avoid a tie.

No one remembered to do this, and the election had been thrown into the House of Representatives, in accordance with the Constitution's rule that the congressmen had the power to choose a president when both candidates lacked a nine-state majority in the electoral college. It soon became apparent that the House was divided—eight states for Jefferson, and six for Burr.

At first, the Federalists saw a chance to nullify the election. They talked of maintaining the 8–6 split and appointing an interim president—perhaps John Marshall, who had just been named chief justice of the Supreme Court by President Adams. James Monroe, the governor of Virginia, warned that a refusal to seat Jefferson could start a civil war. The Democratic-Republican governor of Pennsylvania echoed him.

Various people, notably Congressman Albert Gallatin, thought Burr should come to Washington and make it clear to the Federalists that he would not accept an offer to make him president. Burr chose to remain in Albany, N.Y., serving in the state legislature, and pretending to be preoccupied with preparations for his daughter's wedding. More and more Federalists began to think he represented a solution they could and would tolerate.

Alexander Hamilton, the man who had almost singlehandedly created this impasse, wrote frantic letters to leading Federalists, condemning Burr for almost every sin in the catalogue of evil. He urged them to choose the hated Jefferson, who at least had "pretensions to character." As a decisive vote loomed in the House of Representatives, Gouverneur Morris, now a senator from New York, told Hamilton that the Federalists, "seriously and generally after much advisement" preferred Burr to Jefferson. It was oblique testimony that the Federalist Party was collapsing—and Alexander Hamilton's political career was over.[10]

Thomas Jefferson tried to solve this deadlock with an act of astonishing hypocrisy. On the first day of the New Year and the new century, he took a ferry across the Potomac River at Alexandria, hired a horse, and rode to Mount Vernon to express his sympathy for Washington's death to his presumably still grieving widow. Martha Washington and her granddaughter, Nelly, received him with icy politeness.

Martha Washington had no trouble concluding that Jefferson's motive for his visit was an attempt to win favor from Federalist congressmen who now had the power to decide the election. Martha was soon telling friends that, next to her husband's death, the "detestable" Jefferson's visit was "the most painful occurrence" of her life. He must have known, she added, that she was well aware of his "perfidy." [11]

For seven days and nights, the House of Representatives voted repeatedly without altering the 8–6 division. Finally, Congressman James Bayard of Delaware grew weary of the deadlock. As the lone representative of his tiny state, he had the power to end the impasse. He let it be known that he would be willing to do so if Mr. Jefferson made certain promises: 1. He would not meddle with Hamilton's financial system. 2. America's foreign policy would remain neutral. 3. The Navy would be preserved and gradually increased. 4. There would be no wholesale purge of Federalist officeholders.

This was a solution that George Washington would have undoubtedly approved. Much later, Jefferson would claim he had refused to accept the presidency "with his hands tied." But there is strong evidence that he negotiated through a third party and accepted these conditions. James Bayard switched his vote and Thomas Jefferson became the third president of the United States.

The new chief executive and Vice President Burr exchanged warm letters vowing to ignore the scandalmongers who were claiming that Burr had secretly suggested to certain Federalists that he was willing to become president in Jefferson's place. Simultaneously, the new chief executive began filling his *Anas* with reports of Burr's untrustworthiness. It was the first step to what would soon become a hatred far more virulent than his antipathy for George Washington. [12]

CHAPTER 26

The UnWashington President in His Federal Village

T HE NATION'S NEW LEADER described his presidency as "The Revolution of 1800." The phrase starkly reveals Thomas Jefferson's envy of George Washington, the man who had won the Revolution of 1776. President Jefferson was determined to do as many things as possible the way President Washington did *not* do them.

This program began in Washington, D.C. on March 4, 1801, with Jefferson's trip to the Capitol to give his inaugural address. Instead of riding in a splendid carriage like his predecessors, President-elect Jefferson walked. He was escorted by a company of militia from Alexandria, two of John Adams's cabinet officers, and a few dozen Democratic-Republican congressmen. Ex-President Adams was nowhere to be seen. At four a.m., he had boarded a stagecoach and headed back to Massachusetts, unable to endure facing the man who had defeated him.

Artillery boomed as Jefferson entered the Senate wing of the Capitol, the only part of the building that had been completed. There was no cheering crowd; the population of the District of Columbia was so sparse, it would have been difficult to assemble one.

Symbolism aside, walking was the only realistic option. Jefferson had been staying at a boardinghouse a few hundred yards from the Capitol. Riding in a carriage would have looked pretentious—even silly. But Democratic-Republican newspapers—and later, biographers—seized on this stroll to demonstrate his identification with average Americans. No aristo-crat, he! This was a man of the people!¹

🎴

In the preceding two weeks, Jefferson had worked hard on his inaugural address. He had finished it in time to have printed copies to distribute to the listening congressmen and senators and the eager hands of newsmen. He included a tribute to George Washington, calling him "our first and greatest revolutionary character, whose preeminent services…entitled him to the first place in his country's love." Then, in a voice so soft, few of the one thousand people in the Senate chamber could hear him, Jefferson called for reconciliation and forgiveness.

He urged everyone to "bear in mind that though the will of the major-ity is in all cases to prevail, that will to be right must be reasonable; that the minority possess their equal right which equal law must protect and to violate would be oppression. Let us then, my fellow citizens, unite with one heart and one mind. Let us restore to social intercourse that harmony and affection without which liberty and even life itself are dreary things… Every difference of opinion is not a difference of principle. We have called by different names brethren of the same principle. We are all Republicans, we are all Federalists…"²

It was a much needed plea for political peace. But would the President be able to deliver on its promise? A substantial number of his listeners/readers were in no mood for such a message. The Democratic-Republican politicians who had borne a decade of Federalist slurs and sneers that they were malcontents, traitors, and Jacobins wanted *revenge*. The new presi-dent's Federalist cousin, Chief Justice John Marshall, who administered the oath of office, thoroughly understood their state of mind, having re-cently campaigned for Congress in Virginia.

Marshall divided Jefferson's party into "speculative theorists" like the President, and "absolute terrorists" like Robespierre. If Jefferson did not side with the latter group, Marshall predicted these revenge seekers would "soon become his enemies and calumniators."³

🎴

In pursuit of his proclaimed goal of Republican simplicity, the new president abandoned the levees and receptions of George Washington's presidency. He also declared an end to presidential proclamations. These "monarchical" customs had to be expunged from the presidency to make it more acceptable to the people. These changes drew praise from the Democratic-Republican newspaper chorus.

Even more popular was President Jefferson's cancellation of all internal taxes, and the demolition of the jobs of hundreds of tax collectors. Equally praised was his reduction of appropriations—and salaries—for the army and the navy.

The goal was a shrinkage of federal power—with a special enmity reserved for the Washington-style presidency. President Jefferson saw Congress, the supposed voice of the people, as the central power in the federal government. A small but important step in this direction was the abandonment of the presidential speech at the opening session of a new Congress. Instead, Jefferson sent a written message, which was read aloud by a clerk. It was an example that would be imitated by every president for more than a century. Not until 1912 did a historian by profession, President Woodrow Wilson, decide George Washington had the right idea. A speech reminded Congress that the president was the leader of the government, the only true spokesman for all the people.

Also on the political menu was a shrinkage of the third branch of the federal government, the judiciary. President Jefferson yielded to the wrath of the terrorist wing of his party and repealed the Judiciary Act of 1801. This law had created twenty-six new judges; lame duck President John Adams had made sure they were all Federalists. The legislation also made it easier to move cases from state to federal courts, and gave the latter jurisdiction over land titles. This clause stirred fury in Kentucky and Tennessee, which further tilted the president toward repeal.

Vice President Burr, presiding in the Senate, told Federalist Senator Gouverneur Morris of New York that he disliked the bill. Burr doubted the "equity" of depriving these judges of their gavels when the Constitution stated clearly that federal judges would serve for life and their pay could not be reduced. He wondered if the bill were "constitutionally moral." One of Burr's friends, Senator Jonathan Dayton of New Jersey, had similar feelings, and proposed that the act be "revised and amended" rather than repealed.

When the bill came to a vote in the Senate, enough moderate Democratic-Republicans liked this idea to create a 15–15 deadlock. The Vice President now had a vote, and he tilted toward Dayton, recommitting the bill for further discussion. Before any revisions could be considered, an absent Democratic-Republican senator showed up and it passed, 16–15. Some people said if the Senate had voted by secret ballot, the bill would never have won approval.

Burr's vote to recommit was another reason for President Jefferson to worry about his vice president. He may have been thinking of him when he said, while signing the repeal bill, that the talk of a compromise emanated from "wayward freaks which now and then disturb operations." This was not the language of a man supposedly committed to political reconciliation.[4]

In the afterglow of the president's inaugural address, other transactions escaped the attention of both politicians and newsmen. One of the new chief executive's first moves was an order to his Secretary of the Treasury, Albert Gallatin. He was to examine the U.S. Treasury's books and discover proof of Alexander Hamilton's double-dealing and corruption. Jefferson was hoping for a pretext to junk the whole Hamilton system. This violated the secret promise Jefferson had made to Congressman Bayard of Delaware. There were times when President Jefferson spoke and sometimes acted as if he were one of his party's terrorists.

Gallatin scrutinized the former Treasury secretary's records until his eyes grew bleary and his large nose drooped. The man from Geneva informed the dismayed president he had not found an iota of corruption—and Gallatin's economist head told his Democratic-Republican heart that the Bank of the United States and its funded debt and thriving stock market were vital to the stability of the republic. The bank, he informed Jefferson, had been "wisely and skillfully managed."[5]

Another presidential move got far more publicity—and erased the kind words President Jefferson had said about George Washington in his inaugural address. Less than two weeks after he took office, Jefferson wrote a letter to Thomas Paine, inviting him back to America. Paine had contacted Jefferson the previous October, breaking five years of silence. The pamphleteer was living in Paris on money borrowed from friends. Napoleon's France had no interest in him or his ideas.

The President told Paine that the frigate, USS *Maryland*, would soon bring Congressman John Dawson to France, bearing some modifications of John Adams's treaty of peace for the French to ratify. "Mr. Dawson is charged with orders to the Captain of the *Maryland* to receive and accommodate you," Jefferson wrote.

Paine translated Jefferson's letter into French and published it in a Paris newspaper. The French, who had largely forgotten the agitator, were baffled; the English, who soon read a translation in their papers, were bewildered that the new president would send a warship to bring back a man who had so grossly insulted George Washington, the American they most admired. The reaction in America was a mixture of rage, revulsion, and embarrassment. How could the president write an affectionate letter "to that living opprobrium of humanity, TOM PAINE," raged the Federalist *Gazette of the United States.*

Most editors could not decide what made Paine more opprobrious, the seventy-page collection of expletives he had flung at George Washington or his attack on Christianity in *The Age of Reason,* the book he had written after his bestselling *The Rights of Man.* The Democratic-Republican press was unable to summon anything even approaching enthusiasm for the President's invitation. One paper claimed that Paine was a citizen and therefore entitled to cross the Atlantic in a "public vessel." The President's favorite paper, the *National Intelligencer,* which he had helped bring to the new capital, insisted that everyone should "feel charity for the misfortune of a fellow mortal." [6]

Omitted by the commentators of the day was a probability that this historian finds particularly troubling. President Jefferson must have known that Martha Washington was still alive at Mount Vernon. In letters, she sometime referred to her late husband as "my ever regretted friend." Did it occur to the President that Martha would soon learn he had invited the slanderer of her late friend to return to America as an honored guest of the republic? It made an even greater mockery of Jefferson's visit to Mount Vernon to express his pretended condolences. Remembering the cool reception he had received, perhaps the leader of the Revolution of 1800 did not care.

Another move contradicted the new president's claim that, henceforth, only one nation, the United States of America, was the object of his affections. Four months after Jefferson became president, a smiling Louis Andre Pichon appeared in his office, hoping to arouse his supposedly abandoned passion for France and her Revolution. Pichon had been the man who helped revive John Adams's first peace overture after Foreign Minister Talleyrand's friends, X, Y, and Z, had aborted it. Now the slim charming Frenchman was back in America, still only a *Charge' d'Affaires*, but one with a diplomatic triumph on his escutcheon.

The affable Pichon was encouraged by President Jefferson's cordial greeting. The Charge' cheerfully reported the latest good news from Europe. First Consul Napoleon Bonaparte had regained almost all the territory lost in the resurgence of anti-French sentiment after Admiral Nelson's 1798 victory in the Battle of the Nile. An exhausted England, battered by nine years of seesaw war, would soon sign a treaty of peace with France at Amiens. This semi-surrender restored First Consul Napoleon's access to the world's seas and oceans. Would the President of the United States object if France shipped an army to Santo Domingo to regain control of that troubled island?

The 1789 Revolution had stirred wild violence on the one-third of the island that spoke French and is today called Haiti. The other two-thirds spoke Spanish, as they still do in the modern Dominican Republic. An explosive mix of whites, mulattoes, and slaves had triggered a bloody upheaval that ended with both halves of the island ruled by a gifted black man, Toussaint Louverture. President John Adams, seeing a chance to frustrate a belligerent France, had shipped Louverture's army food and ammunition and weapons, and sent him advice on creating a government. Loverture soon established a stable interracial society which had begun to restore the island's once fabulous prosperity.

President Jefferson's response to Pichon could not have been more positive. He thumped his desk and declared that "nothing would be easier than for us to supply everything for your army and navy, and starve out that black dictator, Toussaint!" The sneering label revealed that President Jefferson remained convinced that blacks were incapable of forming a worthwhile government. He was also oblivious to the danger of letting Napoleon Bonaparte plant a French army within striking distance of American shores. The proposal would have set off alarm bells in George Washington's mind.[7]

Pichon rushed back to his quarters and sent President Jefferson's carte blanche for an invasion of Santo Domingo across the Atlantic to his superior in Paris, Foreign Minister Talleyrand. The XYZ negotiator had survived the transition from the Directory to the Consulate without even the hint of a problem. He and Napoleon Bonaparte saw cynical eye to cynical eye about politics and power. The Foreign Minister had a plan to reduce the cocksure American republic to a submissive satellite. France would snuff out their westward expansion with a "wall of brass" along the Mississippi River.

How to do this? It was all very simple, in Talleyrand's scheming brain. The United States had negotiated President Adams's semi-surrender peace treaty with Napoleon's older brother, Joseph. The very next day, Napoleon's younger brother, Lucien, negotiated another treaty at the country palace of the Spanish king, Carlos IV. This agreement would return to France the immense territory of Louisiana, which King Louis XV had given to Spain in 1763 to compensate them for their losses in the Seven Years War. To prove the new arrangement was between good friends, Napoleon agreed to put King Carlos's son-in-law on the throne of Tuscany—most of northern Italy—and vowed, as any and all listeners would later attest, that he would never give or sell Louisiana to a third power.

Louisiana made Tuscany look like a mere dot on the world's map. Stretching from the Canadian border to the mouth of the Mississippi, and from the western bank of the Mississippi to the Rocky Mountains, it was a third of the continent. Santo Domingo was the pivot on which this gigantic power grab revolved. France was broke. Napoleon—and Talleyrand—remembered when "Saint Domingue," as the French called it, was France's most valuable overseas colony, a cornucopia that produced thousands of tons of sugar from its fertile soil. Bonaparte wanted to restore this flow of francs to the Consulate's treasury.

Within hours of receiving Pichon's message of President Jefferson's cooperation, the First Consul ordered his brother-in-law, General Charles Leclerc, and twenty thousand of his best troops, to prepare for a long voyage and a tropical campaign. Bonaparte was so sure that Leclerc could dispose of Louverture and his "gilded Africans," he gave his beautiful sister, Pauline, permission to accompany her handsome husband.

The campaign on Santo Domingo should not last more than six weeks, Bonaparte told General Leclerc. That would give him plenty of time to reembark most of his army and take possession of New Orleans and Louisiana. Control of the Mississippi's mouth would make it much easier to "persuade" the western Americans to see things from a French point of view. These bumpkins were extremely dependent on the right to ship their grain from New Orleans. A dozen or so regiments stationed along the Mississippi would add to General Leclerc's powers of persuasion. *Vive la France!* would soon become the favorite expression of western Americans—or else.

⚜

President Jefferson and his Secretary of State, James Madison, remained in contented ignorance of this plan. They had many other things on their minds. The President was upset about the warlike statements emanating from Algiers and other Muslim ports in North Africa. He decided to send a hefty portion of the tiny U.S. Navy to deal with these pirates— rather than pay the usual tribute to keep their corsairs away from American ships in the Mediterranean Sea. This decision would have American sailors and Marines fighting and dying in the Mediterranean for the next fourteen years.[8]

President Jefferson had other, somewhat contradictory ideas about the Navy. He thought it was a mistake to let it become too large. Especially wrong was the officers' fondness for frigates and ships of the line. The President thought these oceangoing vessels were prone to behave truculently toward foreign nations, leading to unnecessary wars. What the Navy needed were ships built to defend the nation's ports against intruders. The new president found time to design one of these vessels and order its construction.

It was a long, slim gunboat, carrying two or three cannon. Its outsized sails and oars theoretically gave it speed and the ability to maneuver. Soon there were dozens of these ships on the way. Alas, the Navy's professional officers did not like them. They claimed that they were too fragile. A single blast of their own cannon threatened to turn them into debris. But the President scoffed at these complaints and ordered his brainchild multiplied exponentially.

The President also fretted over the fact that almost all the officers in the minimal U.S. Army of three thousand men were Federalists, thanks to General Hamilton. Jefferson decided to found the military academy Hamilton and Washington had frequently recommended—and appoint only Democratic-Republicans to its student body. To make sure they did not threaten the government, as he believed standing armies were prone to do, the President chose remote West Point, far up New York's Hudson River, as the academy's home.[9]

Another presidential worry emanated from Richmond, Virginia, where newsman James Thomson Callender had just spent six months in jail for violating the Sedition Act. Jefferson had repeatedly supported this consummate smear artist in his attacks on John Adams, Alexander Hamilton, and George Washington. One of the President's first acts was pardoning Callender, on March 16, 1801, a mere twelve days after he took office.

The President also took an extraordinary interest in making sure Callender's $200 fine was remitted. This involved unexpected complications; Jefferson had to fire the Federalist federal marshal, David Meade Randolph, the brother-in-law of the president's son-in-law, Thomas Mann Randolph, because the marshal had supposedly packed the jury with Federalists for Callender's trial. The enraged marshal said he might exact revenge on Callender, who claimed he was afraid to go near him to collect his fine.[10]

Things only got worse. Callender informed the President that he would not be happy unless he became the well-paid postmaster of Richmond. When Jefferson balked, Callender came to Washington, D.C., to argue truculently with James Madison. Callender talked loudly of having information that might force Jefferson to resign his high office. The President sent him $50, which later looked to many people like blackmail.

When it became evident that he was not going to get his government job, the journalist began publishing some of his trove of damaging facts in his newspaper, the Richmond *Recorder*. These included the letters of praise Jefferson had bestowed on his literary efforts and receipts for the money he had given him—and the claim that the President had fathered several children by a mulatto slave named Sally Hemings.

Callender assured his readers it was well-known among Monticello's neighbors that Jefferson had kept Sally as "his concubine" since he returned from Paris. Their romance had begun in the City of Light, when fifteen-year-old Sally had escorted his daughter Maria Jefferson to France. Among the proofs visible at Monticello was a boy named "Tom," who had red hair and a striking resemblance to the President.

Federalist editors leaped on the story. It was reprinted in paper after paper across the nation, often with a poem first published in the Federalist Boston *Gazette*.

Of all damsels on the green
In mountain or in valley
A lass so luscious neer was seen
As Monticellian Sally.

Chorus: Yankee Doodle, who's the noodle
What wife was half so handy?
To breed a flock of slaves for stock
A blackamoor's the dandy

When pressed by load of state affairs
I seek to sport and sally
The sweetest solace of my cares
Is in the lap of Sally.

This was mortification in capital letters for a president who hoped—even expected—to eclipse George Washington. Benjamin Franklin Bache had reprinted British-forged letters portraying Washington in the grip of passion for a loyalist lady in 1776. But no one with even a minimum of intelligence believed them. The Sally Hemings story had plausibility stamped all over it.

Historians are still debating whether Jefferson was guilty of this liaison. In recent years some researchers have advanced what they consider conclusive proof, based on DNA evidence. Other historians have pointed out that there are several kinds of DNA. The one that the accusers cite proves little or nothing about an individual. Not a few people have begun to think that the accusation cannot be proved—or disproved.

All President Jefferson could do was grimly refuse to acknowledge the story. This was not an easy task, since he had once hailed the man who published the tale as a journalist without peer. Callender added additional injury by printing another story, claiming that Jefferson once tried to seduce attractive Betsy Walker, the wife of neighbor John Walker. Now a very angry Federalist, Walker confirmed the journalist's revelation and talked of challenging the President to a duel.

It is hard to resist wondering if the politician who had introduced ideological slurs and sneering accusations into America's political discourse with the aid of Philip Freneau was getting what he deserved. A great many Federalists, notably Alexander Hamilton, who had started a newspaper in New York, the *Evening Post*, thought this was unquestionably the case.

✧

Another problem confronting the President was traceable to a strong Jefferson prejudice—his hatred of cities. He was extremely happy to find himself presiding in semi-rural Washington, D.C. Many—probably most—of the rest of the federal government felt otherwise. By 1800, everyone who had invested money in the District of Columbia's real estate had abandoned the place.

The only completed block of private buildings stood empty and crumbling. On Greenleaf Point, another large cluster of buildings was described by one visitor as looking like "a considerable town which has been destroyed by some unusual calamity." On Rock Creek, a bridge that was supposed to connect the federal city to the rest of the nation—it had been built with symbolic stones from the thirteen original states—had collapsed.[11]

President Jefferson and his fellow Democratic-Republican administrators also found that the District had a strong appeal for those who thought Napoleon or General Hamilton or the ghost of George Washington was persecuting them. More numerous were those who connected the pursuit of happiness to a government job. Only 233 males in the population of 4,000 had more than $100 in cash or property. Welfare, called poor relief in those more candid days, consumed 45% of the District's expenses.

"In the heart of the city," wrote one visitor, "not a sound is to be heard," even by day. "Everything here seems to be in a dead calm," reported a newly arrived congressman. "An absolute supiness overwhelms all." The President's abandonment of internal taxes meant that the Capitol remained unfinished, after completing the wings for the Senate and the House of Representatives. There was no central hall or dome. The two wings were connected by a crude covered boardwalk. Around it clustered the only real community, seven or eight boarding-houses and a few shops.[12]

Most of the year, Pennsylvania Avenue, which linked the Capitol and the President's "palace," was a mile-long morass in which carriages sank to their axletrees. Congress voted $10,000 to build a sidewalk. The contractor used chips from the stone for the Capitol. The result was a surface that sliced open shoes when it was dry; in wet weather it became a kind of glue that often pulled them off a walker's feet.

In the congressional boardinghouses, life was dismal. Even senators slept two or three to a room. They entertained guests in an overheated parlor, "full of noise and confusion." Inevitably, men from New England lived together and ditto for southerners and middle staters. Most remained strangers to each other. Alexander Hamilton's vision of a cosmopolitan New York becoming a capital like London, strengthening the federal union with its arts and culture and creature comforts, had become its stark opposite in President Jefferson's "federal village."

No one put it better than George Washington's friend, Senator Gouverneur Morris. "We want nothing here," he said. "Nothing but houses, cellars, kitchens, well informed men, amiable women, and other little trifles of that kind, to make our city perfect." A French diplomat agreed wholeheartedly. "My God!" he cried. "What have I done to be condemned to reside in such a city?"[13]

Another source of the erosion of the "fraternal affection" that President Washington had seen as essential to the future of the Union was phenomenal congressional turnover, and poor attendance by those who had been elected. President Jefferson often mentioned the size of the Democratic-Republican majority in the Senate or the House of the Sixth Congress—when and if everyone "arrived." Very few congressmen or senators brought their wives to this cultural and culinary desert. One congressman told an old friend that "a banishment of six months to Siberia would not be more disagreeable" than a sojourn in the nation's capital. [14]

All in all, the Revolution of 1800 resembled that other Jefferson fantasy—his worship of the French Revolution. That chimera was about to bring him extremely disturbing news.

CHAPTER 27

How a Mosquito Rescued Thomas Jefferson's Presidency

I N LATE JANUARY 1802, General Victor Leclerc's armada hove off to Santo Domingo. The size of his fleet and army made Toussaint Louverture and his generals suspicious. It was much too large to be the escort of a delegation from Paris, offering a new relationship between France and the semi-independent island. They had recently received a letter from First Consul Napoleon Bonaparte, intimating that some arrangement of that sort was contemplated.

Leclerc called on Henri Christophe, the general in command of the port of Cap Francois, to surrender the city. When Christophe refused, Leclerc's warships and regiments attacked from land and sea. Christophe slaughtered the port's white inhabitants, set the place afire, and retreated into the countryside. An exasperated Leclerc discovered he was in a ruined city where almost all the food was in American-owned warehouses or on ships in the harbor. He was stunned by the prices the proprietors demanded.

The general rushed an agent to New York to borrow a million francs. The agent came back empty-handed. A bankrupt France's credit was worthless. Leclerc bombarded Chargé Andre Pichon with letters, ordering him to browbeat the Americans into making good on their promise to feed his troops. When Pichon sought help from Secretary of State Madison, he got questions instead of answers.

Why was the French army so large, Madison asked? He had heard from several people that part of the army was destined for Louisiana. Was that true? Was there anything to the rumor that the French had acquired this immense territory from the Spanish? On Madison's desk was a letter from Fulwar Skipwith, former consul and now the American commercial agent in Paris, warning him that this transfer had almost certainly taken place, although Talleyrand and Bonaparte repeatedly denied it.[1]

A desperate Chargé Pichon begged Madison for a loan of a million francs. Out of the question, Madison replied. It would infuriate Congress. A Pichon interview with President Jefferson produced soothing phrases about friendship with France but no money.

Meanwhile, General Leclerc, having seized wholesale tons of American owned supplies, was fighting a ferocious war on Santo Domingo. He won battle after battle. He captured Toussaint Louverture and shipped him to France, where he would die in a freezing dungeon. But Leclerc's casualties were shockingly heavy. Suddenly, he learned even worse news from his alarmed surgeons: A strange illness was creeping through the army. Soldiers suddenly grew too weak to carry their muskets. In twenty-four hours came black vomit, yellowing skin, convulsions, and death. It was yellow fever, produced by the bite of the most important and least known political ally in American history—a tiny buzzing female mosquito called *aedes egypti*. In regiment after regiment, whole companies collapsed and died virtually en masse. An appalled Leclerc asked for reinforcements, and Bonaparte sent him another fifteen thousand men. They suffered the same disastrous fate.[2]

Back in Paris, Minister Robert Livingston was asking the same sort of questions that Secretary of State Madison had thrust at Pichon. He was soon convinced that the transfer of Louisiana was a fact and sent the news to his government. A stunned President Jefferson replied that if it were true, America had only one choice: "We must marry ourselves to the British fleet and nation."[3]

In Paris, Envoy Livingston, a Hudson River grandee whose family had ruled much of the Hudson River Valley for generations, declined to panic. Instead, he wrote a clever "memorial" and circulated twenty copies of it throughout the French government. The essay warned them that an attempt to colonize Louisiana would cost a huge amount of money and might lead to war with the United States. Why was France risking the triumphant peace she had fought so long and hard to achieve? Santo Domingo was another expensive proposition. Livingston predicted that "ages will elapse" before the colony "ceased to drain the wealth and strength of France."[4]

The memorial was a seed that would take time to grow. For the moment, such opinions did not seem to matter. In August 1802, a blatantly engineered plebiscite made Napoleon First Consul for Life. A majority of the French people voted against it. But Lucien Bonaparte, the Man of Destiny's younger brother, operating as Minister of the Interior, declared him the victor by three million votes. It was one more ironic touch in the decline and fall of President Jefferson's "polar star," the French Revolution. Somewhere, Edmund Burke, who had died in 1797, was laughing. Tom Paine, marooned in France (Federalist vituperation had persuaded him to reject Jefferson's offer of transportation by U.S. Navy frigate), prudently decided not to attack the First Consul for Life with the sort of invective he had flung at George Washington.[5]

※

On November 2, 1802, General Leclerc died on Santo Domingo. Napoleon was undeterred. He shipped more troops and appointed as new commander, General Donatien de Rochambeau, son of the man who had headed the French Expeditionary Force during the American Revolution. He also ordered another general to embark as soon as possible with twenty thousand men to occupy New Orleans and Louisiana. On board were numerous officers empowered to play civil as well as military roles. Secret orders included bribing Americans to spy and agitate in France's favor—and form alliances with Indian tribes east of the Mississippi River.

Further reassuring the First Consul and his officers was the knowledge that the commander in chief of President Jefferson's army, General James Wilkinson, was Agent 13, a spy on the Spanish payroll. King Carlos paid the general thousands of dollars a year to keep him aware of what the restless western Americans were saying about the moribund Spanish empire. Napoleon was confident that the threat of betrayal—and the promise of more cash—would make Wilkinson a complaisant tool while French grenadiers created Talleyrand's "wall of brass" along the Mississippi.

※

Next came a carefully planned preliminary shock. The Spanish intendant (ruler) in New Orleans abruptly closed the port to American commerce. A huge uproar exploded in the western states and was swiftly echoed in the East. Alexander Hamilton called for war. Historians are now inclined to believe the closure was orchestrated in Paris. King Carlos IV had issued the order the day after he finally signed the documents surrendering Louisiana to France. When the general in command of the army of occupation reached New Orleans, he had orders from Talleyrand to stall endlessly about reopening the port and tell the complaining westerners that he had written to Paris and was expecting an early reply.

No doubt to Talleyrand's amusement, in the same month—September 1802—James Thomson Callender issued his revelation about President Jefferson's affair with Sally Hemings. Would Americans fight under the leadership of a morally degraded president? Worse, the Jefferson administration was totally unprepared for war. What was left of General Hamilton's army—about three thousand men—was scattered in garrisons in the West and South. Much of the tiny American Navy had been dispatched to the Mediterranean to fight the pirates of North Africa.

The military fantasy land in which Jefferson was operating was illustrated by a letter from William C.C. Claiborne, the governor of the Mississippi Territory. Claiborne said he had two thousand militiamen "pretty well organized," and he thought six hundred of them could capture New Orleans "provided there should be only Spanish troops to defend the place." The governor was obviously leaving room to maneuver if Napoleon's army of twenty thousand veteran troops appeared. If that happened, he would almost certainly tell his militiamen to go home.[6]

❦

In the midst of this international tension, Tom Paine arrived in Washington, D.C. He had waited until the Peace of Amiens made ocean travel relatively safe and sailed on a merchant ship. His appearance nonetheless triggered another explosion of abuse from Federalist editors. He was described as such a smelly drunkard, one paper suggested Jefferson might use him for manure at Monticello.

If the agitator had hoped to stay at the President's mansion in Washington, D.C., he was disappointed. Jefferson's two daughters were visiting; both these religious young ladies made it clear that they did not wish to associate with a self-proclaimed heretic and blasphemer. Jefferson persuaded them to tolerate Paine as a dinner companion for a single night.[7]

Matters did not improve when Paine began issuing a series of open letters "To the Citizens of the United States." He lashed out at his Federalist critics in the first one. In the second, he called ex-President Adams every insult in the dictionary. He summed him up by saying he was a man "of a bewildered mind." Adams brooded over this seemingly unprovoked assault, and could only assume his ex-friend Jefferson was somehow responsible.

Paine's third letter was a totally mindless assault on George Washington. He compared the Reign of Terror in France, with its rampant guillotines, to "the Reign of Terror at the latter end of the Washington administration and the whole of that of Adams." He asserted that the leaders of both reigns—Robespierre and Washington—were the same sort of men. The first president was of "such an icy and death-like constitution that he neither loved his friends nor hated his enemies."

Jefferson brushed aside calls to somehow muzzle Paine. He let the editor of the *Aurora* tell people that the President would never dream of interfering with the agitator's right to abuse and smear Washington and Adams because Paine had devoted "so much of his time, health, and talents to freedom." [8]

In Congress, Federalist orators excoriated the Jefferson administration for its cowardly tolerance of the closure of New Orleans. One of the Senate's best speakers, John Ross of Pennsylvania, accused the President of trying to "put to sleep" the spirit of resistance in the western states. Ross was from Pittsburgh, which added weight to his words. The Senator called on Jefferson to summon fifty thousand militia to seize New Orleans before the French arrived. The speech caused a sensation and threw the Democratic-Republicans on the defensive.

Early in 1803, an increasingly desperate President Jefferson decided to send James Monroe to France as an envoy extraordinary. He had orders to buy the port of New Orleans, the lands abutting it, including West and East Florida, which Napoleon had reportedly also acquired from Spain. The envoy was authorized to pay as much as $9 million. The purchase would reassure the western states and keep them loyal to the Democratic-Republican Party. After talking to the President and his secretary of state, a shocked Monroe realized he was being asked to rescue the nation from a ruinous war with France, the country Jefferson had taught him to embrace with such passionate enthusiasm.[9]

In Europe, an uncommonly cold winter had frozen Napoleon's New Orleans army of occupation in its Netherlands port of embarkation. Suddenly, a British naval squadron started patrolling the waters off the Dutch coast—a strange gesture on the part of a nation supposedly at peace with France. The British were worried that the army might head for restless Scotland or Ireland. The peace/truce treaty with Napoleon was beginning to unravel.

In the treaty, London had agreed to withdraw its army from Malta. France was supposed to do likewise from the Netherlands. Neither had done so. Then there was the general whom Bonaparte had recently sent to Egypt and the rest of the Middle East, where he showered mullahs and caliphs with presents and predicted the entire region could be captured by six thousand troops. Another French general had sailed for India with a large staff. Was he hoping to recruit British-hating allies there?[10]

In Paris, the news from Santo Domingo continued to be bad. That tiny ally of the United States, *aedes egypti*, continued to destroy whole regiments. A request for another thirty-five thousand men had just arrived on Bonaparte's desk. Every regiment in the French army shuddered at the mere mention of the island; it had become synonymous with death. Guerilla resistance continued to flare in the interior. Most of the island was now a burned-over worthless wreck—a graphic reminder of Minister Robert Livingston's prophetic memorial.

In France, the secret police told the First Consul for Life that many soldiers in the French Army and a worrisome percentage of the civilians were still republicans, unhappy about the Bonaparte dictatorship. There was only one way to keep these malcontents happy. He had to produce another smashing military victory. Against whom, the First Consul asked himself? The answer leaped in his soldier's soul. There was only one enemy he truly hated: that nation of shopkeepers called Great Britain. But raising and equipping an army and navy large enough to invade their island would take millions of francs—which were currently absent from the French treasury.

On April 10, Easter Sunday, Napoleon summoned Admiral Denis Decres, Minister of the Navy, and Francois Barbe-Marbois, Minister of

Finance, to the palace of St. Cloud, outside of Paris. Both men stared in openmouthed amazement when he told them he was thinking of selling all of Louisiana to the United States. The Admiral protested. He had spent much of the previous year shipping men to Santo Domingo. "It does not become you to fear the Kings of England," he said.

Barbe-Marbois disagreed. "We should not hesitate to make a sacrifice of that which is slipping from us," he said. "War with England is inevitable."

The First Consul for Life said he would ponder both opinions. The next day he summoned Barbe-Marbois back to St. Cloud. "Irresolution and deliberation are no longer in season," Napoleon said. "I renounce Louisiana—the whole colony, without reserve."[11]

Thus did the suspicious ministers of George III, Napoleon Bonaparte's imperial fantasies, and the tireless efforts of *aedes egypti* combine to transform the presidency of Thomas Jefferson from an imminent disaster to a triumph that would echo down the centuries.

CHAPTER 28

An Empire vs. A Constitution

O N APRIL 11, 1803, the same day that Napoleon confided to his advisors his readiness to sell Louisiana, Foreign Minister Talleyrand invited Minister Robert Livingston to his Paris mansion. Livingston went expecting nothing but more double-talk. For over a year, he had been urging Talleyrand to persuade Bonaparte to sell East and West Florida and New Orleans to the United States. He was astonished when Talleyrand asked him if he was interested in buying all of Louisiana.

As if he were talking to a four-year-old, the Foreign Minister explained that without New Orleans, Louisiana was more or less worthless to France. How much would the American government be willing to pay for the whole territory? The dazed Livingston suggested 20 million francs. That was much too low, Talleyrand said. Perhaps he should think it over and contact him tomorrow. Livingston slowly realized the Foreign Minister was serious.

The day before Livingston heard this astounding offer, he had received a letter from Envoy Extraordinary James Monroe, telling him he had landed at Le Havre. Livingston's reply was anything but a warm welcome. He had been infuriated by Monroe's appointment, which he considered a reflection on his abilities. He told Monroe the situation looked hopeless. Only if President Jefferson had already seized New Orleans by force was there any hope of progress toward a negotiated settlement. Otherwise, war seemed inevitable.

Thanks to Talleyrand, Livingston saw a chance to make Monroe even more superfluous. When the new envoy arrived in Paris on April 13,

Livingston greeted him with just enough politeness to allay any suspicion of what he had in mind. During dinner, Finance Minister Barbe-Marbois made an unexpected appearance and told Livingston he was eager to talk with him. When Monroe said he wanted to join the conversation, Livingston claimed it would be inappropriate. The Envoy Extraordinary had not yet been presented to Foreign Minister Talleyrand. Monroe was infuriated. He had heard about the Louisiana offer from his friend Fulwar Skipwith, and suspected Livingston was trying to close the deal without his help.

It was a first glimpse of the huge political importance of the Louisiana Territory. Both men sensed that whoever got the credit for buying it would have a very good chance of becoming a future president of the United States. The next day, Livingston bargained privately with Marbois and settled on a price of 60 million francs—about $16 million. There were many details to settle, and Monroe, once introduced to Tallyrand, joined the discussions. Simultaneously, he wrote a letter to Secretary of State Madison, accusing Livingston of trying to elbow him out of the negotiations.

Monroe wrote an even more whining letter to President Jefferson, telling him his health was bad but he was soldiering on—and thanking him for a warning to be "on my guard." Against whom, it was not clear—perhaps Talleyrand—or Livingston. Monroe assured the President he was "exerting my best energies in the cause in which I came…If I contribute in any degree to aid your administration in the confirmation of the just principles on which it rests, and promotion of the liberty and happiness of my country, it will prove…a delightful mission to me."[1]

Hoping to improve his standing with Madison and Jefferson, Monroe tried to badger the French into lowering their price. Livingston reluctantly went along. The Americans first claimed 40 million francs was their top figure, then 50 million. Marbois became more than a little frantic. He warned them Napoleon could change his mind at any moment. He knew Admiral Decres and Bonaparte's two brothers were telling the First Consul the sale was a huge mistake.

Finally, Marbois lost patience and told them if they did not accept the 60 million francs to which Livingston had agreed in the opening round, the deal was off. The envoys took deep breaths—they were not authorized to spend this huge sum—$250,000,000 in modern money—and said yes. On May 2, 1803, they signed a treaty that added 828,000 square miles to the American nation.

Finance Minister Marbois swiftly arranged with Baring Brothers, one of London's premier banks, and an Amsterdam bank, Hope and Company, to loan the money to the United States. Thanks to Hamilton's financial system, America's international credit was still the best in the world. The British government went along, telling themselves American possession of Louisiana was better than having a Napoleonic presence so close to their restless French subjects in Canada.

Within two weeks, France and Britain were again at war. Napoleon went to considerable trouble to announce the ratification of the Louisiana treaty by his puppet legislature on the same day that the guns began to boom. Without a fleet to defend Louisiana, the Man of Destiny did not want to leave any ground for considering the colony as "still French."[2]

In their negotiations with the French, Monroe and Livingston left unspoken another large worry. What would President Jefferson think of acquiring this huge territory? There was not a word in the Constitution that so much as mentioned the possibility of such an event. Would he—could he—turn his back on his belief in strict construction of the national charter? Would the President have to admit that President Washington and Secretary of the Treasury Hamilton were right when they insisted on the Constitution's implied powers?

Unaware that Louisiana was now American property, in Washington, D.C., President Jefferson was in the midst of another reversal of his political principles. The man who invented the term "Anglomany" for anyone even suspected of having favorable thoughts toward Great Britain asked his cabinet to tell him whether he should seek an alliance with the nation he had hated and denounced for three decades. The cabinet voted 3-2 in favor of seeking the alliance. Secretary of State James Madison commissioned James Monroe to go to London and begin negotiations.[3]

Almost three months had passed since Monroe had embarked for France. The Mississippi remained closed to American commerce. The Federalist press, led by Alexander Hamilton's *Evening Post*, published story after story, mocking and denouncing President Jefferson's timid inaction. Then came news that sent Jefferson into a paroxysm of joy. The Spanish ambassador informed him that Spain was restoring America's privileges in New Orleans.

The President saw a chance to teach the American people a lesson in the power of diplomacy. "To have seized New Orleans as our Federal maniacs wished" would have cost $100 million dollars and "countless lives," he triumphantly declared.

Jefferson seemed to have forgotten that the governor of the Mississippi Territory had told him he could overwhelm the token force of Spanish troops in New Orleans with two thousand militiamen. Also not mentioned was Secretary of State Madison's discovery that the restoration of New Orleans was described only as an "act of benevolence" of the Spanish king. There was no reference to the 1795 treaty, which had given American rights as well as privileges in the port. The Spanish, still assuming French ownership would soon be a fact, were simply arranging things so the blame for another closure—if Napoleon were so inclined—would rest on France.

✨

For the next two months, the western states remained calm and Federalists were reduced to grumbling. Late in June, Secretary of State Madison received the letter Minister Robert Livingston had written on April 13, telling him that France was offering all of Louisiana. Madison immediately gave his wholehearted approval to making the purchase.

The Secretary of State swiftly informed the President, who began leaking the news to Democratic-Republican newspapers. The first announcement came in that Federalist stronghold, Boston, where, on June 30, the *Independent Chronicle* trumpeted "LOUISIANA CEDED TO THE UNITED STATES!" On July 3, confirmation reached Secretary of State Madison in a letter from the retiring Minister to Britain, former New York Senator Rufus King, enclosing a letter from Monroe and Livingston, announcing the success of their negotiations.

Madison rushed the news to President Jefferson, who, in turn, sent it by messenger to the editor of the *National Intelligencer,* which had become a semi-official administration organ. On July 4, the paper published the electrifying news and citizens from the District of Columbia and from Virginia and Maryland rushed to the President's mansion to join a marvelously timed celebration. On the steps of his residence, a beaming Jefferson, flanked by his cabinet, announced the news.

The *National Intelligencer* gave President Jefferson all the credit for the stupendous acquisition, striking a note that would be repeated again and again in the next few months by Democratic-Republican orators and newspapers. "We have secured our rights by pacific action. Truth and reason have been more powerful than the sword," the editor declared. Other papers expanded this approach. The Boston *Independent Chronicle* declared: "The wise, seasonable and politic negotiation of the President, approved and confirmed by Congress, has gloriously terminated to the immortal honor of the friends of peace and good government and to the utter disappointment of the factious and turbulent throughout the union."

⚜

The flabbergasted Federalists now proceeded to cooperate with the President's demolition of their party. They pooh-poohed Louisiana, without bothering to find out what the average voter thought of the purchase. Orator Fisher Ames complained that "we are to give money of which we have too little for land of which we already have too much." Another called Louisiana "a great waste," a wilderness peopled only by wolves and wandering Indians. When the details of the treaty became public, other Federalist leaders were even more exercised. The Boston *Columbian Centinel* cried: "THE ADDITION OF LOUISIANA IS ONLY A PRETENCE FOR DRAWING AN IMMENSE SUM OF MONEY FROM US."

One of the few federalists who kept his head was Alexander Hamilton. In the New York *Evening Post*, he praised the acquisition. It coincided with his vision of America's destiny as the world's most powerful nation. But Hamilton shrewdly concluded that President Jefferson deserved no credit for this vast expansion. "Every man possessed of the least candour and reflection" would see that "unforeseen and unexpected circumstances" were responsible, rather than any "wise or vigorous measures" by the President.

Hamilton did not realize he was talking about *aedes egypti*. In 1803, no one knew the source of the devastating outbreaks of yellow fever that had wrecked the French army in Santo Domingo—and decimated Philadelphia and other cities. At one point, Jefferson blamed the disease on crowding and lack of sanitation, and declared that cities would soon be a thing of the past.

For Hamilton, the best explanation was "the kind interpositions of an overruling Providence." There is a hint of sadness, even regret in these words. The ex-secretary of the treasury may have foreseen that President

Thomas Jefferson was about to overshadow President George Washington for decades to come.

※

In Paris, Robert Livingston was a disappointed man. He arranged for friends to publish his memorial to Talleyrand, arguing against the wisdom of France's trying to colonize Louisiana. He tried to alter the record of when he first discussed the purchase with Talleyrand, making it before Monroe had landed at Le Havre. But he could not escape the date of his exultant letter to Secretary of State Madison about Talleyrand's offer on August 13—the day Monroe arrived in Paris.

Monroe, perhaps advised by the canny Madison, avoided arguing back. Instead, he humbly declared in a letter to Virginia's senators that he deserved no special credit for Louisiana. Napoleon's decision to sell was entirely the product of President Jefferson's masterful diplomacy. Madison chimed in, criticizing Livingston for not waiting until Monroe reached Paris before negotiating. If they had joined forces "under the solemnity of a joint and extraordinary embassy," they might have won a lower price. It need hardly be added that these were words that Monroe felt free to circulate to his supporters.

Livingston had let more than a few friends know that he hoped Jefferson would drop the tainted Aaron Burr and ask the Hudson River aristocrat to be his vice president in 1804. That would position Livingston to run for president in 1808—a possibility that collided with the ambitions of both Madison and Monroe.

Another Livingston gave everyone a glimpse of the political hardball these self-proclaimed Virginia idealists were ready to play. Robert Livingston's brother, Edward, was mayor of New York. In the summer of 1803, he discovered a clerk in his office had embezzled a shocking amount of money. He asked Jefferson's attorney general, Levi Lincoln, if he could have a stay on repaying it. The answer was an icy no. Mayor Livingston had to resign and sell every piece of property he owned to come up with the cash. He had some very harsh words to say about President Jefferson's ingratitude for his family's support in the 1800 elections.[4]

※

In his presidential mansion, Thomas Jefferson was having thoughts that might nullify all these political maneuvers. At a cabinet meeting on July

16, 1803, he told his chief advisors that he felt the Constitution should be amended before they could include Louisiana in the union. He asked them what they thought of a proposed amendment, which he had circulated among them. It was a long, complicated affair that would have divided Louisiana into white and Indian territories.

The cabinet officers hemmed and hawed. It was apparent that no one, including James Madison, agreed with the President. They pointed out that the treaty required ratification within six months of its signing in Paris. That meant the United States had to sign it by October 30. There was no way that an amendment could be circulated and voted on by the seventeen states now in the Union in the next two and a half months.

President Jefferson semi-backed down. He called Congress into special session on October 17. He ordered William C.C. Claiborne, governor of the Mississippi Territory, to summon some of his militiamen to occupy New Orleans. He told General James Wilkinson to support him with a detachment of regulars. But the president continued to fuss over an amendment. In a long letter to his friend Senator John C. Breckinridge of Kentucky, he proposed a new plan.

Jefferson admitted there was no time for a prior constitutional amendment. "The fugitive occurrence" of Napoleon's offer (a covert admission that he had had nothing to do with it) made acceptance a virtual necessity for "the good of their country." But he wondered if after the treaty was ratified, he should ask Congress to join him in an appeal to the nation to approve it with a constitutional amendment.[5]

A letter from Robert Livingston changed everyone's mind. Napoleon seemed close to deciding against the sale. He was grousing that the banks were too slow in delivering the bonds that would pay for the territory. Also worrisome was an explosion of wrath from Spain, because Napoleon had violated his solemn promise not to cede Louisiana to a third party. Livingston urged President Jefferson to "let nothing prevent you from immediate ratification."

The President rushed a letter to Senator Breckinridge, begging him to say nothing about an amendment. Cabinet members got letters imposing the same silence. Even after these precautions, the man who loved to legislate wrote another, shorter draft of an amendment and sent it to his cabinet. Again, they told him it was a waste of time.

Then came a clincher. Senator Wilson Cary Nicholas of Virginia, Jefferson's collaborator on the Kentucky and Virginia resolutions, had heard about the proposed amendment. He begged the President to forget it. The Democratic-Republicans in Congress were splitting into "Old" Republicans and "National" Republicans. The Old Republicans were the radicals that Chief Justice John Marshall had called terrorists. Cary said if they heard about an amendment, they might refuse to approve the treaty.

An agitated President Jefferson, flung back to losing so many arguments with Hamilton during President Washington's presidency, exclaimed that implied powers reduced the Constitution to "blank paper." But there was no other justification for the Louisiana Purchase. It was the death knell of his strict construction theory—a largely invisible triumph that pleased at least one watchful critic, Alexander Hamilton.[6]

On October 17, 1803, Congress convened in special session. The President sent them a carefully worded message, urging the Senate's approval of the treaty, and requesting the House to approve the $16 million price. He credited the acquisition of Louisiana to the "enlightened government of France"—praise of First Consul Bonaparte's dictatorship that must have caused at least a modicum of pain for a man who had seen the French Revolution as the birth of a worldwide triumph of *liberté*. Also extolled was "uncontrolled navigation" of the Mississippi and the elimination of "all dangers to our peace." The President declared he was relying on "the wisdom of Congress" to validate his decision.

Ironically, the man who wrote the message was President Washington's former ghostwriter, James Madison. He made sure there was no hint of constitutional scruples anywhere in the smooth prose. The Senate, led by Senator Wilson Cary Nicholas, approved the treaty the day after they read it. An attempt by the Federalists to call for all the pertinent papers was instantly crushed, and the solons voted their approval by an overwhelming 24–7.

The House of Representatives was a different story. The Old Republicans were in force there. When Federalist Roger Griswold of Connecticut called for background papers, Majority Leader John Randolph tried to silence him with an immediate vote. It passed by a hairbreadth 59-57. The next day, Griswold mentioned the word that the President had tried so hard to suppress. He asked how they could approve the treaty without a constitutional amendment. The "federal village" was apparently not that different from the Washington, D.C metropolis of the twenty-first century, with its inability to conceal secrets.

Griswold added an attack from another angle. How could the Jeffersonians incorporate the people living in Louisiana into the Union? Louisiana should be governed as a territory, the way the British ruled Jamaica or
India. A desperate Majority Leader Randolph repudiated this argument
with the rhetorical equivalent of a roundhouse right to Griswold's Federalist chin. He declared the Constitution's implied powers gave the government the power to incorporate Great Britain or France, if the opportunity
arose. He called for a vote and the Democratic-Republicans, irritated by
Griswold's tone of Federalist superiority, agreed to pay Napoleon his $16
million by a party line vote of 90–25. In New York, we can be sure Alexander Hamilton gleefully declared strict construction was now dead, em-
balmed, and buried.

Another argument erupted in the Senate when the solons discussed
implementing the treaty. Former Secretary of State Timothy Pickering,
now a Massachusetts senator, claimed that accepting Louisiana required
the unanimous vote of every state in the Union. Some Democratic-Republicans, with their frequent apostrophes to the will of the people, were
flustered by this contention. Senator Breckinridge of Kentucky's answer
was as unconstitutional as an American politician could get: he warned all
and sundry that if the treaty were rejected, the western states would secede
from the Union and start their own country. The vote was 24–5 for implementing the treaty.

Knowing how crucial time had become, President Jefferson rushed a
copy of the ratified treaty to Chargé Pichon. He exchanged it with a copy
he had received from Paris. Pichon then hired messengers to take the
confirmation of the sale to New Orleans, along with orders to hand over
the city and the territory to the United States. Meanwhile, Jefferson persuaded Congress to authorize a call for eighty thousand militiamen to
overcome any and all resistance that might erupt in Louisiana. Postmaster Gideon Granger launched an early version of the pony express to get
the necessary documents to Natchez, where the American army of occupation was assembling.

Accompanying the documents was a proclamation by the federal government, warning against resisting the army. Rumors had reached Washington, D.C. of a possible uprising in New Orleans. Along with threats of
meeting force with overwhelming force, the author—possibly Secretary of
State Madison—tried to calm the restless locals with soothing words. He
described President Jefferson as "a philosopher who prefers justice to

conquest." With their cooperation, the kindhearted President would make Louisiana "a garden of peace."

For the next seven weeks, President Jefferson and everyone else in Washington, D.C. fretted over what might be happening in New Orleans. On Christmas Day came hopeful news. Spain had handed over the territory to the French on November 30, with no resistance. This was a huge relief. Thanks to Pichon, there was no doubt that the French would comply with the treaty. Now the only question to be answered was whether the citizens of New Orleans would greet the U.S. army of occupation under General Wilkinson with cheers or gunshots.

While the Americans fretted, on Santo Domingo the final chapter of Napoleon's 1802 invasion was unfolding. Until Bonaparte declared war on England, there seemed to be at least a possibility of victory. Reinforced by another fifteen thousand men, General Donatien de Rochambeau was gradually regaining control of the situation. When news of the renewed global war reached the Caribbean, the British West Indies fleet headed for the island. They blasted French-held seaports and smuggled guns and ammunition to the black rebels.

In August 1803, a desperate Rochambeau asked President Jefferson for a loan of $100,000 to save "the most beautiful possession of France." With the Louisiana treaty on his desk, Jefferson did not reply. By October, Rochambeau was telling Pichon he needed a million francs a month to buy food and ammunition for his men. Once more, Jefferson and Madison ignored the French entreaties. A month later, with the French army reduced to eight thousand men (*aedes egypti* was still at work), Rochambeau surrendered his troops to the British fleet cruising offshore. It would be hard to imagine a more humiliating end to Napoleon's dream of a restored French colonial empire.

In New Orleans, the new French ruler, Prefect Pierre Clement Laussat, informed his mixture of French and Spanish subjects that they would soon be U.S. citizens. The Frenchman said that "the advent of war" [between France and England] had been the reason First Consul Napoleon has sold the territory to President Jefferson. He hailed the transaction as a "pledge of friendship" between the United States and France. He urged the Louisianans to participate in U.S. politics and foresaw a time when they could become a "preponderating influence" in the American government.

In Natchez, General James Wilkinson told Governor Claiborne that there was no need for the six thousand militia he was about to summon for the march to New Orleans. Wilkinson had visited New Orleans a few months earlier and cast a trained eye on the pathetic Spanish garrison of three hundred soldiers. On any given day, half of them were either in prison or in the hospital being treated for venereal disease and similar disorders of garrison life. These were the men that President Jefferson claimed it would have cost $100 million to conquer. Wilkinson ordered 450 U.S. regulars to board boats and join him and Governor Claiborne for a voyage down the Mississippi to the soon-to-be "Queen City" at the mouth of the mighty river.

Wilkinson was looking forward to conferring with Spanish officials in New Orleans. They were $20,000 behind in their secret service payments to him. Spain was as bankrupt as Bonaparte had been before he sold Louisiana. The General was delighted with President Jefferson's purchase. He was sure it guaranteed all his back pay and a lot more cash to come. The acquisition brought the Americans much too close to the gold mines of Mexico. Madrid would be eager to get his advice on how to keep the wild men of the West at bay.

The General and his regulars met no resistance. They were soon standing at attention in the riverside Place d'Armes while the French tricolor came down and the Stars and Stripes ascended the official flagpole. The soldiers fired a volley, saluting the occasion, and cannon boomed on dozens of Americans ships anchored in the river. A cheer rose from a small group of Americans in the watching crowd. A French eyewitness reported it only made "more gloomy the silence and quietness" of the rest of the spectators. Prefect Laussat summed up the prevailing emotion by bursting into tears.

Once more, Postmaster Granger's early version of the Pony Express went to work. Riding day and night, one of their durable band reached Washington, D.C. with the good news on January 14, 1804. President Jefferson instantly informed the *National Intelligencer* and sent an exultant message to Congress. The newspaper struck the leitmotif of the celebration in its rapturous editorial: "Never have mankind contemplated so vast and important an accession of empire by means so pacific and just." [7]

Ignored by these words were the thousands of blacks who had died fighting to defend Santo Domingo against Napoleon's army. The means by which they—with the help of *aedes egypti*—had enabled America to acquire Louisiana were neither pacific nor just. One wonders what Americans would have said if they had known that France's imperial venture had had President Jefferson's enthusiastic approval.

In the next few days, the *Intelligencer* published numerous fictionalized reports of how delighted the citizens of Louisiana were to become Americans. On Friday, January 26, over a hundred Democratic Republican politicians, led by the President, Vice President, and the cabinet, gathered at Stelle's Hotel on Capitol Hill for a celebratory banquet. While three cannon from the Navy Yard shook the windows with a salute, a band played a new song, "Jefferson's March," written for the occasion. A chorus sang an ode of praise for the President. Its signature stanza was:

> *To Jefferson, belov'd of heaven*
> *May golden peace be ever given.* [8]

It is hard to resist noting all these acclamations were a trifle "monarchical." If such tributes had been paid to President Washington, letters from Jefferson, Madison, and Monroe would have flung that term in all directions. Benjamin Franklin Bache and James Thomson Callender would have published indignant essays. Philip Freneau would have again emerged from the wilds of South Jersey to screech his alarm.

After the President and Vice President left the banquet, a toast was drunk to Jefferson. It was prefaced by three cheers. Someone suggested a toast to Vice President Burr. There were no cheers. Not a few senators and congressmen declined to drink it. Relations between Aaron Burr and the President had been sliding downhill for some time. There was talk of the Vice President forming a third party, composed of Federalists and moderate Democratic-Republicans who were put off by the rhetoric of the radical branch of the party.

A lot of people, including President Jefferson, were watching the Vice President closely. When a Federalist senator, a colleague of ex-Secretary of State Pickering, told Burr that New England planned to secede and form a separate nation, the Vice President did not say a word against the idea. Senator William Plumer of New Hampshire became convinced that the Vice President not only thought such a severance would take place—"he thought it was necessary that it should." Behind these words and plans was a growing fear of "imperial Virginia," as one Federalist leader put it. The Old Dominion and her southern satellite states would be in charge of settling and governing Louisiana, reducing the rest of the country to a mere appendage.[9]

Ignoring these gloomy Federalist prophets, the Democratic-Republicans continued to celebrate Louisiana. In late January 2004, no less than five hundred splendidly dressed men and woman gathered for a ball in nearby Georgetown. On the rear wall was a huge illuminated portrait of President Jefferson, framed by military flags. Hard-pressed to see Republican simplicity in this opulent crowd, the *National Intelligencer* said the "plain unblemished walls" were a statement unto themselves. They were devoid of "spectacles that celebrate the achievements of warriors." The words left little doubt that the President's admirers were determined to elevate their hero to a level of reverence well above that enjoyed by that well-known warrior, the late George Washington.

※

Few Americans paid any attention to the stupendous preparations to invade England that Napoleon Bonaparte was undertaking in France, with the help of America's $16 million payment for Louisiana. In camps around the port of Boulogne, on the English Channel, "The Army of England" was already two hundred thousand men strong. Elsewhere, almost as many workmen were building two thousand flatboats, each equipped with a cannon, to blast their way through defenses on British beaches. All Europe watched with awe as frenzied visions of total victory coruscated through France. The disaster of Santo Domingo was as forgotten as the abandoned army in Egypt.

A few thoughtful men in America—especially men with military experience, such as Aaron Burr and Alexander Hamilton—feared that soon after Napoleon dictated a humiliating peace in London's St. James Palace, the Man of Destiny would have fresh thoughts about a new world to conquer on the other side of the Atlantic. He would have no difficulty persuading a terrified Spain to cede the Floridas to him. With most of its navy still fighting Muslim pirates in the Mediterranean, the United States would be unable to prevent the arrival of a large part of the Army of England in this strategic territory. President Jefferson's gunboats, with their thin planking and low decks, would be helpless to prevent it. A single frigate had the firepower of forty gunboats.

East Florida occupied some two hundred miles of the east bank of the Mississippi. It would be a simple matter for the French to close the river for some reason—perhaps a failure to salute their flag on one of the forts erected along the shore. It would help to have the commander of the American Army on the First Consul's payroll. If the United States chose war, General Wilkinson would be an artful collaborator in marching his regulars and militiamen into a catastrophic defeat. Talleyrand's "wall of brass" would rise along the Mississippi, and the Man of Destiny would soon be celebrating the "liberation" of France's captive brethren in Canada. As for President Jefferson's treaty purchasing Louisiana—it would become an amusing scrap of paper in the archives of the French empire.[10]

CHAPTER 29

The Voters Speak the
Language of Praise

L OUISIANA REMAINED A CENTRAL concern in President Jefferson's
administration throughout 1804. He waited impatiently for reports
from an expedition he had sent into the territory, led by one of his former
secretaries, Captain Meriwether Lewis, and a fellow officer, Lieutenant
William Clark. When no news reached Washington, D.C.—everyone underestimated the distances that had to be traversed—the President published a hasty collection of data, "An Account of Louisiana," based on
stories from wandering trappers and imaginative Indians and myths from
speculative books. Among the purported wonders of the new territory was
a mountain of salt on the upper reaches of the Missouri River that was 145
miles long and 130 miles wide. Other details included Indians seven feet
tall and herds of woolly mammoths with gigantic tusks.

The Federalists seized on these unlikely details and ridiculed the President as a gullible pseudo-philosopher—the last man the nation needed to
administer this immense swath of the continent. The editor of the *New
York Evening Post,* Alexander Hamilton's newspaper, wondered if Louisiana's magical wonders also included an "immense lake of molasses...and a
vale of hasty pudding." Others brought up a more practical but equally
hostile point of view. Land prices in the eastern United States were certain
to plummet when people realized there was virtually unlimited fertile
acreage awaiting them west of the Mississippi River.

These brickbats were flung with the knowledge that 1804 was a presidential election year. On February 25, the Democratic-Republicans in Congress caucused to nominate their candidates. Thomas Jefferson was unanimously named for another term as president. For vice president, George Clinton of New York, the man who had persuaded Citizen Genet not to send his destructive open letter to Thomas Jefferson in 1798, won sixty-seven votes, and Senator John Breckinridge of Kentucky won twenty-one. Vice President Aaron Burr received none. President Jefferson's hostility to Burr had become a fixed point in the party's political geography.[1]

༜

Aaron Burr knew he had become persona non grata. At one point, he visited the presidential mansion and offered to go quietly, if Jefferson gave him an overseas appointment that would be worthy of Burr's current political stature. Perhaps minister to Paris? The president talked and talked and talked about what a wonderful idea that was. But in the end, the answer was no.[2]

This evasion probably had something to do with the way the Vice President presided at a Senate trial to impeach a federal judge. Harvard graduate John Pickering had been a Revolutionary War leader in New Hampshire. For a while he was a good judge, first in the state's courts, and then on the federal bench. A fondness for John Barleycorn had damaged his brain and led to bizarre behavior. The Judiciary Act of 1801 had stated that incapacitated judges could be replaced. Jefferson's repeal of the act had returned Pickering to the bench, where his antics soon made headlines. The President's solution was impeachment, which confronted another problem: How could an insane man be convicted of "treason, bribery, or other high crimes and misdemeanors?"

The man who loved to think legislatively had a solution. They would simply avoid mentioning Pickering's insanity. Jefferson exhibited even more disrespect for the Constitution by telling Senator Plumer of New Hampshire that a president should be able to remove a federal judge "on the address of the two Houses of Congress." This opinion became the gossip of the day in Washington, D.C. Senator Gouverneur Morris told Alexander Hamilton the Constitution was "gone."[3]

When Pickering was tried before the U.S. Senate, Vice President Burr did everything in his power to make it difficult for the Democratic-Republicans to ignore the judge's insanity. He ruled that his attorney, Robert Goodloe Harper, would be permitted to appear and read a letter from Pickering's son, testifying to his father's incapacity. When this information had no impact—one senator remarked that he was "resolved not to believe Pickering insane no matter what he heard"—Harper denounced the proceedings and withdrew, declaring he could not defend an insane man.

New England's Federalist senators begged their colleagues not to inflict the disgrace of impeachment on the family of a man who had once been an admirable patriot. The Democratic-Republicans stuck to their plan and convicted Judge Pickering without so much as mentioning treason, bribery, or any other crime. He was guilty because the articles of impeachment said so. Eight senators absented themselves rather than vote either way.

On the same day, the radical branch of the Democratic-Republicans in the House of Representatives reported articles of impeachment against Supreme Court Justice Samuel Chase of Maryland. He had won their enmity with his ferocious attacks on journalists who had been indicted under the Sedition Act. When it came to the federal judiciary, President Jefferson's Revolution of 1800 was becoming much more than a clever phrase.[4]

On wrecked, abandoned Santo Domingo, the only leader left standing was burly, black General Jacques Dessalines. He ripped out the white strip in the French flag and announced the creation of a new nation, Haiti. Next, he marched his army across Haiti and killed every white French man, woman, and child. This was his revenge for Napoleon Bonaparte's invasion, which President Jefferson had so heartily approved. Afterward, Dessalines wrote a letter to the President, expressing his interest in establishing diplomatic relations.

The President responded by asking his son-in-law, Congressman John W. Eppes, to support a resolution in the House of Representatives, refusing to recognize the black republic, and banning all political and commercial contact with it. Everyone knew this was a message from Thomas Jefferson. To drive the point home, Eppes glared around the House chamber. "Some gentlemen would declare Santo Domingo free." (He deliberately refused to call it Haiti.) "If any gentleman [still] harbors such sentiments, let him come forward boldly and declare it. In such case, he would cover himself with detestation."[5]

The resolution was opposed by the Federalists, who wanted to continue to trade with the black republic. But the embargo passed and Haiti
was cut adrift to reel through the next five decades as a rogue nation, ex-
ploited and abused by France and other trading countries. To this day, it
remains an ongoing tragedy. [6]

Around the nation, many Federalist newspapers continued to sneer at Jefferson for paying James Thomson Callender to slander John Adams and
George Washington. The man who had repeatedly proclaimed newspapers vital to the political health of a free society and had recommended
"scission"—secession from the Union—rather than tolerate the Federalists'
Sedition Act changed his mind when he became the nation's prime editorial target. The President wrote to Democratic-Republican Governor
Thomas McKean of Pennsylvania, suggesting that a "few prosecutions of
the most prominent offenders" might make certain obnoxious editors behave. How to explain this anomaly? Jefferson had decided it was perfectly
legal for state governments to muzzle hostile editors. The Bill of Rights'
enshrinement of free speech was limited to the federal government. This
presidential pronouncement swiftly travelled to other states.[7]

In New York, still bossed by George Clinton, the reaction was enthusiastic. The Clintonites decided to indict a young editor named Harry Croswell, who published *The Wasp*, a lively paper in the town of Hudson.
Croswell often dilated on the charge that Jefferson had paid Callender to
slander the two previous presidents.

To guarantee a conviction, the attorney general of New York went
President Jefferson one better in the legal maneuver game. He arrested
Croswell for "seditious libel"—a charge based on the common law of England, which made it a crime to criticize the head of state, whether or not
the accusation were true. No less a personage than Morgan Lewis, the
chief justice of the state's supreme court, presided at the trial. To no one's
surprise, Croswell was convicted. His lawyer appealed this parody of justice to the New York State Supreme Court.

Here was a political wonderland beyond the imaginings of the most
manic Federalist. The author of the Declaration of Independence was now
covertly in favor of using the legal system of the hated British tyrants to
silence his critics. Inevitably, the maneuver awoke a dangerous, not quite
sleeping, bystander, Alexander Hamilton. The former leader of the Feder-

alist Party volunteered to defend Croswell free of charge. Hamilton talked of issuing subpoenas to James Thomson Callender and to President Jefferson to testify in a new trial.[8]

Croswell was an ideal candidate for a Federalist martyr. Few newsmen equaled his skill at skewering the President—and incidentally defending George Washington. Here is his savage laugh at Jefferson's plea that he had given money to Callender only because he was a political refugee from Scotland and was being persecuted under the Sedition Act.

It amounts to this then:

*He (Jefferson) read the book [*The Prospect Before Us*] and…inferred that Callender was an object of charity. Why? One who could be guilty of such foul falsehoods, such vile aspersions of the best and greatest man the world has yet known—he is an object of charity? No! He [Callender] is the very man an aspiring and mean and hollow hypocrite would press into the service of crime. He is precisely qualified to become a tool, to spit the venom and scatter the malicious poisonous slanders of his employer. He is, in short, the very man that a dissembling patriot [and] pretended "man of the people" would employ to plunge the dagger or administer the arsenic.*[9]

The President pretended the Croswell trial was not happening anywhere in his domain. Callender, on the other hand, would have been delighted to testify. Before this delicious (to Federalists) scene could transpire, the newsman was found dead at 3 a.m. on the outskirts of Richmond in three feet of James River water. The coroner pronounced his demise an accident brought on by too much alcohol. But insiders had their doubts. Several months before this ultimate silencing, George Hay, James Monroe's son-in-law, had bashed Callender over the head with a club to encourage his reticence. Many people thought this time some member of the Monroe family or a friend had done a more thorough job.

When the New York State Supreme Court granted a hearing for a new trial, both houses of the state legislature jammed the Albany courtroom to hear Hamilton's plea. Over the next two days, the ex-secretary of the treasury spoke for six hours. His central argument was the importance of the right to prove the truth of an accusation in cases of seditious libel. Hamilton pointed out that the much despised and denounced and now expired Sedition Act had given each accused man the right to respond to his indictment. Hamilton was also apparently aware that

President Jefferson wanted all judges, including justices of the U.S. Supreme Court, removed and/or appointed by a majority vote of Congress. "We ought to resist, resist, resist until we hurl the demagogues and tyrants from their...thrones," Hamilton thundered.

Never was there a case where the truth was so important. "Was Mr. Jefferson guilty of so foul an act as the one charged?" The question catapulted Hamilton into a passionate eulogy of the slandered Washington that one of the judges thought was "never surpassed, never equaled." There was little doubt that the former Treasury secretary was well aware of the competition for ultimate fame that was being waged in this political war.

The mostly Democratic-Republican Supreme Court retired to argue about their decision. The New York legislators went back to their chambers and passed a bill, making the truth a vital part of any attempt to convict a journalist for seditious libel. It remains a landmark event in the nation's erratic progress toward a truly free press. A pleased Hamilton remained in Albany to argue other cases—and take part in another political enterprise of some importance. Vice President Burr was running for governor of New York and was bidding for Federalist support.

҉

The Vice President's candidacy had been preceded by a vicious newspaper and pamphlet war. British-born James Cheetham, editor of New York City's Democratic-Republican paper, the *American Citizen,* suddenly developed an intense dislike of Colonel Burr. Cheetham sent President Jefferson stories blackening Burr's character in every imaginable way. His most serious salvo was *A View of the Political Conduct of Aaron Burr, Esq.* This diatribe accused Burr of trying to steal the presidency in 1800 and plotting to run against Jefferson with Federalist backing in 1804. Cheetham was not shy about using epithets such as "cunning," "wicked," and would-be perpetrator of "an evil of great magnitude." [10]

President Jefferson told Cheetham that his information was "pregnant with considerations" and he would be glad to continue receiving "your daily paper by post." In an era when every paper had a political point of view, this was an oblique way of saying "I agree with you."

Burr did nothing while Cheetham abused him during the closing months of 1803. Suddenly there emerged in bookshops and other stores a pamphlet by one "Aristides" entitled: *An Examination of the Various Charges Exhibited Against Aaron Burr–And a Development of the Character and*

Views of his Political Opponents. It soon became a very hot seller. It refuted Cheetham's assaults and suggested the smelly shoes were on other feet. It accused Jefferson of cutting a deal with the Federalists to break the tie in the electoral college in 1801. It said even more scarifying things about DeWitt Clinton, mayor of New York, and his uncle, Governor George Clinton, with nasty references to the way the governor had once won re-election by invalidating the votes of three upstate counties. President Jefferson's toleration of this gross power play proved he was a "weak and fickle visionary" unable to control "the excesses of democracy."[11]

On December 31, 1803, the President found time to put his worries about Louisiana aside to write George Clinton, assuring him he regarded this pro-Burr assault as a tissue of libels and lies. It was all a "design to sow tares between particular Republican characters." Here was vivid evidence of Jefferson's remarkable ability to stand the truth on its head. It was the Clintons and the President who had started the slander game against Vice President Burr.

In Washington, D.C., President Jefferson maintained a sheen of politeness in his relationship with his vice president. He regularly invited him to dinner, and wrote fretful notes, making sure there was no confusion about the dates. If he was disturbed that Colonel Burr also began dining with mostly Federalist members of Congress, the President did not exhibit an iota of disapproval. Jefferson too invited Federalists to his sumptuous dinners at the presidential residence, hoping to promote his "We are all Republicans all Federalists" stance.

Everyone knew the serious dining at the residence occurred on nights when leading Democratic-Republican senators and congressmen gathered, and the President subtly—and sometimes not so subtly—told them how he wanted them to vote on various matters. The dinners were a central part of Jefferson's program to shrink the presidency to near invisibility in the public eye. Congress—the voice of the people—was now in apparent charge of the nation's destiny. The President supposedly did little more than lend them encouragement.

❦

Vice President Burr's candidacy for the governorship of New York stirred worry on several fronts. Insiders such as Alexander Hamilton knew that there was a tacit agreement with New England's Federalists that if Burr won, he would take the Empire State into their secessionist conspiracy, which was growing more and more formidable. Ex=Secretary of State Timothy Pickering was telling dozens of people that he planned to form an alliance with Great Britain, if they agreed to add Canada to the new nation.

Against this background, Hamilton's antipathy for Burr prompted him to make a speech in Albany, condemning Burr's candidacy. It was dismissed as envy. The former secretary of the treasury had made one blunder too many with his 1800 attack on President John Adams. New York's Federalists made it clear he had no power to change their minds about any political issue.

❧

In Washington, D.C. President Jefferson embarked on another step in the Revolution of 1800. Instead of the formal levees of the Washington and Adams administrations, the President's mansion was open every morning to any and all citizens who wanted to wander in. The President frequently met them in dusty riding clothes or wearing bedroom slippers—outfits that confused the visitors. One man described him wearing "an old brown coat, red waistcoat, and corduroy small clothes, much soil'd, woolen hose, slippers without heels." The visitor thought he was a servant.

The new British ambassador, Anthony Merry, and his large, formidable wife were not amused when the President greeted them in a similar outfit. Merry was wearing full diplomatic regalia—a black coat with gold braid, white breeches, and silk stockings. An infuriated Merry informed Secretary of State Madison that they had been deliberately insulted. Madison told him the President had received the Danish minister in a similar costume. Merry huffily replied that the Dane was a diplomat of the third rank.

With that complaint for a prologue, it was not hard to foresee the Merrys' reaction when Jefferson announced that he had abolished ranks for visiting diplomats. They would all be treated equally at dinners and receptions. Even more disconcerting was another new rule. When a group of guests went in to dinner, they would be seated "pell-mell" at any convenient chair, "with any other strangers invited."

At the Merrys' first presidential dinner, when the service was announced, Jefferson casually offered Dolley Madison his arm. The politically astute Dolley whispered: "Take Mrs. Merry!" but the President ignored her. The Secretary of State tried to make amends by offering the lady his official arm. Ambassador Merry fared even worse. In the dining room, he was about to sit down beside the attractive American wife of the Spanish ambassador when a congressman shoved him aside and seized the chair. "This will be a cause of war!" the bewildered wife exclaimed to her Spanish husband. Merry ended up sitting far below the proverbial salt, at the bottom of the table.

The seething British ambassador and his wife departed in frigid silence the moment they finished their dinners. Merry's report to his superiors in London was thick with outrage. He saw his treatment as an attempt to exhibit the President's hostility to Great Britain and his fondness for France—a claim not without foundation. Jefferson had also invited the French *Chargé d'Affaires*, Louis Andre Pichon, to the same dinner. This was a violation of an unwritten rule that diplomats from countries at war with each other were never expected to mingle.

Merry filled the ears of Federalist senators and congressmen with his fury. Soon the *Gazette of the United States* was attributing the President's "unaccountable conduct" to pride, whim, weakness, and malignant revenge. The timing of this silly contretemps could not have been worse. Many Americans, especially in New England, had begun to see Britain as a champion of freedom in their war with Napoleon Bonaparte's dictatorship.

Ironically, the man who suffered most from the President's leveling of diplomatic distinctions was his devoted disciple, James Monroe. Jefferson had sent him to London to negotiate an alliance to counter Napoleon's plan to occupy Louisiana with an army. When Bonaparte abruptly sold the territory, the President decided Monroe should begin talks to replace the Jay Treaty, which was about to expire.

At first, the tall, affable Monroe and his elegant wife, Elizabeth, were welcomed heartily. George III was so polite, Monroe was forced to repudiate the negative opinion of the monarch from his younger days. The new envoy was emboldened to ask the government to abandon the custom of impressing American sailors into the British navy—the major irritant in the two country's relations. The king and his ministers assured him they would do their utmost to solve the problem.

The worsening war between Britain and France made it difficult for the British to keep that promise. A strong British navy was the key to their national survival. Monroe was soon telling an impatient Secretary of State Madison that there was little hope of a new treaty. Suddenly, the cordial treatment the Monroes had been receiving in London's diplomatic and social circles underwent a stunning change. They were snubbed at dinners and receptions, and Elizabeth Monroe often ended the evening sobbing in her husband's arms.

The reason for the icy boycott was slowly revealed to the Monroes. President Jefferson's treatment of Ambassador Merry and his wife had outraged George III and the entire British upper class. At diplomatic receptions and dinners, Monroe informed Secretary of State Madison, "we have no fixed place and preference seems to be given to Portugal, to Naples, Sardinia, etc., powers which have not one hundredth part of [our] political weight." The President showed no inclination to help his ostracized diplomat by abandoning his pell-mell rules for White House dining.[12]

In New York, another drama was in its second act. Vice President Aaron Burr was running for governor. For a while his prospects looked good. Alexander Hamilton, stung by the Federalists' rejection of his advice, declared himself neutral. His newspaper, the *New York Evening Post*, backed Burr. So did ex-Governor John Jay, and former Federalist gubernatorial candidate Stephen Van Rensselaer, "the Patroon," whose thousands of tenants on his Hudson River estates were ordered to vote for the Colonel. The Clintons [NYC Mayor DeWitt and Governor George] nominated as Burr's opponent Judge Morgan Lewis, chief justice of the Supreme Court, the presider at Harry Croswell's conviction for seditious libel. Their literary hit man, James Cheetham, received orders to destroy Burr's reputation with all the ferocity and lack of regard for the truth that were the hallmarks of his methods.

Cheetham described Burr as a lawyer who had plundered the inheritances of his clients, as a sadist who had lashed enlisted men almost to death during the Revolution, as a sexual degenerate who had ruined the reputations of countless New York women, and as a political outcast who had been repudiated by both political parties. On April 26, 1804, the day the polls opened, the editor claimed that the Vice President had tried to attract the black vote by guaranteeing them an elegant supper at his Greenwich Village mansion, Richmond Hill. As a warm-up, he staged a ball at which "a considerable number of gentlemen of color" offered a toast to "a union of all honest men." The editor of the *Evening Post* declared that never in the history of New York politics had any newspaper stooped so low.

President Jefferson continued to receive daily deliveries of the *American Citizen*, putting him in close touch with the election. He was undoubtedly pleased by the result. Although Vice President Burr won New York City by some one hundred votes, he was virtually annihilated in most upstate counties. Chief Justice Morgan Lewis won in something very close to a landslide. The Washington *Intelligencer*, the President's semi-official mouthpiece, praised New Yorkers for standing "firm to their principles" and rejecting "acts subversive of the public good."[13]

For the next three weeks, a deeply depressed Aaron Burr ignored sympathy letters from friends and business associates. Also ignored were triumphant sniggers from James Cheetham, who gloated that the defeat virtually guaranteed Colonel Burr's ruin, financially as well as politically. The newsman was right about the financial side. Burr had helped to charter a new bank in New York which would have been eager to give a newly elected governor unlimited credit. In the Colonel's mailbox lay letters from numerous ex-friends, asking for the immediate repayment of long overdue loans.

On May 23, a totally unexpected visitor materialized on Burr's doorstep: General James Wilkinson, commander in chief of America's army. Wilkinson secretly shared with Burr a detestation of President Jefferson. The general regarded the commander in chief's cost-cutting reduction of the regular army's salaries and troop levels as a personal insult. At one point, Congress had considered demoting Wilkinson from brigadier to colonel; Vice President Burr had intervened and restored his rank.

This professional double-talker brought interesting news from New Orleans, which he had occupied with his 450 regulars in January. The city was seething with rage at the man who had purchased Louisiana. The President had inflicted on them a government that was little short of a dictatorship. There was no legislature. All the power was in the hands of the appointed governor, William C.C. Claiborne.

Without quite admitting he was on Madrid's payroll, General Wilkinson told Burr that local Spanish officials in West Florida were ready to believe anything he told them. All in all, it was an ideal moment for enterprising men to carve off a lucrative chunk of Spain's empire. The most tempting prize was Texas, an immense territory peopled by a handful of Mexicans and a few wandering Indians. Just over the horizon was Mexico—a country that possessed gold and silver beyond calculation. If all went well, it might not be difficult to persuade certain states, such as Kentucky and Tennessee, to join them in a secessionists' western empire.

Burr did not hesitate to express his interest in this daring enterprise. First, however, he had some business to settle with Alexander Hamilton. A letter in the Albany *Register* reported that Alexander Hamilton had spent not a little time denouncing Burr while he was in the state capital three months ago. The letter writer mentioned a few epithets and added that there was "a still more despicable opinion" of Colonel Burr that he declined to specify.

The Vice President—Burr still had nine months left in his term—wrote a letter to Alexander Hamilton demanding an explanation of the phrase, "a more despicable opinion." The tone was insulting. Hamilton knew it was a challenge to a duel. In a gentleman's code of honor, dodging such a letter impugned a man's courage. That rendered him ineligible to command an army. Beyond the horizon still loomed the possibility of New England's secession, and civil war. Looming even larger was Bonaparte's invasion of Britain; its success would be followed by renewed imperial interest in America. Either or both crises would overwhelm the leadership abilities of Thomas Jefferson. An American with a military reputation would be needed to rescue the republic.

On July 11, 1804, Colonel Burr and General Hamilton met in Weehawken, New Jersey, across the Hudson River from New York, where dueling was illegal. Burr killed Hamilton with his first shot. It was the greatest imaginable favor anyone ever did for Thomas Jefferson. The duel destroyed Hamilton literally and Burr politically, removing the only two men with the stature and skills to oppose the Revolution of 1800. It also inflicted a fatal wound on New England's secessionist conspiracy. Most Federalists rediscovered their enthusiasm for the fallen Hamilton, and regarded Burr with loathing as his murderer. The plot floundered to an embarrassed halt.

Colonel Burr did not accept his political destruction. Within three weeks of the duel, he was in Philadelphia, talking to British ambassador Anthony Merry, who was in the City of Brotherly Love to be treated for a medical problem. Burr explained a plan that had been growing in his mind since his conversation with Brigadier General Wilkinson. He asked Merry if the British government would cooperate with a general who led an army of western soldiers down the Mississippi to capture New Orleans, and surge from there to Texas where he would call on the western states to join them in a new confederacy. All they needed was a half-million dollars and a British naval squadron at the mouth of the Mississippi to close the river if President Jefferson called on the American navy to stop this revolution in the making.

The ambassador thought of how often President Jefferson had insulted him at his "pell-mell" dinners. Merry was soon writing a letter marked *most secret* to his superiors in London, telling them the current Vice President of the United States had given him a proposal "to effect a separation of the western part of the United States." [14]

For while, it looked as if a half dozen of President Jefferson's more dubious political chickens were coming home to roost as nightmare fowls.

๛

Before these disasters could occur, the presidential campaign of 1804 intervened. It was the first opportunity for American voters, as distinguished from political orators and newspaper editors, to express their opinion of the Louisiana Purchase. Local Democratic-Republican leaders did not hesitate to make Louisiana the heart of their campaigns.

In Washington, D.C., President Jefferson had decided to remove the chance of another tie in the electoral college between members of the same party. Among the more important topics at his political dinners was an amendment to the Constitution, providing that a party's nominees for president and the vice president would run on a single ticket. In August, he was pleased to inform Secretary of State Madison that South Carolina and Tennessee were about to ratify this Twelfth Amendment, making it the law of the land. [15]

Typical of the presidential campaign's electioneering was a celebration in New York on May 12, 1804, the approximate first anniversary of the day Robert Livingston and James Monroe signed the agreement to buy Louisiana. At sunrise, every cannon in the forts on the Battery, at the foot of Manhattan Island, and on nearby Governors Island, roared "a Grand National Salute." Every major building in the growing city and all the ships in the harbor hoisted the Stars and Stripes. While church bells pealed triumphantly, Mayor Dewitt Clinton, fresh from his and his Uncle George's triumph over would-be governor Aaron Burr, organized a procession in City Hall Park.

Through the city's streets, to the rattle of drums and the shrill of fifes, marched dozens of the city's militia companies, gleaming muskets on every shoulder. At the head of this military host, the commander carried a white silk banner with the reason for this celebration printed on it in large letters. EXTENSION OF THE EMPIRE OF FREEDOM IN THE PEACEFUL, HONORABLE AND GLORIOUS ACQUISITION OF THE IMMENSE AND FERTILE REGION OF LOUISIANA IN THE PRESIDENCY OF THOMAS JEFFERSON

Behind the marchers came the city's leading political organization, the Tammany Society, whose votes had helped make Thomas Jefferson president in 1800. They carried a fifteen-foot-long muslin map of the Mississippi River and the 828,000 square miles of Louisiana. The crowd of onlookers had no trouble getting the message. The cheers were loud and lusty. More than one man among the applauders saw himself becoming a proud and prosperous western landowner in the not-too-distant future.

In the fall of 1804, Thomas Jefferson and New York's George Clinton ran for the nation's highest offices against Charles Cotesworth Pinckney of South Carolina and Rufus King of New York. The Democratic-Republicans carried every state in the Union except Connecticut and Delaware. In the electoral college, they won by a staggering 162–14.

Even Massachusetts, the state that Timothy Pickering had envisioned as a bastion of his secessionist conspiracy, succumbed to the magical promises of the Louisiana Purchase. In Congress, Democratic-Republican majorities remained gigantic. Thomas Jefferson seemed on his way to transcending George Washington as the man who was first in the hearts and heads of their countrymen.[16]

CHAPTER 30

The Improbable Failures of a Triumphant Second Term

As the Democratic-Republicans celebrated their triumph, on the other side of the Atlantic, a related political drama was heading for a climax as well. The desperate British, so fearful of a Napoleonic invasion that George III took the precaution of hiding the crown jewels deep in the countryside, dispatched a band of sixty French exiles with orders to assassinate the Man of Destiny. When Napoleon's secret police detected the plot, he suspended plans for the invasion and launched a massive manhunt to round up his would-be killers.

When they were captured, the culprits confessed they had a co-conspirator living just across France's border in the principality of Baden. He was a relative of the executed Louis XVI, the Duc d'Enghien. The British secret police had funneled him thousands of pounds, with the understanding that the moment Napoleon expired, Enghien would rush to Paris and become Louis XVI's heir. The First Consul seized the hapless Enghien and executed him by firing squad, outraging the crowned heads of Europe.

Bonaparte decided it was time to abandon his current political title. He told his followers that as long as he reigned as First Consul, he would be the target of other murderous intrigues. The only solution was for him to take the title of emperor of France and name a line of succession in his family. The obedient French newspapers immediately began telling their readers the importance of giving the Man of Destiny a crown. His yesmen in the legislature vociferously agreed. Next came a plebiscite with the same fake results as the Consul for Life vote. The Corsican adventurer and his greedy family became the official rulers of France.

After a threat of a Napoleonic thunderbolt heading in his direction, Pope Pius VII decided to protect the large swatch of central Italy he ruled from Rome. He came to Paris to crown the new monarch on December 2, 1804. As the pontiff raised a jeweled coronet to place on the imperial head, Napoleon snatched it out of his hands and crowned himself, dissipating once and for all any lingering illusion that he represented the glorious 1789 Revolution in the name of *liberté*.

An imperial France astride Europe was the international background against which President Thomas Jefferson celebrated his reelection. He did not confess anywhere, to anyone, even to himself in his *Anas,* that he had been totally wrong in his vision of a French "empire of liberty" emanating from Paris. He also did not admit his landslide reelection was the result of acquiring Louisiana with very little discernible thought or effort on his part. On the contrary, the President was already beginning to congratulate himself for this achievement, a process that would grow more explicit with time.

For the moment, the President benignly tolerated extravagant praise from his followers. One wrote a long poem, bemoaning France's failure to live up to "bright freedom's early dawn." As for Haiti, the writer ridiculed the ability of blacks to produce a workable government, much less a free one. Writing off Europe and Africa in one sweep, this party-line bard concluded that only in America did the world's hunger for liberty have any hope of fulfillment.

The nameless poet justified his assertion with a rhapsodic list of the Democratic-Republican leaders in charge of the nation.

> *Lo, Gallatin sublimely stands*
> *While finance brightens in his hands*
> *His grateful country proud to own*
> *And smile on her adopted son*
> *No less great Madison shall claim*
>
> *Of public gratitude and fame*
> *But MORE the man whose lofty soul*

O'erlooks, combines, directs the whole
Yes, Jefferson.... [1]

Among the numerous politicians who called at the presidential mansion to congratulate President Jefferson was Vice President Aaron Burr. To demonsrate his friendship, President Jefferson invited Vice President Burr to dinner not once but several times in the next weeks. Burr was also cordially saluted by Secretary of State Madison and Secretary of the Treasury Albert Gallatin. Neither they nor the President were troubled in the least by the fact that the Vice President had been indicted for the murder of Alexander Hamilton in New York and New Jersey.

At least as eager to befriend Colonel Burr was Senator William Branch Giles of Virginia. He was one of the radical Old Republicans who backed the President's attack on the judiciary. Giles persuaded ten Democratic-Republican colleagues to sign a letter to New Jersey's governor, asking him to quash the Vice President's indictment for murder. Giles and his fellow Virginian, House Majority Leader John Randolph, were looking forward to impeaching Associate Justice of the Supreme Court Samuel Chase, and they wanted and needed the cooperation of the Vice President, who would preside at the trial.[2]

Like most politicians, Giles and Randolph thought cordiality would assure Burr's cooperation. They were also fairly certain that Colonel Burr, having been smashed by the Jefferson-Clinton axis in his run for governor of New York, would be awed into virtual servitude by the staggering dimensions of the President's reelection victory.

❁

In the Chase impeachment trial, Thomas Jefferson saw an opportunity to revamp the Constitution to make it more sensitive to the voice of the people. Chief Justice John Marshall was undoubtedly right when he called Jefferson a speculative theorist. But behind this figure was another Thomas Jefferson, who still secretly believed the earth belonged to the living and there was a constant danger of lingering "Anglomany" turning into monarchism or a dictatorship that would stifle the voice of the people.

The number of Federalist judges appointed by Presidents Washington and Adams was a prime reason for this worry. After Justice Chase was convicted, the President had a proposal ready to present to Congress.

First, he would warm up key leaders in the Senate and the House at several of his political dinners in the presidential mansion. He would reiterate and amplify his already stated opinion that Congress could and should remove any federal judge, including those currently on the Supreme Court, by a majority vote of the Senate and the House. Congress could then appoint whomever they pleased, with a reminder that the new judges had better listen to the voice of the people as it emanated from the nation's legislators—behind whom stood their enormously popular chief executive.

҈

Would anyone dare to defy President Jefferson's landslide mandate? The answer was a startling yes. In New Orleans and elsewhere in the purchased territory, thousands of new subjects of the United States had not been permitted to participate in the election. Their dissatisfaction with the autocratic government Jefferson had designed for them was acute. Their mood was worsened by the continuing ineptitude of the governor of the territory, William C.C. Claiborne. He could not speak a word of French and made no attempt to learn the language. The Governor soon became convinced he was surrounded by insurrectionists and bombarded the President with anxious letters.

In December 1804, these surly semi-citizens of the United States sent three delegates to Washington, D.C. to state their grievances. With them they carried an impressive "Remonstrance" written by former Mayor Edward Livingston of New York, now a confirmed Jefferson hater. The document was designed to embarrass the author of the Declaration of Independence. It asked why the right to vote and trial by jury had become "problems" in Louisiana. They demanded the citizenship rights guaranteed them in the Louisiana treaty, including statehood. They threatened to take the first available ship to France and demand justice from Emperor Napoleon Bonaparte.

The now royal ruler of France had returned to the English Channel to ready his two hundred thousand-man "Army of England" for the invasion of Britain. To test his flatboats he sent several thousand men into the heaving channel in dirty weather. Over five hundred men drowned, but the Man of Destiny was undiscouraged. He told one aide that even if it cost twenty thousand men to get the army ashore in Britain, it would be a small price to pay.

Rather than arouse this formidable opponent, who reportedly also talked of another invasion of Santo Domingo, President Jefferson reluctantly agreed to an act that Congress would pass on March 2, 1805, in the closing days of his first term. It gave the territory of Louisiana an elective assembly of twenty-five members. They were also guaranteed statehood when their population reached 65,000. But they were barred from importing slaves, unless they came with immigrants from the United States—and recent land grants by their former Spanish rulers were considered void.

These negatives produced a continuing dissatisfaction, which the Louisiana delegates did not attempt to conceal. One of the most sympathetic listeners was Vice President Burr. He was especially interested when they told him that would-be revolutionists from Mexico were walking the streets of New Orleans proclaiming their desire to win independence from the deadening hand of Spain. This was the sort of information that encouraged an embittered politician to find new meanings in that great Jeffersonian phrase, "the pursuit of happiness."

※

On February 4, 1805, the U.S. Senate convened for the impeachment trial of Judge Samuel Chase. Vice President Burr's preparations were dramatically different from the trial of Judge Pickering, which had taken place with little or no alteration of the Senate chamber. The Vice President ordered the two-story high walls draped in brilliant crimson cloth. Every politician in Washington knew what he was doing. He was saying that the trial was on a historical par with the 1788 impeachment of Warren Hastings, the Viceroy of India, in the British House of Lords.

Everyone also knew that the corrupt, imperious Hastings had been impeached at the insistence of Edmund Burke, the Irish orator who had predicted the French Revolution would descend from the glorious democratic sunrise of 1789 to the sordid dictatorship it had now become. Was Colonel Burr suggesting that President Jefferson's Revolution of 1800 was heading in the same direction?

The Vice President had carpenters erect a new semi-circular gallery in front of the permanent one. The senators' desks were moved out and their crimson leather chairs arranged in tiers. The members of the House sat facing the senators in more tiers of green covered seats. Further back, open to the public, was the permanent gallery, with room for over four hundred spectators.

Vice President Burr had his chair placed in the center of the chamber, against a wall. In two enclosed areas nearby sat the House managers of the impeachment, led by John Randolph, and Justice Chase with his battery of top-flight lawyers to defend him. The chamber looked more like a theater than a courtroom. One Federalist senator said the Vice President made the trial "a great, interesting, and super spectacle."[3]

The staging was designed to dismantle the Democratic-Republican impeachment program. Throughout the month of January, Burr had watched Senator William Branch Giles telling fellow solons that impeachment was not a particularly significant or dramatic process. Senator John Quincy Adams overheard Giles express his contempt for an independent judiciary. The Virginian told another senator that every justice on the Supreme Court except one, who was a Democratic-Republican, "must be impeached and removed." This included Chief Justice John Marshall, whom Jefferson—and Giles—especially hated.

"A removal by impeachment," Giles declared, "was nothing more than a declaration by Congress to this effect—you hold dangerous opinions and if you are suffered to carry them into effect you will work the destruction of the nation." At another point he described the process as merely saying, "We want your offices" so we can give them to "men who will fill them better." It had nothing to do with that nonsense about high crimes and misdemeanors in the Constitution. There was no need for a trial and its arguments. All Justice Chase had to do was show up, and the senators could vote to oust him and go back to their boardinghouses.[4]

This was American Jacobinism, showing its face—and teeth—in Washington, D.C., where it was virtually impossible to summon protestors to oppose it. If Congress had been meeting in New York or Philadelphia, the two previous capitols, such talk would have aroused demonstrators by the thousands. It was one more evidence of the danger of Thomas Jefferson's romance with his federal village.

More evidence of underlying terrorism was supplied by Chief Justice John Marshall. In 1804, in a ruling that laid the foundation for judicial review, one of the bedrock principles of the modern American republic, Marshall had declared that the high court had the power to rule an act of Congress unconstitutional. This obiter dicta had infuriated President Jefferson and the Old Republicans. Now, trying to save his job, Marshall started telling people Congress might have the right to review Supreme Court decisions and overrule them by a majority vote.

Vice President Aaron Burr was not even slightly interested in such equivocations and evasions. This trial was step one in his revenge on Thomas Jefferson. He insisted that it was extremely serious constitutional business—which was nothing less than the truth. Burr has been so abused by his contemporaries and later historians, another possible motive has been lost. He may well have been deeply sincere in his apparent conviction that the future of the republic was at stake in this trial. He was one of the most successful lawyers in the nation. He had served with distinction in the Revolution and his ancestry went back to the earliest arrivals in New England. If anyone felt he had an inherited stake in the United States of America, it was Aaron Burr.

As the trial began, a Democratic-Republican senator strolled around the Senate chamber munching an apple. The Vice President impaled him with a blazing rebuke that sent him reeling to the nearest refuse bin. Burr was equally hard on another solon who showed up wearing a loose floppy coat, in the nondescript style popularized by President Jefferson at his mansion. The Vice President also insisted on everyone listening to Judge Chase when he replied to the charges against him.

The bulky, white-haired jurist had a formidable reputation and a personality to match it. He had been one of the first Americans to defy Britain's assertion of the right to tax the colonies and a fiery backer of armed resistance in 1775. He had signed the Declaration of Independence for his native state, Maryland. He was an impressive-looking man, with a suave, confident bearing.

Chase's answers revealed his defenders' strategy. He denied again and again that he had violated any law or committed a crime in his behavior on the bench. He noted that the district judges who had served with him, and apparently agreed with his sentiments and rulings, had not been impeached, implying he was the victim of a vendetta. He admitted that he had criticized the Democratic-Republican Party and the Jefferson administration, especially in a charge he gave to a jury in Baltimore in 1803, in which he predicted the nation would soon sink into "mobocracy." Chase dared the prosecution to prove that this was "seditious" or even unusual, in the light of comments by other judges, whom he quoted at length.

President Jefferson strenuously disagreed with the Justice. When he first heard Chase's mobocracy description of his administration, he wrote a letter to one of the House of Representatives' leaders, Maryland Congressman Joseph Nicholson, asking: "Ought this seditious and official attack on the principles of our Constitution...to go unpunished? And to whom so pointedly as yourself will the public look for the necessary measures? I ask these questions for your consideration. For myself, it is better that I should not interfere."

The President meant, of course, *publicly* interfere. He was unquestionably interfering by writing the letter. Every congressman who read it—we can be sure there were many—knew that the President of the United States was asking for Chase's impeachment. Some readers might wonder why Jefferson called Chase's remarks "seditious" when he had vehemently defended the right of newspaper editors and congressmen to make similar remarks, prompting the Federalists to pass the Sedition Act in 1798. [5]

Part of Justice Chase's confident manner emanated from his personal convictions, but it was no doubt bolstered by retaining Luther Martin, the attorney general of Maryland, to head his defense team. Martin was considered the best trial lawyer in America and was a good friend of Vice President Burr. He was also unmatched in his hatred for Thomas Jefferson. When Martin wanted to insult a man, he said he was "as great a scoundrel as Thomas Jefferson." During Burr's run for the governorship, Martin had written him a warm letter, wishing him a "compleat triumph" over his enemies.[6]

Martin and his fellow lawyers mauled the largely emotional arguments of John Randolph, William Branch Giles, and their fellow prosecutors. Martin was especially effective when he accused the Jeffersonians of trying to destroy the Supreme Court. He said he was defending not only his friend Judge Chase, but his fellow citizens against a scheme to demolish a bulwark of their liberty.

On the last day of the trial, Vice President Burr made a crucial ruling on a proposal from Senator James Bayard of Delaware, the man who had masterminded the Federalist deal that broke the electoral deadlock in Congress in 1801. Bayard proposed that each senator be required to vote on whether Judge Chase was guilty of high crimes and misdemeanors. This challenge to the Judge Pickering precedent triggered a wild argument between Old Republicans, National Republicans, and Federalists in which several senators asked the Vice President to rule the proposal was out of order. Burr stonily refused, and the proposal passed by a single vote, 17–16.

This meant the senators were forced to focus on the facts of the case rather than on the prosecutors' declamations on monarchism, Anglomany, and Chase's violation of the popular will in his brusque assaults on the

Democratic-Republican Party. On March 1, Vice President Burr addressed the chamber in a sonorous judicial voice. "You have heard the evidence and arguments adduced on the trial of Samuel Chase, impeached for high crimes and misdemeanors," he said. "You will now proceed to pronounce distinctly your judgment on each article."

The secretary of the Senate read each article to every senator, and asked him whether it proved Chase guilty of a high crime or misdemeanor. The process took two hours, while the spectators watched in hushed suspense. The secretary handed the results to Vice President Burr, who solemnly declared: "Samuel Chase Esquire stands acquitted of all the articles exhibited by the House of Representatives." The Old Republicans had fallen far short of winning a two-thirds majority on almost every article.

Federalist senators gazed at Colonel Burr with dazed disbelief. One confided to his journal that Hamilton's killer had "done himself, the Senate and the nation proud." A Federalist newspaper said Burr had presided "with the dignity and impartiality of an angel but with the rigor of a devil."[7]

The infuriated Democratic-Republican congressmen withdrew to their own chamber, where they indulged in ferocious condemnations of the Chase verdict. Randolph, Giles, and the other Old Republicans put together a call for a constitutional amendment allowing any federal judge to be removed by a majority vote of Congress. Another amendment, aimed at the moderates who declined to vote for impeachment, would enable a state legislature to recall a senator by a majority vote, if he dared to displease them.

There is no surviving record of what President Jefferson thought of these proposals. But there are glimpses. One senator told his diary that "it seems to be a great and primary object with him never to pursue a measure if it becomes unpopular." This suggests the moderate Thomas Jefferson was now in control. Another hint comes from a witness who reported that Secretary of State James Madison was wryly amused—and pleased—by the Old Republicans' agitation over their defeat. This was not surprising. They were trying to eviscerate his Constitution.

In 1820, when Jefferson was seventy-seven years old, he told one friend that he still thought there should be some way to make federal judges show a sense of "responsibility" to public opinion. The idea that they should be independent of the will of the nation in a republican government still outraged him. William Short was unquestionably correct when he said Thomas Jefferson never changed his mind.[8]

The Chase acquittal cast a shadow over President Jefferson's second inauguration, which took place on Monday, March 4, 1805, only three days after the trial. The President's oratorical skills were far from mesmerizing, and he was further handicapped by his audience's memories of a remarkable farewell speech outgoing Vice President Aaron Burr had given in the Senate on the previous Saturday. It had been a deeply moving statement of his pride and pleasure in presiding over the U.S. Senate and a paean to the body's importance, which reduced several listeners to tears. Some people may have suspected it was Burr's way of demonstrating his unquestioned superiority to the new vice president, George Clinton.

This became all too apparent when Clinton began presiding over the Senate. Jefferson's silver-haired executive partner struck one diary-keeping senator as "old and feeble...His voice is weak—I cannot hear the one half of what he says—he has a clumsy, awkward way of putting a question. What a vast difference between him & Aaron Burr!" Another diarist, Senator John Quincy Adams, noted many of the same defects and concluded: "A worse choice...could scarcely have been made." [9]

For his second inaugural, President Jefferson did not walk the muddy mile between his mansion and the capitol. Instead, he rode in a carriage accompanied by his secretary and a groom. He gave his inaugural speech in a Senate chamber crowded with spectators. But most of them were not members of Congress. Perhaps signaling their unhappiness with the outcome of Judge Chase's trial, the national legislature had adjourned the previous night, and most of them were heading home while the President spoke.

Jefferson read his speech in a low, barely audible voice. But the *National Intelligencer* had copies of it in print in the day's edition. It was chiefly a summary of what his administration had accomplished. The national debt had been reduced, the expenses of the tiny federal government had been trimmed, and America had remained at peace with all the world's nations.

The latter claim was not the case, if the Muslim pirates in Algiers and other ports along the North African coast were regarded as nations. The President's undeclared war with them was now in its fourth year. A few

minor victories had been won at sea, and several of the city-states had negotiated treaties of peace. But Pasha Yussef Karamali remained defiant
behind his formidable forts at Tripoli. His posture was strengthened by an
extremely embarrassing American blunder. The frigate USS *Philadelphia*
had run aground in Tripoli's harbor, and its three hundred-man crew had
been forced to surrender.

In spite of cries of pain from Secretary of the Treasury Gallatin about
the cost, the President was forced to send reinforcements, swelling the
expeditionary force to five frigates, three brigs, and three schooners as well
as numerous smaller vessels. The navy remained stymied by Tripoli's forts
until, in 1805, an enterprising American civilian named William Eaton, a
former consul at Tunis, launched an unorthodox land war with the help of
a handful of U.S. Marines. Eaton recruited a ragtag force of five hundred
Arabs, Greeks, and Albanians who marched overland from Egypt and intimidated Yussef into negotiating a treaty of semi-peace. The Pasha forced
the United States to pay him $60,000—at least a million dollars in mod-
ern money—to free the *Philadelphia*'s crew.

Numerous congressmen were outraged by this costly pseudo-victory
and said harsh things about President Jefferson. Worse, a kind of guerilla
war continued at sea, forcing the commander in chief to keep two or three
warships on duty in the Mediterranean for the rest of his second term.
Jefferson's contention that a navy could entangle a nation in foreign wars
came true in a very ironic way. The man who issued the warning became
both entangler and entangled.[10]

The military sideshow off North Africa was by no means the only sword
rattling that President Jefferson pursued in his second term. In 1803, soon
after the Louisiana Purchase, the President and his Secretary of State convinced Congress that the Spanish colony of West Florida was included in
the acquired territory. Congress passed a bill, organizing the area around
Mobile for the collection of customs. But Spain, angry over Napoleon's
sale of Louisiana without consulting them, insisted the land still belonged
to them. The President's envoy to Madrid, James Monroe, got nowhere in
months of wearisome negotiations.

A stalemate ensued until December 1805, when the President, in his
annual message to Congress, made it clear he was ready to use force to
seize the disputed area. This was a dangerous thing to say. In 1804, Spain

had joined France in the war against England, which meant Emperor Napoleon Bonaparte was in the picture as well. For a while, to Secretary of State Madison's distress, President Jefferson talked of making an alliance with England to support his obsession with West Florida.

Suddenly, the President sent another message to Congress, reporting that war with Spain might not be necessary. Majority leader John Randolph, the President's partner in the attempt to impeach Judge Chase, was summoned to the presidential mansion and told that Florida could be obtained by paying $2 million in bribes to certain French and Spanish officials.

Randolph exploded. This was a violation of his Old Republican principles. The hot-tempered Virginian went back to Congress and denounced the President for deserting the purism of Old Republicanism. Implicit in Randolph's wrath was the Federalist refusal to pay bribes to Foreign Minister Talleyrand's friends, Messrs. X, Y, and Z. How could the President risk the reputation of the Democratic-Republican Party by violating a principle the monarchists and Anglomen had upheld?

Buoyed by the party's massive majorities in both houses, Jefferson ignored Randolph and persuaded Congress to vote the money. The fiery congressman called those who voted for the bribes "pages of the presidential water closet"—the 1805 term for toilet. He organized about twenty similar minded Old Republicans into a third party, the "Tertium Quids." These "Third Somethings" would soon give the President more than a few restless nights.[11]

All this war talk and money talk in regard to Spain came to nothing. Napoleon, growing more and more surly toward the Americans, abruptly decided West Florida should remain in Spanish hands. This left a large number of western Americans in a very unhappy mood. During these months of many words and little action, Aaron Burr had been travelling through the west, talking to politicians such as Andrew Jackson in Tennessee. Their widely shared desire to drive the Spaniards into the Gulf of Mexico was the sort of thing the former vice president was hoping to hear. In St. Louis, Burr found his friend General Wilkinson, now the governor of the Louisiana Territory, equally enthused by the wrath the President had stirred up against Spain.

An even larger worry was America's relationship with Great Britain, which was again showing signs of desperation in the renewed war with Napoleon. Parliament added destructive new rules to the Royal Navy's blockade of Europe, which entitled His Majesty's captains to seize American merchant ships almost at will. While admiralty courts debated their fates, the ships lay inert in various harbors in England and the West Indies, their hulls and their cargoes rotting and their owners fuming. In six months, Philadelphia alone lost one hundred ships, valued at $500,000.

Soon British warships cruised off every American port, ready to board any ship that emerged. At first President Jefferson did nothing but step up construction of his worthless gunboats. In his State of the Union message in December 1805, he went much further, recommending the construction of six ships of the line—seventy-four gun craft that were the battleships of the era. Unfortunately, Congress declined to pay for them. The President's long-standing fear of military despotism from standing armies and navies was not easily altered by a sudden embrace of moderate realism a la George Washington. Congressman John Randolph and his Quids were quick to join this fray on the Old Republican side, with ruinous effect.[12]

The grievance against Britain that stirred America's deepest emotions was the Royal Navy's readiness to induct into their ranks any sailor on a captured ship whom they suspected of being a British subject, or worse, a deserter from one of their men of war. Senator John Quincy Adams called it an "authorized system of kidnapping upon the ocean." The British admitted to seizing three thousand men during these years of global war. Americans claimed it was double that figure. [13]

The British were totally intransigent on this issue. In London, envoy James Monroe persisted in a long and wearisome series of discussions. As we have seen, Jefferson's "pell-mell" etiquette added to his woes. The President sent William Pinkney, Attorney General of Maryland, to assist him with fresh instructions. The move infuriated Monroe, much as his special embassy had angered Robert Livingston in Paris. Finally, the two weary diplomats signed an agreement that would supposedly replace the hated Jay Treaty, without quite resolving the impressment issue.

When President Jefferson read the document, he found it unsatisfactory. The British promised to offer "immediate redress" to any American mistakenly kidnapped. This was better than nothing. But Jefferson's hatred of Britain convinced him that his spokesmen could and should obtain a total abandonment of impressment, plus a public apology.

Equally irritating to the President was a clause in which America surrendered the right to bar British imports as a form of protest. Jefferson refused to abandon this tactic, which had worked well in the years preceding the American Revolution. President Washington might have signed the treaty, with the proviso that this clause would be dropped. But President Jefferson's British hatred led him to inform the dismayed Monroe and Pinkney that he would not even submit their effort to the Senate. In retrospect, this decision would become a major step down the slippery slope to the War of 1812.[14]

CHAPTER 31

The President vs. The
Chief Justice

ABSORBED BY FOREIGN POLICY, President Jefferson remained oblivious to a conspiracy that was taking shape on his western frontier. Aaron Burr was recruiting a thousand-man army in western New York, Pennsylvania, and Ohio. Ambassador Merry's letter requesting British assistance had failed to win a response in London. The ex-vice president had refused to be discouraged by this rebuff. Nor did his hunger for revenge diminish when Jefferson and Secretary of State Madison abandoned their threats of war with Spain to deal with the British assault on America's merchant ships. Burr was betting on what he saw and heard from several visits to Washington, D.C.

John Randolph's revolt was threatening Jefferson's control of Congress. "Administration is damned," Burr gleefully informed General Wilkinson. The President's failure to do anything about British depredations on the high seas or Spanish intransigence in Florida was convincing many people that the Man from Monticello was not a strong president in the George Washington tradition.[1]

An aggressive move by Spain added to Burr's hopes. The Spanish had sent thirteen hundred men across the Sabine River to seize a slice of land east of this stream, which supposedly marked Louisiana's border with Texas. The President had ordered General Wilkinson to challenge them. A war with Spain seemed theirs for the starting. Burr rushed messengers to New Orleans to inform Wilkinson that he and his volunteers were about to board boats to descend the Mississippi and begin their attack on Texas.

Burr did not know that General Wilkinson had been dismayed by the British failure to respond to Ambassador Merry's letter. The General had been especially disappointed by the British dismissal of Burr's request for a badly needed $500,000 to finance the expedition. Wilkinson had also been unnerved by rumors of Burr's plan that had gotten into several western newspapers. The General arrested Burr's messengers and rushed letters to President Jefferson declaring he had just uncovered a nefarious plot to revolutionize the West and start a war with Spain. Other letters went to the Spanish governor of East Florida and the imperial viceroy in Mexico City, revealing Agent 13's good deed and demanding an appropriate reward.[2]

President Jefferson went berserk. Gone was the philosophical detachment he had displayed in the past, when he had spoken almost casually about the eventual separation of the western states from the Union. Now he became a Unionist with a passion that rivaled George Washington. Jefferson knew Burr was trying to deprive him of the Louisiana Territory—the greatest—and perhaps only—noteworthy achievement of his presidency.

The man who had serenely announced there would be no "monarchical" proclamations issued while he was president now unleashed one. He announced—and denounced—a plot to destroy the Union, and ordered the U.S. Army and federal officials in the West to treat Burr and his volunteers as traitors. When the colonel and his flotilla reached Natchez, U.S. soldiers arrested them at gunpoint. Burr tried to flee, but was quickly captured and shipped to Richmond, Virginia for a trial and possible execution.

The enraged President announced to Congress and the country that Burr was guilty "beyond question." This was a reckless thing for a president with a law degree to say about a man before he even reached a courtroom. In Washington, D.C., Chief Justice John Marshall decided he was not going to let Thomas Jefferson hang the man who had rescued the Supreme Court from Democratic-Republican destruction. The Chief Justice announced he would personally preside over Aaron Burr's trial for the crime of treason.[3]

※

If there was a man on earth Thomas Jefferson hated more than George Washington, it was John Marshall. The President suspended all other federal business to superintend Aaron Burr's trial. When the attorney general, Caesar Rodney of Delaware, withdrew from the case, explaining he had no enthusiasm for prosecuting a man who had once been a friend, the President appointed George Hay as his replacement. This was the same man who had battered James Thomson Callender over the head with a club for revealing Jefferson's supposed liaison with his slave, Sally Hemings. In spite of—or perhaps because of—this unorthodox demonstration of loyalty, the President had appointed him the federal attorney for Virginia.

Chief Justice Marshall staggered Prosecutor Hay by announcing that he could find probable cause for a trial on only one count: the misdemeanor of waging war against Spain, a country with whom the United States was at peace. As for the evidence of treason presented thus far—the cipher letter that General Wilkinson had seized from Burr's messengers in New Orleans—it was much too weak to take seriously. The General himself was still en route from New Orleans to testify at Burr's trial.

The Chief Justice saw no reason to send the ex-vice president to prison while awaiting better proof. Quoting the famed British jurist, William Blackstone, Marshall said he could not allow "the hand of malignity" to seize an individual and deprive him of his liberty.

Among the politicians crowding the Richmond courtroom, there was not one who failed to recognize whose hand was being accused of malignity. As they sat in stunned silence, Marshall set May 22, 1807, as the trial date.[4] When news of this ruling reached the Presidential mansion, a tantrum ensued. An enraged President Jefferson sent letters whirling to his leaders in Congress, urging them to revive the proposed constitutional amendment that had loomed over the trial of Justice Chase, permitting any federal judge to be removed by a majority vote of Congress.

The Chief Justice's reply to this threat did nothing to moderate President Jefferson's tantrum. Marshall insisted on the importance of adhering strictly to the Constitution—another thrust certain to make a former strict constructionist squirm. Treason was a charge that was "most capable of being employed as the instrument of those malignant and vindictive passions which may rage in the bosoms of parties struggling for power."[5]

The presidential residence all but vibrated with President Jefferson's rage. Soon dozens of federal marshals were heading west to find proof that Burr intended to create a new empire out of a "scissionist" Tennessee, Kentucky, and perhaps Ohio, plus conquered Texas and Mexico. In seven frantic weeks, the federal agents collected a mini-army of 140 witnesses who were ordered to struggle across the Alleghenys to Richmond without an hour's delay. This roundup cost $100,000—well over a million dollars in modern money. Secretary of the Treasury Gallatin must have blanched at the hole this outlay punched in the precariously balanced federal budget, which was no longer supported by domestic taxes.[6]

In Richmond, ex-Vice President Burr enjoyed the hospitality of numerous leading citizens. He added four lawyers to his defense team. The most important was his friend Luther Martin, the successful defender of Judge Chase against the accusations of the man he still called "that scoundrel, Jefferson." By the time the trial resumed on May 22, 1806, the population of Richmond had leaped from five thousand to ten thousand. Many of these newcomers were westerners, led by Andrew Jackson, who repeatedly proclaimed that the President was a would-be tyrant and General Wilkinson was an abominable liar.[7]

A steaming Senator William Branch Giles was among the Democratic-Republican politicians on the prospective grand jury that federal attorney George Hay assembled. Jefferson's neighbor and closest collaborator in Congress, Senator Wilson Cary Nicholas, was also there. Echoing the President's disregard for legal niceties, Giles had proclaimed Burr guilty on the floor of the Senate. Both men were startled when Chief Justice Marshall permitted Burr, serving as his own attorney, to challenge each grand juror. The ex-vice president acidly suggested that Giles and Nicholas would have difficulty pretending they were impartial. Red-faced and fuming, the two senators withdrew.[8]

Almost every other juror admitted he thought Burr was guilty. One of the few who said they would wait to hear the evidence was Congressman John Randolph, who was definitely not there to obey President Jefferson's orders. Chief Justice Marshall coolly appointed him the jury's foreman.

Next, Burr asked Marshall's approval of another motion, designed to send President Jefferson's blood pressure soaring to new and dangerous heights. Burr asked the Chief Justice to order the President to come to Richmond with all possible speed, bringing with him the papers pertinent to the case. A frantic Federal Attorney Hay insisted subpoenaing the President was out of the question. Luther Martin and his fellow defense attorneys seized this opportunity to descant on President Jefferson's "peculiar" relationship to the case. The Chief Justice cautioned them not to allow the "heat of debate" to produce extreme sentiments. But he did nothing to stop them—and he issued the subpoena.[9]

Unlike a king, the Chief Justice said, the president was no more immune to a subpoena than any other citizen. He might have wryly added that Democratic-Republican principles virtually demanded this policy. Only if President Jefferson could prove that his job was consuming his "whole time" would he be permitted to stay in his Washington, D.C. mansion. Marshall added that it was "apparent" the President had plenty of time to spare.

Once more, even the most comatose political insider got the implication: each year, the President spent the summer months in Monticello, leaving clerks to run the federal government in sweltering Washington, D.C. Further bolstering the subpoena, Marshall remarked that it was obvious the President "wished" to convict his former vice president. That made it necessary for the court to give the defendant all possible assistance.

When Federal Attorney Hay frantically protested the word "wished," Marshall admitted he might be right, and substituted "expected." He refused to change this word, in spite of Hay's continued unhappiness. All this was, of course, reported in newspapers and in letters to the presidential mansion. President Jefferson replied that he was ready to surrender Wilkinson's letter to him, but he would be the judge of what other papers he might reveal to the court. As for coming to Richmond—his "paramount duties" as chief executive made this impossible.

As the red-faced Hay read this response to Chief Justice Marshall, many spectators in the courtroom may have asked themselves if President George Washington would ever have let himself get into such a contretemps. Such thoughts were even more probable when General James Wilkinson finally arrived in Richmond in a uniform virtually oozing gold braid. With every well-liquored breath, Spain's Agent 13 exhaled righteous wrath against his former partner, Burr. Federal Attorney Hay had a long talk with the General and informed the President he was convinced of his "unsullied integrity." An overjoyed Jefferson added a warm letter of welcome to his favorite soldier. The faceless operatives running Madrid's secret service must have exchanged covert congratulations for all the money they had paid Agent 13. How many other agents had been able to totally bamboozle a nation's ruler?

Grand Jury Foreman John Randolph had a very different welcome for President Jefferson's key witness. He called Wilkinson "the most finished scoundrel that ever lived." The General's performance on the stand added weight to that opinion. Under cross-examination from a Burr attorney, Wilkinson admitted that he had erased much of the cipher letter he had seized from Burr's messengers. When another defense lawyer asked Wilkinson if he had had prior knowledge of Burr's purported plot, the General declined to answer on grounds of possible self- incrimination. [10]

Swallowing his disgust, Federal Attorney Hay summoned some fifty witnesses to testify that Burr had taken command of a thousand well-armed men on an island in the Ohio River near the town of Marietta. These witnesses claimed to have listened to plans to seize control of Texas, followed by a call for the western states to join them in a new confederacy, whose first task would be the conquest of Mexico. The grand jurors indicted Burr for plotting to attack Spain's empire—and for treason against the United States.[11]

Burr's jury trial was another public spectacle. It took place in the spacious hall of the Virginia House of Delegates to accommodate the huge crowd of onlookers. General Wilkinson was caught in numerous lies and contradictions by the defense lawyers. A distressed Federal Attorney Hay told the President he was no longer a believer in his star witness's unsullied integrity. Jefferson, apparently by an act of will, ignored this denunciation and bombarded Hay with suggestions on other ways to obtain a conviction.[12]

Several witnesses testified to hearing Burr discuss his plans. But had he committed an "overt act" that could be described as treasonous? The legal contest soon revolved around this question. No one had opposed the Burr expedition on their trip down the Mississippi. No one had fired a single shot when federal soldiers called on them to surrender in Natchez.

Federal Attorney Hay focused on the day that Ohio militia under the command of General Edward Tupper had raided the plotters' island camp. One witness claimed that the Burrites had leveled their muskets at them and forced a hasty retreat. But no one corroborated the incident, and General Tupper denied seeing a leveled gun anywhere. Burr's attorneys asked the Chief Justice if there was any point in hearing similar non-evidence from the rest of President Jefferson's 140 witnesses.[13]

Marshall agreed that it would be a waste of time. He ordered both sides to make their closing arguments. Luther Martin spoke for three days, denouncing the prosecution as a plot engineered by the scoundrel President Jefferson. Prosecutor Hay, doing his utmost to overcome the missing overt act, reiterated again and again that the assembled army was proof of Burr's treason. Finally, it was time for the Chief Justice's decision.[14]

Marshall spent a full weekend composing his judgment on President Jefferson's prosecution. He solemnly declared that assembling an army was not enough to convict Aaron Burr of treason. As long as there was no proof of an overt act, he remained beyond the reach of the law. It was one of the most important decisions Marshall ever wrote. Henceforth, no future American prosecutor would be able to convict opponents for theoretical or putative treason. The Chief Justice cited reams of authorities to support his conclusion.

Marshall also noted that the government's attorneys had hinted that he faced impeachment if he ruled for Burr. "That this court does not usurp power is most true," the Chief Justice said. "That this court does not shrink from its duty is no less true." It was an unmistakable challenge to the President to dare try to remove him. [15]

The jury retired to ponder the case within the framework that the Chief Justice had decreed—and returned in less than an hour to declare that Burr was "not proved to be guilty under this indictment by any evidence submitted to us." Burr's attorneys protested this wording but the Chief Justice let it stand. However, he wrote "not guilty" in the trial record. Within a week, the still enraged President Jefferson sent a copy of the proceedings to Congress, and renewed his call for an amendment to enable him to remove any federal judge if a two-thirds majority of Congress approved. The President called Luther Martin "a federal [federalist] bulldog," and talked of prosecuting him, based on hearsay evidence that the attorney had been involved in Burr's revolutionary plans.

Any senator or representative who read the details of General Wilkinson's embarrassing performance on the witness stand almost certainly concluded that the President's pursuit of vengeance was fatally flawed. Nevertheless, Jefferson's demand for the amendment was sent to committees in the Senate and House.

Senator William Branch Giles went beyond the President's attempt to reduce the federal courts to an appendage of the party in power. The hotheaded Old Republican introduced a bill calling for the death penalty for anyone who assembled to resist a federal law, as well as for anyone who assisted such an assembly, even if he were not present when the arrests were made. It made the penalties under the Sedition Act seem trivial. In the hysterical atmosphere that President Jefferson had generated, Giles's bill passed the Senate, but it was rejected by the House of Representatives. A similar fate befell the President's demand for a constitutional amendment to demolish the independence of the federal judiciary.[16]

Burr's attorneys easily defeated attempts to convict him of waging war against Spain, and he was soon a free man. Travelling north, he stopped in Baltimore and a menacing mob surrounded his hotel. The ex-vice president was forced to flee into the night. It was the first glimpse of the average American's reaction to Burr's acquittal. A huge majority was infuriated. Why? Louisiana again. The thought that the ex-vice president had attempted to deprive them or their children or grandchildren access to those 828,000 square miles of fertile land was grounds for detestation and even murder.[17]

In New York, Burr's home territory, the reaction was equally hostile. An outcast, Burr fled to Europe, hoping to persuade either the French or the English to back his no longer viable scheme. In the United States, the purchaser of Louisiana remained a popular hero. If Thomas Jefferson had managed to hang Aaron Burr, he would have won cheers in every city and town in America. But historians, looking back on the trial, find it difficult to avoid a shudder at the President's unWashington performance.

CHAPTER 32

The Final Defeat of the UnWashington President

A MONG THE POLITICAL CLASS, the excesses of the Burr trial had not a little to do with what one historian has called the "ungluing" of the Democratic-Republican Party in the closing years of President Jefferson's second term. In the House of Representatives, John Randolph and his Tertium Quids remained on the offensive against the President. Revived Federalists collaborated with them whenever possible.[1]

Another reason for Jefferson's loss of prestige and control was the ongoing conflict with the Royal Navy on the oceans. American hopes of ending British impressments had expired when Jefferson rejected Monroe's treaty. But the President persisted in demanding a complete surrender of London's claim to the right to inspect American merchantmen to make sure they were not violating London's blockade of Napoleonic France.

Events in Europe worsened the situation for the Americans. Napoleon shelved his plan to invade England. Instead, he turned east and won stupendous victories over the Prussians and the Austrians, giving him control of almost every European port. Deciding to win by ruining the British economy, the Man of Destiny issued decrees banning all trade with the island nation. Ships of neutral countries were liable to seizure if they had so much as visited a British port. The British responded with new Orders in Council, creating a tighter blockade of Bonaparte's continent. The two belligerents in effect declared commercial war on the ships of every other trading nation. The British admiral in Halifax, Nova Scotia, issued an order to the squadron patrolling off Virginia to board any and all ships, including men of war, to seize deserters from the Royal Navy.

Meanwhile, President Jefferson was still fighting his undeclared war with the Muslim pirates off North Africa. A new fifty-gun American frigate, the USS *Chesapeake* was ordered to join this seemingly interminable struggle. On June 22, 1807, the warship was put to sea for the long voyage. Suddenly, lookouts shouted that a British man of war was heading toward them. HMS *Leopard* surged alongside and demanded the right to board the *Chesapeake* to search for deserters.

When the American frigate's captain refused to submit to such an indignity, the *Leopard* opened fire at point blank range, killing three Americans and wounding eighteen. The unprepared, mostly untrained crew of the *Chesapeake* surrendered. A boarding party seized four men, only one of whom was a British-born deserter. The other three were Americans who had been impressed a few months earlier from a merchant ship. They had escaped from another frigate in the British squadron and joined the Chesapeake's crew.[2]

The nation exploded. Calls for war blossomed in dozens of newspapers. President Jefferson broke his no proclamation rule again and barred all British warships from American ports. He summoned Congress to meet two months earlier than its next scheduled session, and intimated they might be asked to declare war to settle once and for all the "long train of injuries and depredations under which our commerce has been afflicted on the high seas for years past." He summoned all America's merchant ships home as soon as possible, and ordered dozens more of his gunboats built to defend the nation's harbors. He also asked the states to mobilize an army of one hundred thousand militiamen and discussed the possibility of conquering Canada.[3]

The President was dismayed to find his cabinet deeply divided about these measures. Secretary of State Madison was in full agreement with his enraged leader. But Secretary of the Treasury Gallatin disliked the President's entire message. He told Jefferson the country was totally unprepared for war with the British.

Secretary of War Henry Dearborn warned the President that it would take months for the understaffed federal government to persuade the states to muster one hundred thousand militiamen to serve in a federal army. Secretary of the Navy Robert Smith told Jefferson he was making a huge mistake, linking the attack on the *Chesapeake* with the British impressment policy. The captain of HMS *Leopard* was clearly at fault. Why imperil a chance for an advantageous negotiated peace or at least truce with a "manifesto against the [whole] British government?"[4]

Jefferson was suddenly in the same presidential hot seat that George Washington had occupied when half his cabinet disagreed with the other half. By August, the President was semi-backing down and thinking of war with Spain rather than Great Britain. "Our southern defensive force can take the Floridas, volunteers for a Mexican army will flock to our standard...Perhaps Cuba will add itself to our Confederation," he told the startled Madison. Aside from the wildly unrealistic dimensions of these thoughts, the President did not seem to realize that he was virtually admitting Aaron Burr's game plan had some merits.[5]

The British tried to avoid a war by admitting that the attack on the *Chesapeake* had been a blunder. They relieved the captain of HMS *Leopard,* offered to pay reparations for the dead and wounded, and said they were ready to return the three seized Americans. The British-born deserter was, however, hanged in Canada. President Jefferson stubbornly insisted he would be satisfied only with the complete abandonment of impressments. He dismissed the British offer as "unfriendly, proud and harsh."

Soon the President was cheering new victories by Napoleon. He informed Madison that if he had to choose between George III and Bonaparte, he leaned toward the Corsican. "I say, 'Down with England!'" he cried, as his long-running hatred of the British overcame his judgment.

A harried Secretary of the Treasury Gallatin warned Jefferson that public opinion was now hostile to a war over the *Chesapeake.* Most people, especially in New England and the Middle States, were satisfied with the British semi-apology and offer of compensation. The outrage over the attack on the warship had evaporated. Unfortunately, Gallatin's wise advice was overwhelmed by the latest news from Europe. A new British decree declared naturalization papers of British-born American seamen would be disregarded in impressment operations. Any and every Briton was liable to seizure. From Paris came word that, henceforth, American ships would be treated as former friends and seized without mercy.

On December 18, 1807, President Jefferson responded with a new and truly astonishing message to Congress. He wanted approval for a measure that would protect American ships and seamen from all "the belligerent powers of Europe." How was this to be done? By an "inhibition of the departure of [all] our vessels." With almost no discussion of its merits, Congress passed the Embargo Act, which forbade American ships to trade with Britain, France, and every other nation in the world.

A leading historian has called this move "the greatest example in American history of ideology brought to bear on a matter of public policy."[6] Americans would soon discover how President Jefferson, the apostle of minimal government, ruled, when the people rejected one of his theories.

Once more, Secretary of the Treasury Gallatin disagreed with the President's policy, this time vehemently. He accused Jefferson and his Secretary of State of reacting much too hastily. Gallatin went even further, with words of warning that deviated sharply from standard Democratic-Republican thinking. "In every point of view, privations, sufferings, revenue, effect on the enemy, politics at home, I prefer war to a permanent embargo." The Secretary of the Treasury added words that remain to this day a standing rebuke to all ideologues: "Governmental prohibitions do always more mischief than had been calculated, and it is not without much hesitation that a statesman should hazard to regulate the concerns of individuals as if he could do it better than themselves."[7]

President Jefferson ignored Gallatin. He confused the Secretary of the Treasury and other critics by urging Congress to prepare the nation for war. At first, he apparently did not see the embargo as more than a temporary device. But it dawned on the President and his cabinet that announcing a six-month limit was self-defeating. Both Jefferson and Madison hoped to force Britain to negotiate on their terms. This leverage would only be achieved if the King and his ministers were frightened by fear of permanent damage to their economy.

Unfortunately, another Jefferson policy, the abolition of all internal taxes, forced the President to allow the British to continue to export goods and products to America in British ships. The duties on these imports were needed to keep the federal government solvent. This contradiction at the heart of the embargo would prove to be a fatal flaw.[8]

In January 1808, another important matter seized President Jefferson's attention—the choice of his successor. He strongly preferred James Madison. But he had to deal with angry cries from New York that it was their turn to have a president. There sat Vice President George Clinton waiting for the call. John Randolph and his Quids backed James Monroe and said nasty things about Madison's fragile health and lack of leadership qualities. But the President made his choice very clear, and not many politicians were ready to challenge the purchaser of Louisiana. On January 23, 1808, the congressional Democratic-Republicans caucused and nominated Madison almost unanimously. Aging, incompetent George Clinton was again nominated for Vice President.

With the Federalist Party in ruins, Madison was a certain victor in the fall elections. There was no campaign worth mentioning, in the modern sense of the word. Even if the Federalists had remained a viable party, it would have been a strange one-issue contest. The nation was totally absorbed by the burden that President Jefferson had inflicted on them: the embargo.

⚜

The President soon found himself forced to explain to puzzled citizens and critics in Congress, such as John Randolph and his Quids, the reasoning behind this totally unexpected experiment. Secretary of State Madison rushed three anonymous articles into print in the *National Intelligencer*. He called the embargo a noble alternative to war. It was a chance for Americans to show the world that "we will flinch from no sacrifices which the honor and good of our nation demand from virtuous and faithful citizens."

This was the ideological rhetoric that had almost destroyed the Americans in 1776. The satisfaction of being virtuous was supposed to be the only motivation for a true patriot. Realist General Washington's response to this theory had been *interest;* nothing political was ever accomplished without appealing to people's self-interest or hope of some reward. Alas, the so-called Revolution of 1800 had blurred, if not destroyed, the value of Washington's wisdom.[9]

In Congress, Democratic-Republican ideologues decreed that all parts of the nation should prove their virtue by suffering mutually under the embargo. They persuaded Congress to ban the export of all farm crops as well as manufactured products. Meanwhile, the Secretary of War reported that there was no hope of the states recruiting one hundred thousand militia for the army. Jefferson responded by calling for eight additional regiments for the regular army at a cost of $4 million.

John Randolph and his Quids mocked this proposal. Didn't it violate the Democratic-Republican principle of no standing army in time of peace? The eight regiments raised the number of regulars to ten thousand men, hardly enough to defend a single state, much less the whole nation. The unreality of Democratic-Republican military thinking was underscored by laying keels for another 188 worthless gunboats. [10]

During his governorship of Virginia in 1779, Jefferson had revealed a lack of enthusiasm for enforcing laws that people disliked, such as the requirement to serve in the militia. This approach soon became the case with his war preparations in 1808. Half-hearted attempts to raise men for the new regular army regiments floundered as badly as the call for the states to muster one hundred thousand militiamen. The U.S. Military Academy at West Point, a school that might have supplied officers to this program, had been neglected. It was an educational orphan, without a faculty, a curriculum, or soldierly standards of admission.

✿

Meanwhile, Americans began to feel the impact of the embargo. Ships rotted at anchor in dozens of ports. Thousands of unemployed sailors swarmed in the streets. Merchants went bankrupt. Congress grimly tightened the federal screws. The legislators made it a crime to export goods or food to Canada and Spanish Florida. Armed sloops patrolled the coasts and inland waterways to make sure no one was carrying banned food beyond the nation's borders. One newspaper wryly wondered what was going on. Wasn't the embargo supposed to protect and preserve America's merchant fleet? Now Vermont farmers were being told that it was a crime to sell their pigs in Canada.

The President's new rules inspired a New York Congressman, Barent Gardenier, to make an angry speech, asking this and other questions. Why was the President determined to block every hole "at which the industry and enterprise of our country can find vent?" Gardenier concluded that Jefferson's Anglophobia and his long love affair with France was the explanation. "Darkness and mystery overshadow this House [of Representatives] and the whole nation," Gardenier roared. "We sit here as mere automata, we legislate without knowing."

Even in Virginia, people besides John Randolph began to lose faith. John Taylor, one of the most faithful—and voluble—Jefferson supporters, was one of the many who were troubled by doubts. In a long private letter, he condemned the embargo as a policy that would "impoverish farmers, enrich the lawless [smugglers], drive our seamen into foreign service, drain the treasury...break our banks—and fail to achieve a better treaty" than the one Monroe had negotiated.

In New York, the Albany *Gazette* wondered why so little had been done to prepare for war. "Where are our defenses?" the editor asked, declaring New York Harbor and the entire Hudson River Valley were easy pickings for a well-armed, aggressive enemy. The paper concluded New Yorkers were the victims of an "anti-commercial spirit" emanating from Virginia.[11]

If the editor had had access to President Jefferson's private correspondence, he would have been convinced that this charge was true. As criticism poured into Washington, D.C. from all parts of the nation, the President only grew more determined to maintain the embargo. "I place immense value in the experiment being fully made to see how far this embargo may be an effective weapon in the future as well as on this occasion," he told Secretary of the Treasury Gallatin on May 27, 1808. "I set down [dismiss] the exercise of commerce, merely for profit, as nothing when it carries with it the danger of defeating the objects of the embargo."

The exercise of commerce merely for profit. These were the words of a man who hated banks and stock markets and dismissed the embargo's criticisms as "Federalist maneuvers and intrigues." It would be hard to imagine a chief executive more out of touch with the American people.[12]

Further complicating matters, President Jefferson sabotaged the embargo by repeatedly telling correspondents and American diplomats abroad that he had never imagined the ban would last so long. In July 1808, he told a correspondent he thought it would end in the fall or winter. If it was still the law, "Congress will have to act."

There was another hallmark of the Jeffersonian presidency. *Congress will have to act.* Not the president of the United States will have to act—words that would have come without hesitation from George Washington, who had insisted foreign relations were the president's responsibility.[13]

The more stubborn and inflamed about his ideological voyage President Jefferson became, the more ferociously he turned to enforcing the embargo at the point of federal guns. He proclaimed the border area between Canada and the United States in a state of insurrection and had federal marshals and regular army soldiers patrolling it day and night. He told the governor of New York how important it was to "make individuals feel the consequences of daring to oppose a law by force."

The man who had launched a minimal federal government in the Revolution of 1800 was acting more and more like Napoleon Bonaparte and others who believed that might made right. President Jefferson declared he alone knew "the real needs of the American people," and he was determined not to allow "unprincipled adventurers" to commit "crimes against their country."

In January 1809, Congress passed a truly appalling enforcement act. It made a joke out of the Fourth Amendment, barring unreasonable searches and seizures. Anyone who loaded food or goods on an American ship would henceforth need a federal permit. Federal inspectors would have the right to ban anyone they suspected of illegal intentions from going to sea. The President grew especially angry at Massachusetts, where outwitting the embargo had become a way of life. Their opposition "amounted almost to rebellion and treason," he raged. The Bay State's legislature passed a defiant resolution declaring that they would not "willingly become the victims of a fruitless experiment."[14]

By this time, the cost of the embargo was becoming visible in dollars and cents, with Massachusetts the chief victim. Almost half the merchantmen in the nation sailed from her ports. In carrying charges alone, ship owners had lost $15 million. In 1808, American exports dwindled from $103 million to $23 million. Imports sank by more than half, from $144 million to $58 million. If we translate these numbers to modern money, we are talking about billions. The American economy ground to a paralyzed halt. Many people in the Bay State began to hate Virginians—a root cause of the future Civil War.[15]

🎐

The fantasies that President Jefferson and Secretary of State Madison communicated to Congress and the Democratic-Republican party faithful collapsed as the embargo lurched toward a full year. Both Britain and France found sources of food elsewhere in the world. The starvation the President liked to imagine he was inflicting on Britain never happened.

Instead of thinking seriously about a new course of action, President Jefferson drifted. He devoted many hours to helping the Connecticut writer, Joel Barlow, gather material for a history of his administration that would glorify the Revolution of 1800 and justify the embargo. In his annual message to Congress in December 1808, the President merely reported that the French and British had both rejected his offers to abandon the embargo if they repealed their decrees and orders in council.

Nevertheless, the President declared the embargo had demonstrated "the patriotism of our fellow citizens" and "the moderation and fairness which govern our councils." The embargo also had an educational side. It had awakened Americans to "the necessity of uniting in support of the laws and rights of their country." Best of all, it had "saved our mariners and our vast mercantile property."

Missing was any admission that the embargo had been a failure. The unspoken message was the President's conclusion that the abolition of America's commerce remained preferable to surrendering to French and British tactics. Then came words that virtually proclaimed the bankruptcy of Thomas Jefferson's presidency: "It will rest with the wisdom of Congress to decide on the course best adapted to such a state of things."

These were words that President George Washington would never have spoken. He had seen what the wisdom of Congress produced in the American Revolution—disorganization, bankruptcy, and imminent defeat. It was why he and James Madison had created the office of the president—to offset the inability of legislative bodies to *govern*. Here was the fatal flaw of the ideologue who loved to legislate but not to enforce, implement, or lead. Thomas Jefferson's surrender of the president's authority and prestige at this moment of crisis would send a message oozing through the next decades of American history, repeatedly sapping the will and power of the federal government.

The President's followers began blaming the American people for the embargo's failure. "We have been too happy and too prosperous," Secretary of the Treasury Albert Gallatin told his wife. He condemned Americans for considering "as great misfortunes" the supposedly minor privations that the embargo inflicted. Senator Wilson Cary Nicholas condemned "our people" for their readiness to "crucify their leaders" for not submitting to Britain and France while a hefty percentage of them could hardly wait to begin "pursuing after the[ir] lucrative trade." Another Jefferson friend, Archibald Stuart, summed up this Democratic-Republican paroxysm by declaring the American people were "avaricious, enterprising, and impatient of restraint." [16]

These were the traits that George Washington and Alexander Hamilton had considered crucial for the creation of a great nation. They would have disagreed with the loaded adjective, avaricious, and suggested a less hostile term—perhaps profit-minded. But they would have unquestionably disapproved the underlying loathing for business and finance that permeated the Revolution of 1800, thanks to the predilections of its leader.

Meanwhile, seeds of "scission" (secession) were sprouting in New England. The governor of Connecticut declared that the state had the right to "interpose their protecting shield between the right and liberty of the people and the assumed power of the federal government." Massachusetts declared the embargo was "unconstitutional and not legally binding on the citizens of this state." The Virginia and Kentucky Resolutions were coming back to life to torment their authors. When someone accused Old Republican Senator William Branch Giles of encouraging a military despotism with the embargo's enforcement tactics, he piously declared the President was only seeking the power to "carry into effect a great national and Constitutional object." These meaningless words would have fit comfortably in the mouth of Napoleon Bonaparte. More than a few people did not hesitate to point this out.

All this controversy had a debilitating effect on President Jefferson. Well before the end of his second term, he virtually withdrew from the duties and responsibilities of his high office. He shipped his books and furniture back to Monticello and wrote self-pitying letters to his daughter Martha, longing for her company and the affection of her numerous children. On March 4, 1809, Jefferson's last day in office, Congress repealed the embargo. On this mournful note, the Revolution of 1800 ended and President Jefferson retreated to Monticello.

The contrast between President George Washington's departure to Mount Vernon at the summit of his popularity, leaving behind his Farewell Address to echo through the centuries, and Thomas Jefferson's return to Monticello in an aura of confusion and failure, underscores the importance of seeing the difference between these two men as a great divide in America's journey to world power.

As James Madison took over as president and Thomas Jefferson departed for Monticello, his admirers in Washington, D.C. pretended the failure of the embargo had never happened. The *National Intelligencer* hailed the ex-president as if he were still the conquering hero of the Louisiana Purchase. "Never will it be forgotten as long as liberty is dear to man that it was on this day Thomas Jefferson retired from the supreme magistracy amid the blessings and regrets of millions," the editor declared.

At the presidential mansion, a group of local citizens gathered to praise Jefferson's "mild and endearing virtues" and thank him for presiding in such friendly fashion over their federal village. Jefferson was deeply touched and replied with words that testified to his deep love of his country.

"The station which we occupy among the nations of the earth is honorable but awful. Trusted with the destinies of this solitary republic of the world, the only monument of human rights, and the sole depository of the sacred fire of freedom and self government...all mankind ought...with us to rejoice in its prosperous and sympathize with its adverse fortunes, as involving everything dear to man. And to what sacrifices of interest or convenience ought not these considerations to animate us? To what compromises of opinion and inclination to maintain harmony and union among ourselves and to preserve from all danger this hallowed ark of human hope and happiness?" [17]

Thomas Jefferson's gift for inspiring words should persuade the readers of this book to summon forgiveness and rueful—or better, sympathetic—admiration for this deeply conflicted man. Every nation needs a voice of hope and promise as well as a model of realistic leadership that will enable these visions of an ideal tomorrow to survive. In George Washington, Americans have been blessed with a primary example of this kind of leadership. Like him, our greatest presidents have valued the visionary side of our heritage, but resisted the demands and pretensions of ideologies as well as the envies and angers of party politics.

CHAPTER 33

The Transformation of
James Madison

A T President James Madison's inaugural ball in 1809, one observer noted that the new chief executive soon became "spiritless and exhausted." His face was so "woebegone" people began to wonder if he had the strength to stand, much less dance. Madison confessed to one guest that he would have much preferred to be home in bed. A woman partygoer described him as "a small man quite devoid of dignity." [1]

Even his critics admitted that Madison was a charming and lively conversationalist in private. Unfortunately, the presidency required a strong public personality. James Madison simply did not have one. His fragile health, his slight physique, his timid public manner—he trembled visibly as he began his inaugural address—were the virtual opposite of his two predecessors, Washington and Jefferson, and was almost as starkly opposed to John Adams, who was a superb orator.

At Jefferson's suggestion, Congress had begun nominating the presidential candidates of the Democratic-Republican Party. The practice inclined many senators and congressmen to look on the chief executive with domineering eyes. The phrase "King Caucus" quickly became shorthand for the legislators' attitude toward the nation's chief executive. He was their servant, and they welcomed the chance to let him know it at almost every opportunity.

The President's responsibility for foreign policy, something George Washington thought he had established, all but vanished in this new arrangement. Congress served notice of this reversal on Madison almost immediately when the legislators refused to ratify Albert Gallatin as his choice for secretary of state. Radical Old Republican Senator William Branch Giles was behind this rejection. He thought he deserved the job, which he saw as a stepping-stone to the presidency.

Robert Smith, Jefferson's Secretary of the Navy, pushed his own candidacy, which was backed by his brother, a powerful and corrupt Maryland senator. President Madison abandoned Gallatin and accepted Smith as the secretary of state, ignoring his barely concealed contempt for "Little Jemmy," a nickname many congressmen began using. Quid leader John Randolph summed up the choice in his usual savage style. If Smith could spell, he said, "he ought to be preferred to Giles."[2]

When President Jefferson left office, he had vowed a total withdrawal to Monticello. He even circulated a letter to officials in Washington announcing that under no circumstances would he recommend anyone for a federal job. Jefferson seldom if ever intruded on Madison's day-to-day administration of the government. But Madison wrote his predecessor numerous letters, reporting on his problems and frustrations. Jefferson responded to these messages with strong opinions about what should be done.

In negotiations with the British to replace the expired Jay Treaty, Jefferson urged his successor to make sure that this hated document was never "quoted or looked at or even mentioned." The new president should rely on America's "forbearing yet persevering system" of embargoes and semi-embargoes. Napoleon had recently routed a British army that attempted to oppose his occupation of Spain. After gloating over the British defeat, Jefferson speculated that Bonaparte, with the control of Madrid's South American empire in his grasp, might be willing to let America buy the Floridas and Cuba.

Jefferson thought President Madison could browbeat the Man of Destiny by threatening to aid revolutions in Mexico and other Spanish colonies. To reassure the Emperor that America had no ambitions in South America, Jefferson recommended erecting a column on "the southernmost limit of Cuba" with the inscription "Ne Plus Ultra" [No More Beyond This Point] on it.

Next, Madison might look to Canada, which Jefferson called "The North," and seize that huge chunk of the continent. Then "we should have such an empire for liberty as she has never surveyed since the creation."

Best of all, Jefferson continued, these acquisitions could be defended without a navy. "Nothing should ever be accepted which would require a navy to defend it," he virtually decreed.[3]

※

In 1810, Secretary of the Treasury Gallatin asked Congress to renew the charter of the Bank of the United States for another twenty years. A Senate committee approved the proposal, but the measure was savagely attacked by John Randolph's Quids and numerous Old Republicans. The result was a Senate deadlock, which gave Vice President George Clinton the deciding vote.

Still hungry for revenge against the long-dead Alexander Hamilton, the aging New Yorker voted no. War with either France or Britain loomed just over the horizon and the federal government was now no longer able to borrow money. Gallatin saw deficits swelling and requested a rise in import duties. Congress turned him down and told him to borrow $5 million. They had no idea where or how he should manage this feat, or the interest rates he would have to pay.

President Madison urged a larger army and navy to deal with the increasing probability of war. Congress, still clinging to the Jefferson gospel of reducing the federal debt to zero, slashed defense appropriations. Within a year, Gallatin would inform the President that the federal government did not have enough money to pay the salaries of the few dozen departmental clerks in Washington, D.C.

※

Oblivious to this Democratic-Republican fiscal unrealism, a group of new congressmen, led by thirty-four-year-old Henry Clay of Kentucky, began calling for war with Britain. Newspapers soon dubbed these combative politicians the War Hawks. They had little or no interest in the main issue that had preoccupied Presidents Jefferson and Madison, America's maritime rights. Most of the leading War Hawks were from the West. Their motive was Canada.

Like ex-President Jefferson, they saw the colony's vast, mostly unpopulated acres as another bonanza for future generations of Americans, almost rivaling Louisiana. Best of all, the British, still fighting for their survival against Emperor Bonaparte, had only a comparative handful of soldiers defending the border.[4]

A secondary War Hawk motive was the Midwest's dwindling number of Indians. The tribesmen were led by a Shawnee chief, Tecumseh, and his half-blind prophet brother, Tenskwatawa, who preached independence from the white man and an end to drinking his destructive rum. These new leaders were not much of a threat. At best they could summon four thousand widely scattered warriors. There were at least one hundred thousand western white men of fighting age to oppose them.

In Washington, D.C., and at Monticello, meanwhile, ex-President Jefferson and President Madison were travelling down another track to war. Their decade-and-a-half-long animosity to Great Britain was a powerful factor in their discussions. A sentimental attachment to a long vanished revolutionary France convinced them that the British, not the Emperor Napoleon, was America's chief foe. For two years, they ignored a stream of reports about seizures of American vessels by Napoleon's warships and privateers. President Madison repeatedly insisted, "The national faith was pledged to France."[5]

In a letter to Democratic-Republican William Duane, now editor of the Philadelphia *Aurora* (Benjamin Franklin Bache had died of yellow fever), Jefferson saw this decision for war with Britain uniting the nation into an irresistible force, like an ancient Roman phalanx. The triumph would not be a party victory. He dismissed that term as "false and degrading." It would be a national victory because "The Republicans are the nation!"[6]

Then came news that the French navy, hoping to cut off the flow of American grain to British regulars and Spanish guerillas still fighting Napoleon's forces in Spain, were burning American merchant ships wherever they seized them. Congress began calling for war with both England and France. One Democratic-Republican leader cried that "the devil himself could not tell which government…is the most wicked." President Madison ignored these waverers and urged Congress to vote for war with Britain before the legislators adjourned in the spring of 1812.

In the House of Representatives, where War Hawk Henry Clay had become Speaker, there was a prompt vote for gunfire, 79–49. This was not the unanimity that a country needed to inspire men to risk their lives, but it was still a hefty majority. The Senate was a different matter. It took them four full days to report the President's war message out of committee. After weeks of divisive debate, the solons finally approved an assault on Canada, 19–13. The votes of both houses revealed that the war had virtually no support in New England or the Middle States.[7]

As this divisive vote for battle took charge of America, the British de-cided to abandon their Orders in Council and try to negotiate a new com-mercial treaty to replace the expired Jay agreement. This news did not reach the United States for another two months. If George Washington had been president, he probably would have suspended military operations and informed Congress that the war was over. But the hatred for the Brit-ish that Madison shared with Jefferson combined with presidential sub-mission to the will of Congress to ignore this conciliatory overture. Thus, America lurched into one of the more dubious wars she has ever fought.

⚗

The regular army consisted of about seven thousand men scattered in twenty-three garrisons throughout the nation. The Navy had six frigates, three sloops of war, and seven smaller vessels plus 170 of Jefferson's gun-boats. These pseudo-warships cluttered harbors from Boston to Savannah, but no officer with any talent or ambition could be persuaded to command one. The British had a navy with six hundred men of war at sea and ready to fight. The pinchpenny Congress adjourned on July 6, 1812 without vot-ing a cent to expand America's matchbox fleet. Jefferson's mindless hatred of a navy remained unchallenged. [8]

Winning a war, Thomas Jefferson maintained, was merely a matter of finding good generals and colonels. There was no need for trained troops or that awful thing, a large regular (aka standing) army. "It is nonsense to talk about regulars," he told James Monroe when the latter became Madi-son's secretary of war. "They are not to be had among a people so easy and happy...as ours." Militia, properly inspired by their leaders and the pre-sumed patriotic fervor of all true Democratic-Republicans, could defeat Britain's "mercenaries" anytime. President Madison followed this reversal of George Washington's approach to war-making like the Jeffersonian true believer he had become. [9]

Unfortunately, neither Madison nor his predecessor had a clue about the qualifications of a winning general. As his senior commander, Madison chose Jefferson's former secretary of war, sixty-one-year-old Henry Dear-born, who had grown grossly overweight thanks to his cushy job as Collec-tor of Customs in Boston. He had fought well at Bunker Hill and other Revolutionary War battles, but had never risen above second-in-command of a regiment.

Other appointees were around the same age and had achieved similar middle-level ranks in the Revolution. Some were even more unhealthy than Dearborn. Brigadier General William Hull, who also served as governor of the Michigan territory, had not entirely recovered from a stroke.

Overseeing these aging soldiers was Madison's Secretary of War, William Eustis, a Massachusetts doctor who had also served in the Revolution but had no experience in supervising an army. Since Madison did not bother to appoint a commander in chief, Dr. Eustis was responsible for overseeing operations in nine different military districts, an obvious impossibility. As the war approached, he spent much of his time revising the army's training manual, and reading ads in magazines to find where he could buy hats and shoes at bargain prices. As a whole-hearted Jeffersonian believer in militia, Dr. Eustis also hated West Point. He reduced appointments to a trickle, and transferred cadets all over the landscape, bringing the school to a complete stop for the better part of a year.[10]

Madison's Secretary of the Navy was a Southern planter named Paul Hamilton, who had seldom set foot on a warship and was much too fond of alcohol to think clearly most days. One congressman described him as "about as fit for his place as the Indian Prophet [Tenskwatawa] would be for Emperor of Europe." Secretary Hamilton was a firm believer in Jeffersonian defensive naval tactics. He ordered America's handful of frigates and sloops to remain in various harbors and join the ex-president's gunboats in opposing enemy attempts to invade these home waters.[11]

Most Democratic-Republican politicians were convinced that the Canadians were ready to switch sides at the first glimpse of an American flag. Ex-President Jefferson told one correspondent that victory would be "a mere matter of marching." It was the same illusion that had produced the Continental Congress's ruinous invasion of Canada in 1775. Jefferson and Madison, having no interest in military matters, were oblivious to this harsh lesson.[12]

On land, the war was a series of military disasters. General William Hull led twenty-two hundred men in an attack on upper or western Canada. When a British general with even fewer men besieged him in Detroit, Hull surrendered lest his men be massacred by the Indians in the British ranks. The bemused British announced that the Michigan territory was now part of Canada, pushing America's northern border back to the Ohio River.

General Dearborn was supposed to be in charge of the attack on eastern Canada. But numerous minor illnesses prevented him from leaving the comforts of Boston. The impatient Democratic-Republican governor of New York launched another army at British-held Fort Niagara. About six hundred regulars crossed the Niagara River and seized high ground. The New York militia discovered scruples about leaving their home state and declined to support them. The regulars were forced to surrender.

General Dearborn finally responded to desperate pleas from Secretary of War Eustis, and in November left the comforts of Boston to take command of a six thousand-man army at Plattsburgh, on Lake Champlain. When his militiamen realized they might spend a freezing winter in Canada, they, too, decided to stay home.

Only on the ocean did America's fighting men distinguish themselves in 1812. Someone persuaded Secretary of the Navy Hamilton to abandon the Jeffersonian strategy of keeping the frigates and other ships in ports. Sent to sea, the sailors amazed the British—and the Democratic-Republicans—by defeating British frigates in nine of ten encounters.

These victories inspired Congress to junk Jefferson's anti-Navy doctrine. In late November 1812, the House Committee on Naval Affairs voted to build four ships of the line and six heavy frigates. The Committee defended this decision in a labored statement that claimed it was "a bright attribute of the tar [sailor] that he has never destroyed the rights of the nation" (unlike that terrible Jeffersonian monster, a standing army.)[13]

An obviously unhappy ex-President Jefferson sighed that "frigates and 74s [ships of the line] are a sacrifice we must make, heavy as it is, to the prejudices of a part of our citizens." In other words, Congress, the supposed voice of the people, had just told him that on naval matters, he did not know what he was talking about. President Madison signed the bill without a comment.[14]

The 1812 naval victories stirred widespread celebrations, but they had little or no impact on the war. By 1813, the British navy had so many warships in American waters, American men of war did not dare to venture from their harbors. Napoleon's disastrous 1812 invasion of Russia and a surge of hatred for the arrogant Bonapartes elsewhere in Europe had tilted the long war in Britain's favor.

In 1813, the American army's attacks on Canada were a replay of 1812. President Madison gave Thomas Jefferson's favorite general, James Wilkinson, command of eight thousand troops for a waterborne assault on Montreal via the St. Lawrence River. Spanish Agent 13 collided with French Canadian militia who stopped him seventy miles short of his objective in what most generals would consider a skirmish. Wilkinson ingloriously retreated. A smaller army, marching from Plattsburgh, also abandoned the fight after an equally minor defeat. The year ended with not a single American soldier in Canada.

Further south, a British fleet sailed from Bermuda and ravaged towns along the Virginia coast and in Chesapeake Bay. From Monticello came a long disquisition on how gunboats could save the situation by defending the mouth of the great bay. Jefferson admitted that "ridicule had been cast on this instrument of defence." He blamed the criticism on the "prejudices of the gentlemen of the Navy." He was still convinced that in "shoaly" water, the gunboats could damage enemy warships and flee up rivers and creeks beyond the reach of larger men of war.[15]

President Madison earnestly assured his predecessor that the new Secretary of the Navy, William Jones, was "not unfriendly to gunboats." This was a barely white lie. Jones, a former ship captain, detested Jefferson's creations. He called them "receptacles of idleness and objects of waste." Virtually quoting the Secretary of the Navy but omitting his name, Madison told Jefferson his gunboats had been judged "too slow in sailing and too heavy for rowing." By 1815, there would not be a Jefferson gunboat left in the U.S. Navy.[16]

Early in 1814, truly ominous news arrived from Europe. Emperor Napoleon, having lost a half-million men in his invasion of Russia, was on the brink of surrender to a British-led coalition of armies. In April, the Man of Destiny abdicated his throne and agreed to spend the rest of his days on the tiny island of Elba off the Italian coast. The exultant British decided they could now teach their American cousins some military lessons they would never forget.

Plans were made to invade the United States from Niagara, Lake Champlain, and New Orleans. Hard fighting by American regulars, who had learned some lessons from two years of defeats, stopped the Niagara thrust. Meanwhile, a twenty-two-ship British squadron appeared off the Chesapeake escorting forty-five hundred men with orders to ravage the coast and if possible, attack Washington, D.C .

With the army's scant supply of regulars fighting on the Canadian border, President Madison had to rely on militia. The President summoned ninety-five thousand of these theoretically patriotic amateurs to defend the federal village. A mere sixty-five hundred responded to their president's call. Madison accompanied these temporary soldiers to the battlefield, hoping that his presence would inspire them.

Led by an incompetent general named William Winder, the militiamen made a stand at the village of Bladensburg, five miles from Washington. While President Madison watched, the British infantrymen charged. The militiamen fired a single volley and ran, sweeping General Winder and the President away in the terrified mob.[17]

The British marched to Washington, D.C., where they almost captured Dolley Madison, who had refused to leave the presidential residence in spite of several warnings. The British burned the mansion and every other public building in Washington, D.C., except the patent office. It was a national—and presidential—humiliation that was almost beyond belief. A month later, when the House of Representatives convened for a special session of Congress, they voted 79-37 to abandon President Jefferson's federal village.

The city of Philadelphia assured the government they would be welcomed back and even designated buildings they could use. Madison, with his wife Dolley's encouragement, rejected the idea, even though it was emanating from the supposed voice of the people, Congress. For the next four months, Congress debated abandonment of Washington, D.C., while Dolley and her husband hosted numerous dinners (in a rented private mansion) to persuade them to change their minds.

As Madison grappled with the defeatism permeating Congress, a naval victory on Lake Champlain did wonders for everyone's morale. A ten thousand-men British army headed down this long, narrow lake, which served as a kind of invasion highway into the heart of New York state. A thirty-year-old navy commander named Thomas Macdonagh smashed the enemy's escorting fleet in one of the most important military victories in American history. The British army abandoned their invasion and retreated to Canada. The news had not a little to do with Congress deciding to stay in Washington, D.C.

There was little else to cheer Madison's collapsing administration in 1814. A "mediation commission" the President had sent to Europe to explore the possibility of peace drew no response from London. The federal government was unable to borrow money from American state banks and was reduced to selling bonds for forty cents on the dollar. In the fall of 1814, the Secretary of the Treasury told the President the country needed $50 million to escape bankruptcy. There was no hope of raising such a sum, and the government defaulted on payments due to reduce the national debt.

The Secretary of the Treasury informed the Democratic-Republican majority in Congress that it was time to start taxing everything in sight, including western whiskey. He also urged the revival of the Bank of the United States. The latter was a gulp too large for Congress, even though President Madison recommended it. But the congressmen and senators succumbed to a tax program far heavier than anything perpetrated by those awful monocrats, Alexander Hamilton and George Washington.[18]

New England was talking secession again, and openly trading with the enemy in Canada and the West Indies. The British army in Canada had recovered from its repulse on Lake Champlain and was preparing for a bigger, probably successful invasion. The only spark of hope came from Tennessee, where Andrew Jackson, that admirer of Aaron Burr, had magically emerged as a winning general. In a confrontation with the large and powerful Creek Indian nation, who were backed by the Spanish, he had shattered the Indian army and knocked them out of the war.

President Madison promoted Jackson to major general and put him in charge of defending New Orleans. Early in 1815, he defeated an army of British regulars, ending Europe's dream of controlling the Mississippi River and the politics of the western states. The news reached Washington, D.C. just as delegates from a convention held in Hartford, Connecticut, by the New England states arrived in town. They came demanding a revision of the Constitution to give them semi-independence—or they would secede from the Union. After watching congressmen and others celebrating the glorious news from New Orleans, they slunk out of town without presenting their ultimatum.

Almost simultaneously, a treaty of peace arrived in the still fire-blackened capital. Commodore Macdonough's victory on Lake Champlain had convinced the British that peace with their best overseas customer might be a better solution than more fire and sword. The treaty did not mention impressment or neutral rights, theoretically the two causes of the war. But President Madison signed it without consulting ex-President Jefferson, and Congress ratified it unanimously.

Three years of seesawing between victory and defeat had changed President Madison's mind about fighting a war Jefferson-style. In a message to Congress, he informed them that the experience had demonstrated the importance of "skill in the use of arms and the essential rules of discipline"—in a word, the training that a regular army gave the men in its ranks. He added that the "present system" of relying on militia was unlikely to inculcate these virtues in American soldiers. In line with this new thinking, Madison urged an expansion of the U.S. Military Academy.

When Congress did not respond to these pronouncements, the President created on his own authority the office of Permanent Superintendent of the Military Academy—a major step toward an organized and functioning school for the soldiers who would lead Americans in future wars.

In 1816, the last year of Madison's term, the new leadership-oriented President persuaded Congress to think nationally in ways that would have pleased George Washington. Congress chartered a second Bank of the United States and revived Secretary of the Treasury Alexander Hamilton's Report on Manufactures—the last step in his program to create a great commercial republic. In line with this innovation, Madison persuaded the legislators to sponsor the nation's first protective tariff to guard new American industries against foreign [mostly British] competition.

Supporting these revivals of President Washington's policies was Chief Justice John Marshall, who rejected the state of Maryland's attempt to challenge the new Bank of the United States. In *McCulloch vs Maryland*, Marshall struck down Jefferson's notion that the Constitution was a compact between the states. Instead, he insisted "the government of the Union...is emphatically and truly a government of the people." While the federal government was "limited in its powers," the Constitution gave it the "discretion" to use the means required to apply these powers "in the manner most beneficial to the people."

Thomas Jefferson was horrified by President Madison's embrace of the Bank of the United States. Writing to his son-in-law, Congressman John Eppes, the ex-president saw America heading for a future of "debt, bankruptcy and revolution." Exhuming his dictum, "The Earth Belongs to the Living," he called Madison's policy a "slavish" imitation of Great Britain. There was no need for a Bank of the United States to loan the government money. Treasury notes could pay for a war just as easily as borrowing from an unconstitutional monster like the BUS.

When Jefferson broached this idea to Madison, the President stunned his former mentor by dismissing his plan and his reasoning. Madison pointed out that printing Treasury notes was not terribly different from the 1776 Continental Congress's printing millions of dollars of paper money, which ended up with the government bankrupt and the dollars "not worth a continental." Even more appalling [to Jefferson], Madison declared the new Bank of the United States should be modeled on the Bank of England.[19]

Over the next several years, Jefferson grew more and more enraged by John Marshall's judicial decisions, which consistently stressed federal power and made the Supreme Court the ultimate arbiter. In 1823, Jefferson reverted to the cry of the long defunct anti-federalists—the Constitution was a plot to "consolidate" the states out of existence. He wrote a letter full of violent denunciations to William Branch Giles, who had become governor of Virginia. Instead of the Supreme Court, Jefferson proposed a plan to resolve clashes between the states and the federal government by letting the people decide disputes at state conventions.

When Jefferson showed the letter to James Madison, he again earnestly but firmly disagreed with his lifelong friend. Madison argued with almost irresistible force for judicial review and the supremacy of the Supreme Court. He pointed out that calling conventions every time the states and the federal government disagreed would soon destabilize the politics of the nation. Jefferson retreated into silence.

If we include the vigorous leadership President Madison gave Congress in his final year in office and his embrace of the Bank of the United States, a protective tariff and internal taxes, it is no exaggeration to say that experience, that best of all teachers, had forced James Madison to rethink his long devotion to President Thomas Jefferson and reconsider his once angry opposition to President George Washington.

Madison was much too polite—and too fond of Jefferson as a friend—to put his transformation into blunt words before Jefferson's death in 1826. The two men worked closely together on a praiseworthy retirement project—the founding of the University of Virginia. Even here there were glimpses of disagreement. As the university neared opening, they discussed the texts that should be listed as required reading for the law school, a branch of education in which, Jefferson declared, "we are the best judges." He recommended the Declaration of Independence, the Federalist, and the 1798 and 1800 Virginia Resolutions as well as English sources, such as John Locke and Algernon Sidney.

Madison politely (as always) but firmly objected. He argued that none of these texts, though rich in fundamentals, should be recommended as biblical-like repositories of The Truth. He particularly dismissed the Virginia Resolutions as much too partisan. Instead, Madison suggested merely calling the list the "best guides" to the principles of American government, giving the next generation the freedom to construct their own beliefs. Then, without any hint of apology or pleading, Madison suggested adding George Washington's Farewell Address.

Two years after Jefferson's death in 1826, Andrew Jackson revived and even enlarged George Washington's tradition of the strong president—and James Madison made his political transformation explicit. In 1832, a clash between Vice President John Calhoun and his followers in South Carolina about a state's right to protest a protective tariff escalated into a constitutional crisis. Calhoun espoused the Jeffersonian doctrine that the national charter was a compact between sovereign states, which meant a state could "nullify" a federal law that it found hostile to its interests. From there it was only a step to the claim that a state had the right to secede from the Union in order to protect its citizens' rights to life, liberty, and the pursuit of happiness. Among Calhoun's most vociferous supporters was William Branch Giles of Virginia.

President Jackson was not a constitutional scholar, but his private secretary was a young man named Nicholas P. Trist, who had married one of Thomas Jefferson's granddaughters. Trist's grandmother, Elizabeth Trist, had run the boardinghouse at which Madison and Jefferson had stayed during their congressional years in Philadelphia. This personal link enabled Trist to bring the eighty-one-year-old ex-president into the dispute, with remarkable results.

Madison published a vigorous rebuttal of the nullifiers' claims. He insisted that the Virginia and Kentucky Resolutions were merely statements of opinion, with no claim to being legal principles. He was especially fierce on Calhoun's embrace of Jefferson's proposal to settle disputes between the states and the federal government by calling state conventions. The ex-president cited his essay in *The Federalist*, which argued that the Supreme Court was the best and only way to settle such differences.

Chief Justice John Marshall had been following this contest with close attention. He informed the world that Madison's demolition of Calhoun gave him "peculiar pleasure." Madison was also repudiating Thomas Jefferson but Marshall diplomatically omitted his name. The fourth president, the Chief Justice said, "was himself again, [avowing] the opinions of his best days." [20]

Calhoun, Giles, and their backers in other southern states dismissed Madison as an old codger with a fading memory of what he really thought and meant in 1798. They had "incontestable" proof that Thomas Jefferson believed in the doctrine of nullification. He had written it into his Kentucky Resolutions. To Madison's dismay, he discovered in his papers a draft of Jefferson's resolutions, with the dreaded word in the Master of Monticello's own hand.

Although he was ravaged by the infirmities of old age, with his wife Dolley's help, Madison hurled himself into the argument. He insisted that Jefferson did not mean nullification as Calhoun was using it, to justify a single state's defiance of the government. Madison stressed with almost visible desperation his friend's lifelong commitment to majority rule. More important, in his letters to Nicholas Trist, intended for President Jackson, Madison reiterated that the federal union was indissoluble, perpetual—and crucial to the future happiness of nation.

When the South Carolinians summoned a convention that declared the latest federal tariff was null and void, and proclaimed their readiness to defend their stand with gunfire, President Andrew Jackson had ready a Madisonian reply that was tailored to the Tennesseean's convictions and temperament. "The Constitution of the United States…forms a *government*, not a league…It is a government in which all the people are represented, and which operates on the people individually, not upon the states." That meant the United States "was a *nation,*" and secession would destroy it. "Do not be deceived by names," Jackson warned. "Disunion by armed force is *treason.*"

For a few days South Carolina blustered defiance. But when President Jackson obtained from Congress the right to summon an army, and grimly promised to invade the state at the head of ninety thousand men, the hot-heads in Charleston collapsed. It was a replay of George Washington's destruction of the Whiskey Rebellion. In Montpelier, James Madison applauded. He wrote a letter of congratulation to ex-War Hawk Henry Clay, who had persuaded Congress to pass a more moderate tariff bill that made South Carolina's capitulation less humiliating.

❦

For the rest of his life, fears for the future of the Union disturbed ex-President Madison's sleep. "What madness for the South," he sighed, when reports convinced him that many southerners were still talking nullification and secession. Looking for greater safety in disunion, he said, would be "jumping into the fire for fear of the frying pan." Madison worried that the next crisis would involve "the Negro, or slavery question." President Andrew Jackson voiced the same fear. As Madison brooded on this possibility, he decided to leave a message to his fellow Americans.

Madison called it "Advice To My Country." It began with a paragraph describing it as "issuing from the tomb"—it would not be published until after his death (in 1836). But it was "the experience of one who has served his country in various stations through a period of forty years, who espoused in his youth, and adhered through his life, to the cause of liberty, and who has borne a part in most of the great transactions which will constitute epochs of its destiny."

> The advice nearest my heart and deepest in my conviction is, that the Union of the States be cherished and perpetuated. Let the open enemy to it be regarded as a Pandora with her box opened, and the disguised one as a Serpent creeping with his deadly wiles into Paradise.[21]

Those words marked the final transformation of James Madison. He had abandoned the divisive ideology that emanated from Thomas Jefferson's Monticello and returned to the sunny piazza of Mount Vernon as a partner of that realistic visionary, George Washington. It is a journey that every man and woman in America can and should take—now and in the future.

Epilogue

B Y THE TIME JAMES Madison wrote those resounding farewell words, no one realized that he was repudiating Thomas Jefferson and affirming George Washington. Madison avoided a specific reference to either man—ironic proof that he was still emotionally trapped between them. To explain himself would have required a veritable treatise on their differences, which would have been extremely painful for Madison to write. He would have had to face not only their clashing views on the importance of the Union. At least as significant was their disagreement over the powers of the presidency and the role of Congress in governing the nation. Washington's views had been obliterated from the public mind. The man responsible for this historical erasure was Thomas Jefferson.

Throughout Jefferson's presidency, and in the two decades of his life after he returned to Monticello, he waged a persistent campaign to portray Washington as a symbol of American nationhood with virtually no content to the image but his role as a noble, nonpartisan father of the country. As Jefferson put it in his first inaugural address, Washington was "our first and greatest revolutionary character" whose "preeminent services entitle him to the first place in his country's love." There is not a hint in these words of the decisive president who smashed the secessionists of the Whiskey Rebellion, deflated the so-called Democratic Societies and their adoration of France, and persuaded Americans to accept the less-than-perfect John Jay treaty with England as a price worth paying for peace—all feats that Thomas Jefferson had dismissed with sneers and loathing.

By 1813, Jefferson had begun to rewrite the history of Washington's administration. "General Washington did not harbor one Principle of Federalism," he insisted." Note the use of "General" instead of "President." When Chief Justice John Marshall published his biography of

Washington, making it very clear that President Washington was not only a Federalist, he abhorred Jefferson's Democratic-Republicans for their mindless worship of France, their readiness to ignore the Consitution and discuss—and even plan—to fracture the Union, Jefferson dismissed the book as a tissue of lies put together for "electioneering purposes." In his heart, Jefferson maintained, Washington was a "small r" republican, which meant he could never have agreed with the monarchists and Anglomen who peopled the Federalist party.[1]

Standing the truth on its head in this way, Jefferson succeeded in making the Federalists guilty of twisting Washington's reputation into a parody of the real president. They had "gone some distance toward sinking his character by hanging theirs on it, and by representing as the enemy of republicans him, who of all men, is best entitled to the appellation of the father of that republic which they were endeavoring to subvert." There was, Jefferson admitted, opposition "to the course of [Washington's] administration," but that simply was an effort "to preserve Congress pure and independent of the Executive," to restrain the administration to republican forms and principles, and not permit the Constitution "to be warped in practice into all the principles and pollutions of their favorite English model." The Republicans, "devoted to the present Constitution," had never threatened the national charter, as Chief Justice Marshall claimed. They merely resisted "Anglomany & Monarchy."[2]

By blending Washington into this imaginary history, Jefferson made it difficult and finally impossible for average Americans to remember their clashing visions of the federal government. These differences have persisted throughout the nation's history. We have seen how close Jefferson's political heirs in the Democratic Party came to fracturing the Union in the 1830s by embracing his view that the federal government was a compact between the states, which could be dissolved by a majority vote of any state. Coupled with this contention was his idea that a state could nullify an act of Congress if they thought it impinged on their rights. When these ideas collided with New England's abolitionist crusade against slavery, the bloodbath of the Civil War became inevitable. More and more, it looked like Washington's vision of the central importance of the federal Union was heading for history's dumpster.

It slowly became apparent that millions of Americans had absorbed a profound respect—even a love—of the Union. Washington's Farewell Address played a large part in this sentiment. Not a few historians believe that the Union was the primary emotion—not hatred of slavery—that galvanized the nation to resist the South's secession.[3] At least as important was the election of Abraham Lincoln, a man who was a believer in the implied powers of the presidency, thanks to his long apprenticeship in the Mid-Nineteenth Century Whig Party, who considered themselves the heirs of the Federalists. He had no hesitation about wielding unprecedented authority as commander-in-chief. He suspended habeas corpus and other rights, issued the Emancipation Proclamation and a stream of executive orders that bypassed Congress in the name of urgency. One might call him the unJefferson President. Without his extraordinary, often almost extra-legal leadership, the Union would not have survived its four-year ordeal.

When an assassin's bullet ended Lincoln's presidency, another divide in the conflict between Jefferson and Washington came to the fore. Angry members of Congress invoked Jefferson's view of the national legislature as the nation's true ruler. Thaddeus Stevens, the leader of the Republicans in the House of Representatives, sounded the battle cry: "Though the President is Commander-in-chief, Congress is his commander, and God willing, he shall obey...He and his minions shall learn that this is not a government of Kings and Satraps but a Government of the people, and that Congress is the people."[4] Stevens and his Senate ally, Ben Wade of Ohio, set up the Joint Committee of Fifteen, composed of six senators and nine congressmen, a body that operated like a British cabinet, making regular reports to Congress and drafting legislation. They rammed through a series of punitive laws that were a cruel parody of Lincoln's hopes of reconciliation and made Reconstruction a hated word in the South.[5]

The Joint Committee also drafted legislation aimed at drastically reducing the powers of the president. Early in 1867, they passed laws that kept Congress in continuous session if it so inclined, and added the power to call itself into special session, a privilege hitherto reserved to the chief executive. They struck at his role as commander in chief by ordering President Andrew Johnson to issue all military orders through General Ulysses S. Grant, and forbidding Johnson to remove Grant or transfer him to another post without the Senate's consent. To cripple the president's patronage powers, they passed a Tenure of Office Act, which made it a "high misdemeanor" for him to fire any federal official without their approval.

When Johnson challenged this latter law by dismissing Secretary of War Edwin Stanton, Congress impeached him. Most of the charges dealt with the Tenure of Office Act, but the President's accusers threw in a final article that revealed the real nature of the clash: he was guilty of "defaming Congress." Fortunately for the future of the country, some Republican senators began to have second thoughts about what their party was doing. "Once set the example," said Lincoln disciple Lyman Trumbull of Illinois, "and no future president will be safe who happens to differ with a majority of the House and two-thirds of the Senate on any measure deemed by them important." This was an almost exact description of the kind of government President Jefferson tried to achieve in the impeachment of Judge Samuel Chase.[6]

In the final vote, Trumbull and six other Republican senators destroyed their careers rather than give Congress this ultimate power, which a majority was eager to grasp. The vote, thirty-five for conviction, nineteen against, was one short of the needed two-thirds majority.[7]

Although Johnson was acquitted, he emerged from the ordeal a shattered president, who barely ventured out of the White House for the rest of his term. Thaddeus Stevens's dictum that Congress and the people were identical became the virtual law of the land. "The executive department of a republic like ours should be subordinate to the legislative department," Ohio Senator John Sherman remarked a few years later, as if he were discussing something as obvious as the changing of the seasons.

Forty years of weak presidents and an ever more powerful Congress began. Of thirteen pieces of major legislation passed between 1873 and 1897, presidential initiative was responsible for only one. Senator George F. Hoar of Massachusetts remarked that most senators of this era would have considered a message from the White House, asking their vote on a bill, a "personal affront." If a senator visited the White House, it was "to give, not to receive advice." Thomas Jefferson would have loved every year of this era. George Washington would have been appalled.[8]

With this lofty attitude came a paradoxical hallmark of congressional government—rampant corruption. Credit Mobilier, a holding company that was organized to build the Union Pacific Railroad, purchased congressmen and senators in wholesale lots. The Russian ambassador sold Alaska to the United States with similar tactics. With power the only test of legitimacy, the Senate became the headquarters of political bosses such as Roscoe Conkling of New York, Simon Cameron of Pennsylvania, and Zachariah Chandler of Michigan. Presiding over state and city machines fueled by immense amounts of graft, they inspired Henry Adams to remark in his novel, *Democracy*, that the United States "had a government of the people, by the people, for the senators." Only half in jest, Mark Twain wrote: "It could probably be shown by facts and figures that there is no distinctly American criminal class except Congress."[9]

Viewing this scene with high-minded dismay in 1884, a college professor named Woodrow Wilson put an astute finger on the fundamental flaw of congressional government: it was impossible to fix responsibility for decisions emanating from a body composed of hundreds of politicians. "Nobody stands sponsor the policy of the government," Wilson wrote. "A dozen men originate it; a dozen compromises twist and alter it; a dozen officers whose names are scarcely known outside Washington put it into execution." [10] Wilson decided the only answer to congressional government was a strong presidency. "The president is at liberty, both in law and in conscience, to be as big a man as he can," he concluded. Wilson might have realistically added: "As big as President George Washington." But he, too, had lost touch with the reality of Washington's presidency.[11]

For almost twenty years after Wilson declared the need for a strong president, his words remained in the realm of prophecy. The presidents of the late nineteenth century fought an essentially defensive battle against congressional attempts to further erode their office. In these struggles, it became increasingly clear that public opinion tended to favor the president, who was elected by all the people and could, with considerable effectiveness, claim to be their spokesman.

In 1901, the assassination of William McKinley brought Theodore Roosevelt into the White House and a new assertion of presidential power began. Roosevelt's initiatives in foreign policy, such as the creation of the Panama Canal, his dispatch of the Great White Fleet on a world tour, his challenges to the country's "malefactors of great wealth," left Congress gasping in his wake. Executive orders created national forests from public lands, initiated anti-trust prosecutions, and settled a coal strike by threatening to seize the mines.

Roosevelt identified himself with the "Jackson-Lincoln theory of the presidency," maintaining it was "not only his right but his duty to do anything that the needs of the nation demanded, unless such action was forbidden by the Constitution or the laws." How ironic—and sad—that even this gifted man, who wrote as well as read serious history books, did not realize he was walking in George Washington's footsteps. It is one more proof of the devastating way Thomas Jefferson wrote Washington's presidency out of America's meaningful past.[12]

The argument between presidents and Congress by no means ended with Theodore Roosevelt. His successor in a larger-than-life-size presidency was his cousin Franklin Roosevelt, who seized command of Congress and the nation from the moment he took office in the Depression-wracked America of 1933. He had obviously absorbed the example of his cousin Theodore. In an interview with the *New York Times* on November 13, 1932, a week after his election, FDR said: "The presidency is not merely an administrative office. That is the least of it...It is preeminently a place of moral leadership....Without leadership alert and sensitive to change, we are all bogged up or lose our way." George Washington would have applauded these words.

Along with moral leadership and a tidal wave of legislative proposals, Roosevelt added a new ingredient to the president's relationship with Congress—the merciless use of the veto. He rejected 631 measures of Congress—more than all 31 of his predecessors together. Presidential leadership, as Roosevelt practiced it, was by no means synonymous with harmony. It was often accompanied by the sound of gnashing congressional teeth.[13] During World War II, Roosevelt expanded the powers of the presidency to global proportions, creating dozens of federal agencies spending billions of dollars with blank checks supplied by a passive Congress. As the war wound down, there were signs that many senators and representatives in both parties were unhappy with the endless stream of diktats from the White House. If FDR had lived, he would have faced a Congress as surly and hungry for power as the one Andrew Johnson had confronted.

The lawmakers lost no time trying to intimidate Roosevelt's successor, Harry S Truman, ignoring virtually all his legislative proposals. When the Republicans won control of both houses of Congress in 1946, Senator William Fulbright suggested Truman should appoint a Republican as secretary of state and resign. With no vice president, this putative leader of the opposition would become president. This was congressional government beyond even Thomas Jefferson's dreams. Compounding the irony, it was also an attempt to transform the American presidency into a British model.

This fantasy of congressional supremacy was aborted by a snort of contempt from Truman—and by a new historical phenomenon: the Cold

War. The confrontation with Communism institutionalized the president's role as a world leader who towered above Congress. Over the next two decades, the executive branch expanded exponentially. The presidential budget rose from $10 million to $38 billion. By the late 1950s, it was eight hundred times larger than Congress's budget.[14]

By 1964, Congress was considered an almost superfluous department of the American government. Senator Joseph A. Clark of Pennsylvania pointed this out in plaintive detail in his 1964 book, *Congress, The Sapless Branch*. George Washington would have been deeply troubled by this imbalance. He never tried to deny the importance of Congress's role in our government.

Under Presidents Johnson and Nixon, executive power reached a new zenith. While waging war in Vietnam with the thinnest of congressional mandates, Johnson was the first chief executive who chose not to spend huge amounts of money voted by Congress for pet projects such as federal highway and housing programs—in 1967, a staggering $10.6 billion, 6.7% of the federal budget. The policy, called impoundment, was continued by Richard Nixon with even more ruthless regularity. By 1973, Nixon had impounded funds for over one hundred federal programs, arguing that it was within his constitutional power as the guardian of the nation's fiscal stability. [15]

Nixon's overwhelming electoral victory in 1972 over Senator George McGovern, a leading congressional spokesman against the war in Vietnam, seemed to zoom his presidency into the very empyrean of political power—until a seemingly insignificant burglary and the White House's fumbling attempt to cover it up produced the political earthquake called Watergate.

Once more, Congress laid the presidency low and our second era of congressional government began. In quick succession, after abandoning South Vietnam, the lawmakers asserted jurisdiction over the CIA, and in the War Powers Act, put the president on a sixty-day leash if he sent troops into a conflict without their approval. In the Congressional Budget and Impoundment Control Act of 1974, they arrogated unto themselves total power to decide how much to spend and spend and spend.[16]

In 1976, when the voters sent a Democrat to the White House, Congress made it clear that far more than a clash of political parties was behind their revolt against Nixon and his successor, Gerald Ford. The Democratic chairman of the House International Affairs Committee,

Clement Zablocki, announced: "We are not going to roll over and play dead just because Jimmy Carter is president." Before his first year in office was over, Carter was complaining vehemently about Congressional interference and usurpation.

This central issue of the Great Divide—the relationship between the president and Congress—continues to trouble voters and candidates and incumbents. Some historians, virtually echoing Thomas Jefferson, warn against an imperial president. But there are equally strong reasons to worry about an imperial congress. There is no final answer to this problem. President Washington confronted several attempts to assert congressional power in foreign policy, most of them led by his former partner in the creation of the presidency, James Madison. Washington refused to yield an iota of his authority in this crucial realm. He simultaneously remained respectful of Congress's rights and powers, and never attempted to interfere with them, even when they were investigating one of his most valued cabinet members, Alexander Hamilton.

A history of Washington's presidency should become required reading for every man and woman in America. Equally important is the history of our first unWashington president, Thomas Jefferson. A knowledge of the alternatives they offered the nation will be an invaluable resource as America faces a future in which the Great Divide will undoubtedly create new problems. Ultimately, our ability to resolve these challenges can and should rest on George Washington's visionary conviction of the importance—even the necessity—of the president's role as the nation's elected leader. Thomas Jefferson's fear of excessive presidential power and his passionate belief in the importance of individual freedom can also play a part in the eternally fascinating pursuit of that elusive goal, the happiness of the United States of America.

Acknowledgments

I have long been a believer in the adage that every historian stands on the shoulders of previous historians. That is especially true for this book. It was inspired by a unique historical treasure trove created by a great scholar of the American past—James Morton Smith, director emeritus of Delaware's Henry Francis du Pont Museum. In the 1980s and early 1990s, Dr. Smith collected and edited *The Republic of Letters, The Correspondence Between Thomas Jefferson and James Madison*. Along with chapters of his wise commentary, these three green covered volumes contain copies of the 1,250 letters that Thomas Jefferson and James Madison exchanged between 1776 and 1826. Dr. Smith gave me a set of these books when I invited him to speak at the New York American Revolution Round Table twenty years ago. Nothing can approach the revelations I discovered while reading and rereading their pages.

The Great Divide is also a culmination of many years of research for earlier books such as *1776: Year of Illusions, Washington's Secret War: The Hidden History of Valley Forge*, and *The Perils of Peace, America's Struggle for Survival After Yorktown*. In these books, George Washington grew steadily in my mind as a figure not merely of symbolic importance, but as a leader who deserves to be consulted and pondered by anyone who seeks to understand the American presidency.

In 1970, President Harry S Truman awoke me to the centrality of this office when he told me one night in Independence, Missouri, that he considered the presidency the greatest political achievement of the mind of man—and George Washington was responsible for its creation. Without the man from Mount Vernon's insistence on the need for the president to be coequal with Congress, Mr. Truman declared, the office's other progenitors, James Madison and Alexander Hamilton, could never have persuaded the Americans of 1787 to risk giving so much power to a single individual.

My research on Thomas Jefferson began a long time ago, when I decided to write an "intimate" biography that would focus largely on his personal relationships with his wife, his daughters, and his grandchildren. The inspiration for this book came from *The Domestic Life of Thomas Jefferson* by his granddaughter, Sarah N. Randolph. That book had an extraordinary impact on its readers. It revived Jefferson's reputation, which was in tatters after the Civil War. Both sides had found grave fault with his views on secession and slavery. Rather than attempt to deal with these complexities, the book portrayed the private Jefferson, a man who unquestionably had enormous charm.

For *The Great Divide*, I am in more immediate debt to my wife, Alice, a gifted writer in her own right, who has been the same source of advice and encouragement that she has been in my previous books. Also important has been my youngest son, Richard Fleming, whose computer skills and readiness to explore the digital history available on the Internet have once more been a great resource. Similar gratitude goes to another researcher—now also a well-praised historian—Steven Bernstein. He has helped me, with the same dependability and intelligence he displayed in earlier books.

Four librarians deserve my special thanks. First is Mary Thompson, Research Historian of the Fred W. Smith National Library at Mount Vernon. Few scholars in the nation can match her knowledge of George Washington's life—or her readiness to share the documentation for it. Next is Mark Bartlett (and his entire staff) at the New York Society Library, a unique repository of books and tradition that numbers George Washington, Alexander Hamilton, and John Jay among its early borrowers. Next is Lewis Daniels, head of the Westbrook, CT public library, who combines the high tradition of American libraries with his combination of courtesy and enthusiasm for the nation's history. Finally, Gregory Gallagher, chief librarian at the Century Association in New York, who has helped me find obscure books with remarkable skill and rapidity.

I also want to thank my editor at Da Capo Press, Robert Pigeon, whose advice and insights have often added depth to these pages. Similar gratitude goes to my agent, Deborah Grosvenor. There are many others who have my thanks—particularly fellow historians with whom I have discussed aspects of this narrative. All these people and books have been part of what I hope is a new synthesis of events and ideas that will help us better understand the presidency and the conflicts that this crucial office has stirred in the emergence of the United States of America.

Notes

FRONTISPIECE QUOTATIONS

1. The Papers of George Washington, Digital Edition (Hereafter PGW Digital), ed Theodore J. Crackel, Charlottesville, Va 2008. Letter to Henry Knox, February 25, 1787.
2. The Papers of Thomas Jefferson, Digital Edition (hereafter PTJ Digital), ed Barbara B. Oberg and J. Jefferson Looney, Charlottesville, Va 2008-2014. Jefferson to William Short, January 3, 1793.
3. The Papers of James Madison, Digital Edition (hereafter PJM Digital), ed J.C.A. Stagg. Charlottesville, Va 2010. Speech at the Constitutional Convention, June 26. 1787.

INTRODUCTION

1. William Parker Cutler and Julia Perkins Cutler. *Life, Journal and Correspondence of Rev. Manasseh Cutler* (2 vols, Cincinnati 1888), 2: 56-57.
2. Stuart Leibiger, *Founding Friendship, George Washington, James Madison and the Creation of the American Republic*, (Charlottesville, Va: 1999), 1-9
3. George Washington to John Jay, Aug. 15, 1786, PGW Digital .
4. Peter H. Henriques, *Realistic Visionary, A Portrait of George Washington*, (Charlottesville:, 2006).
5. Thomas Jefferson to John Adams, Dec. 28, 1796, PTJ Digital.

CHAPTER 1

1. Joseph Manca, *George Washington's Eye, Landscape, Architecture and Design at Mount Vernon*, (Baltimore, Md 2012), 31. This book is an extraordinarily good way of seeing Washington through the house he designed to suit his own needs, with a constant emphasis on "republican simplicity."
2. John C. Fitzpatrick, editor. *The Writings of George Washington*, (Washington, DC 1937, Vol. 26), 232.
3. Douglas Southall Freeman, *George Washington*, (New York: 1948-57), Vol. 3 *Planter and Patriot*, 520, GW to RH Lee Aug. 29, 1775. Letter to Lund Washington, Aug. 20, 1775. Letter to Joseph Reed, WGW IV, 165, 240-41.
4. Freeman, Vol. IV, 194, note 118.
5. Dave R. Palmer, *George Washington's Military Genius*, (Washington DC: 2012, 126. Lt. General Palmer is a former superintendent of West Point.
6. GW to Major General Wm Heath, Dec. 18, 1776, PGW Digital.
7. Letters of Delegates to Congress (hereafter, LDC) Vol. 8, Lovell to Samuel Adams, Jan. 20, 1778 (Library of Congress, 1976-2000), 618-19.
8. Philip Pappas, *Renegade Revolutionary, The Life of General Charles Lee* (New York: 2014), 256-273
9. Speech to the Officers of the Army, Mar 15, 1783, *George Washington Writings*, The Library of America, 1997, 10-11.

10. GW to Joseph Jones, May 31, 1780. WGW, Vol 18, 443-4. Also see GW to Madison, Nov. 5, 1786. "Thirteen sovereignties pitted against each other and all tugging at the federal head will soon bring ruin on the whole."

11. Henry Knox to George Washington, Oct. 23, 1786, PGW Digital.

12. Washington to Henry Lee, Oct. 31, 1786, Writings of Washington, Vol. 29, 34.

13. GW to JM, Nov. 5, 1786, WGW, Vol. 29, 51.

14. Leibiger, *Founding Friendship*, 61.

15. Walter Stahr, *John Jay, Founding Father* (New York: 2010), 215-217.

16. Papers of James Madison, PJM Digital.

17. James Madison to GW, Feb. 21, 1787, PGW Digital.

18. Washington to Henry Knox, Mar. 21, 1787, Washington Writings, Library of America, 640.

CHAPTER 2

1. Pauline Maier, *American Scripture, Making the Declaration of Independence* (New York: , 1997), 147-149. This superbly researched book casts Jefferson's role in writing the document in a new, far more realistic light.

2. Smith, James Morton, editor, *The Republic of Letters* [hereafter, ROL], *The Correspondence between Thomas Jefferson and James Madison, 1776-1826*, Vol 1, (New York:1995), 38.

3. Madison (JM) to Jefferson, (TJ) May 6, 1780, ROL, Vol. 1, 138.

4. Jefferson to William Fleming, June 8, 1779. PTJ Digital.

5. JM to TJ, May 6, 1780, ROL, Vol. 1, 137-9.

6. Dumas Malone, *Jefferson The Virginian, Vol. 1* (Boston: , 1948), 324-5

7. Madison and the Virginia Congressional Delegation to Gov. Jefferson, Oct. 5, 1780, ROL, Vol. 1, 146-7.

8. William Maxwell, ed. *Virginia Historical Register and Literary Notebook*, Vol III, 1850, John Page to Theodoric Bland, 196.

9. JM to TJ, Apr 3, 1781, ROL, Vol. 1, 180.

10. TJ to GW, Oct. 28, 1781, PTJ Digital.

11. Malone, *Jefferson the Virginian*, 364-5.

12. Ibid, 366.

13. TJ to James Monroe, May 20, 1782, PTJ Digital.

14. JM to TJ, Jan. 15, 1782, ROL, Vol. 1, 209-11.

15. TJ to GW, Jan. 22, 1783, GW to TJ, Feb. 10, 1783, PTJ Digital.

16. Varnum Lansing Collins, *The Continental Congress at Princeton* (Princeton, NJ: 1908), 248-49

17. TJ to JM, Jan. 1, 1784, ROL, Vol. 1, 290. Also see 276, editorial commentary.

18. TJ to GW, April 16, 1784, PTJ Digital.

19. In Philadelphia, Washington pushed hard for abandoning the hereditary principle. The delegates to the meeting reluctantly agreed, but insisted that the decision would have to be approved by all the state chapters. Most chapters never gave their approval. The Cincinnati remains hereditary to this day. But Washington's admonitions persuaded them to eschew political participation as a group.

20. TJ to JM, May 8 & 11, 315-16, ROL, Vol. 1.

21. TJ to JM, July 1, 1784, ROL, 321.

CHAPTER 3

1. Leibiger, *Founding Friendship*, 85. Madison's exact words were: "No member of the convention appeared to sign the instrument with more cordiality than he [Washington]."

2. GW to Lafayette, June 18, 1788, PGW Digital.

3. JM to TJ , April 23, 1787, ROL, Vol. 1, 439.

4. TJ to JM, Jan 30, 1787, ROL, Vol. 1, 438. Also see TJ to William Stephens Smith, Nov. 13, 1787, PTJ Digital.

5. TJ to JM, Jan 30, 1787, ROL, Vol. 1, 436. Also see Dumas Malone, Vol. 2, *Jefferson and the Rights of Man*, Boston 1951, 164-5.

6. Jefferson to John Adams, Nov. 12, 1787, PTJ Digital.

7. TJ to WS Smith, Sept. 28, 1787, PTJ Digital.

8. ROL, TJ to JM Dec. 20, 1787, ROL Vol. 1, 512. Also see PTJ Digital, same date.

9. Ibid, ROL, 518, also in PTJ Digital.

10. Ibid, ROL, 514, also in PTJ Digital.

11. GW to AH, Aug. 28, 1788, PGW Digital. Also see Ron Chernow, *George Washington, A Life* (New York: 2010), 544.

12. GW to AH, Aug 28, 1788, op. cit. Leibiger, *Founding Friendship*, 89.

13. JM to GW, Nov. 18, 1787, PJM Digital.

14. GW to JM, Oct. 10, 1787, PGW Digital. Also see Leibiger, 91.

15. GW to Patrick Henry, Benjamin Harrison, and Thomas Nelson Jr., Sept 24, 1787, *The Documentary History of the Ratification of the Constitution*, Digital edition, John P. Kaminski et al eds, 2009. GW to JM, Oct. 22, 1787, PGW Digital. George Clinton's Remarks Against Ratifying the Constitution, July 11, 1788, *Documentary History of Ratification*, op. cit.

16. TJ to Alexander Donald, Feb. 7, 1788, TJ to Wm Carmichael, Dec. 15, 1787, Doc. Hist of Ratif, op. cit. Also see Andrew Burstein and Nancy Isenberg, *Madison and Jefferson*, (New York: 2010), 180

17. Debates in Virginia Convention, *Documentary History of Ratification*, op. cit.

18. Pauline Maier, *Ratification, The People Debate the Constitution, 1787-1788*, New York 2010, 267. Moncure Conway, *Omitted Chapters of History Disclosed in the Life and Papers of Edmund Randolph*, New York, 1888, 108. Also see Leibiger, 94.

19. Burstein-Isenberg, *Madison and Jefferson*, 180. Also see Ralph Ketcham, *James Madison*, Newtown, Conn 1971, 263.

20. James Monroe to TJ, July 12, 1788, PTJ Digital. Also see Burstein-Isenberg, *Madison and Jefferson*, 183.

21. GW to Jonathan Trumbull Jr. July 28, 1788. PGW Digital. Also see Leibiger, Founding Friendship, 96.

CHAPTER 4

1. TJ to JM July 31, 1788, PJW Digital. JM to TJ, July 24, 1788, PJM Digital.

2. JM to GW, June 27, 1788, PJM Digital.

3. Burstein-Eisenberg, *Madison and Jefferson*, 188. Leibiger, *Founding Friendship*, 98.

4. JM to TJ, Oct 8, 1788, PJM Digital, JM to GW, June 27, 1788, PJM Digital, GW to Henry Knox, April 1, 1789, PGW Digital.

5. Memorandum of a discussion of the President's Retirement, May 5-25, 1792. PJM Digital. Madison here recalls his early conversations with Washington about his plan to retire "as soon as the state of the government would permit."

6. GW to Henry Knox, April 1, 1789, PGW Digital.

7. Robert Hendrickson, *Alexander Hamilton Vol II*, 1789-1804 (New York, 1976), 540-1.

8. Leibiger, *Founding Friendship*, 105.

9. JM to TJ, May 27, 1789. PTJ, Digital. In this letter, Madison tells Jefferson who is being appointed or considered for cabinet posts. He praises the "moderation and liberality" of Congress.

10. Richard Norton Smith, *Patriarch, George Washington and the New American Nation* (Boston, 1991), 37

11. JM to TJ, May 23, 1789, P TJ, Digital. Here Madison tells Jefferson about the disagreement over titles The Papers of JM also contain a memo, "Title for the President," which contains Madison's speech in the House, objecting to Adams's titles.

12. Conor Cruise O'Brien, *The Long Affair, Thomas Jefferson and the French Revolution, 1785-1800* (Chicago, 1996), 78. TJ to JM, July 29, 1789, 626-7, ROL, Vol. 1.

13. Leibiger, *Founding Friendship*, 112-13.

14. GW to JM, May 12, 1789. Also see Leibiger, *Founding Friendship*, 113, and Chernow, *Washington*, 595.

15. GW to JM, Sept 23, 1789, PGW Digital.

16. Alvin M. Josephy Jr., *On the Hill, A History of the American Congress* (New York, 1979), 58–60.

CHAPTER 5

1. TJ to Lafayette, Apr. 11, 1787, PTJ, Digital, op. cit.

2. Alexis de Toqueville, *The Old Regime and the French Revolution*, new translation by Stuart Gilbert (New York, 1955), 107.

3. Toqueville, 173, cites evidence that France's prosperity increased enormously in the 1780s. But the antiquated, corrupt government passed few if any benefits along to the people at large. As a result, Toqueville writes, "the steadily increasing prosperity, far from tranquilizing the population, everywhere promoted a spirit of unrest."

4. Howard C. Rice, Jr. *Thomas Jefferson's Paris*, Princeton, 1976, 116–17. Merrill D. Peterson, *Thomas Jefferson and the New Nation*, New York, 1970, 376–77.

5. O'Brien, *The Long Affair*, 53

6. Ibid, 58–9

7. Rice, *Thomas Jefferson's Paris*, 117

8. Rice, Ibid.

9. Simon Schama, *Citizens, A Chronicle of the French Revolution*, (New York, 1989), 405-6.

10. O'Brien, *The Long Affair*, 62–3.

11. TJ to Comte Diodati, Aug 3, 1789. PTJ, Digital, op. cit. The letter was written little more than two weeks after the assault on the Bastille. Count Diodati was a diplomat who represented a small German state, Mecklinburg-Schwerin, at the court of Versailles.

12. TJ to JM, September 6, 1789, ROL, Vol. 1, 631–36. Also in PTJ Digital, same date.

CHAPTER 6

1. Burstein-Eisenberg, *Madison and Jefferson*, 213.

2. Lewis Reifsneider Harley, *The Life of Charles Thomson, Secretary of the Continental Congress and Translator of the Bible from the Greek*, Philadelphia, 1900, 112. (ebook)

3. Woodrow Wilson, *Congressional Government*, Boston, 1900, 45. It would take a hundred years for another gifted political thinker. In this great book, Wilson noted that the chief problem with Congress as a governing body was its sheer number. No one had to take responsibility for crucial decisions.

4. David Stuart to GW, July 14, 1789, PGW Digital.

5. Andrew Burstein, *The Original Knickerbocker, The Life of Washington Irving* (New York, 2006), 7.

6. Douglas Southall Freeman, *George Washington*, Vol. 6, *Patriot and President* (New York, 1954), 240.

7. James Thomas Flexner, *George Washington and the New Nation*, Vol. 3, Boston, 1970, 229-30. Also see Freeman, Vol. 6, 243–5.

8. Ibid.

9. There is a good account of this hatred of a standing army in my book, *The Perils of Peace* (New York, 2007), 308-9. It was undoubtedly a disease in the public mind, which ran rampant for well over a decade.

10. Howard Taubman, *The Making of the American Theater* (New York, 1965), 42-44.

CHAPTER 7

1. O'Brien, *The Long Affair*, 67-8

2. Isaac Kramnick, *The Rage of Edmund Burke* (New York, 1977), 31. Also see Schama, *Citizens*, 457-8.

3. JM to TJ, Oct. 8, 1789, PJM Digital.

4. GW to TJ, Jan 21, 1790, TJ to GW, Dec. 15, 1789, PGW Digital.

5. GW to TJ, Jan 21, 1790, PGW Digital. JM to TJ , ROL, Vol. 1, 639.

6. JM to TJ, Feb. 4, 1790, ROL, 650-53.

7. Flexner, Vol. 3, 235-8.

8. Henderson, *Hamilton*, Vol. 1, 342-4.

9. Ibid 541-2.

10. Stanley Elkins and Eric McKitrick, *The Age of Federalism* (New York, 1993), 124–5.

11. JM to TJ, Jan. 24, 1790, ROL, Vol. 1, 649-50. Also see Elkins and McKittrick, *Age of Federalism*, 136 and Hendrickson, *Hamilton II*, 27.

12. Benjamin Rush to JM, Mar 10, 1790, PJM Digital.

13. Josephy, *On the Hill*, op. cit., 69-70. Also see John Steele Gordon, *Hamilton's Blessing* (New York 2010), 24.

14. GW General Orders May 21, 1783. This contains Washington's advice to his departing troops not to sell their notes and securities at a discount—from Writings of GW, John C. Fitzpatrick, Ed.

15. GW to David Stuart, June 15, 1790, PGW Digital.

16. Malone, Vol II., 253-4.

CHAPTER 8

William McClay, *Sketches of Debates in the First Senate of the United States*, 1880, 212.

2. JM to TJ, June 9, 1793, PTJ Digital.

3. James Grant, *Party of One* (New York 2005), 363.

4. Extract from a Speech of Edmund Burke, Feb. 9, 1790. PTJ, Digital.

5. O'Brien, *The Long Affair*, 80.

6. Franklin B. Sawvel, ed. *The Anas of Thomas Jefferson* (New York, 1970), 31.

7. TJ to John Page, May 4, 1786, PTJ Digital.

8. AH to Edw Carrington, May 26, 1792, Papers of AH, Digital Edition, ed by Harold C. Syrett, 2011. Joseph J. Ellis, *Founding Brothers* (New York, 2000), 57.

9. *Journal of Wm McClay, US Senator from Pennsylvania* (New York, 1790), 178.

10. Jefferson's Account of the Bargain on Assumption and Residence Bills, 1792. PTJ, Digital.

11. McClay, *Journal*, 309-328.

12. O'Brien, *The Long Affair*, 83.

13. Stephen Decatur, Jr., *The Private Affairs of George Washington, from the Records and Accounts of Tobias Lear, Esquire, His Secretary.* (New York, 1969), 169.

14. Elkins and McKitrick, *The Age of Federalism*, 633-4.

CHAPTER 9

1. Flexner, *George Washington and the New Nation*, Boston, 1989, Vol 3, 278.

2. Ibid 278-9.

3. Final version of *An opinion on the Constitutionality of an Act to Establish a Bank*—Feb 21, 1791. PAH Digital. Also see The Federalist 44, Philadelphia, 1877.

4. Malone, Vol. 2, 343.

5. PAH, op. cit., Final Version.

6. Paul Leicester Ford, *The True George Washington* (Philadelphia, 1896,244.)

7. GW to David Humphries, July 20, 1791, PGW Digital. JM to TJ, July 10, 1791, PJM, Digital. Also see ROL, Vol. 2, 667

8. GW Diary of Southern Trip, Notes on NC, SC and GA, PGW Digital.

9. GW to Officials of Fredericksburg, Va, Apr 9, 1791, PGW Digital.

10. Chernow, *Washington*, op. cit., 673.

11. Smith, *Patriarch*, op. cit., 109.

12. TJ to JM, July 24, 1791. PTJ Digital. Also see ROL, Vol. 2, 700-01.

13. JM to TJ, Aug 8, 1791, PJM Digital, ROL, 705-6. Also see Leibiger, *Founding Friendship*, 137.

14. GW to David Humphries, July 20, 1791, PGW Digital.

15. John Brewer, *The Sinews of Power, Money and the English State*, 1699-1783 (Taylor and Francis E library, London). This is a revelatory book that explains the roots of 18th Century England's power.

16. Elkins and McKittrick, *Age of Federalism*, op. cit., 53.

17. Jacob Axelrad, *Philip Freneau, Champion of Democracy*, 204-8

18. Forest McDonald, *Alexander Hamilton* (New York, 1979), 241. Smith, *Patriarch*, op. cit., 132.

19. JM to TJ, Oct 3, 1794, PJM Digital. ROL, ibid Vol. 2, 857.

20. Thomas Paine, *Rights of Man, Being an Answer to Mr. Burke's attack on the French Revolution, Vol 1*. (London, 1791), 23.

21. TJ to John Adams, July 17, 1791, PTJ, Digital.

22. TJ to JM, May 9, 1791, PTJ, Digital. ROL, 687-8.

23. Prospectus of the Society for Establishing Useful Manufactures, Aug. 1791, PAH Digital.

24. For the *National Gazette*: The Union, Who Are Its Real Friends? Mar. 31, 1792, PJM, Digital. ROL, Vol. 2, 709.

CHAPTER 10

1. Freeman, Vol 6, 336-37. This account is based on Tobias Lear's recollection of the stormy scene.

2. Richard H. Kohn, *Eagle and Sword, The Beginnings of the Military Establishment in America* (New York, 1975), 104-7.

3. Ibid. On 73-88, Kohn has a good discussion of the roots of Congress's hostility to a standing army. It was led by ideologues like Elbridge Gerry of Massachusetts, who persuaded the state's legislature to order their congressional delegation to "oppose…the raising of a standing army of any number…in time of peace." (61)

4. Ibid, Kohn, 113-15.

5. McDonald, *Alexander Hamilton*, 247.

6. Ibid, 248.

7. Ibid, 249.

8. Letters from Anonymous, Jan. 3 and Jan. 20, 1792, PGW Digital.

9. Malone, Vol. 3, 401.

10. Jefferson, *Anas*, Feb. 29, 1792, 51-56.

11. Ibid.

CHAPTER 11

1. 2010, Memorandum on a Discussion of the Presidsent's Retirement, May 5, 1792. PJM, Digital.

2. GW to JM, May 20, 1792, PGW Digital. TJ to JM, June 4, 1792, PTJ Digital.

3. Jefferson, *Anas*, July 10, 1792, 83-86.

4. Edmund Randolph to GW, Aug 5, 1792, PGW Digital.

5. Forrest McDonald. *The Presidency of George Washington* (Wichita, KS 1974), 93.

6. GW to AH, Aug 26, 1792, PAH Digital.

7. Jefferson, *Anas*, Oct. 1, 1792, 88-92.

8. Ibid.

9. Ibid.

10. TJ to JM, Oct. 1, 1792, JM to TJ, Oct. 9. 1792, ROL, Vol. 2, 740-42.

11. John C. Miller, *Alexander Hamilton and the Growth of the New Nation* (New York, 1959), 333-342.

12. Jefferson, *Anas*, Dec. 17, 1792, 100.

13. Malone, Vol 3, *Jefferson and the Ordeal of Liberty*, 476, Ron Chernow, *Alexander Hamilton*, New York, 2004, 417.

14. John P. Kaminski, *George Clinton, Yeoman Politician of the New Republic*, (Madison, Wis, 1993), 223-5. Jefferson told one correspondent it seemed impossible "to defend Clinton as a just or disinterested man." Madison thought Clinton should resign.

15. TJ to JM, Dec. 12, 1792, Jan 18. 1793, Feb. 21-27, 1793, ROL, Vol. 2, 760-64. All these letters deal with the attempt to oust Hamilton. The last is Jefferson's draft of Giles's Resolutions. Also available in PTJ Digital, with slightly different dates and titles. The editors of the Digital Edition note that Jefferson had assured President Washington in a Sept. 9, 1792 letter that he was determined "to intermeddle not at all with the legislature." Thus it was not surprising "that he went to great lengths to conceal his part in this affair."

CHAPTER 12

1. O'Brien, *The Long Affair*, 114.

2. George Green Shackelford, *Jefferson's Adoptive Son, The Life of William Short*, 1759-1848 (Lexington Ky, 1991), 115-18. Also see Malone, Vol. 2, 15, 149-50.

3. O'Brien, *The Long Affair*, 116

4. Schama, Citizens, 555. Also see O'Brien, *The Long Affair*, 117.

5. Jefferson, *Anas*, 69.

6. JM to Edmund Pendleton, Dec. 18, 1791, PJM Digital. For use of party name, see Alfred F. Young, *The Democratic-Republicans of New York: The Origins, 1763-1797*, 1967, Williamsburg, Va.

7. O'Brien, The Long Affair, 130-31.

8. Flexner, Vol 3, *George Washington and a New Nation*, 355-56.

9. Jefferson, *Anas*, 69.

10. O'Brien, *The Long Affair*, 129-30.

11. TJ to Lafayette, June 16, 1792, PTJ Digital.

12. Schama, *Citizens*, 597.

13. Ibid, 600.

14. Wm Short to TJ, July 20, 1792, PTJ, Digital. This long letter vividly describes the madness in France. Also see Harlow Giles Unger, *Lafayette* (New York, 2002), 282-86.

15. O'Brien, *The Long Affair*, 137.

16. Ibid, 138.

17. JM to The Minister of the Interior or the French Republic, April 1793, PJM Digital. David Freeman Hawke, *Paine* (New York, 1974), 258.

18. O'Brien, *The Long Affair*, op. cit., 140.

19. Chernow, *Hamilton*, 432.

20. O'Brien, *The Long Affair*, 641.

21. Schama, *Citizens*, 640.

22. Ibid, 642.

23. Jefferson, *Anas*, Dec. 27, 1792, 100-101.

24. TJ to Wm Short, Jan 3, 1793. PTJ Digital. In *The Long Affair*, Conor Cruise O'Brien considers this letter so important, he quotes it in full. He notes that Dumas Malone, Jefferson's best known biographer, "refrains from quoting any part of it." Also, that "a little earlier," he (Malone) had referred to Jefferson's "personal distaste for disorder and violence."

25. Shackelford, *Jefferson's Adoptive Son*, op. cit., 67-8.

26. Schama, *Citizens*, op. cit., 668-70.

27. *National Gazette*, Apr 20, 179. In his old age, Jefferson admitted Freneau had gone too far. He admitted he would not have voted to execute the king, if he had been a member of the French legislature. Malone, Vol. 3, 61.

28. Elkins and McKittrick, *The Age of Federalism*, 356-7. Ketcham, *James Madison*, 337-39.

CHAPTER 13

1. AH to GW, Apr 5, 1793, PGW Digital. Hamilton received the news from "a respectable merchant" in Lisbon, Portugal. GW to TJ, Apr. 12, 1793, PGW Digital. In a later letter, GW told Gouverneur Morris that his "primary objects" were "to preserve the country in peace if I can, and to be prepared for war if I cannot." GW to GM, June 25, 1794, PGW Digital.

2. Schama, *Citizens*, 686-7. Knee breeches were worn by the upper class. The poor wore long, loose trousers.

3. Ibid, 687.

4. Malone, Vol. 3, 64.

5. Jefferson, *Anas*, Apr 18, 1793, 118-19.

6. Freeman, Vol. 7, *First in Peace*, 44-48.

7. Malone, Vol. 3, 69-70.

8. TJ to JM, Apr. 28, 1793, ROL, 769-70.

9. TJ to James Monroe, May 5, 1793, ROL, 771.

10. JM to TJ, May 8, 1793, ROL, 772-3.

11. TJ to Monroe, op. cit., 771

12. Elkins and McKittrick, *Age of Federalism*, 330-31.

13. GM to GW, Jan. 6, 1793, PGW Digital.

14. O'Brien, *The Long Affair*, op. cit., 155-6.

15. Flexner, *George Washington, Vol. 4*, Anguish and Farewell (1793-99), 41.

16. TJ to James Monroe, May 5, 1793, PTJ Digital. The letter is enclosed in a letter to Madison, TJ to JM, May 5, 1793, ROL, Vol. 2, 770-2.

17. Freeman, Vol. 7, 71-2.

18. TJ to JM, May 19, 1793, ROL, 774–6.

19. Elkins and McKitrick, *Age of Federalism*, 344.

20. Freeman, Vol. 7, 76-77.

21. Flexner, Vol. 4, 45.

22. Jefferson, *Anas*, 124-5.

23. TJ to JM, June 9, 1793, June 19, 1793, ROL, Vol. 2, 781, 786.

24. Schama, *Citizens*, 787.

CHAPTER 14

1. *Correspondence between the Hon. John Adams, President of the United States, and the late Wm. Cunningham, Esq.*, Boston, 1823, 34.

2. TJ to James Monroe, May 5, 1793, ROL, 771.

3. Meade Minnigerode, *Jefferson Friend of France 1793. The Career of Edmond Charles Genet* (hereafter, *Genet*) (New York: 1928), 223.

4. O'Brien, *The Long Affair*, 162.

5. Minnigerode, *Genet*, 224-5.

6. O'Brien, *The Long Affair*, op. cit., 171-5. The author cites two other scholars who have studied Genet, and concluded that Jefferson "knowingly" assisted the envoy in his projects to seize Louisiana and Canada for France.

7. Flexner, Vol. 4, 52–3.

8. TJ to JM, June 9, 1793, ROL, 780-2.

9. Freeman, Vol. 7, op. cit. 90.

10. Minnigerode, *Genet*, 265.

11. Jefferson, *Anas*, July 15, 1793, Malone, Vol. 3, 114-15.

12. Freeman, Vol 7, 102.

13. Flexner, Vol IV, 58-9.

14. Ibid, 59.

15. Notes on Neutrality Questions, July 13, 1793, PTJ, Digital edition.

16. TJ to JM, July 7, 1793, ROL, 753.

17. Ketcham, *James Madison*, 344-45. Also see Freeman, Vol. 7, 105-6.

18. Minnigerode, *Genet*, 270-71.

19. Ibid, 209-10.

20. Notes on Cinet [Cabinet] Meeting on Edmond-Charles Genet, July 23, 1793, PTJ Digital.

21. TJ to JM, Aug. 18, 1793, ROL, 808-9.

22. Minnigerode, *Genet*, 236.

23. Ibid, 232-35.

24. O'Brien, *The Long Affair*, 180-1.

25. TJ to JM, Sept. 1, 1793, ROL, 813.

CHAPTER 15

1. Jefferson, *Anas,* 161–66.

2. TJ to JM, Aug. 11, 1793, ROL, Vol. 2, 802-5.

3. TJ to Gouverneur Morris, Aug. 16, 1793, PTJ Digital. This letter includes a copy of the official letter requesting Genet's recall.

4. Flexner, Vol. 4, 85.

5. Jefferson, *Anas*, Nov. 28, 1793.

6. James C. Ballagh, ed., *The Letters of Richard Henry Lee*, Vol. 2, , (New York, 1911-14), 563.

7. GW to Edmund Randolph, Dec. 24, 1793, PGW Digital.

8. TJ to GW, Dec. 31, 1793, PTJ Digital, GW to TJ, Jan. 1, 1794, PGW, Digital, TJ to Wm Giles, Dec. 1, 1795, PTJ Digital.

9. TJ to Horatio Gates, Feb. 3, 1794, PTJ Digital. Vow to Langdon, *Literary Diary of Ezra Stiles*, Vol. III (New York, 1901), 489. TJ to JM, April 27, 1795, ROL, Vol. 2, 877-8.

10. AH to Edw Carrington, May 26, 1792, PAH, Digital. Margaret A. Hogan, C. James Taylor, *My Dearest Friend, Letters of Abigail and John Adams* (New York, 2007), 349. Joseph J. Ellis, *First Family, Abigail and John Adams* (New York, 2010), 167. JA to AA, Dec. 26, 1793, Adams Papers Digital Edition, C.J. Taylor, ed. (Charlottesville 2008-14).

11. Forrest McDonald, *The Presidency of George Washington*, (Lawrence KS 1974), 137.

12. Ibid.

CHAPTER 16

1. Elkins and McKittrick, *Age of Federalism*, 382-3.

2. A Century of Lawmaking for a New Nation, U.S. Congressional Documents and Debates, 1774-1875, House of Representatives, 3rd Congress, 1st Session, January 1794 (Annals of Congress), 406-09.

3. Elkins and McKittrick, *Age of Federalism*, Tonnage and Shipping Chart, 382. By 1796, American tonnage would swell to 675,046 tons and British numbers would dwindle to 19,669.

4. A Century of Lawmaking, 3rd Congress, 1st Session, 390-91.

5. JM to TJ, Mar 2 1794, ROL, Vol. Two, 831-2. Elkins and McKittrick, Age of Federalism, 388.

6. Ketcham, *James Madison*, 351.

7. GW to Henry Lee, Oct 16, 1793, PGW Digital. Proclamation on Expeditions Against Spanish Territory, Mar. 24, 1794 (By the President). A Century of Lawmaking, 3rd Congress, 1st Session.

8. Freeman, Vol. 7, 156-7.

9. Elkins and McKittrick, *Age of Federalism*, 389.

10. JM to TJ, Mar 9, 1794 . 834-5. JM to TJ, Mar 14, 1794, 837, ROL, Vol. 2. Also see Ketcham, *James Madison*, 351.

11. James Monroe to TJ, Mar 16, 1794, PTJ, Digital.

12. Elkins and McKittrick, *Age of Federalism*, 390.

13. Ibid, 393.

14. James Monroe to GW, Apr. 8, 1794, GW to Monroe, Apr. 9, 1794, PGW Digital.

15. JM to TJ, May 25, 1794, ROL, 844-5.

16. Gouverneur Morris to GW, June 25, 1794, PGW Digital.

17. TJ to James Monroe, Apr 24, 1794, PTJ Digital.

18. GW to TJ, Apr 24, 1794, PGW Digital.

19. GW to Henry Lee, Aug 26, 1794, PGW Digital.

CHAPTER 17

1. Freeman, Vol. 7, 183.

2. Alexander Hamilton to GW, Aug. 2, 1794, PGW, Digital. Elkins and McKittrick, *Age of Federalism*, 461-3.

3. Thomas P. Slaughter, *The Whiskey Rebellion*, New York, 1986, 209

4. Proclamation, Sept 25, 1794, PGW Digital.

5. GW to Henry Lee, Aug. 26, 1794, PGW Digital.

6. Slaughter, *Whiskey Rebellion*, 186.

7. Ibid, 190-91.

8. Ibid, 216.

9. Ibid, 215-16.

10. Journal of the House of Representatives of the United States, 1826, 233-36.

11. JM to Monroe, Dec. 4, 1791, PJM Digital.

12. TJ to JM, Dec. 28, 1794, ROL, Vol. 2, 866-68.

13. TJ to James Monroe, May 26, 1795, PTJ Digital.

14. Not until a year after the Whiskey Rebellion did Jefferson admit to anyone that he was aware of the mass murders of the French revolution. "What a tremendous obstacle to the future attempts at Liberty will be the atrocities of Robespierre," he exclaimed to his friend Tench Coxe. TJ to Coxe, June 1, 1795. PTJ Digital.

15. Eugene P. Link, *Democratic-Republican Societies*, 1790-1800, (New York, 1942), 200-209.

CHAPTER 18

1. Conway, *Omitted Chapters* in *The Life and Papers of Edmund Randolph*, 231. Also see Kohn, Eagle and Sword, 215-16.

2. Richard N. Cote, *Strength and Honor, The Life of Dolley Madison* (Mt. Pleasant SC, 2005), 103.

3. Slaughter, Whiskey Rebellion, 219-20.

4. Flexner, Vol. 4, 203.

5. O'Brien, *The Long Affair*, 208-9.

6. Freeman, Vol. 7, 226.

7. Paul David Nelson, *Anthony Wayne, Soldier of the Early Republic* (Bloomington Ind., 1985), 272.

8. Freeman, Vol. 7, 237, note.

9. Samuel Flagg Bemis, *Jay's Treaty, a Study in Commerce and Diplomacy* (New York, 1923), 153-4.

10. *Aurora*, June 1, 1795.

11. Donald Henderson Stewart, *The Opposition Press of the Federal Period* (Albany NY 1968), 199-200.

12. Chernow, *Hamilton*, 486-7.

13. Malone, Vol. 3, op. cit., 246.

14. Ibid, 247, 249.

15. Hendrickson, *Hamilton*, Vol. 2, 339-41.

16. Flexner, Vol. 4, 212.

17. TJ to James Monroe, Sept 6, 1995, PTJ Digital.

18. Defence No. 1, July 1, 22, 1795 (published in the New York *Argus* or Greenleaf's *New Daily Advertiser*), PAH Digital.

19. TJ to JM, Sept 11, 1795, ROL, Vol. 2, 885.

20. TJ to Edward Rutledge, Nov. 30, 1795, ROL, Vol. 2, 889.

21. Address on the Jay Treaty, Aug. 13, 1795, PAH Digital.

22. Washington's Seventh Annual Message to Congress, Dec. 8, 1795, PGW Digital, Presidential Series, Proclamations and Addresses.

CHAPTER 19

1. JM to James Monroe, Dec. 20, 1795, PJM Digital. Address of the House of Rep to the President, Dec. 4, 1795, PJM Digital.

2. William Sullivan, *Familiar Letters of Public Characters on Public Events from the Peace of 1783 to the Peace of 1815* (Boston, 1834), 59-60.

3. JM to TJ, Feb. 29, 1796, ROL, Vol. 2, 921-22.

4. JM to TJ, Mar 6, 1796, ROL, Vol. 2, 924-6.

5. JM to TJ , April 11, 1796, ROL, Vol. 2, 930-31.

6. TJ to James Monroe, Mar 21, 1796, ROL, Vol. 2 890-91.

7. TJ to JM, Mar. 27, 1796, ROL, Vol. 2, 927-8.

8. JM to TJ, April 4, 1796, ROL, Vol. 2, 923-30.

9. Ibid.

10. JM to TJ, Apr. 18, 1796, ROL, Vol. 2, 933-34.

11. Ibid.

12. Ibid.

13. JM to TJ, May 1, 1796, ROL, Vol. 2, 936-7. In a Committee of the Whole, a legislative body is considered one large committee. Its purpose is the encouragement of discussion and debate on a difficult issue.

14. JM to TJ, May 22, 1796, 938-9, ROL, Vol. 2., 938-9.

15. Ketcham, *James Madison*, 365.

16. JM to TJ, May 22, 1796, op. cit. above.

17. Flexner, Vol 4, 277-8. Also see Freeman, Vol. 7, 384

18. Flexner, Vol. 4, 280-1.

19. Elkins and McKittrick, *The Age of Federalism*, 508.

20. Freeman, Vol. 7, 395-6.

21. Richard Norton Smith, *Patriarch*, 270.

22. Harlow Giles Unger, *The Last Founding Father, James Monroe and A Nation's Call to Greatness* (New York, 2009), 124-5.

23. TJ to JM, Jan 3, 1798, ROL, Vol. 2, 1011-14.

CHAPTER 20

1. GW to AH, May 15, 1796, *The Writings of George Washington from the Original Ms Sources*, Electronic Text Center, U of Virginia.

2. Robert F. Dalzell Jr. and Lee Baldwin Dalzell, *George Washington's Mount Vernon, At Home in Revolutionary America*, 1998, 213. A copy of the 1792 speech by Madison was enclosed in the letter to Hamilton. The Text of the Farewell Address is available in PGW, Digital, Presidential Series, Proclamations and Addresses.

3. Felix Gilbert, *To The Farewell Address*, Princeton, 1961, 115-136.

4. http:// gwpapers.virginia.edu, presidential series, 1788-179 7.

5. Joseph Ellis, *His Excellency George Washington* (New York 2004), 245.

6. Moncure D. Conway, Writings of Thomas Paine, Vol. 3 (New York, 1895, 243-252.

7. Harrison Clark, *All Cloudless Glory, the Life of George Washington*, Vol. 2 (Washington, DC 1996), 349-50. Clark recounts a conversation between Benjamin West, the American-born

painter, and Rufus King, the American ambassador to London, in which West describes George III using these words.

CHAPTER 21

1. Hendrickson, *Hamilton* II, op. cit., 375-82.

2. Phocion IV, October 19, 1796, *Gazette of the United States*, Newsbank/Readex Data Base: America's Historical Newspapers New York Public Library Microform. Phocion was an Athenian statesman, known for his leadership abilities and his modest lifestyle.

3. Phocion VIII, Oct. 24, 1796, *Gazette of the United States*, Newsbank/Readex op cit

4. Grant, *Party of One*, op. cit., 377-78.

5. O'Brien, *The Long Affair*, op. cit., 225-6.

6. Minnigerode, *Genet*, 396-97. In an appendix, Minnigerode reprints Genet's entire letter, 413-25.

7. Peterson, *Thomas Jefferson and the New Nation*, 570.

8. TJ to JM , Dec. 17, 1796, ROL, Vol. 2, 944.

9. John Adams to Abigail Adams, Jan 14, 1797, quoted in ROL, V2, 895. Also see Grant, Party of One, 379.

10. TJ to JM, Jan. 1, 1797, JM to TJ, Jan 8, 1797, TJ to JM, Jan. 30, 1797. ROL, V2 , 945.

CHAPTER 22

1. Malone, Vol 3, 295.

2. TJ to JM Jan. 8, 1797, ROL, Vol 2, 955.

3. James Iredell to his wife, Hannah, Feb. 24, 1797, G.J. McCree, *Life and Letters of James Iredell*, 2 volumes (New York, 1857). Iredell was a Justice of the U.S. Supreme Court.

4. Wm Loughton Smith to Rufus King, Apr 3, 1797, ROL, Vol. 2, 966, note.

5. Richard R. Rosenfeld, *American Aurora: A Democratic-Republican Returns* (New York, 1997), 243

6. Grant, *Party of One*, op. cit., 379.

7. Ibid, 385.

8. Ibid, 386.

9. Chernow, *Hamilton*, op. cit., 525.

10. TJ to JM, June 8, 1797, ROL, Vol. 2, 979-81.

11. TJ to Elbridge Gerry, June 21, 1797, ROL, 971.

12. JM to TJ, Aug. 5, 1797, ROL, Vol. 2, 973, 990-92.

13. James Thomson Callender, *History of the United States for 1796*, Philadelphia, 1797, 204, PTJ Digital. TJ to James Monroe, July 15, 1802. Fawn M. Brodie, *Thomas Jefferson, An Intimate History* (New York 1974), 304.

14. JM to TJ, Oct. 20, 1797, ROL, Vol. 2, 973, 993.

15. GW to AH, Aug 21, 1797, PAH Digital.

16. JM to TJ Aug 5, 1797, ROL, Vol 2, 973-4. 990-92

17. TJ to John Wise, Feb. 12, 1798, ROL, Vol. 2, 996.

18. TJ to Angelica Church, Jan. 11, 1798, ROL, Vol 2, 995.

19. O'Brien, *The Long Affair*, 242

20. Ibid

21. Jean Edward Smith, John Marshall, *Definer of a Nation*, New York, 1996, 126, 190.

22. O'Brien, *The Long Affair*, 244-45.

23. TJ to JM Feb. 15, 1798, ROL, Vol. 2 997-8, 1019-20.

24. Grant, *Party of One*, 389-90.

25. O'Brien, *The Long Affair*, 246.

26. Grant, *Party of One*, 398.

27. TJ to JM April 5, ROL, Vol. 2, 1035-6. Grant, *Party of One,* 391.

28. TJ to JM, April 28, 1798, JM to TJ Apr 15, 1798, ROL, Vol. 2, 1001-2

29. Grant, *Party of One*, 394.

30. Ibid, 397.

31. Nathan Miller, *The U.S. Navy: An Illustrated History*, Annapolis, 1977, 42-43.

32. John Adams to GW, June 22, 1798, PGW Digital.

33. Grant, *Party of One*, 405-7.

CHAPTER 23

1. Comments on Monroe's *A View of the Conduct of the Executive of the United States*, circa March 1798, PGW Digital.

2. Freeman, Vol. 7, 476-77.

3. Malone, Vol. 3, 308-9.

4. John Nicholas to GW, Feb 22, 1798, PGW Digital.

5. TJ to JM, June 7, 1798, ROL, Vol. 2, 1057-8.

6. TJ to JM June 21, 1798, ROL Vol. 2, 1008-9, 1060-1062.

7. ROL, V2, 1010 (editorial comment).

8. TJ to JM, June 21, 1798, ROL, Vol. 2, 1061-2.

9. Jefferson to Martha Jefferson Randolph, Apr. 5, 1798, 159-60.

Jefferson to Martha Jefferson Randolph, Apr. 5, 1798, 159-60.

9 Jefferson to Martha Jefferson Randolph, Apr. 5, 1798. Edwin Morris Betts and James Adams Bear Jr., eds, *The Family Letters of Thomas Jefferson* (Columbia, Mo, 1966), 159-60.

10. Jefferson to Martha Jefferson Randolph, May 17, 1798, ROL, Vol. 2, 1063.

11. ROL, Vol 2, 1010, editorial comment.

12. James Morton Smith, *Freedom's Fetters, The Alien and Sedition Laws and American Civil Liberties* (Ithaca, NY, 1956), 14.

13. Jefferson to Samuel Smith, Aug. 22, 1798, ROL, Vol. 2, 1066.

14. Jefferson's Draft of the Kentucky Resolutions, ROL, Vol. 2, 1069-70.

15. ROL, Vol. 2, 1070-1.

16. JM to TJ, Dec. 29, 1798, ROL. Vol. 2, 1085. Editor James Morton Smith cites this letter when he writes: "In no case since their exchange of views on "the earth belongs to the living" did the Father of the Constitution differ so fundamentally with the Author of the Declaration of Independence." ROL, Vol. 2, 1072.

17. TJ to S.T. Mason, Oct. 11, 1798, PTJ Digital.

18. Joseph E. Fields, ed., *Worthy Partner, the Papers of Martha Washington* (Westport Ct. 1994). Martha to Mary Stead Pinckney, April 20, 1799, 319-20.

19. Joan M. Jensen, *The Price of Vigilance*, New York, 1956, 24-45. Also see: Harold Holzer, *Lincoln and the Power of the Press, New York, 2014*. "Lincoln 'pulled no punches in defending press suppression' in wartime," Holzer writes. But the President also made it clear that when the war ended, editorial freedom would be restored. For the internment of the Japanese, see Geoffrey R. Stowe, *Perilous Times, Free Speech in Wartime* (New York, 2004), 286-302.

20. GW to Patrick Henry, Jan. 15, 1799, PGW Digital.

21. Henry Mayer, *A Son of Thunder, Patrick Henry and the American Republic* (New York, 1986), 471-2. Henry was dying of stomach cancer.

22. GW letter to AH, Feb. 25, 1799, PGW Digital.

23. Theodore Sedgwick to AH, Feb. 19, 1799, PAH Digital.

24. TJ to JM, Feb. 19, 1799, ROL, Vol. 2, 1097-98.

25. Page Smith, *John Adams*, Vol. II (New York, 1962), 1102-11.

CHAPTER 24

1. Mayer, *A Son of Thunder*, 471-2 for Henry's election and death.

2. Jonathan Trumbull, Jr. to GW, June 22 and Aug. 10, 1799 and GW replies, July 21 and Aug. 30, 1799, PGW Digital, Retirement Series.

3. GW to James McHenry, Nov 17, 1799, PGW Digital, Retirement Series

4. Smith, *Patriarch*, 351-2. Also see Freeman, Vol. 7, 619.

5. Malone, Vol. III, 413. Ketcham, *Madison*, 397.

6. AH to Theodore Sedgwick, Feb. 2, 1799, PAH Digital.

7. TJ to JM, Jan. 30, 1799, ROL, Vol, 2, 1090-91.

8. Burstein and Isenberg, *Madison and Jefferson*, 345.

9. Ibid.

10. TJ to JM, Aug 23, 1799, ROL, Vol. 2, 1118-19. Jefferson mentions Madison's "visit" in this letter. Also see ROL, 1108-9. Editor James Morton Smith writes that "Madison thought Jefferson had pushed his compact between the states theory too far" and blundered into his "fateful—perhaps fatal—theory of 'scission' or "secession."

11. O'Brien, *The Long Affair*, 248-9.

12. Burstein and Isenberg, *Madison and Jefferson*, 348.

13. Ibid, 348.

14. Patrick J. Garrity, *A Sacred Union of Citizens: George Washington's Farewell Address and the American Character* (Lanham MD 1996) 1. A Century of Lawmaking for a New Nation, U.S. Congressional Documents and Debates, 1774-1875, House of Rep 6th Congress, 1st Session, 194.

15. Smith, *Patriarch*, 359

16. Axelrad, *Philip Freneau*, 344

17. Edward G. Lengel, *General George Washington*, New York 2005, 358. Lengel, who is a professor of history at the University of Virginia and editor-in-chief of the Washington Papers, notes that in 1814, Jefferson remarked that in his sixties, Washington's "memory was already sensibly impaired by age, the firm tone of his mind for which he been remarkable, was beginning to relax, its energy was abated, a listlessness of labor, a desire for tranquility had crept upon him and a willingness to let others act and even think for him." "In fact," Lengel states "Washington lost no mental acuity [even] in retirement."

CHAPTER 25

1. Burstein and Isenberg, *Madison and Jefferson*, 350.

2. TJ to John Breckinridge, Jan 29 1800, PTJ, Digital. Also see ROL, Vol. 2, 1112 .

3. JM to TJ, ROL, Feb 14, 1800, and Apr 4, 1800, ROL, Vol. 2, 1113. TJ to Thomas Mann Randolph, Feb. 2, 1800, PTJ Digital.

4. Malone, Vol III, op. cit., 484-5.

5. Charles O. Lerche, Jr. *Jefferson and the Election of 1800, A Case Study in the Political Smear,* William and Mary Quarterly, Oct. 1948, 472. Also see Burstein-Isenberg, *Madison and Jefferson,* 355.

6. Malone, Vol III, op. cit., 490-1. Adrienne Koch, *Jefferson and Madison, The Great Collaboration* (New York 1950), 212.

7. Milton Cantor, *Great Lives Observed (*Englewood Cliffs NJ, 1972), 108.

8. JM to TJ, Nov. 11, 1800, ROL, Vol. 2, 1153.

9. ROL, Vol. II, 1139-40. Also see Ketcham, *James Madison*, 405.

10. Mary Jo Kline, ed. *Political Correspondence and Public Papers of Aaron Burr* (hereafter PAB), 2 vols, Princeton, NJ, 1983, 485-7, Gouverneur Morris to AH, Jan 26, 1801, PAH Digital.

11. John Cotton Smith, *The Correspondence and Miscellanies of the Hon. John Cotton Smith, LLD* (New York,1847, 224-5). Smith was a member of the group of politicians who visited Mount Vernon early in 1802. Also see Don Higginbotham, *Virginia's Trinity of Immortals: Washington, Jefferson and Henry and Their Fractured Relationships,* Journal of the Early Republic. Winter 2003, 521-543.

12. Jefferson, *Anas,* 223-28.

CHAPTER 26

1. Peterson, *Thomas Jefferson and the New Nation*, 654-5.

2. Malone, Vol 4, op. cit., 15-20.

3. Leonard Baker, *John Marshall, A Life in the Law* (New York, 1974), 359. Marshall stated this opinion in a letter to Charles Cotesworth Pinckney, Mar 4, 1801, the day he administered the oath of office to President Jefferson.

4. Richard E. Ellis, *The Jeffersonian Crisis* (New York, 1971), 50-52.

5. James Alexander Hamilton, *Reminiscences of James A. Hamilton* (New York, 1869), 122.

6. David Freeman Hawke, *Paine* (New York, 1974), 344.

7. Winthrop Jordan, *White Over Black, American Attitudes toward the Negro, 1550-1812* (Chapel Hill, NC, 1968), 376-77.

8. Jack Sweetman, *American Naval History*, Naval Institute Press, Annapolis, MD 1984, 20-38. The shooting war ended in August, 1815. A final treaty of peace was not signed until 1816.

9. Robert Cowley and Thomas Guinzberg, eds., *West Point, Two Centuries of Honor and Tradition* (New York, 2002), 18-19.

10. Malone, Vol. 4, 208.

11. James Sterling Young, *The Washington Community, 1800-1828*, New York, 1966, 21-23.

12. Ibid, 26.

13. Unger, *The Last Founding Father*, 172.

14. Craig R. Hanyan, DeWitt Clinton, *Years of Moulding*, unpublished Ph.D. thesis, Harvard U. 1964, 266. DeWitt Clinton took a dim view of the federal village during the years he served as one of New York's senators.

CHAPTER 27

1. Ketcham, *James Madison*, 414–415.

2. Robert Debbs Heinl and Nancy Gordon Heinl, *Written in Blood, the Story of the Haitian People, 1492–1971* (Boston 1978), 110–113.

3. Jefferson to Robert R. Livingston, Apr 18, 1802, PTJ Digital.

4. George Dangerfield, *Chancellor Robert R. Livingston of New York, 1845–1813* (New York, 1960), 334-337.

5. Steven Englund, *Napoleon, A Political Life* (New York, 2004), 217.

6. Malone, Vol. 4, 324–5.

7. Hawke, *Paine*, 353–56.

8. Ibid, 357–8.

9. Unger, *The Last Founding Father*, 155–58.

10. Dennis A. Castillo, *The Maltese Cross, A Strategic History of Malta* (Westport, Ct., 2003), 126.

11. John Kukla, *A Wilderness So Immense, The Louisiana Purchase and the Destiny of America* (New York, 2004), 254-257. Also see E. Wilson Lyon, *The Man Who Sold Louisiana: The Career of Francois Barbe-Marbois* (Norman, OK, 1942).

CHAPTER 28

1. *The Writings of James Monroe*, Vol. IV, New York, 1902, 9-12.

2. Alexander DeConde, *This Affair of Louisiana*, New York, 1976, 161–174.

3. Malone, Vol 4, 256.

4. W. B. Hatcher, *Edward Livingston, Jeffersonian Republican and Jacksonian Democrat*, (Baton Rouge, LA, 1940), 93-99.

5. Malone, Vol 4., 313–14

6. Ibid, 318–19

7. Ibid, 338

8. Everett Somerville Brown, ed. *William Plumer's Memorandum of Proceedings in the United States Senate (1803-1807)*, New York, 1923, 123. Also see Jerry W. Knudson, *Newspaper Reaction to the Louisiana Purchase*, Missouri Historical Review, Oct. 1953, 207. For poem, see: Patricia L. Dooley, ed, *The Early Republic, Primary Documents on Events from 1799 to 1820* (Westport, CT, 2004), 147.

9. Brown, ed. *Plumer's Memorandum*, 517-18.

10. Alan Schom, *Napoleon Bonaparte*, New York, 1997, 314-327. Carola Oman, *Napoleon at the Channel*, New York, 1942, 98-111.

CHAPTER 29

1. Jefferson, *Anas*, Dec. 31, 1803, Jan. 2, 1804, 222–3.

2. Ibid, Jan. 26, 1804, 224–28.

3. Ellis, *The Jeffersonian Crisis*, 71–2.

4. Kline, PAB 849. Brown, ed: *Plumer's Memorandum*, 147-77. Ellis, *The Jeffersonian Crisis*, 73-5. Annals of Congress, House of Representatives, Eighth Congress, 1st Session, 813.

5. A Century of Lawmaking in a New Nation, U.S. Congressional Documents and Debates, 1774-1875, Annals of Congress, House of Representatives, 9th Congress, 1st Session, 515-16.

6. Tim Mathewson, *Jefferson and the Non-Recognition of Haiti*, American Philosophical Society, Vol. 140, No 1, Mar. 1966, 24-88.

7. Leonard W. Levy, ed., *Freedom of the Press from Zenger to Jefferson* (New York, 1966), 364. In Part Five, "The Special Case of Thomas Jefferson," 327-76. Levy included over a dozen letters from Jefferson upholding a free press, and wryly noted that with Jefferson it was necessary to distinguish rhetoric from reality.

8. Hendrickson, *Hamilton* II, op. cit., 596-609.

9. *The Wasp*, Aug. 23, 1802.

10. Milton Lomask, *Aaron Burr*, 2 Vols (New York 1979-83), Vol. 1, 317. Also see Herbert S. Parmet and Marie B. Hecht, *Aaron Burr, Portrait of an Ambitious Man*, New York, 1967, 185.

11. Samuel Wandell and Meade Minnigerode, *Aaron Burr*, 2 vols. (New York, 1925), Vol 1, 245-46.

12. Unger, *The Last Founding Father*, 174.

13. Arthur Bryant, *Years of Victory*, New York, 1945, 53-54.

14. Kline, PAB, 891-2

15. TJ to JM, Aug 3 1804, ROL, Vol 2. 1331. "No time should be lost in publishing officially the final ratification," Jefferson wrote.

16. Isaac Newton Stokes, *The Iconography of Manhattan Island*, 1498-1909 (New York, 1915-28), Vol. 5, 1422.

CHAPTER 30

1. Burstein and Isenberg, *Madison and Jefferson*, 426-27.

2. Kline, PAB, op. cit., 898-99. Also see David O. Stewart, *American Emperor, Aaron Burr's Challenge to Jefferson's America* (New York, 2011), 76-78.

3. Baker, *John Marshall*, 429.

4. Ibid, 424.

5. Jefferson to Joseph H. Nicholson, in Bruce Peabody, *The Politics of Judicial Independence, Courts, Politics and the Public*, Baltimore 2011, 77.

6. Kline, PAB op. cit., 861-62.

7. Lomask, Aaron Burr, Vol. 2, 367.

8. Malone, Vol. 4, *Jefferson the President*, First Term, 482.

9. John P. Kaminski, *George Clinton*, 275.

10. Miller, *The U.S. Navy*, 52-60.

11. Josephy, *On The Hill*, 132.

12. Malone, Vol. 5, 410, 481.

13. Ibid, 401.

14. Ibid, 405-13.

CHAPTER 31

1. Kline, PAB, op. cit. 968.

2. Ibid, 973-80. Parmet and Hecht, *Aaron Burr,* 270.

3. Baker, *John Marshall*, 462-3.

4. Ibid, 464.

5. Ibid, 465. Also see *The Papers of John Marshall*, Digital Edition, edited by Charles F. Hobson Vol. 7, 17.

6. Malone, Vol. 5, 303. Burstein and Isenberg, *Madison and Jefferson*, op. cit., 446.

7. Thomas P. Abernethy, *The Burr Conspiracy*, New York, 1954, 234-5.

8. Parmet and Hecht, *Burr*, 288.

9. Baker, *Marshall*, 477. Also see Malone, Vol. 5, *Jefferson the President, Second Term*, 314.

10. Lomask, *Aaron Burr*, Vol. 2, 208.

11. Baker, *John Marshall*, 507-9.

12. Abernethy, *Burr Conspiracy*, 249.

13. Baker, *John Marshall,* 501, Lomask, *Burr,* Vol. 2, 267-9.

14. Baker, *John Marshall,* 507-9.

15. Lomask, *Burr*, Vol 2, 281. *Papers of John Marshall*, Vol. 7, 115.

16. Josephy, *On the Hill*, 134.

17. Parmet and Hecht, *Burr*, 309.

CHAPTER 32

1. Josephy, *On The Hill*, 134.

2. Malone, Vol. 5, 416 -22. The patrolling British warships regularly sent men ashore to buy fresh water, vegetables, and other supplies in Norfolk. Desertion from these landing parties was frequent.

3. Burton Spivak, *Jefferson's English Crisis,* Charlottesville, Va, 1979, 87.

4. Ibid, 89.

5. TJ to JM, Aug 16, 1807, ROL Vol. 3, 1486.

6. Gordon Wood, *Empire of Liberty* (New York, 2009), 649.

7. Malone, Vol. 5, 482.

8. Forrest McDonald, *The Presidency of Thomas Jefferson* (Lawrence KS, 1976), 107

9. GW to John Bannister, April 21, 1778, PGW Digital. This five-page letter is a veritable treatise on how to raise and maintain a successful army.

10. Wood, *Empire of Liberty*, 652.

11. Burstein and Isenberg, *Madison and Jefferson*, 455. Also see Spivak, *Jefferson's English Crisis,* 116-17.

12. Ibid, 117, note.

13. Ibid, 118.

14. Malone, Vol. 5, 652.

15. Wood, *Empire of Liberty*, 655.

16. Spivak, *Jefferson's English Crisis,* 151-2. The author describes the American nation as a "rudderless ship" in the last year of Jefferson's presidency.

17. Malone, Vol 5, 653-4, 667-68.

CHAPTER 33

1. Josephy, *On the Hill*, 139.

2. Ketcham, *James Madison,* 482.

3. TJ to JM, April 27, 1809, ROL, Vol. 3, 1568. Also see PJM Digital, same date.

4. Donald R. Hickey, *The War of 1812, A Forgotten Conflict,* Champaign Ill, 2012, 60.

5. Ibid.

6. Peterson, *Thomas Jefferson,* 931.

7. Ketcham, *James Madison*, op. cit., 529.

8. Spencer C. Tucker, *The Jeffersonian Gunboat Navy*, Columbia, SC, 1883, 10, 103, 107.

9. TJ to to Monroe, Oct. 16, 1814, PTJ Digital.

10. Cowley and Guinzberg, eds, *West Point*, 24-5. Thanks to Eustis, the number of cadets dwindled to one.

11. Ketcham, *James Madison*, 522.

12. TJ to William Duane, Aug. 4, 1812, PTJ Digital.

13. Annals of Congress, House Committee on Naval Affairs, Nov. 27, 1812, 12th Congress, 2nd Session, 1812. Also see Thomas Clark, *Naval History of the United States*, Vol. 1, Philadelphia, 1814, 230, 234.

14. TJ to James Monroe, Jan. 1, 1815, PTJ Digital.

15. TJ to JM, May 21, 1813, ROL, Vol. 3, 1719-20. Also see same in PTJ Digital.

16. JM to TJ, June 6, 1813, ROL, Vol 3, 1721-22. See same in PJM Digital.

17. http://pgparks.com/War_of_1812/History/The _Battle_of_Bladensburg. htm. Also see Walter Lord, *The Dawn's Early Light* (New York, 1972), 23-24, 139.

18. Ketcham, *James Madison*, 588-89.

19. TJ to JM, Sept. 24, 1814, JM to TJ Oct. 10, 1814, ROL Vol. 3, 1744-47. Also see Burstein and Isenberg, *Madison and Jefferson*, 527.

20. James Morton Smith commentary, ROL, Vol 3, 1989-91.

21. Ketcham, *James Madison*, 671.

EPILOGUE

1. Brian Steele, *Thomas Jefferson Remembers George Washington*, in *Sons of the Father, George Washington and His Proteges,* edited by Robert M.S. McDonald, Charlottesville, VA 2013, 88.

2. Ibid, 89.

3. Gary W. Gallagher, *The Union War* (Cambridge, 2011). This entire book is a tribute to the power of the Union as a motivating force.

4. Josephy, *On The Hill*, 228.

5. James L. Sundquist, *The Decline and Resurgence of Congress,* Washington DC, 1981, 26.

6. Josephy, *On The Hill*, 231

7. Ibid. 232

8. Sundquist, *Decline and Resurgence of Congress*, 28.

9. Josephy, *On the Hill*, 240.

10. James McGregor Burns, *Congress on Trial,* New York, 1949, 147.

11. Ibid, 164.

12. Sundquist, *Decline of and Resurgence of Congress*, 32.

13. James Burnham, *Congress and the American Tradition,* Chicago, 1959, 108.

14. Ibid, 139.

15. Gordon S. Jones and John A Marini, eds, *The Imperial Congress, Crisis in the Separation of Powers* (New York, 1988), 156-7.

16. Ibid, 158.

Index